TO SEMIOTICS AND LINGUISTICS

This *R...* ...lex
and cl... ...ons
special ...ires
in the ...

- key ...cepts such as ... No renewal ... and
  syn...
- key ...
- key ... the
  Pra...

The R... ...d of
semio... ...eful
ready-...

Paul ... *The*
Ameri... ...He is
the ed... ...ader
in Co...

Routledge Companions

Routledge Companions are the perfect reference guides, providing everything the student or general reader needs to know. Authoritative and accessible, they combine the in-depth expertise of leading specialists with straightforward, jargon-free writing. In each book you'll find what you're looking for, clearly presented – whether through an extended article or an A–Z entry – in ways which the beginner can understand and even the expert will appreciate.

Routledge Companion to Global Economics
Edited by Robert Beynon

Routledge Companion to Feminism and Postfeminism
Edited by Sarah Gamble

Routledge Companion to The New Cosmology
Edited by Peter Coles

Routledge Companion to Postmodernism
Edited by Stuart Sim

Routledge Companion to Semiotics and Linguistics
Edited by Paul Cobley

THE ROUTLEDGE COMPANION
TO SEMIOTICS AND LINGUISTICS

Edited by
Paul Cobley

London and New York

First published 2001
by Routledge
11 New Fetter Lane, London EC4P 4EE

Simultaneously published in the USA and Canada
by Routledge
29 West 35th Street, New York, NY 10001

Routledge is an imprint of the Taylor & Francis Group

© 2001 selection and editorial matter Paul Cobley;
individual chapters, the contributors

Typeset in Times New Roman by
Keystroke, Jacaranda Lodge, Wolverhampton
Printed and bound in Great Britain by
Biddles Ltd, Guildford and King's Lynn

British Library Cataloguing in Publication Data
A catalogue record for this book is available from the British Library

Library of Congress Cataloging in Publication Data
Routledge companion to semiotics and linguistics / edited by Paul Cobley.
p. cm.
Includes bibliographical references and index.
1. Semiotics. 2. Linguistics. I. Cobley, Paul, 1963–
P121 .R692 2001
410—dc21 2001019312

ISBN 0–415–24313–0 (hbk)
ISBN 0–415–24314–9 (pbk)

To semiotician, linguist and, as he himself said
of Peirce, that 'incomparable polymath',
Thomas A. Sebeok and to
the memory of William C. Stokoe, champion
of 'sign' and signs

CONTENTS

NOTES ON CONTRIBUTORS

Initials of authors who contribute to Part II appear after each entry.

Jean Aitchison is Professor of Language and Communication at the University of Oxford. She is the author of a number of books, including (on language change) *Language Change: Progress or Decay?* (3rd edn) and *The Seeds of Speech: Language Origin and Evolution*.

Myrdene Anderson is Associate Professor of Anthropology and Linguistics at Purdue University, Indianapolis. Her publications include *On Semiotic Modeling*, *Refiguring Debris – Becoming Unbecoming, Unbecoming Becoming*, and *Cultural Shaping of Violence* (each co-edited). (**MA**)

Edna Andrews is Professor of Slavic Linguistics and Cultural Anthropology, and Chair, Department of Slavic Languages and Literatures, Duke University, North Carolina. Her monographs include *Lotman and the Semiotics of Culture*, *The Semantics of Suffixation in Russian*, and *Markedness Theory: The Union of Asymmetry and Semiosis in Language*. (**EA**)

Eugen Baer is Professor of Philosophy at Hobart and William Smith Colleges in Geneva, New York, USA. His publications include *Semiotic Approaches to Psychotherapy* and *Medical Semiotics*. (**EB**)

Kristian Bankov is Lecturer in Semiotics at the New Bulgarian University and at Sofia University, Bulgaria. Among his publications in semiotics are 'Text and Intelligence', in *Snow, Forest, Silence: The Finnish Tradition of Semiotics* and *Intellectual Effort and Linguistic Work* (forthcoming). (**KB**)

Bernard Burgoyne is Professor of Psychoanalysis and Head of the Centre for Psychoanalysis at Middlesex University. He is a Member of the European School of Psychoanalysis, and is the editor of *Drawing the Soul* and (with Mary Sullivan) of *The Klein–Lacan Dialogues*. (**BB**)

Rocco Capozzi is Professor of Contemporary Italian Literature, semiotics and literary theories at the University of Toronto. He is the author of *Bernari. Tra fantasia e realtà, Scrittori, critici e industria culturale, Leggere* Il Nome della Rosa *e l'intertestualità* and is the editor of *A Homage to Moravia* (1992), *Scrittori e le poetiche letterarie in Italia* and *Reading Eco*. (**RC**)

Paul Cobley is Reader in Communications at London Guildhall University. His publications include *Introducing Semiotics* (with Litza Jansz), *The American*

Thriller: Generic Innovation and Social Change in the 1970s and *The Communication Theory Reader* (editor). (**PC**)

Nikolas Coupland is Professor and Chair of the Centre for Language and Communication Research at Cardiff University (Wales, UK). He is, with Allan Bell, founding editor of the *Journal of Sociolinguistics*. His publications include *Dialect in Use*, *Language, Society and the Elderly* (with Justine Coupland and Howard Giles), *Sociolinguistics: A Reader and Coursebook*, and *The Discourse Reader* (the last two with Adam Jaworski). (**NC**)

John Deely is a Professor in the graduate programme of the Department of Philosophy of the University of St Thomas in Houston, Texas. His books include *Basics of Semiotics*, *New Beginnings*, *The Human Use of Signs: Elements of Anthroposemiosis* and *The Four Ages of Understanding: The First Postmodern Survey of Philosophy from the Ancient Times to the Turn of the Twenty-first Century*. (**JD**)

Roy Harris is Emeritus Professor of General Linguistics at the University of Oxford. His publications include *The Language Makers*, *The Language Myth*, *The Language Machine*, *The Language Connection* and *Signs, Language and Communication* (1996). His translation of Saussure's *Cours de linguistique générale* was awarded the Scott Moncrieff prize. (**RH**)

Nathan Houser is Director of the Peirce Edition Project and Professor of Philosophy at Indiana University–Purdue University, Indianapolis. He is general editor of the projected thirty-volume *Writings* of Charles S. Peirce, co-editor of *The Essential Peirce*, and is the author of many articles on Peirce's logic and semiotics. (**NH**)

Ray Jackendoff is Professor of Linguistics and Cognitive Science at Brandeis University, where he has taught since 1971. He is author of *Semantics and Cognition*, *Consciousness and the Computational Mind*, *The Architecture of the Language Faculty*, *Foundations of Language* and, in collaboration with Fred Lerdahl, *A Generative Grammar of Tonal Music*.

Adam Jaworski is Senior Lecturer at the Centre for Language and Communication Research at Cardiff University. His publications include *The Power of Silence* and *Silence: Interdisciplinary Perspectives*. One of his forthcoming books is *Key Concepts in Language and Society* (with Nikolas Coupland). (**AJ**)

Adam Kendon studied biology and psychology at Cambridge and Oxford. At present affiliated to the University of Pennsylvania and the Istituto Universitario Orientale in Naples, he studies gesture as a component of communication in face-to-face interaction. Most recently he has published a critical English edition of Andrea de Jorio's 1832 treatise on Neapolitan gesture. (**AK**)

Gunther Kress is Professor of Education/English at the Institute of Education, University of London. His publications include *Language as Ideology*, *Social*

Semiotics (both with Robert Hodge), *Reading Images: The Grammar of Visual Design* (with Theo van Leeuwen), *Before Writing, Early Spelling*, and (both forthcoming) *Multimodal Teaching and Learning* and *Multimodality*. (**GRK**)

Kalevi Kull teaches biosemiotics in the University of Tartu, Estonia. His publications include *Lectures in Theoretical Biology* (co-editor), a special volume of *Semiotica* about Jakob von Uexküll (editor) and papers about the recognition concept of species, semiotic aspects of evolution, history of biosemiotics, and ecosemiotics. (**KK**)

Svend Erik Larsen is Professor of Comparative Literature at Aarhus University, Denmark. His publications include *Sémiologie littéraire, Tegn i brug* (translated as *Signs in Use*, forthcoming), *Actualité de Brøndal* (editor), and *Gärten und Parks* (editor). (**SEL**)

Mikle D. Ledgerwood is tenured Professor of French and Technology and Education at the State University of New York at Stony Brook (USA). His publications in semiotics include *Images of the 'Indian' in Four New-World Literatures, New Approaches to Medieval Textuality*, and articles on semiotics, cyberspace and textuality. (**MDL**)

Robin Melrose is Principal Lecturer in English at the University of Luton, UK. His publications include 'The margins of meaning: arguments for a postmodern approach to language and text' and 'The seduction of abduction: Peirce's theory of signs revisited'. (**RM**)

Floyd Merrell is Professor of Semiotics and Spanish American cultures and literatures at Purdue University. His publications include *Unthinking Thinking: Jorge Luis Borges, Mathematics, and the 'New Physics', Peirce, Signs, and Meaning, Sensing Semiosis* and *Simplicity and Complexity*. (**FM**)

Paul Perron is Professor of French and Principal of University College, University of Toronto. His publications include *A. J. Greimas and Narrative Cognition* and *Analyzing Cultures* (with M. Danesi), *Balzac: Sémiotique du personnage romanesque* and *Semiotics and the Modern Quebec Novel*. (**PP**)

Susan Petrilli teaches Semiotics and Philosophy of Language at Bari University, Italy. Her publications include, *Che cosa significa significare?, Materia segnica e interpretazione, Su Victoria Welby. Significs e filosofia del linguaggio, Teoria dei segni e del linguaggio*, and (with Augusto Ponzio) *Fuori Campo, La comunicazione globale, Signs of Research on Signs, Man as a Sign, Signs, Dialogue, and Ideology*. (**SP**)

Augusto Ponzio is Full Professor in Philosophy of Language at Bari University, Italy, where he also lectures in text semiotics and general linguistics. He is Head of the Department of Linguistic Practices and Text Analysis and Director of a doctoral programme in language theory and sign sciences. His publications include *Production linguistique et idéologie sociale, Metodologia della* *formazione linguistica, La revolución Bajtiniana, Sujet et alterité, Sur Emmanuel Lévinas*, and *La comunicazione*. (**AP**)

Bent Preisler is Professor of English Language and Society at Roskilde University, Denmark. His publications include *Linguistic Sex Roles in Conversation, A Handbook of English Grammar on Functional Principles* and *Danskerne og det Engelske Sprog*. (**BP**)

Raphael Salkie is Principal Lecturer in Language Studies at the University of Brighton. His publications include *The Chomsky Update* and *Text and Discourse Analysis*, and he is the editor of the journal *Languages in Contrast*. (**RS**)

Kim Christian Schrøder is Professor of Communication at Roskilde University, Denmark. His publications include *The Language of Advertising, Media Cultures: Reappraising Transnational Media* and numerous articles about audiences' use and reception of mass-mediated discourses. (**KCS**)

Thomas A. Sebeok is Distinguished Professor Emeritus of Linguistics and Semiotics and Senior Fellow in the School of Information Sciences at Indiana University. He served as the General Editor of the *Encyclopedic Dictionary of Semiotics* (2nd edn, vols 1–3, 1994), and is Co-editor of *Semiotics: A Handbook on the Sign-Theoretic Foundations of Nature and Culture* (vols 1–2, 1997; vol. 3, forthcoming). (**TAS**)

Pippa Stein is an English teacher-educator at the University of the Witwatersrand, Johannesburg. Her research interests are semiotics and multiliteracies. She has published in the *TESOL Quarterly* and the *Harvard Educational Review*. (**PS**)

William C. Stokoe, Professor Emeritus of Gallaudet University, Washington, DC, taught language and culture there and investigated and described American Sign Language, giving that name to a language denied language status for millennia. His publications include *Sign Language Structure, A Dictionary of ASL, Gesture and the Nature of Language* (with David Armstrong and Sherman Wilcox), and *Language in Hand*. He died in 2000. (**WCS**)

Peeter Torop is Professor and Head of the Department of Semiotics at the University of Tartu, Estonia, vice-president of EAS and co-editor of *Sign Systems Studies*. His major publications include *Total Translation, Dostoevsky: History and Ideology, Signs of Culture*, 'Tartu School as School', and 'The Position of Translation in Translation Studies'. (**PT**)

Jef Verschueren is a Research Director of the Flemish Fund for Scientific Research and Professor of Linguistics at the University of Antwerp. He is the founder and secretary-general of the International Pragmatics Association. His publications include *Handbook of Pragmatics* (co-edited with Jan-Ola Östman, Jan Blommaert and Chris Bulcaen), *Debating Diversity* (co-authored with Jan Blommaert), and *Understanding Pragmatics*. (**JV**)

ACKNOWLEDGEMENTS

As editor it falls to me to write this section of the volume. However, what I would like to acknowledge is that this book is wholly a collective venture. It could never have come about without the co-operation of an international community of scholars in semiotics and linguistics. All the scholars whose endeavour is to be found in this volume have been a pleasure to work with. It is hoped that their dedication to knowledge and its dissemination, as well as the friendly spirit of collaboration in which the work was carried out, are reflected in this book. I'm happy to say that I have made some very good friends as a result of working on this dictionary; I'm sad to say that I have also lost one in the final weeks before this book went into production.

There are some individuals whose names are not represented in this book who have equally been part of its collective authorship. Peter Pugh, Jeremy Cox and, of course, Richard Appignanesi, are a rare breed: visionaries who can delegate. Their presence can be felt in this book even if their names are not visible. Similarly, Duncan Heath and Andrew Furlow have been instrumental in maintaining the good feeling which helped to completion the volume you hold in your hands.

Finally, the usual disclaimer: although this book is a collective venture, it should be pointed out that any mistakes within its pages are not to be attributed to contributors. From first to last, I was assigned the task of preventing errors.

Paul Cobley
London
2000

USING THIS BOOK

The Routledge Companion to Semiotics and Linguistics presents up-to-date information on the key questions within its subject area. It is designed to allow the reader to navigate the subject with ease, through cross-referencing within the volume and by means of indications for further enquiry.

The book is divided into two parts. Part I: Semiosis, communication and language, consists of an introduction and ten short chapters. Each of these chapters broadly answers one from a series of likely questions about semiotics and linguistics in the early twenty-first century (see Introduction). Part II: Key themes and major figures in semiotics and linguistics, consists of a dictionary of semiotics and linguistics, containing a wealth of information on terms used in the subject area as well as biographical entries on influential individuals.

CROSS-REFERENCING

The cross-referencing procedure takes place throughout the volume. Any topic or name which has an entry in Part II of the volume will, on its initial appearance, be printed in **bold** type. This is the case for the chapters in Part I as it is for the entries in Part II. On those occasions when an entry does not explicitly mention a name or topic which nevertheless bears some relevant further information on the entry, it will be followed by 'See also' with the cross-reference printed in CAPITALS.

Cross-referencing from entries in Part II of the volume to chapters in Part I of the volume will occasionally take place. To avoid confusion, references to chapters in Part I are indicated by giving the author's name in underlined type; for example, Harris, Jackendoff, Salkie, and so on. Despite the cross-referencing in the volume, both Part I and Part II can, of course, be used on their own terms: as a free-standing collection of essays or as a far-reaching dictionary of semiotics and linguistics.

The identity of the author of each entry in Part II is indicated by bold initials at the end of the entry.

FURTHER READING

Each of the chapters in Part I of the volume is followed by five recommendations for further reading. The only exception to this is Chapter 1, 'Nonverbal communication' whose topic is probably by far the largest in the volume. This chapter starts the volume off by providing a valuable comprehensive list of readings, one each for the main areas of the topic in question.

Further reading recommendations continue into Part II. The entries in this section are of three different sizes (small, medium and large). Large entries such as **code** are followed by three recommendations for further reading; medium-sized entries such as **semantics** are followed by one recommendation for further reading; and the smaller entries such as **noun** have none.

BIBLIOGRAPHICAL REFERENCES

When reference is made to a published work, for example in the following fashion, 'Halliday's linguistic work has culminated in his extensive description of English in functional terms (1985)' or 'However, most sentences can only be understood against a set of background assumptions which effectively define a context (Searle 1978)', the reference to the work is to be found in the References at the end of the volume and not at the end of the specific chapter or entry.

One peculiarity of the subject area must be mentioned in respect of bibliographical references. In Peirce scholarship it has been customary to refer to the standard edition of his works, the eight-volume *Collected Papers*, which usually appears in bibliographies as follows:

Peirce, C. S. (1931–58) *Collected Papers of Charles Sanders Peirce*, ed. A. Burks, C. Hartshorne and P. Weiss, Cambridge, MA: The Belknap Press of Harvard University Press.

However, when scholars make reference to the *Collected Papers* they invariably use a short-hand method which consists of naming the number of the volume and the number of the section within the volume; thus, 'The symbol is the sign "in consequence of a habit (which term I use as including a natural disposition)" (4.531)'. To make matters slightly easier and to help prevent any confusion in the process of cross-referencing, this book will retain the numbering of volume and section but will designate the *Collected Papers* by the initials, *CP*: thus, 'The symbol is the sign "in consequence of a habit (which term I use as including a natural disposition)" (*CP* 4.531)'.

Note that not all of Peirce's work appears in the *Collected Papers* and that much of his work is also published elsewhere: this includes original places of publication (for example, journals such as *The Monist*), the chronological edition of his writings currently being published by the Peirce Edition Project, as well as other, shorter collections of Peirce's essays, notes and letters.

Part I
SEMIOSIS, COMMUNICATION AND LANGUAGE

Introduction

Paul Cobley

The pursuit of signs

It would be difficult to imagine someone who was not interested in communication; someone who, for one reason or another, was never engaged in investigating the nature of specific messages or even the nature of messages in general. Such a person would be someone who had failed to ponder how children learn to use language, how pets and animals indicate their desires, how long the gap is between lightning and a thunderclap, how difficult it is to understand computer manuals, how the heart beats faster in situations of fright, how brand names might encapsulate both products and consumer desires, how music can be soothing, how people can be placed socially and regionally by their accents, how some actors are accomplished in the theatre but unsuited to films (or vice versa), how some citizens of the United States raise their middle finger as an obscene gesture while their counterparts in Britain stick up their middle and index fingers, how certain foods begin to smell after a period of decay, how Internet search engines invariably offer barely relevant information, how tabloid newspapers are different from broadsheet ones, and how mobile phone users so frequently seem to be 'on the train'.

In short, it would be a person who is not concerned with the working of **sign**s; and the length and diversity of this relatively short list should give an indication of the impossibility of such a person's existence. Indubitably, humans have harboured an intense interest in signs, and it is an interest which not only predates verbal investigation of human significance but was also vital to the survival of our early nonverbal hominid ancestors (see, for example, Foley 1997, pp. 43–6). This seems to be the case whether the orientation to signs was manifest through tool-making or hunting or through language and the development of culture.

Perhaps unsurprisingly, given its centrality in culture, the scrutiny of the nature of signs has commonly been conducted through a distorting human lens. In these instances, signs have usually been considered to be connected to the human capacity for language and ensuing cultural products, with a bias towards the verbal. Thus, it is easy to imagine that the study of signs, **semiotics**, in spite of a long lineage which will become apparent throughout this volume, is somehow a matter of analysing language and discovering how various artefacts and processes of human culture are analogous to it.

There are some good reasons for this misapprehension. Classic humanities subjects such as philosophy, history and literary studies, as well as the newer topics such as communications, media and cultural studies have been infiltrated and, in

3

the latter case, probably *created* by the currency of certain strains of thought: **structuralism**, **poststructuralism** and postmodernism, all of which, somewhat problematically, are commonly attributed to the late twentieth-century Parisian intelligentsia. The fact of the matter is that 'structuralism' hails, originally, from Czechoslovakia and Russia. Furthermore, semiotics has thrived in countries such as Italy, Estonia, Finland, the Slavic states and the United States, not to mention countries such as China and Japan. However, as a result of historical and institutional circumstances, 'semiotics' has mistakenly become associated with structuralism/poststructuralism in Britain, in some universities in the United States, and in Paris.

This association, to a varying extent, has been forged by references to the work of a Swiss linguist, Ferdinand de **Saussure**, who projected the idea of **semiology**, a 'science' of signs. Thus, *linguistics* has been seen to be intimately related to the study of the sign, allowing the proliferation of a number of perspectives in the human sciences – in anthropology, philosophy, sociology and literary theory, especially – which have been guided, directly or indirectly, by Saussurean and post-Saussurean linguistic principles.

Yet, there can be little doubt that the psychologistic theme of Saussure's *Course in General Linguistics* ([1916] 1974) has frequently been undermined by attempts to erect a study of the sign in his name. The crux of the matter is the two-sidedness of the linguistic sign; for Saussure, a sign is made up of a 'sound image' and a 'concept', both of which are in the mind of the sign user. For reasons that are unclear, numerous interpreters of Saussure, in extending his work to other domains, have treated the 'sound image' as a material phenomenon rather than the mental one that he describes. It is possible that this might have been exacerbated by the 1959 English translation of the *Course*: despite the appearance of a further, more circumspect, English version of Saussure in 1983, the potentially misleading translation of his names for the two sides of the linguistic sign – **signifier** and **signified** – had stuck. The idea was abroad that Saussure's linguistics, following the transformation of the linguistic sign into a generalizable function, provided a convenient gateway to other cultural phenomena. Indeed, in the 1960s Roland **Barthes** somewhat lightheadedly proclaimed semiology to be a mere subset of the master discipline, linguistics (1967a, p. 8).

In light of the fact that such a pronouncement appears in the literature, let us be clear and dogmatic that the very localised study of the *linguistic* sign, a sign type used by humans alone, is only one component of the study of the sign in general. Admittedly, it is not a minute part of sign study because language is so complex and, apparently, so close to home that global academia has, for some time, instituted linguistics as a major discipline. However, the very human phenomenon of language is just one aspect of **semiosis**, the action of signs in general, throughout the universe. Put this way, language looks very small compared to the array of signs engendered by all interactions between living cells.

And the emphasis on the 'living', here, is deliberate. The distinction between what is animate and what is not helps to define two terms within semiosis which are often used in very loose ways. *Communication* is a form of semiosis which is concerned with the exchange of any messages whatsoever: from the molecular code and the immunological properties of cells all the way through to vocal sentences. **Signification** is that aspect of semiosis which is concerned with the value or outcome of message exchange and is sometimes given the name '**meaning**', a word that is fraught with **polysemy**. Both phenomena are indigenous to living, animate matter and, indeed, semiosis has been seen as the 'criterial attribute of life' (Sebeok 1994, p. 6). Given that this is the case, what is needed for the study of semiosis is a theory of the sign which is capable of covering the almost unimaginable expanse of different types of sign activity.

SEMIOTICS AND LANGUAGE

While semiology might have seemed to be, in some limited twentieth-century intellectual circles, the final word on the sign and, especially, the human phenomenon of language, work from two other perspectives thrived. First, linguistics in the latter part of the century was thoroughly re-invigorated by the project of Noam **Chomsky** and his co-workers. His positing of an innate human propensity for language – more accurately, a **Universal Grammar** – profoundly re-orientated linguistic study. Second, three key figures – Charles **Morris**, Roman **Jakobson** and Thomas A. **Sebeok** – two of whom were schooled in and contributed to modern linguistics, worked tirelessly to broaden the remit of sign study beyond the merely vocal. For all three, the sign theory of **Peirce**, itself a re-formulation of the ancient doctrine of semiotics, was pivotal in their attempts to investigate the breadth of communication and signification.

Above all, what must be mentioned immediately with regard to both the enterprises of Chomskyan linguistics and modern semiotics as shaped by these pioneers is the resultant problematization of the commonly utilized term 'language'. On at least half a dozen occasions in the foregoing the word has already been used almost as if it referred to an easily comprehensible entity. What will become apparent from the rest of this volume is that while language is now widely accepted to be central to the definition of what it is to be human, there is no consensus on what language actually is. The one point of agreement that does exist, however, is that English, Turkish, Chinese, and American Sign Language (ASL), for example, are to be considered as languages; 'body language', music, animal communication systems, and other semiotic devices like traffic signals, on the other hand, are not.

Chomsky's work presented a serious challenge to both common sense and academic understandings of language as a material phenomenon made up of words, sentences and so forth which facilitate human communication. As discussed elsewhere in this volume, after Chomsky it has become necessary to investigate the possibility that language is more adequately seen as a system of knowledge in the mind of humans. A 'cognitive revolution' has therefore been required to attempt to disentangle the relations between 'language', 'mind' and 'brain'.

Jakobson's studies of the **icon**ic and **index**ical qualities of vocal signs and his discussions of their role in certain speech disorders also challenged the frequently assumed **symbol**ic status of language. But even more important in approaching the elusive definition of language, perhaps, was the work, led by biology, of Morris and Sebeok. In particular, the latter's investigations into animal communication – captured in the self-coined designation, **zoosemiotics** – revealed a considerable amount about the *human* capacity for communication and signification. Contrary to the more credulous commentators on the attempts of experts to teach a limited repertoire of signs to captive primates, Sebeok's writings have repeatedly demonstrated the *exclusively human* propensity for what is to be understood as *language*. In turn, the very 'humanness' of language has facilitated the study of early humans, with the language capacity as a defining feature of the species.

The search for origins, of course, is by no means a foolproof way of discovering why we do what we do today. Frequently, searches for origins – of the universe, of life, of language – meet a dead end, by dint of asking the wrong questions or through lack of proper evidence. However, what is known about early humans provides some important evidence for classifying 'language', 'communication' and 'speech'. It is thought that early hominids (*Homo habilis*, about two million years ago) harboured a language, **grammar** or **modelling** 'device' in their brains. *Homo erectus* (about one and a half million years ago), with an increased brain size over his/her predecessor, also possessed the capacity, an as yet unrealized ability to learn a sophisticated human verbal communication system. However, verbal encoding and decoding abilities only came into use about 300,000 years ago with early *Homo sapiens*. Humans therefore possessed the capacity for *language* long before they started to implement it through *speech* for the purposes of verbal *communication*. Prior to the verbal form, communication would have taken place by nonverbal means, a means that humans continue to use and refine today (see Sebeok 1986a and 1991a; cf. Corballis 1999).

What had been clear to many linguists, at least from Wilhelm von **Humboldt** onwards, was that languages consist of a finite set of rules and a finite set of lexical items which together can, potentially, generate an infinite number of different word combinations. Even Saussure seems to subscribe to this idea in distinguishing *langue* from *parole*, although his use of the word 'règle' certainly does not correspond to Chomsky's 'rule' and he does not formally present *langue* as a generative system (see <u>Harris</u>). The product of applying the finite set is **syntax** or syntactic structure; yet even with the *seemingly* very social notion of generative 'rules' and their socially useful product, language resists being defined as a purely 'cultural' phenomenon in the sense of existing somehow separate from nature. Chomsky's contention is that at least some generative rules are inexorable in the same sense as rules of logic which humans are constrained to obey without even being aware that they know them. Hence 'rules' are not something that humans 'agree on' through social interaction.

To be sure, the study of language cannot proceed through the dissection of human brains; linguistics, instead, has had to work backwards by examining actual language use in order to be able to theorize the constitution of the mental system which precedes it. Yet the problem remains: the search for a definition of language needs to take account of a human faculty which pre-exists its verbal manifestations. Organisms other than humans are not aided in their communication by the syntactic component; that faculty is, at root, a biological one specific to the species *Homo*.

SEMIOTICS AND SCIENCE

As Roy Harris notes in this volume, linguistics has repeatedly been called a science, for institutional reasons rather than as a reflection of the belief that the discipline is characterized by rigorous methodologies for ascertaining scientific **truth**. A great deal of endeavour in fields other than linguistics, within the rubrics of structuralism and poststructuralism, although taking its cue from Saussure's linguistics and his projected 'science' of signs has implicitly or explicitly eschewed science. A discipline such as literary theory has had a protracted history of bracketing itself off from scientific developments. Cultural studies, on the other hand, have almost enshrined the principle in their legislature.

Roland Barthes' *Mythologies* ([1957] 1973c), a text repeatedly cited in studies of media and culture at a time when the disciplines were making inroads into academia, embodied a position which, arguably, encouraged an isolationist stance. Principally, Barthes claimed to have written *Mythologies* because he was impatient at the feigned 'naturalness' of popular cultural artefacts; he goes on to say that he 'resented seeing Nature and History confused at every turn' (ibid., p. 11). This theoretical *leitmotiv* was to recur in cultural studies, especially in books aimed at students. Usually it was transformed into a 'culture vs. nature' argument in order to expose, with the help of semiology, the 'constructedness' of popular texts (see, for instance, Hebdige 1979; Fiske 1989a, 1989b, 1991; Chambers 1986 and reflexive surveys of the field such as Brantlinger 1990 and Turner 1990).

'Culture/nature' as a distinction was nicely facilitated by the fact that English unlike, say, German, already possessed two seemingly custom-made terms. On other occasions the opposition was amplified through discussions of identities and the invocation of **Lévi-Strauss'** anthropology and/or **Lacan**ian psychoanalysis (see, for example, some of the essays in Woodward 1997). Broadly the same opposition of culture (as 'constructed') and nature (as divorced from culture and unknowable) informed a general poststructuralist critique of science (Robertson *et al.* 1996). Here, the scientific enterprise was seen as prone to arbitrary assertions of its own 'natural' objectivity and truth.

There can be no doubt that the concept of science has been traversed by relations of power which have obscured truth and objectivity. Moreover, it is clear that a great deal of injustice, not to mention physical damage, has been perpetrated as a result of ideology predetermining what is to be understood as 'scientific'. One has only to look at the case of the Soviet agriculturalist, Lysenko, to find sad evidence of this (see Lecourt 1973). The issue is raised here in order to highlight some matters of concern for the future study of signs, including those verbal ones which are made possible by the human propensity for language. While semiology might have fostered a 'culturalist' impulse, in the sense of proclaiming itself a science which would be governed by its own *internal* pursuits, this is not an option for the future of semiotics, nor has it ever been, in spite of the fact that some areas have been and will continue to be resolutely devoted to the study of 'cultural' artefacts.

C. P. Snow famously dissected the dilemma of the separation of scientists and 'literary intellectuals' in 1959 when he referred to the 'two cultures' (1993). He painted a vivid picture of learned individuals from different disciplines wilfully refusing to talk to each other and, as a result, becoming further entrenched in their own concerns. When newspapers, magazines and journals returned to review his arguments in 1999, they tended to conclude that little had changed in the intervening years. It is true, too, that Sebeok has recently lamented that the 'number of scholars who nimbly scud back and forth between the "two cultures" remains heartbreakingly small' (1996b, p. 94).

Yet, if there was ever an intellectual arena which not only welcomed scholars to negotiate the ravine separating cultural analysis and science, but also *necessitated* such movement, it is semiotics. This is especially the case following the 'cognitive revolution' in the study of language; but there are other reasons, too. The final years of the twentieth century witnessed Copernican developments in the study of the sign. The residue of the efforts of scientists such as **Uexküll**, Morris, Hediger and Prodi became crystallized in **biosemiotics**. Sebeok, Emmeche, Hoffmeyer, Krampen, Kull and others worked to thoroughly re-orientate semiotics, effecting a resurgence whose roots actually lay in the symptomatology of ancient medicine. To use the parlance of poststructuralism and postmodernism, cultural semiotics (or **anthroposemiotics**) was *decentred* by the growing awareness that it was embedded in a far larger network than itself, a network that incorporated animal semiosis, plant semiosis and even bacterial semiosis.

The implications of biosemiotics – the sheer complexity and vastness of semiosis – are quite startling. They are not, however, reasons for downheartedness about the impetus of semiotics in general. In fact, quite the reverse. Where Saussure's semiology was constrained by its provenance in linguistics, Peirce's doctrine of signs is liberating by virtue of its flexibility across disciplines. Peirce himself was ever the scientist, not just in the major job he carried out for the US Coast and Geodetic Survey (see Brent 1998), but also the way in which his 'semeiotic' was totally interwoven with the 'assertion and interpretation' that are the hallmark of science (see **abduction**, **firstness**, **secondness**, **thirdness** and **interpretant**; see also Hookway 1992, pp. 118–44). Peirce set himself the task of constructing a method by which the life of science might enter into a true representation of all reality. From the outset, he envisaged a sign theory that would be comprehensive rather than localized. As he wrote to Lady **Welby**:

> Know that from the day when at the age of twelve or thirteen I took up, in my elder brother's room a copy of Whateley's *Logic*, and asked him what Logic was, and

getting some simple answer, flung myself on the floor and buried myself in it, it has never been in my power to study anything – mathematics, ethics, metaphysics, gravitation, thermodynamics, optics, chemistry, comparative anatomy, astronomy, psychology, phonetics, economics, the history of science, whist, men and women, wine, metrology, except as a study of semeiotic.

(1966, p. 408)

Semiotics, so conceived, embraces animate nature and human culture; it incorporates scientific analysis with cultural analysis; and it surveys the continuity of semioses within language as well as those outside.

QUESTIONS OF SEMIOTICS AND LINGUISTICS

The breadth of the doctrine of signs is undoubtedly great; the present volume therefore focuses on the relation between semiotics and linguistics, especially how the latter is one part of the former, and also how the driving force of post-Chomskyan linguistics is related to the larger domain of the sign. The first part of the book poses the questions that the intelligent lay person would most likely ask of semiotics and linguistics in the early twenty-first century. These are as follows:

- In light of the fact that linguistics is a part of semiotics and in light of the fact that linguistics concentrates on *verbal* communication, what does *nonverbal* communication consist of and how widespread is it?
- If semiotics is the study of the sign across verbal and nonverbal realms, and Charles S. Peirce is so prominent in formulating this study in the modern world, what is his theory of the sign and how can it be applied to different communicational phenomena?
- Given that humans use both verbal *and* nonverbal signs, what might be the origins of language?
- Language can be perceived in its physical manifestations; it is also something that is mental, too; but things that are mental cannot simply be attributed to the physiology of the brain – so what is the relation between 'language', 'thought', 'mind' and 'brain'?
- Language use does not happen in a vacuum: there are other people to take into account, as well as worldly factors such as situation, poverty, discrimination and so on – what does this entail for the study of the way that humans use signs?
- Surely humans don't just use language for blandly communicating one fact or another; they often have a purpose or use language for some kind of action – what does contemporary linguistics make of this?
- Furthermore, languages have been mutating and dying throughout human history even though it is sometimes commonly imagined that each language is an unchanging structure, or even a tool, constant as the North Star and ready to be used – how does this change happen?
- If semiotics, and linguistics within it, are able to meaningfully address the above

issues in the early twenty-first century, it is probably because of developments in the field during the recent past which have either directed research in a particular way or have broken new ground; one of the most famous names in twentieth-century linguistics has been Chomsky – why?

- The other most famous name in linguistics during the same period is Saussure who would have had his own imperatives for language study – what has been the fate of linguistics after his death?

- If signs and communication are so important in the contemporary world, and if verbal language has had such a key role to play in human life, how important is it in relation to those concerns which consume humans today – identity and power relations?

Each of these questions is addressed in a short chapter in Part I of this book. Sections on 'Further Reading' at the end of each chapter, as well as cross-references to entries in Part II of the volume, provide indications for addressing the questions further (see Using this book, pp. xv–xvi).

Part I therefore begins with a contribution on the broad topic of nonverbal communication. In a considerable feat of concision, Thomas A. Sebeok provides a rich portrait of the kind of communication that takes place between 'all known living organisms'. Covering semioses as diverse as those among prokaryotes, among fish, or between conductors and orchestras, he draws attention to the way in which organisms – including humans – depend on **model**s or, to use the word arising from biosemiotics, *Umwelten*. Chapter 1 provides an indispensable perspective on the place of verbal language within the wider nonverbal universe.

Next, Floyd Merrell's contribution presents a down-to-earth exposition of a topic which has bewildered but excited scholars for over a hundred years: Peirce's concept of the sign. By means of familiar examples Merrell gets behind the sometimes difficult terminology of American philosophy's most outstanding figure. At different times in his life Peirce argued that there were three, ten, sixty-six or even 59,049 classes of signs (1966, p. 407). Merrell follows Peirce in showing that the classes can be broken down, that semiotics is far from being mere taxonomy and that there are 'no all-or-nothing categories with respect to signs'. Chapter 2 demonstrates one certainty, however: that semiosis is characterized by an in-built potential to continue.

Complementing the forward thrust of semiosis, perhaps, is the impulse to look back. The quest for the origins of language is certainly as old as linguistics itself and its intractability has sometimes led to its prohibition by linguistic societies as a topic for discussion (see Sebeok 1986a, p. 172). This has not stopped scholars pursuing the subject, however, as witnessed today by the existence of a major society and annual conference which provides an international forum for new findings and theories in the area (see the web pages at *http://welcome.to/LOS*). The late William C. Stokoe returns to the topic of the origins of language in this volume. Famous for his work in the field of **sign language**s, especially the way in which he was able to argue the language-like properties of ASL and thus contribute to deaf people's push for self-determination (see Maher 1996), Stokoe here in Chapter 3 demonstrates how language is embedded in nonverbal communication once more. Specifically, he argues *contra* Chomskyan linguistics that the quest for origins needs to pay more attention to **gesture**: the semiotic power of the latter, he suggests, has all too often been underestimated. That deaf and hearing infants both use hand and arm gestures for some months before speech as well as the fact that gestures, through hand/eye/brain co-ordination, are 'powerful stimulants to mind', are some of the good reasons to foreground gesture in the investigation of language origins.

Yet, 'mind', 'brain', 'thought' and 'language' are all difficult entities with no easy definitions. Ray Jackendoff in Chapter 4 therefore provides a characteristically lucid essay to help the reader navigate the minefield of the contemporary cognitive approach to language. He explores the relations between the perceptual and motor systems which are responsible for 'mapping from the external world into thought and from thought into action'. The complexity of the processes involved is considerable and the chief task at present is to identify the main sub-systems and investigate their interactions. It may be the case that there are no easy answers here; but Jackendoff enables the non-specialist to gain a grasp of what the right questions might be.

The actual use of language is not only a matter of perceptual and motor systems. Language users find themselves tangled up in diverse social, economic and political co-ordinates which, in their global dominance, are so immediate and pressing that the cognitive basis for language is taken for granted. In Chapter 5 on 'Sociolinguistics and social semiotics', Gunther **Kress** addresses the social co-ordinates inscribed in the use of verbal communication. Initially a sociolinguist, Kress has sought to move beyond the terrain of mainstream linguistics in order to attempt to address the wider domain of semiosis, in particular humans' increasing proclivity for 'multimodality'. His chapter therefore focuses on a state of affairs in 'which language is just one of a number of modes of communication, all of which are culturally and socially shaped'. While language might be 'natural' in its basis, Kress' chapter helps to show that the choice and mixture of semiotic **modes** is influenced by factors deemed cultural.

One important part of semiotics, and a major force in contemporary linguistics, is the (sub)discipline of **pragmatics**. As Jef Verschueren shows in Chapter 6, pragmatics has frequently been depicted as a component of linguistic theory in general as if, like other components such as **phonetics**, **phonology** or **morphology**, it had a highly defined object of study. Thus, it has frequently been the case that pragmatics has been seen to be concerned with linguistic categories related somehow to 'context' (for example, **deixis** or **pronoun**s). In a fecund way, Verschueren revisits the originary moment of pragmatics in the work of Morris and shows that pragmatics' reach is so long that it should properly be seen as a distinct perspective on language. Specifically, he calls pragmatics 'a functional perspective' because of its focus on the human *use* of language. The broad, interdisciplinary nature of such a perspective therefore suggests a strong link with social semiotics within the domain of semiotics in general.

One of the most pressing issues in the study of language in the twentieth century has been that of 'agency', the extent to which humans are able to unproblematically dictate what takes place in communication. As should become clear towards the end of Part I of this volume, pragmatics and social semiotics have been especially implicated in this issue. However, one area where the question has been explicitly raised for hundreds of years and continues to be broached in everyday conversation beyond the bounds of institutionalized linguistics, is the process of 'language change'. Jean Aitchison, one of the contemporary period's most talked-about theorists of language change, presents an admirably level-headed contribution on this topic that has caused so much blood to boil and so much hot air to be expelled. As she shows in Chapter 7, human predilections are undoubtedly part of the process, but this is not the end of the matter. Not only is it in the very character of language to change, it is also part and parcel of ongoing communication, both human and animal.

Debates about language change may have been going on longer than debates about the central figure of late twentieth-century linguistics. Nevertheless, Raphael Salkie's chapter on the work of Noam Chomsky begins by showing that it is important to prevent the clouding of an assessment of Chomsky's work by the many myths and illusions surrounding it. Salkie cuts through these myths in a refreshingly forthright way, showing the relation of Chomsky's linguistics to philosophy and science, as well as hacking through the verbiage which sometimes shrouds the concepts of the language faculty and Universal Grammar. As Chapter 8 makes clear, although his work is controversial, Chomsky has worked through an impressive research project and maintained a remarkable record of intellectual achievement.

The other major figure in twentieth-century linguistics, Saussure, did not live to see the fulfilment of his recommendations for research into language. In a persuasive and highly original contribution, his English translator, Roy Harris, surveys linguistics after Saussure and assesses the extent to which the three main aims of linguistics defined in the *Course* have been met in the years since its publication. Chapter 9 does two invaluable things: it provides an Olympian overview of the objectives of the confusingly variegated linguistic field of the last eighty or so years; and it revisits Saussure's agenda for linguistics which has so frequently been distorted by the refractive action of structuralism, poststructuralism and other, putatively semiological, work.

Part I of this volume concludes with a chapter on **discourse**, a topic that has been almost omnipresent since Saussure but has failed to find a stable home amidst the myriad of disciplines and situations in which it is invoked. Although the very term implies movement and continuation, the work of Nik Coupland and Adam Jaworski has been useful in offering some stability and, indeed, for emphasizing the sense in which discourse itself might work to provide coherence and closure. Chapter 10 begins by examining different definitions of discourse, one of which is simply to do with language use that is greater than the **clause** or the sentence. The concentration on the determinants and consequences of language use once more brings the topic into close contact with **sociolinguistics**, social semiotics and pragmatics but Chapter 10 also discusses what was previously a catch-all phrase, **discourse analysis**, giving it a degree of focus as an approach, especially in relation to the method of **conversation analysis**. The result is a riveting diagnosis of 'language reflecting social order but also language shaping social order, and shaping individuals' interaction with society'.

THE ANCIENT DOCTRINE OF SIGNS AND SEMIOTICS IN THE PRESENT

In the early years of the twenty-first century questions of power, identity and language have assumed an unprecedented importance in human life. Who we are and our relations to the power of others have been constant themes in social existence in modernity. Although socio-economic factors are obviously paramount, these questions have repeatedly been formulated in terms of the human verbal faculty, specifically through the struggle over national languages (cf. Hobsbawm 1992, pp. 52–62). However, it seems that that struggle is about to be superseded. John Deely writes that the current, 'postmodern', period

> coincides with a breakdown of the modern national linguistic compartmentalizations, as a new global perspective begins to emerge beyond national differences of language. This emerging perspective is based not on a unity of natural language, as in the previous three epochs, but on the achievement of an epistemological paradigm capable of taking into account the very mechanisms of linguistic difference and change as part of the framework of philosophy itself. This movement, the postmodern development, is coming to be based especially in the work of the American philosopher Charles Sanders Peirce, with its leading premiss that 'the highest grade of reality is only reached by signs'.
>
> (1994a, p. 44)

Deely's is not the only argument about the escalation of the sign's dominion in the contemporary world, although it is definitely one of the few that is not overwhelmed by cultural pessimism. In fact, his work shows how current semiotics represents a resurgence of the immensely fruitful doctrine of signs to be found in ancient Greek and Latin philosophy (see **Stoics and Epicureans** and **Poinsot**). In the face of current human dilemmas of signification, semiotics, with its distinguished history of tenacity, is likely to prove crucial. It demonstrates how verbal communication is embedded in a far larger universe of nonverbal communication; how even humans are not restricted to speech for their semioses; how humans use different modes for communication; how language is a faculty specific to the genus *Homo*; and, perhaps most important of all lest humans get carried away with their hubris, that the 'semiosic' capacity is synonymous with life, thus placing humans in an environment where they are intimately related to both animals and plants.

1

Nonverbal communication

Thomas A. Sebeok

All known living organisms communicate exclusively by nonverbal means, with the sole exception of some members of the species *Homo sapiens*, who are capable of communicating, simultaneously or in turn, by both nonverbal and verbal means.

The expression 'by verbal means' is equivalent to some such expression as 'by means of speech', or 'by means of script', or 'by means of a **sign language**' (e.g., for use in a deaf group), that are, each, manifestations of any prerequisite **natural language** with which human beings are singularly endowed. However, not all humans are literate or can even speak: infants normally do develop a capacity for speaking, but only gradually; some adults never acquire speech; and others lose speech as a result of some trauma (e.g., a stroke) or in consequence of aging. Such conditions notwithstanding, humans lacking a capacity to verbalize – speak, write, or sign – can, as a rule, continue to communicate nonverbally.

A terminological note might be in order at the outset. The word 'language' is sometimes used in common parlance in an inappropriate way to designate a certain nonverbal communicative device. Such may be confusing in this context where, if at all, 'language' should be used only in a technical sense, in application to humans. Metaphorical uses such as 'body language', 'the language of flowers', 'the language of bees', 'ape language', or the like, are to be avoided.

Nonverbal communication takes place *within* an organism or *between* two or more organisms. Within an organism, participators in communicative acts may involve – as message sources or destinations or both – on rising integration levels, cellular organelles, cells, tissue, organs, and organ systems. In addition, basic features of the whole biological organization, conducted nonverbally in the *milieu intérieur*, include protein synthesis, metabolism, hormone activity, transmission of nervous impulses, and so forth. Communication on this level is usually studied (among other sciences) by subdomains of **biosemiotics** labeled protosemiotics, microsemiotics, cytosemiotics, or, comprehensively, endosemiotics.

Internal communication takes place by means of chemical, thermal, mechanical, and electrical **sign** operations, or **semiosis**, consisting of unimaginably busy trafficking. Take as an example a single human body, which consists of some 25 trillion cells, or about 2,000 times the number of living earthlings, and consider further that these cells have direct or indirect connections with one another through messages delivered by signs in diverse modalities. The sheer density of such transactions is staggering. Only a minuscule fraction is known to us, let alone understood. Interior messages include information about the significance of one somatic scheme for all of the others, for each overall control grid (such as the immune system), and for the entire integrative regulatory circuitry, especially the brain.

The earliest forms of interorganismic communication in our biosphere are found in prokaryotes – that is, mostly one-celled creatures lacking a nucleus. These are commonly called bacteria. In the last two decades, bacterial associations have come to be viewed as being of three sorts: localized teams, a single global superorganism; and in interactions with eukaryotes (which are familiar life forms composed of cells having a membrane-bounded nucleus, notably animals and plants, but also several others). Localized teams of great complexity exist every-where on earth: there are intestinal bacteria, dental plaque bacteria, bacterial mats, and others. There is of course a very large bacterial population in both soils and in the sludge at the bottom of bodies of waters. Such teams busily draw upon information fitting particular sets of circumstances, especially as regards the exchange of genetic information. A distinguished bacteriologist has noted that, in this way, a local bacterial team can adopt sophisticated communicative survival strategies, that is, it can function for a certain period of time as a single multicellular organism (see Sonea and Panisset 1983).

Importantly, all bacteria, worldwide, have the potential to act in concert, that is, in the manner of a boundless planetary aggregation, as a sort of vast biological communications network – an Internet, if you like. This ensemble has been characterized as a superorganism, possessing more basic information than the brain of any mammal, and whose myriad parts are capable of shifting and sharing information to accommodate to any and all circumstances.

The bacterial superorganism created environmental conditions conducive to the evolution of an entirely different life form: the eukaryotes. Bacteria exploited them as habitats as well as used them for vehicles to advance their further dispersal. Indeed, eukaryotes evolved in consequence of a succession of intimate intracellular associations among prokaryotes. Biologists call such associations symbioses, but as these crucially entail diverse nonverbal communicative processes, they might more generally be characterized as forms of biological *semioses*. Biosemioses between bacterial entities started more than a thousand million years ago and are thus at the root of all communication.

Both in form and as to variety of their communicative transactions, animals are the most diverse of living creatures. Estimates of the number of animal species range from about 3 million up to more than 30 million species. Since the behavior of every species differs from every other – most of which are in any case scarcely fathomed – it will be evident that only a few general observations about these can be made here.

Animals communicate through different channels or combinations of media. Any form of energy propagation can, in fact, be exploited for purposes of message transmission. The convoluted ramifications of these can only be hinted at here. Take acoustic events as one set of illustrations of this. Since sound emission and sound reception are so ubiquitous in human communication, it may come as something of a surprise how rare sound is in the wider scheme of biological existence. In fact, the great majority of animals are both deaf and dumb. True hearing and functional sound-production are prevalent – although by no means universal – only among the two most advanced phyla: the (invertebrate) Arthropods and the (vertebrate) Chordates (to which we also belong). Among the former, the insects far outnumber the rest of the animal kingdom. Sound is most widespread in the Orthoptera among these, including grasshoppers, especially the katydids, mantises, and cockroaches, and the cicadas, of the order of Homoptera. Possessing the most complex of arthropodan sound-producing mechanisms, they also have well-developed hearing organs on the forepart of their abdomen. The Coleoptera, or beetles, contain quite a number of noisy forms. By contrast, sound-use is rather rare among the Arachnids, which include ticks, mites, scorpions, and spiders.

As we come to the vertebrates, it becomes useful to distinguish not only nonverbal from verbal but also nonvocal from vocal communication, and to introduce yet further discriminations with the advent of tools. The vocal mechanism that works by means of a current of air passing over the cords, setting them into vibration, seems to be confined to ourselves and, with distinctions, to our nearest relatives, the other mammals, the birds (endowed with a syrinx), the reptiles, and the amphibians; although some fish do use wind instruments as well, they do so without the reed constituted by our vocal cords. So far as we know, no true vocal performances are found outside the land vertebrates or their marine descendants (such as whales).

Humans communicate via many channels, only one of which is the acoustic. Acoustic communication among us may be both verbal *and* vocal, such as, of course, very commonly, as we speak. But so-called alternative sign languages (see **sign languages [alternate]**) developed by emitters/receivers to be employed on special occasions or during times when speech is not permitted or is rendered difficult by special circumstances are, though generally verbal, not vocal. In this category are included North and South American Indian sign languages, Australian aboriginal sign languages, monastic communication systems actualized under a religious ban of silence, certain occupational or performance sign languages as in pantomime theater or some varieties of ballet. Unvoiced signing may also be freely chosen in preference to speech when secrecy is desired, for instance, when a baseball catcher desires to keep the batter ignorant of the next type of pitch to be made; or if a criminal wishes to keep certain messages from witnesses. More complex sign languages used for secrecy are those employed by religious cults or secret societies where ritual codes are meant to manipulate problematic social relationships between 'insiders' vs. 'outsiders'.

Acoustic communication in humans may, moreover, be somatic or artifactual. This is well illustrated by contrasting humming or so-called 'whistle talk', produced by the body alone, with 'drum signaling', which requires some sort of percussion instrument (or at least a tree trunk). Sometimes nonverbal acoustic messages – with or without speech – are conveyed at a remove, from behind masks, through inanimate figures, such as puppets or marionettes or through other performing objects. Again, acoustic somatic communication might be vocal, like a fearsome shriek, or non-vocal, like snapping one's fingers to summon a waiter. Furthermore, in humans, nonverbal communication in the acoustic mode, in all known communities, has been artfully elaborated into a large variety of musical realizations. These might be accompanied by a verbal text (as in a song), or crooned without lyrics, or be produced by all sorts of musical instruments, or be embedded in an enormously complex, multi-dimensional work of art, like an opera. Thus, while the overture to Mozart's *Don Giovanni* is a pure sonata-allegro, the enchanting duet between the Don and Zerlina, 'Là ci darem la mano', (Act I, Scene 7) immediately following a *secco* (i.e. purely verbal) recitative, gives way to a melody solo then voices intertwining, climaxing in a **gesture** of physical touching and, dancelike (i.e. 6/8 meter) skipping off-stage arm in arm ('Andiam, andiam mio bene' . . .). An opera being the supremely syncretic art form, Mozart's musical code, with Lorenzo da Ponte's libretto, is in this scene supported by a host of additional nonverbal artistic codes, such as mime, scenery, setting, costuming, and lighting, among others (as, elsewhere in the same opera, dancing, the culinary art, and even statuary).

Perhaps somewhat less complicated but comparably fused artistic structures include sound films. These usually partake of at least four **code**s: one visual, three auditory, including speech, music, and sound effects. Circus acrobatic performances, which are realized through at least five codes: the performer's dynamic behavior, his social behavior, his costume and other accessories, the verbal accompaniment, and the musical accompaniment furnish still another blended artistic achievement. The dazzling complexity of the messages generated by theater events (Hamlet's 'suit the action to the word, the word to the action' providing but a modest start) can only be hinted at here.

Another interesting sort of nonverbal communication takes place during conducting, which can be defined as involving the elicitation from an orchestra with the most appropriate minimum choreographic gestures of a maximum of acoustical results. In a public setting, the conductor connects not just with the members of the orchestra but also with the audience attending the concert. The gestures shaped by his entire upper body equipment – including hands, arms, shoulders, head, eyes – are decoded by the onlookers through the visual channel, transformed by the players into sound, which is then fed back to the audience. (Operatic conductors often mouth the lyrics.)

The functional advantages or disadvantages of the different channels of communication have never been fully analysed, but certain statements can be made about acoustic communication in these respects which, other things being equal, apply to animals including man. A clear disadvantage, in contrast for instance to molecular traces such as pheromones, or chemical messengers which tend to persist over time, is the ephemeral character of sound. To counteract this, humans eventually had recourse to writing and, more recently, introduced all sorts of sound recording devices. This defect may be outweighed by several advantages sound has over other media. For one thing, sound is independent of light and therefore can be used day or night. For another, it fills the entire space around the source and therefore does not require a straight line of connection with the destination. Also, it involves a minuscule expenditure of energy. In most animals, sound is produced solely by the body – ordinarily, no tool is required. In the case of man, it can also be modulated to vary from intimate whisper to long-distance shouting.

In summarizing what is known of the acoustic behavior of vertebrates, we can only scratch the surface here. Among fish, as in the insects, sound-production seems to occur but sporadically. Almost all are in the Teleosts, and their methods are, Huxley tells us, of three distinct kinds: by stridulation of one hard part against another (grinding their teeth, for instance); by expulsion of gas (a sort of breathing sound); or by vibrating their gas bladder. Some fish hiss like a cat, some growl, some grunt like a pig, others croak, snore, or croon, some bellow, purr, buzz, or whistle, one even vibrates like a drum. And of course fish can hear (although their auditory powers vary considerably).

Most amphibians cannot hear and seldom produce any sound but a weak squeak, but frogs and toads are quite noisy in highly diverse ways. Reptiles can in general hear better; yet few produce sounds (though crocodiles roar and grunt). Birds signify by sounds, given and received, but, more comprehensively, by so-called *displays* – stereotyped motor patterns involved in communication – which also include visual movements and posturing. Birds produce a huge variety of vocalizations, ranging from short, monosyllabic calls, to long, complicated sequences, their songs. Some birds can more or less faithfully reproduce, that is to say, 'parrot', noises of their environment, imitating those of other species, notably even speech-sounds. The communication systems of birds, which have been well studied for many centuries, are so heterogeneous that they cannot be dealt with here adequately. The same must be said of their multifarious, often dazzling, visible displays – stereotyped motor patterns – including their sometimes spectacular plumage (e.g., in peacocks or birds of paradise) and their constructs (as in bower-birds).

Mammals have elaborate auditory organs and rely on the sense of hearing more than do members of any other group, but they also, like many birds, communicate, if sporadically, by nonvocal methods as well. A familiar example of this is the drumming behavior in the gorilla, produced by clenched fists beating on the chest. Echolocation refers to the phenomenon where the emitter and receiver of a train of sounds is the same individual; this is found in bats as well as marine mammals, such as certain species of whales and dolphins. (The capability of blind people to navigate by echolocation has not been proved.) Some vertebrates like rats, mice, gerbils, and hamsters communicate in a range inaudible to normal human hearing, by ultrasonic calls. (Analogously, the most effective color for the social bees seems to be ultraviolet, a spectrum beyond unaided human vision.)

All carnivores (cats, dogs, hyenas, etc.) as well as all primates more or less vigorously vocalize, including man's closest relatives, the apes. But the characteristic performances of these creatures are both so rich and varied – ranging from the relatively silent orangutans to the remarkably diverse 'singing' gibbons – that describing these would demand a book-length treatment. Instead of attempting to even sketch these here, it's worth emphasizing that apes do not communicate verbally in the wild and that, furthermore, even the most strenuous undertakings to inculcate any manifestation of any natural language in captive apes – contrary to insistent claims made in the media – have uniformly failed.

Attempts to teach language-like skills to apes or to any other animals (such as captive marine mammals or pet birds) have been extensively criticized on the grounds that the Clever Hans effect, or fallacy, might have been at work. Since this phenomenon has profound implications for (among other possible dyads) man–animal communications of all sorts, an account seems in order here. In brief, a stallion named Hans, in Berlin at the turn of the century, was reputed to be able to do arithmetic and perform comparably impressive verbal feats, responding nonverbally to spoken or written questions put to him by tapping out the correct answers with his foot. Elaborate tests eventually proved that the horse was in fact reacting to nonverbal cues unwittingly given off by the questioner. Ever since that demonstration of how unintended cueing can affect an experiment on animal behavior, alert and responsible scientists tried to exclude the sometimes highly subtle perseverance of the effect.

It later turned out that there are two variants of the Clever Hans fallacy: those based on self-deception, indulged in by Hans's owner/trainer and other interrogators; and those performances – with 'wonder horses', 'talking dogs', 'learned' pigs or geese – based on deliberate trickery, performed by stage magicians and common con 'artists' (portrayed over many centuries). Deceptive nonverbal signaling pervades the world of animals and men. In animals, basic shapes of unwitting deception are known as mimicry. This is usually taken to include the emulation of dangerous models by innocuous mimics in terms of visible or auditory signals, or distasteful scents, in order to fool predators. In humans, deceptive communications in daily life have been studied by psychologists; and on the stage by professional magicians. Various body parts may be mendaciously entailed, singly or in combination: gaze, pupil dilation, tears, winks, facial expression, smile or frown, gesture, posture, voice, etc.

A consideration of mainly acoustic events thus far should by no means be taken for neglect of other channels in which nonverbal messages can be encoded, among them chemical, optical, tactile, electric, thermal, or others. The chemical channel antedates all the others in evolution and is omnipresent in all organisms. Bacterial communication is exclusively chemical.

Plants interact with other plants via the chemical channel, and with animals (especially insects, but humans as well), in addition to the usual contact channels, by optical means. While the intricacies of plant communication (technically known as the discipline of phytosemiosis) cannot be further explored here, mention should at least be made of two related fields of interest: the pleasant minor semiotic artifice of floral arrangements; and the vast domain of gardens as major nonverbal semiosic constructs. Formal gardens, landscape gardens, vegetable gardens, water gardens, coral gardens, Zen gardens are all remarkable nonverbal contrivances, which are variously cultivated from Malinowski's Trobriands to traditional Japanese *kare sansui* (dry garden), to Islamic lands, China, and, notably so, in France and England.

Smell (olfaction, odor, scent aroma) is used for purposes of communication crucially, say, by sharks and hedgehogs, social insects such as bees, termites, and ants, and such social mammals as wolves and lions. It is less important in birds and primates, which rely largely on sight. In modern societies, smell has been roundly commercialized in the olfactory management of food and toiletry commodities, concern with repulsive body odor and tobacco products. Perfumes are often associated with love and sexual potency.

The body by itself can be a prime tool for communication, verbal as well as nonverbal. Thus, in animals, it is well known that dogs and cats display their bodies in acts of submission and intimidation, as famously pictured in Charles Darwin's book on *The Expression of the Emotions* (1998), in Figs 5–8 (dogs) and Figs 9–10 (cats). There are many striking illustrations in Desmond Morris's field guide (1977) and in the photos assembled by Weldon Kees (Ruesch and Kees 1956) of how the human frame is brought into habitual play. Professional wrestling is a popular entertainment masquerading as a sport featuring two or a group of writhing bodies, groaning and grunting, pretending in a quasi-morality play to vie for victory of good vs. evil; the players interacting with one another, but, more importantly, communicating with a live audience. Performances like this differ from legitimate bouts like boxing and collegiate wrestling, or sports like tennis matches, and group events, such as soccer or cricket, in that the outcome of the contest is hardly in suspense.

Dance is one sophisticated art form that can express human thought and feeling through the instrumentality of the body in many genres and in many cultures. One of these is Western ballet, which intermingles with sequences of hand and limb gestural exchanges and flowing body movements and a host of such other nonverbal protocols that echo one another, like music, costumes, lighting, masks, scenery, wigs, etc. Dance and music usually accompany pantomime or dumb shows. Silent clowns or mimes supplement their body movements by suitable make-up and costuming.

Facial expressions, pouting, the curled lip, a raised eyebrow, crying, flaring nostrils, constitute a powerful, universal communication system, solo or in concert. Eye work, including gaze and mutual gaze, can be particularly powerful in understanding a range of quotidian vertebrate as well as human social behavior. Although the pupil response has been observed since antiquity, in the last couple of decades it has matured into a broad area of research called *pupillometry*. Among circus animal trainers it has long been an unarticulated rule to carefully watch the pupil movements of their charges, for instance, tigers, to ascertain their mood alteration. Bears, to the contrary, are reported to be 'unpredictable', hence dangerous precisely because they lack the pupil display as well as owing to their inelastic muzzle, which thus cannot 'telegraph' an imminent attack. In interpersonal relationships between human couples a dilation in pupil size acts in effect as an unwitting message transmitted to the other person (or an object) of an intense often sexually toned interest.

Many voluminous dictionaries, glossaries, manuals, and sourcebooks exist to explicate and illustrate the design and meaning of brands, emblems, insignia, signals, **symbols**, and other signs (in the literal, tangible sense), including speech-fixing signs such as script and punctuation, numerical signs, phonetic symbols, signatures, trademarks, logos, watermarks, heraldic devices, astrological signs, signs of alchemy, cabalistic and magical signs, talismans, technical and scientific signs (as in chemistry), pictograms, and other such imagery, many of them used extensively in advertising. Regulatory signs (NO SMOKING), direction signs deployed at airports (PASSPORT CONTROL, MEN, WOMEN) or in hospitals (PEDIATRICS), international road signs (NO PASSING) are commonly supplemented by **icon**s under the pressure of the need for communication across language barriers, certain physical impairments, or comparable handicaps.

The labyrinthine ramifications of optical communication in the world of animals and for humanity are boundless and need to be dealt with separately. Such sciences as astronomy and the visual arts since prehistoric times naturally and mainly unfold in the optical channel. Alterations of the human body and its physical appearance, from non-permanent, such as body painting, or theatrical make-up, or routine hair service, to quasi-permanent metamorphoses, by dint of procedures as body sculpture, e.g., the past Chinese 'lotus foot' or Western 'tight-lacing' customs; infibulation, cicatrization, or tattooing; and, more generally, plastic surgery, all convey messages – frequently, as reconstruction, cosmetic in intent, in female breast size – by nonverbal means. The art of mummy painting in Roman Egypt was intended to furnish surrogates for the head by which to facilitate silent communication of a deceased individual during his or her passage to the afterlife.

An intriguing variety of nonverbal human communicative-behavior-at-a-remove is a bizarre form of barter, known since Herodotus, modern instances of which are still reported, is called by ethnographers 'silent trade'. No immediate channels are usually involved. What does happen is something like this: one party to a commercial transaction leaves goods at a prearranged place, then withdraws to a hidden vantage point to watch unobserved, or maybe not. The other party then appears and inspects the commodity. If satisfied by the find, it leaves a comparable amount of some other articles of trade.

The study of spatial and temporal bodily arrangements (sometimes called *proxemics*) in personal rapport, the proper dimensions of a cage in the zoo or of a prison cell, the layout of offices, classrooms, hospital wards, exhibitions in museums and galleries, and a myriad other architectural designs – involves the axiology of volume and duration. A map is a graphic representation of a milieu, containing both pictorial or iconic and non-pictorial or symbolic elements, ranging from a few simple configurations to highly complex blueprints or other diagrams and mathematical equations. All maps are also indexical. They range from the local, such as the well-known multicolored representation of the London Underground, to the intergalactic metal plaque on Pioneer 10 spacecraft speeding its way out of our solar system. All organisms communicate by use of models (*Umwelt*s, or self-worlds, each according to it species-specific sense organs), from the simplest representations of maneuvers of approach and withdrawal to the most sophisticated cosmic theories of Newton and Einstein. It would be well to recall that Einstein originally constructed his **model** of the universe out of nonverbal signs, 'of visual and some of muscular type'. As he wrote to a colleague in 1945:

> The words or the language, as they are written or spoken, do not seem to play any role in my mechanism of thought. The psychical entities which seem to serve as elements in thought are certain signs and more or less clear images which can be 'voluntarily' reproduced and combined.

Later, 'only in a secondary stage', after long and hard labor to transmute his nonverbal construct into 'conventional words and other signs', was he able to communicate it to others (see Hadamard 1945).

FURTHER READING

Because all living things communicate nonverbally, the literature on the subject as a whole is astronomical. Therefore, the following references are arbitrarily restricted to just one English entry for main topics discussed in this article. Topics are listed in alphabetical order.

Aboriginal sign languages

Umiker-Sebeok, J. and Sebeok, T. A. (eds) (1978) *Aboriginal Sign Languages of the Americas and Australia*, vols I and II, London: Plenum.

Acoustics

Busnel, R.-G. (ed.) (1963) *Acoustic Behaviour of Animals*, London: Elsevier.

Acrobats

Bouissac, P. (1985) *Circus and Culture: A Semiotic Approach*, London: University Press of America.

Advertising

Nadin, M. and Zakia, R. D. (1994) *Creating Effective Advertising Using Semiotics*, New York: Consultant Press.

Animal communication

Sebeok, T. A. (ed.) (1977) *How Animals Communicate*, Bloomington, IND: Indiana University Press.

Animal sounds

Huxley, J. and Koch, L. (1938) *Animal Language: How Animals Communicate*, New York: Grosset and Dunlap.

Animals and humans

Sebeok, T. A. (1990) *Essays in Zoosemiotics*, Toronto: Toronto Semiotic Circle Monograph Series No. 5.

Apes

Sebeok, T. A. and Umiker-Sebeok, J. (eds) (1980) *Speaking of Apes: A Critical Anthology of Two-Way Communication with Man*, London: Plenum.

Bacteria

Sonea, S. and Panisset, M. (1983) *A New Bacteriology*, Boston, MA: Jones and Bartlett.

Bird display

Armstrong, E. A. (1965) *Bird Display and Behaviour*, New York: Dover.

Bird song

Catchpole, C. K. and Slater, P. J. B. (1995) *Bird Song: Biological Themes and Variations*, Cambridge: Cambridge University Press.

Clever Hans

Sebeok, T. A. and Rosenthal, R. (eds) (1981) *The Clever Hans Phenomenon: Communication with Horses, Whales, Apes, and People*, Annals of the New York Academy of Sciences, vol. 364, New York: Academy of Sciences.

Clothes

Lurie, A. (1981) *The Language of Clothes*, New York: Random House.

Communication (general)

Sebeok, T. A. (1991) 'Communication', in *A Sign Is Just A Sign*, Bloomington, IND: Indiana University Press, pp. 22–35.

Conducting

Schuller, G. (1997) *The Compleat Conductor*, London: Oxford University Press.

Dance

Hanna, J. L. (1979) *To Dance Is Human: A Theory of Nonverbal Communication*, London: University of Texas Press.

Deception

Schiffman, N. (1997) *Abracadabra! Secret Methods Magicians and Others Use to Deceive Their Audience*, Amherst, MA: Prometheus Books.

Echolocation

Busnel, R.-G. and Fish, J. F. (1980) *Animal Sonar Systems*, London: Plenum.

Einstein's letter

Hedamard, J. (1945) *An Essay on the Psychology of Invention in the Mathematical Field*, Princeton: Princeton University Press.

Emotions

Darwin, C. (1998) *The Expression of the Emotions in Man and Animals*, Introduction, Afterword and Commentaries by P. Ekman, New York: Oxford University Press.

Endosemiotics

Uexküll T. von *et al*. (1993) 'Endosemiotics', *Semiotica* 96: 5–51.

Faces

Landau, T. (1989) *About Faces*, New York: Doubleday.

Film

Metz, C. (1974) *Language and Cinema*, The Hague: Mouton.

Gardens

Ross, C. (1998) *What Gardens Mean*, London: University of Chicago Press.

Gaze

Argyle, M. and Cook, M. (1976) *Gaze and Mutual Gaze*, Cambridge: Cambridge University Press.

Gestures

Morris, D. *et al*. (1979) *Gestures: Their Origins and Distribution*. New York: Stein and Day.

Hands

McNeill, D. (1992) *Hand and Mind: What Gestures Reveal about Thought*, Chicago: University of Chicago Press.

Infants

Trevarthen, C. (1990) 'Signs before speech', in T. A. Sebeok and J. Umiker-Sebeok (eds), *The Semiotic Web 1989*, Berlin: Mouton de Gruyter, pp. 689–755.

Lying

Ekman, P. (1985) *Telling Lies: Clues to Deceit in the Marketplace, Politics, and Marriage*, London: W.W. Norton.

Manwatching

Morris, D. (1977) *Manwatching: A Field Guide to Human Behaviour*, London: Jonathan Cape.

Maps

Turnbull, D. (1989) *Maps Are Territories: Science is an Atlas*, Chicago: University of Chicago Press.

Modeling

Anderson, M. and Merrell, F. (eds) (1991) *On Semiotic Modeling*, Berlin: Mouton de Gruyter.

Monks

Umiker-Sebeok, J. and Sebeok, T. A. (eds) (1987) *Monastic Sign Languages*, Berlin: Mouton de Gruyter.

Music

Wright, C. (1996) *Listening to Music*, St. Paul/Minneapolis: West.

Objects

Krampen, M. (1995) 'Semiotics of objects', in T. A. Sebeok and J. Umiker-Sebeok (eds), *Advances in Visual Semiotics*, Berlin: Mouton de Gruyter, pp. 515–535.

Performing objects

Proschan F. (ed.) (1983) *Puppets, Masks, and Performing Objects from Semiotic Perspectives, Semiotica* 47: 1–361.

Piano

Rosen, C. (1999) 'On playing the piano', *New York Review of Books* 46 (16): 49–54.

Pictorial

Sonesson, G. (1989) *Pictorial Concepts: Inquiries into the Semiotic Heritage and its Relevance for the Analysis of the Visual World*, Lund: Lund University Press.

Plants

Krampen, M. (1994) 'Phytosemiotics', in T. A. Sebeok (ed.), *Encyclopedic Dictionary of Semiotics*, Berlin: Walter de Gruyter, pp. 726–730.

Proxemics

Hall, E. T. (1968) 'Proxemics', *Current Anthropology* 9: 83–108.

Pupil

Janisse, M. P. (1977) *Pupillometry: The Psychology of the Pupillary Response*, London: John Wiley.

Road signs

Krampen, M. (1983) 'Icons of the road', *Semiotica* 43: 1–204.

Semiochemistry

Albone, E. S. (1984) *Mammalian Semiochemistry: The Investigation of Chemical Signals between Mammals*, Chichester: John Wiley.

Sign languages (deaf)

Stokoe, Jr., W. C. (1972) *Semiotics and Human Sign Languages*, The Hague: Mouton.

Signs and symbols

Frutiger, A. (1989) *Signs and Symbols: Their Design and Meaning*, New York: Van Nostrand Rheinhold.

Smell

Classen, C. *et al.* (1994) *Aroma: The Cultural History of Smell*, London: Routledge.

Social organs

Guthrie, R. D. (1976) *Body Hot Spots: Anatomy of Human Social Organs and Behavior*, New York: Van Nostrand Reinhold.

Space

Sommer, R. (1969) *Personal Space: The Behavioral Basis of Design*, Englewood Cliffs, NJ: Prentice-Hall.

Speech surrogates

Sebeok, T. A. and Umiker-Sebeok, J. (eds) (1976) *Speech Surrogates: Drum and Whistle Systems*, vols I and II, The Hague: Mouton.

Tattooing

Sanders, C. R. (1989) *Customizing the Body: The Art and Culture of Tattooing*, Philadelphia: Temple University Press.

Theater

Carlson, M. (1990) *Theatre Semiotics: Signs of Life*, Bloomington, IND: Indiana University Press.

Visual

Ruesch, J. and Kees, W. (1956) *Nonverbal Communication: Notes on the Visual Perception of Human Relations*, Berkeley, CA: University of California Press.

Wrestling

Barthes, R. (1973) 'The world of wrestling', in *Mythologies*, trans. A. Lavers, London: Paladin.

2
Charles Sanders Peirce's Concept of the Sign

Floyd Merrell

How signs happen

In its simplest form, the Peircean **sign** has been defined as something that relates to something else for someone in some respect or capacity. Now at this point I'm afraid that's about as clear as mud. So obviously, my first task is to spell out the gist of this definition insofar as I am capable in a few brief pages.

Peirce's sign sports three components (Figure 2.1). What usually goes for a sign in everyday talk Peirce called a **representamen**. He did so in order to distinguish the representamen from the other two sign components, that, as we shall note, can become signs in their own right. The representamen is something that enters into relation *with* its **object**, the second component of the sign. I will allude to Peirce's object as the 'semiotic object', for it is that to which the sign relates. The semiotic object can never be identical to the 'real' object, since according to Peirce our knowledge is never absolute. Our knowledge can be no more than an approximation to the 'real' world exactly as it is, or better, is becoming. Hence, in a manner of putting it, the 'semiotically real object' we smell, taste, touch, hear, and see is never identical to the 'really real object'. We simply can't know the world just as it is becoming: our minds are too limited and it is too subtle and complex. Consequently, since this 'real object' cannot be completely known once and for all, it can never be more than 'semiotically real' for its interpreters. The third component of the sign is the **interpretant**. It is, roughly speaking and sufficient for our purpose, close to what we would usually take as the sign's meaning. The interpretant relates to and mediates between the representamen and the semiotic object in such a way as to bring about an interrelation between them at the same time and in the same way that it brings itself into interrelation *with* them.

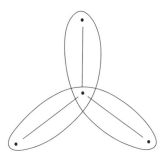

Figure 2.1 The Peircean sign

What I mean by mediation is that a sign component acts as an *intermediary* between the two other sign components. In this act of mediation, most prevalent in the interpretant, the sign component becomes involved with its two companions in such a manner that all three enter into interrelated interdependency. A fully-fledged sign must have a representamen, a semiotic object, and an interpretant, and each of these sign components must enjoy the company of the other two. If not, there is no sign. Sit down to the dinner table and you usually have at the very least a knife, a fork, and a spoon before you. You cut into your steak with the knife, take your soup with the spoon, and dig into your veggies with the fork. All three are necessary to make up your eating utensils. Take any of them away and you either have to drink your soup, pick up your steak with your fork and take bites out of it, or nudge your string beans onto your spoon with your finger.

That is, in your culture, unless you are eating on the run or at a picnic or some such thing, you usually expect three tools for gobbling down your daily fat and cholesterol: knife, fork, and spoon. The spoon gets you started. The knife spreads some butter on a roll. The fork impales a baby carrot. Three different operations? Not really. At the same time, they are all part of one operation: dining. In light of my rather trite culinary metaphors, with respect to the sign, we experience the representamen. It directs our attention to the semiotic object. Then we get some sort of meaning, the interpretant, as a result of the representamen's interrelation with the semiotic object and their own interrelation with the sign's meaning.

As I mentioned above in a somewhat mysterious way, each of the three sign components can become any of the other two components, depending upon the circumstances. For example, a representamen can be a caricature of Winston Churchill found in a history textbook. The semiotic object can be Churchill at Yalta, Russia, in 1945, when he was seated with F. D. Roosevelt and Josef Stalin. The interpretant of the sign consists of the relation between the caricature and the actual figure caught up in an earth-shaking historical event. This event aids us in drawing meaning (the interpretant) from the sign with respect to: our knowledge of World War II, the defeat of the Third Reich, the rise of Russia's international political stock as a result of its role in the war, Stalin's power move, Roosevelt's bad health that rendered him less diplomatically effective than he might otherwise have been, and Churchill's astute, occasionally prophetic, views. All this emerges from a solitary caricature. But that is not all. Subsequently, the semiotic object, Churchill as a physical specimen of humankind, can become a representamen whose own semiotic object is his scowl in the photograph at Yalta. The interpretant, a mediative interrelationship between the man and his facial expression, becomes stubborn pride and dogged persistence in the effort to defeat what Churchill conceived as terribly destructive forces. Or perhaps the original interpretant, Churchill at Yalta, can become a representamen. In such case the Yalta Conference itself can become the semiotic object, and the interpretant has to do with the outcome of the meeting between the three world leaders. Notice that each sign began with a representamen. The representamen interrelated with its semiotic object. Then the semiotic object became a representamen in its own right. Still later, the interpretant became a representamen that subsequently took on its own semiotic object and interpretant.

Another example. The representamen may be a cloud of smoke that suddenly appears over a cluster of silver-tipped spruce in the Rocky Mountain National Park in Colorado. A Ranger spies the sign. Immediately a semiotic object, fire, comes to mind. Then there is an interpretant that mediates and brings the representamen and semiotic object together to create the concept of a dangerous situation that demands immediate action. The Ranger calls for help, and moves in for a closer look. There's the fire! The semiotic object suddenly becomes the representamen whose semiotic object points toward the physical destruction that the flames are wreaking on the natural habitat. A quickly constructed interpretant tells the Ranger that the condition is more severe than she had originally suspected. The apparent danger, from her original interpretant, becomes a representamen that provokes a semiotic object involving a nearby campground. An interpretant involving danger comes into the picture. The thought of danger evokes yet another representamen, campers, the semiotic object for which is the combination of flames surrounding and trapping human beings. The interpretant brings on the emerging concept of victims of yet another forest fire during this hot, dry summer season. Signs become other signs, which in turn give way to more signs, and the stream flows on.

Yet another example, if I may. You are pumping iron in your basement while the TV blares out an athletic event. Then a commercial disturbs your concentration on your weights. You hear 'Coke is it!' Ah, yes. You're sweating, panting, and ready for a break. You head for the refrigerator upstairs. But wait a minute. 'Coke' is what? There was nothing actually said in the commercial about quenching your thirst. In fact, you weren't even watching the boob tube. You were only listening to it while bench pressing big pounds and grunting appropriately. So where's the bite to the sign? The bite is in that sound, 'Coke!', that you've heard hundreds of times. It is nothing more than a syllable, a simple representamen. But you have become so familiar with it, like millions of other people throughout the world, that it immediately translates you into a feel for its semiotic object, a bottle or can of the cold, brown, effervescent stuff. Your tongue suddenly feels a little drier, your body a little hotter and sweatier, your muscles a bit more weary. You come in tune with the proper interpretant, with hardly any need consciously and conscientiously to think it or say it. Soon, with a can of 'Coke' in hand and once more at the bench and contemplating your iron, your previous semiotic object has become a representamen, its own semiotic object is the contented cool feeling in your stomach and your gut, and the interpretant is that pause that relaxes. Now, your limp, slumping posture becomes yet another representamen that interrelates with your prior sweaty, exhausted, somewhat dehydrated condition as semiotic object. And the interpretant? It's the mediated interrelation, the interdependent emergence of your loose and limber condition. Relax a little more. After all, there's no sense in overdoing it. Enough pain and little gain for one day. You remain flopped on the sofa soon to become glassy-eyed before the one-eyed monster. Signs evoke and provoke more signs, which in turn bring on more signs, without end.

A TALE OF THREE SIGNS

The most basic classes of signs in Peirce's menagerie are **icon**s, **indices**, and **symbol**s. An icon is a sign that interrelates with its semiotic object by virtue of some resemblance or similarity with it, such as a map and the territory it maps (a photograph of Churchill is an icon of the original item). An index is a sign that interrelates with its semiotic object through some actual or physical or imagined causal connection. A weathervane obediently moves around to point (indicate, index) the direction of the wind due to the action of the wind on the object (smoke was for the Ranger an index of fire).

A symbol is somewhat more complicated. The series of signs in the above paragraph highlights with a symbol, 'Coke', a sign whose interpretation is a matter of *social convention*. One of the best qualifications of Peirce's symbol is a linguistic sign whose interrelation with its semiotic object is *conventional*. This is to say that there is no necessary natural link (as with the index) or a link due to some resemblance or similarity (as with the icon) between the representamen and the semiotic object. The phonetic sounds or the inscribed letters 'Coke' have no necessary connection to the actual item. The sounds are in the beginning in some form or other *arbitrary*. They could have been virtually any other sounds or marks on paper. For instance, we could all get together and agree that 'Coke' should be replaced by 'Schlarch'. If over time whenever we said or heard or wrote or read 'Schlarch' we thought about that familiar soft drink, we would have our own little social convention regarding a symbol and its semiotic object and interpretant. We wouldn't communicate much with anyone outside our group. But that's OK. When amongst ourselves we would get along fine. Our conventional symbolic sign would serve our purposes quite well. We are now obviously *motivated* by the sign, 'Schlarch'. We are motivated by it because in our little **speech community** we have experienced, we experience, and in the future we expect we will experience, the 'pause that relaxes' as 'Schlarch'. This new sign has become an increasingly entrenched part of our collective, conventional semiotic activities. The interrelations within the sign between representamen, semiotic object, and interpretant are now much more than merely arbitrary.

So we have icon, index, and symbol. Peirce's basic triad: 'One, Two, Three'. 'One' is preceded by 'Zero', that 'emptiness' from whence the sign emerged. And 'One, Two, Three' are potentially followed by 'more', 'many more', up to 'Infinity', since 'Coke' or any other sign can be – and probably will be in the case of 'Coke' – repeated virtually without end. 'Zero, One, Two, Three, . . . Infinity'. It has a certain ring to it, doesn't it? This apparently simple counting game calls for a consideration of Peirce's categories.

THE CATEGORIES

Engendering and processing signs and making them meaningful are more than merely getting information out of them or making sense of them. It is a matter of an intricate interplay between what Peirce called **firstness**, **secondness**, and **thirdness**. Firstness, secondness, and thirdness make up Peirce's categories by means of which **semiosis** – the process of signs becoming signs – is qualified and cognized by way of **semiotics** – the process of rendering signs meaningful. Peirce developed the categories in order to account for the feeling, sensation, experience and conceptualization of signs. Since sign processing, from feeling to conceptualization, is just that, process, signs can have no determinable and self-ordained closure. The categories in this manner might be considered tendencies rather than forms, conditions of becoming rather than static signs attached to things. Or, commensurate with physicist Werner Heisenberg's (1958) concept of the quantum world, the categories are *possibilities* and *potentialities* more than *actual* essences. As possibilities, firstness inheres; as actualities, secondness emerges, and as potentialities for future signs becoming signs, thirdness comes into the picture. These categories make up Peirce's fundamental triad of relations as follows:

1 Firstness: what there is such as it is, without reference or relation to anything else.
2 Secondness: what there is such as it is, in relation to something else, but without relation to any third entity.
3 Thirdness: what there is such as it is, insofar as it is capable of bringing a second entity into relation with a first one and it into relation with each of them.

'One, Two, Three'. It seems as simple as that. But from simplicity, complexity emerges. If we include 'Zero' and 'Infinity' along with 'One, Two, Three', then you can see why. Nevertheless, in schematic form, to all appearances the categories are quite straightforward. Firstness is *quality*, secondness is *effect*, and thirdness is *product in the process of its becoming*. Firstness is possibility (a *might be*), secondness is actuality (what *happens to be* at the moment), and thirdness is potentiality, probability or necessity (what *would be*, *could be*, or *should be*, given a certain set of conditions).[1]

In art, firstness might be a two-dimensional rectangular patch of color on a Picasso canvas. Secondness in such case would be that patch's interactive inter-relations to other rectangular, triangular and irregular patches in the painting. Thirdness would be the viewer's putting them all together into an imaginary three-dimensional image as if seen from the front, from the back, from the right side, from the left side, from above, and from below, all in simultaneity. In poetry, firstness is a few lines as marks on paper in terms of their 'possibility' for some reading somewhere and somewhen by some poetry lover. Secondness is their actual reading and their interrelation with the reader's present mindset and memories of the past and readings of many other lines of poetry. Thirdness is the reader's interaction with the poetic lines in such a manner that meaning emerges for her at that particular moment. In everyday life, firstness is a double arch of bright yellowness in the distance. Secondness is the interrelation established by some hungry observer between the curved, elongated yellowness and a colorful building underneath it. Thirdness is recognition of that familiar establishment as McDonald's.

However, like all schematic categorizations, this one is somewhat deceptive. In reality, firstness, in and of itself, is not an *actual* concrete quality (like, for example, a mere sensation of the color and form of an apple that we might be looking at at this moment). It is nothing more than a possibility, a pure abstraction – abstracted, separated from everything else – as something enjoying its own self-presence and nothing more: it cannot (yet) be *present* to some conscious semiotic animal *as* such-and-such. It is an entity without defined or definable parts, without antecedents or subsequents. It simply *is what it is* as pure possibility.

What is perceived belongs to the category of secondness. It is a matter of something actualized in the manner of *this* happening *here, now, for* some contemplator of the sign. As such it is a particularity, a singularity. It is what we had before us as firstness, such as for example, a vague 'red' patch without there (yet) existing any consciousness of it or its identification as such-and-such. Now, a manifestation of secondness, it has been *set apart from* the self-conscious contemplator, willing and ready to be *seen as*, say, an apple. However, at this point it is not (yet) an 'apple', that is, it is not a word-sign identifying the thing in question and bringing with it a ponderous mass of cultural baggage regarding 'apples' (the particular class of apples of which the one before us is an example, what in general apples are for, their role in the development of North American culture, in folk lore, in fairy tales, health lore, and so on). At the first stage of secondness, the apple is hardly more than the possibility of a physical entity, a 'brute fact', as Peirce was wont to put it. It is one more thing of the furniture of the self's physical world. It is **otherness** in the most primitive sense. If firstness is what *is as it is* in the purest sense of possibility, secondness is pure negation insofar as it is *other*, something other than that firstness.

Thirdness can be tentatively qualified as that which brings about mediation between two other happenings in such a manner that they interrelate with each other in the same way they interrelate with the third happening as a result of its mediary role. This mediation creates a set of interrelations the combination of which is like firstness, secondness, and thirdness twisted into a Borromean knot (recall Figure 2.1). The knot clasps the categories together by means of a central 'node' in such a way that they become interrelatedly, interdependently conjoined by the virtual 'emptiness' of the 'node.' Due to the mediary role of thirdness, each of the categories can intermittently play the role of any of the other categories. Yet at a given space–time juncture, one of the three will be a first, one a second, and one a third. This *semiosic interdependence* would not have been possible without thirdness, for without it, there is just one damn thing and its other, an other damn thing and that which preceded it. As Lawrence Welk says in his oldie show, 'A one, a two, . . .' and then the band comes to life – well, almost. Without the third element, the band, there would be no music. Just as the numbers are preceded by 'Zero', 'silence', 'emptiness', so also, once begun, the band must go on, potentially to

'Infinity' – or at least until the music stops. Without thirdness, without the music, there is no semiosis and no life.

To summarize, firstness is *possibility* (a *might be*), secondness is *actuality* (what *is*), and thirdness is *potentiality*, *probability*, or *necessity* (what *could be*, *would be*, or *should be*, given a certain set of conditions). Firstness, in and of itself, is not an identified concrete quality of something (like, for example, the raw feeling of some body of water we might happen to glance at). It is nothing more than a possibility, a pure abstraction – abstracted, separated from everything else – as something enjoying its own self-presence and nothing more: it cannot (yet) be present to some conscious semiotic observer as such-and-such. It is an entity without defined or definable parts, without antecedents or subsequents. As such it is the bare beginning of something from 'emptiness,' of something from the possibility of everything; it is at once everything and nothing, it simply *is*, as possibility.

Now, I must concede that I have oversimplified Peirce's concept of the sign inordinately. However, what needed to be written has been written, I would hope. At least it has become evident that, since in the Peircean tradition virtually anything can be a sign, the definition of a sign must indeed be of the most general sort. It is not simply a matter of the question 'What *is* a sign?' but 'What *is it like to be* a sign?' and 'What does a sign *do*?' Signs are not special kinds of things, but rather, anything can be a sign if it manifests sign functions. The Peircean sign is often taken as something that *stands for* something *to* someone *in* some respect or capacity. However, with respect to the mind-set of our contemporary milieu, I must express my displeasure with the concept of a sign's 'standing for' (as well as 'referring to', 'corresponding to', and 'representing') something. More properly, a representamen, when at its best, interrelatedly and interdependently emerges with all other signs. At the same time, it interrelates and participates with something (its respective semiotic object). And, in light of the above definition, the representamen and its semiotic object are mediated by a third term, the interpretant. As a result of such mediation, the sign takes on value, **meaning**, and importance as a representamen doing its thing along with its neighbors within the vast river of semiosis – the process of signs becoming other signs. The sign also interdependently interrelates and participates with some interpreter, who is in the act of processing the sign. What is of utmost importance, all three sign components, representamen, semiotic object, and interpretant, can become themselves, signs – that is, representamens.

In light of our 'Coke' example, human communities unfortunately place undue priority on the symbolic mode. The human tendency is to 'linguicize' (symbolize) all signs. This tendency has become endemic in our increasingly wordy cultures. Yet, in the affairs of everyday life, all three sign types, icons, indices, and symbols, never cease to make their presence known. For example, a McDonald's franchise can be the semiotic object of a sign consisting of a billboard with a replica (icon) of the Golden Arches for a carload of hungry stomachs. Or the Golden Arches can be the (indexical) representamen that brings on its semiotic object, the colorful building that invariably finds itself next to familiar arches. In both cases the meaning or value (interpretant) attributed to the class of all McDonald's establishments interrelates with the physical structure of a particular McDonald's feeding trough. Then the car rounds a curve in the highway, and: There are the Golden Arches! Which brings on the boisterous evocation, 'Chow time!' (symbol). In another possible scenario, the word 'McDonald's', accompanied by its conventional meaning and value, can be the representamen for that which the passengers of a fast-moving vehicle are in search. Then the physical structure makes its appearance as the semiotic object actualized, and both are mediated by the interpretant to give the sign value and meaning. Finally, car securely parked, passengers pour out, licking their chops. They enter. The aromas, the din, the employees barking orders, money out of one set of hands and into another one, a walk past munching mouths, the feel of unrelenting plastic seats, the bland taste. All are signs. Most of them are basically pre-symbolic icons and indices. We live in a world of icons and indices more than a world of words (symbols).

Signs can also become other signs and in the process take on radically distinct meanings, depending upon the set of experiences and the expectations of the signs' interpreters. A rock is just a nuisance when in the back yard of your neighbor who has taken up gardening as a pastime. He transfers it from one place to another, often threatening to get rid of it or bury it a few feet under. The rock (representamen) is a sign, whose semiotic object (this rock here, which disturbs otherwise pleasant gardening experiences) interrelates with a sense of frustration, given the sign's negative value and meaning (its interpretant). The sign would be better off in somebody else's back yard as far as he is concerned. One day while you are chatting with him across the fence, you spy the rock. But, . . . what's that? Why it is no rock at all. It is a fossil! You reveal your discovery to your neighbor friend, and are met with 'Yeah? Well get it off my hands if you like. I'm tired of looking at it.' His 'rock' (representamen$_1$), with a negative interpretant, became another sign, your 'fossil' (representamen$_2$), the 'rock' that has now taken on a positive interpretant. The sign became, was transformed into, another sign. In the process the semiotic object became something entirely different than what it was, and the interpretant became something radically distinct as well.

Comparable sign transformations occur daily. They are commonplace in all walks of life. They even occur in that most rigorous of disciplines, physics. The ancient Greek, Democritus, believed atoms to be solid, impenetrable spheres. This concept is entirely incompatible with the notion of 'clouds'. However, in the twentieth century, physicist Erwin Schrödinger convinced the scientific community that 'atoms' have nothing to do with 'solid, impenetrable spheres' at all. Rather, they are more like 'clouds', or so to speak, 'wave packets'. Democritus's atoms became Schrödinger's atoms. The two atoms are well nigh incompatible with each other, though the same word, 'atoms', prevailed. Moreover, in both cases a metaphor inhered. Why a metaphor? Because metaphors have a habit of saying what a thing *is* by saying what it *is not*. Thus they are among the most efficient agents of sign change. 'Men are beasts' is true. Well, at least 'men' are 'beasts' as far as the woman making the statement and other women and perhaps even a few men are concerned. Yet 'men' are not 'beasts', according to the customary classification of the word 'beasts'. The sign 'beasts' becomes what it was not, 'men', and at the same time 'men' become what they ordinarily are not, 'beasts'.

Even effects can do an about-face and become causes, and vice versa, depending upon incessantly shifting perspectives. Cause–effect sequences appear largely indexical. The wind 'causes' a weathervane to point in the direction of its blowing; the rising temperature 'causes' the mercury column in a thermometer to rise. If we were children or poets we could conceive of a mercury rise 'causing' the temperature to go up. Smoke is ordinarily not considered the 'cause' of fire. But if a smoker falls asleep in bed and the mattress catches fire, it could be said that the 'smoke' was the 'cause' of the fire. The 'cause' of a plane crash might have been attributed to the weather. Then evidence showed that the pilot had too much to drink, and the 'cause' becomes the 'effect' of alcohol which in turn created the 'cause' of the accident. In exceedingly more complex situations, cause and effect are not as clear-cut. Does poverty 'cause' teen pregnancies or do teen pregnancies 'cause' conditions that contribute to poverty? An answer can't be pinpointed. Consequently, arguments can be presented in favor of both factors as whether 'cause' or 'effect', depending on the viewpoint.

These sign *transformations* are the product of what I will call sign *translations*. Iconically speaking, Democritus's 'atoms' become Schrödinger's 'atoms', or indexically speaking, a 'cause' becomes an 'effect'. These translations are chiefly the result of the ways and means of language use, of symbols. Icons bring two compatible signs together into what is conceived as essentially one sign. Indices link signs together in what appears to be as natural a process as can be. Symbols, in contrast, are at their best when breaking signs up and putting them into pigeon-holes. Thus we have 'good' and 'evil', 'true' and 'false', 'men' and 'women', 'right' and 'left', 'black' and 'white', and all such discriminations. Thus signs, symbolic signs, can be authors of radical translations: Democritean 'atoms' to Schrödingerian 'atoms', 'teen pregnancy' as 'cause' to 'effect', and so on.

Translations can require as radical a switch as Spanish writer Miguel de Cervantes's Sancho Panza taking a windmill to be just another windmill, while his lord, the venerable Don Quixote, sees a giant or a dragon lumbering toward him. They are as unruly as Bill Clinton considered by one citizen as 'our president and a damn good one, whose private life is his own and none of my business', while for another citizen, he 'is an embarrassment to our country and should be impeached'. But actually, why can't virtually any and all combinations of words and images and things change radically over time? Such radical change becomes evident when one takes into account that 'atoms' have been (1) solid impenetrable spheres; (2) spheres with hooks on them so as to hold onto other spheres and make molecules; (3) like a plum pudding; (4) like the solar system; (5) largely vacuous; (6) like a hazy cloud; (7) the source of over 200 subatomic particles; and (8) virtually nothing at all? – each of these eight views have actually been attached to 'atoms' at one period or another in the history of science. Which is more bizarre, the delirious outpouring of Don Quixote, or the utterance 'An atom is a hazy cloud' reaching the ears of Democritus of old or chemist John Dalton in the early part of the nineteenth century? What is a moose for one party may by some quirk of the imagination be a salamander for another one: a goose taken as a gander is much too tame for this game.

In this light, I would rephrase the customary Peircean definition of the sign as: *anything that interdependently interrelates with its interpretant in such a manner that that interpretant interdependently interrelates with its semiotic object in the same way that the semiotic object interdependently interrelates with it, such correlations serving to engender another sign from the interpretant, and subsequently the process is re-iterated.* Now that was another mouthful. Yet it's basically the way of all signs, I would submit, with stress on the notions of inter-dependency, correlations, interrelatedness, and above all participation. I have taken my cue once again from Peirce, according to whom a sign is something by means of which we know something we did not previously know.

THE THREE SIGN TYPES SCHEMATIZED

Now, everything I have written in this section suggests that a sign can be in varying degrees iconic, indexical, and symbolic, all at the same time. A sign's evincing one sign type does not preclude its manifesting some other sign type as well. There are no all-or-nothing categories with respect to signs. As one sign type is, another sign type can become, and what that sign was may become of the nature of the first sign that the second sign now is. Putting things into neat pigeon-holes might allow us some security, but it is a tenuous game, since signs simply cannot stand still. Their incessant dance cannot help but whisk us along the semiosic stream, in spite of our stubborn need for stability. In sum, we have Table 2.1.

Table 2.1 Sign types

Sign type	Icon	Index	Symbol
semiotic mode	similarity	causal or natural relation	convention
practical examples	photograph painting diagram touch of silk musical note sweet smell	smoke for fire symptom for disease thermometer for heat crash for falling log feel of fur for cat tail sour taste for lemon	word insignia Morse code logical sign algebraic sign
how to make and take them	feeling sensation	perception inference action-reaction	learning by instruction and by doing

Practical examples of icons include obvious signs: photographs, paintings, diagrams (and figures and caricatures). The smooth feeling of a piece of fabric reminds one of silk through the association of resemblance. A musical note is an auditory sign that one can sense is comparable to a note in a particular tune. The relation is tentative established between the note overheard and a note from the repertoire of tunes one has stored in one's memory bank. A sweet smell in the chemistry laboratory reminds one of bananas or pineapple, which is appropriate for a class of compounds called esters. In each case there is a vague association by virtue of a commonality between the feeling one has now and one's memory of past feelings. But, I must emphasize, the feeling is no more than a feeling at the outset. For that reason the feeling remains vague, indefinite, relatively uncertain. No *other* of the sign, the sign's semiotic object or its interpretant, has at this point entered the scene. There has not been any determination of the class of signs to which this particular sign here and now belongs. Those signs can come a fraction of a second later, as we shall observe below.

Smoke for fire, a symptom for a disease, a thermometer for gauging the amount of heat in the atmosphere. These are all are visible signs that lead one to the sign's other, whether by the shock of a pleasant to disconcerting surprise, or by acknowledgment of what was expected to be the case. A loud crash caused by a log or any other large object is auditory, the feel of an elongated furry object is identified as a cat, and the acrid taste of some yellow liquid is related to a lemon. These signs are nonvisual, yet their function is as indexical as visual signs. Then these signs can be qualified in terms of the magnitude of the fire, the type and severity of the disease, and the numerical value of the temperature. All that comes later, however. For now, we are in indices of the basic sort. Proceeding on down the semiosic stream brings on at least the rudiments of language use, of symbols.

Words, the Morse code, and logical and algebraic signs, are for the most part arbitrary in the beginning though in their practice they have become conventional and they motivate their makers and takers customarily to respond along predetermined pathways. Insignias, as well as flags, shields, banners, and labels insofar as there is no necessary connection between the sign and the physical world object, act, or event with which they interrelate, are ordinarily not set out in linear strings, as are natural and artificial language. They are most properly symbols, nonetheless. They are not made and taken in terms solely of feelings and sensations or by perception and inferential process or habitual actions and reactions. On the contrary. They must be learned by explicit instruction. This instruction is for the most part imparted through symbolic signs.

Suppose in high school you are learning to fill out a tax form. You are given verbal instructions and a booklet to read. There are still gaps: questions, vagueness, uncertainty. In order to fill in some of these gaps, you learn by observing what parents, teachers, and other role models do when they do their taxes. These examples serve fundamentally as icons. Then you try to duplicate what you have observed. The icons are extended. They merge with indices, for you have become the other of the original examples when you attempt to image that original in iconic fashion.

Thus, learning begins to take place, by virtue of icons, indices, symbols. Then by much practice, speculation, contemplation, and perhaps even meditation, you can, over time, become proficient at the semiotic activity in question.

NOTE

1 For further, Almeder (1980); Hookway (1985); Merrell (1995a, 1995b); Savan (1987–88), for a consideration of Peirce's sign theory, see Sebeok (1976a, 1991b, 1994) and Sheriff (1989, 1994), for a collection of Peirce's writings, Hoopes (1991), Peirce (1992).

FURTHER READING

Merrell, F. (1995) *Peirce's Semiotics Now: A Primer*, Toronto: Canadian Scholars' Press.
Merrell, F. (1997) *Peirce, Signs and Meaning*, Toronto and London: University of Toronto Press.
Peirce, C. S. (1992) *The Essential Peirce: Selected Philosophical Writings*, vol. 1, (ed.) N. Houser and C. Kloesel, Bloomington: Indiana University Press.
Savan, D. (1987–88) *An Introduction to C. S. Peirce's Full System of Semeiotic*, Toronto: Victoria College.
Sebeok, T. A. (1994) *Signs: An Introduction to Semiotics*, Toronto: University of Toronto Press.

3

THE ORIGINS OF LANGUAGE

WILLIAM C. STOKOE

INTRODUCTION

Human curiosity begins early, perhaps as soon as the infant begins to reach for something that comes into view, and certainly well before it first attempts speech. Curiosity about language, however, can begin only after there already exist languages to be curious about, and to speculate with. Thus, in the creation myths of many cultures, a benevolent totem animal or spirit or god speaks with the first humans, or leaves it to them to bestow names on the earth's flora and fauna. Such myths are naïve but natural. In a sense they are also logical: the naïve observer can only think of language in terms of the words one knows. The observer therefore supposes that humans must have been given language, just as infants always have been, by a benign other who already knows which spoken words mean what.

These supernatural 'others' are not acceptable as scientific postulates explaining the origin of language. The skeptic's first question will be, 'Who taught Elohim-Yaweh, or the Cosmic Serpent or Turtle, or the First Mother what each word meant?' There is no answer but 'Have faith!'

Recent attempts to determine how language may have begun are related to attempts to explain consciousness or mind. Gerald Edelman's four recent books, especially *The Remembered Present: A Biological Theory of Consciousness* (1989), bring the state of the art in neuroscience to bear on the problem. Merlin Donald, in *Origins of the Modern Mind* (1991), traces the evolutionary trail from the chimpanzee, through *Homo erectus* (1.5 to 0.2 million years ago), to modern humans in three cultural stages: episodic, mimetic, and linguistic (the latter he identifies with spoken language only). Mike Beaken, in *The Making of Language* (1996), sees language as the result of 'labour', cooperation in problem solving: 'Put simply, labour is the social production of the means of life, and the highest development of social behaviour' (ibid., p. 23). Armstrong, Stokoe, and Wilcox (*Gesture and the Nature of Language*, 1995) look beyond gesture as normally used by speakers to the signs of extant sign languages and find therein clues to the possible origin of syntax. *The Hand: How its Use Shapes the Brain, Language, and Human Culture* (1998) by Frank R. Wilson not only updates the classic works on the hand by Bell and Napier with current physiology and paleontology but also adds the direct observations of a practicing neurologist, concluding that the human hand-cum-brain has evolved with the capability of doing everything humans do, including the production of language **sign**s.

A completely different approach is taken by Noam **Chomsky** (1957), Derek Bickerton (1995) and Steven Pinker (1994), in these and other works on language. Their view is that syntactic structure, not its physical manifestation, separates language as abstract or **Universal Grammar** from every other kind of communication. Chomsky concluded in 1957 that infants could not possibly learn the **rule**s needed to create these structures from the incomplete language they hear, and that therefore the rules must be genetically implanted.

The present state of the art of brain science and neuroscience, however, finds no biological reality corresponding with such rules. Fourteen of the most eminent neuroscients, writing in the Spring 1998 issue of *Dædalus* (127.2), emphasize that the brain is not a computer; it contains no nerves or modules stocked with blueprints of the universe, no rules of anything remotely like Universal Grammar. Thus, it seems more profitable to listen to what these scientists have to say and investigate the possibility that language evolved naturally in a species that itself had evolved within the latest to emerge, our branch of the primate order.

INVESTIGATING LANGUAGE EVOLUTION

Investigate has a more respectable **connotation** than speculate, and looking critically at tracks or traces or clues – vestiges – is literally the procedure to be followed here. First, though, it may be useful to speculate on how and when the trail was lost. Serious philosophical thought about the origin of language, as well as the ability to preserve myths in scriptures, had to wait for the invention and widespread use of writing (which also made possible the first **grammar** 4,000 years ago). Myths are supposed to have been orally circulated long before language could be written – approximately 10,000 years ago. By most modern estimates speech is thought to go back between 40,000 and 140,000 years before that. But certain vestiges as clues may point to a beginning of genuine language much earlier, perhaps as much as a million years ago. One such vestige is the persistence of **sign language**s, some of them used as an alternate to speech by certain tribal peoples, others used as their first or only language by deaf people (see **sign languages [alternate]** and **sign languages [primary]**).

Another vestige is the persistence of common **gesture**s even though the vast majority of the world's languages are speech driven. As the visible activity of virtually everyone who interacts using speech, gestures have been treated as optional and dispensable adjuncts to language (as written texts and telephony make them). Gestures have recently been studied as output from the same source as the speaker's vocal output (McNeill 1992). Nevertheless, their present appearance, interpretation, and universal use do not necessarily indicate how gestures may have been used in former ages.

What led to losing the track of language ages ago, leads theorists today to argue that language could not have evolved. Bacon called this common fallacy 'the idol of the marketplace' – the widespread belief that the way everybody does a thing is the only way it ever has been done. It may seem that everyone born speaks and understands one spoken language, or more, but deaf people everywhere, many who can neither hear nor speak, use fully functional sign languages. Deaf persons who sign and see their language instead of hearing and speaking it make up about ¹⁄₁₀₀₀ of the total population. This amounts to a considerable number, yet unsupported claims that deaf people's signing is no language at all have long hidden the truth. Real sign languages are alive and functioning and may contain clues to the way that **meaning**, even language-structured meaning could have begun to be shared in human populations.

VISION AND HEARING

Essential for finding the track of language all the way from its beginning to its present form is appreciating the difference between vision and hearing. With our eyes and brains we see 'what is there' – everything stationary and in motion within sight. With our ears and brains, however, we can detect only rapid variation in air density. Only when vocally produced sound waves have distinctive patterns that allow them to become conventionally associated with something else, can hearing them tell us much. When a stretch of speech does mean something, it is because members of a community possess a convention linking those speech patterns to those meanings. Such a convention must go back to the beginning of speech, but of course it constantly – though very slowly – changes, even as language does.

But getting meaning did not have to wait for a spoken language convention. A hominid creature can interpret some kinds of signs directly with no need for a convention. For example, when any of us (or a home-raised chimpanzee) points upward with a hand, it would be a very strange observer who did not associate that gesture with the concept we know as 'up'. We can conceive of 'up' and 'down' because we are bipedal animals and because our body and brain evolved from earlier species in the human lineage. Meanings like 'up' and 'down' have been associated with human vision and movement for a very long time, thus they have become conventionally as well as naturally linked to their meanings. (They are both an **index** and a **symbol**.) Pointing up and down also may have taken hominids a step closer to full consciousness and language, because these actions introduce a crucial feature of any language system – contrast. Opposition in the concepts is represented both by visible changes and by strongly felt opposing actions of the same muscle sets. We feel the difference between a gesture meaning 'up' and one meaning 'down', just as we feel the difference between measuring with hands something large and something small.

Other primates than ourselves have not been found to point intentionally, although we commonly speak of the instinctive 'freeze-motion' and fixed gaze of many social animals as pointing. The critical issue is consciousness. Chimpanzees, as Gerald Edelman notes, have primary consciousness (1989, Ch. 9). The chimpanzee Washoe was raised among signing and voluntarily non-speaking humans, by Allen and Beatrix Gardner and their hearing and deaf associates. When Washoe signed 'YOU ME GO-OUT' (using three signs of American Sign

Language, [ASL]), she was obviously aware of what she was asking for, and she it was who decided which human companion her hand for 'you' pointed at.

But these are clues needing interpretation. Washoe was exposed to signs of American Sign Language, as they are represented in the *Dictionary of ASL* (1976). ASL is of course the language of a dynamic modern microculture (Hall 1994), but the signs Washoe was able to learn and use appropriately suggest of course that the ancestor of *Pan* and *Homo* did not only have the capability of forming concepts but, in the right circumstances, of using and understanding visible representations of those concepts.

To extrapolate from fact to possibility: chimpanzees do not much use overt pointing naturally; modern humans point a great deal. It therefore seems likely that members of early hominid species (e.g., *Australopithicines*, *Homo habilis*) would have used manual pointing to some extent. With pointing many kinds of meanings can (and a million years ago could) be expressed and understood. The pointing hand and its movement, when seen and interpreted in the growing brain, can make, for instance, the full set of personal indications: 'you, me, him, her, them', and also 'us' as either 'you and me' or as 'other(s) and me'. It can designate directions: 'up, down, there, here, that way, this way'. It can even indicate transparently a few kinds of movement: 'come, go'.

Once such pairs of signs with meanings became well understood and regularly used within a social group, nuances in the hand–arm configuration could introduce new meanings; like 'mine', which, for many users of sign languages and 'natural' gestures, presses the hand's palm to the body in a natural show of possession; and consequently, turned outward, can signify 'yours', 'his', etc. Metaphorically, the hand pushes away the conceived-of object.

Using even a few of these sign-meaning pairs would have conferred great survival value on a hominid group. Being able to sign directions and indicate persons, as well as what property belonged to whom, would have enhanced group cohesiveness. It would also have enabled the collective, as Beaken's (1996) thesis holds, to accomplish what no individuals working separately could do. At the same time these signs for concepts would have brought the modern mind closer. Sign-concept pairs lead to a new level of brain circuitry. Concepts formed and manipulated in various circuits of the brain are characteristic of primary consciousness; but with direct, transparent, visible representations of concepts (Edelman 1989), the representations themselves become percepts, and thus additional concepts. Thus the brain's function grows as what is seen is sorted, conceptualized, represented, and the whole process repeated once more, now with percept and concept and representation interconnected in what Edelman calls 're-entrant mappings' in the brain. Note too that the brain, except in disease, keeps separate the representations and the things themselves – 'the map is not the territory'.

The behavior of chimpanzees who see something happening 'over there' shows that they have knowledge of a sort about what happened; but a hominid in the same situation, might see and point 'over there', and a member of the group might also see the gesture and recognize that it is directing attention to what happened there.

Such an exchange would do more than communicate the obvious meaning; it would imply that each of the participants has begun imputing mind or intentions to the other.

VERBAL AND NONVERBAL SIGNS, SENTENCES AND WORDS

Manual actions that are signs, that are interpreted as denoting something other than themselves, are commonly taken to be the equivalent of words – even when they are labeled nonverbal. In the search for the origins of language and its evolutionary trail, however, the common conceptions associated with *word* are misleading. The Chomskyan revolution in linguistics had the good effect of diverting disproportionate attention from words and sounds and meanings to structure and syntax. Unfortunately, however, its philosophical basis is Cartesian; it separates the by-definition, perfect *competence* of the ideal speaker (itself a Platonic idea) from the flawed *performance* of us mortals, the actual users of language. The paradigm that Chomsky's revolution overthrew (as understood by Austin, Bloch, Carroll, Smith, Trager and other anthropological and descriptive linguists) did not take words as the center of language but only as 'the entry point'. Their investigations led, in one direction, from words to **morpheme**s, **phoneme**s, **phone**s, and physiological foundations. In the other direction the investigators looked to **morphology**, including **syntax**, and semology (what phrases and sentences mean). But even scientists sometimes fall into the path of least resistance, and for younger linguists working within that once data-based paradigm it must have seemed easier and more profitable to concentrate on phonology than on investigating actual usage to see how words and sentences mean.

Of course, as Smith and Trager emphasized in the Linguistic Society of America's Summer Institute in 1957, language is a system; a system operates only when its **component**s are in harmony; and close analysis of words apart from sentences gets one no closer to the lost track than does a close analysis of the rules of grammar which neglects meaning and the human users of a language. This dictum about systems leads after four decades to restatement in the form of a paradox:

> Sentences cannot exist without words,
> but words cannot exist without sentences.

Less tersely put, we must have noun-like and verb-like signs before we can construct sentences, but the only way to know what signs are noun-like and what are verb-like is their use in sentences. For example, we cannot know whether a use of *run* is as **verb** or **noun** unless we find it as part of a longer stretch of English.

This consideration might be thought to impede the search for language origins and evolution but asking which came first, chicken or egg, did not seriously impede progress in biology. Knowing that sentence and word make sense only together – within the system – may even help turn attention in the right direction. The popular idea of language seems to be that to make a sentence one puts words into a sequence as required by grammar rules. This is not so different from the current theory that one begins with the rules, creates a tree structure, and then replaces the symbols at the ends of its branches with words from the **lexicon**. If the paradox holds, however, this procedure will not work, because the words in the lexicon must already be sorted by kind, and that sorting had to come from their roles in sentences. Recognizing that sentence and word are really inseparable, are not hierarchical, are but two aspects of a single system can refine our conception of what we are looking for when we look for language origins. Neither 'the first word' nor 'the first sentence' are likely to present themselves separately to view. Instead, we are likely to find word and sentence combined in something else.

If we turn aside from language for a moment to the parallel search for the origins of mind, this statement by Marcel Kinsbourne can be illuminating:

> experience is not a composite assembled out of its parts. The contrary position – that experience is carved out of a less differentiated whole – gains plausibility. While no truly apt metaphor for how the brain works comes to mind, 'crystallizing out' seems more fitting than 'assembling together'.
>
> (1998, p. 246)

Paraphrasing Kinsbourne, a sentence is not assembled out of words, but words are crystallized out of a less differentiated whole. But such a whole or matrix, pregnant with language, cannot be found in speech. The crystallizing process will not work with, for instance, the utterance, 'Black!' when that utterance means 'I want my coffee without cream or sugar.' The parts are all to be found in the question, not in the answer, although the answer is understood to be referring exactly to them. Speech does not provide undifferentiated wholes, perhaps because it never had to. Speech comes in already separate parts; not just the familiar 'parts of speech' but words, morphemes, phonemes, sounds; and it is true that these are indeed put together in strings, not crystallized out. But if speech began as a surrogate for manual expression of an already sophisticated visible language, obviously its wholes would long before have been crystallized into components.

GESTURE AS SYMBOL

A great many gestures are indeed still undifferentiated wholes. Even the two or three chimpanzee gestures reliably observed among wild animals fit the case. One of these is made with supinated forearm and slightly cupped hand pulled from the direction of another toward self. It expresses, in one translation: 'Please, you give me some of that food.' (The animal's demeanor strongly implies the 'please'; for a dominant animal snatches food from another, while a suppliant's whole body expresses subordination.)

Although chimpanzees have not crystallized out its parts, the parts are all there in the begging gesture they make: the hand is configured as if holding a piece of food (noun object); held forward it directly indicates the hoped for food possessor (**pronoun** subject, self); then its inward movement indicates with its direction and termination the transitive verb of giving as well as beneficiary (noun indirect object).

David McNeill sees human gestures as differing from speech: 'The gesture is thus a symbol, but the symbol is of a fundamentally different type from the symbols of speech.' Nevertheless, he finds gestural and guttural symbols accomplishing the same purpose:

> In language, parts (the words) are combined to create a whole (a sentence); the direction is thus from part to whole. In gestures, in contrast, the direction is from whole to part. The whole determines the meanings of the parts (thus it is 'global').
>
> (1992, p. 19)

The two kinds of symbol naturally differ, as sound differs from light and hearing from vision; and McNeill's term 'global' here seems equivalent to Kinsbourne's 'undifferentiated whole'. Any disagreement would seem to come from their aims – McNeill's to determine the relationship of gesture to speech in the behavior of modern human subjects, Kinsbourne's to trace the origins of mind, and thus of language.

What seems most likely in the present context is that early hominids first used and understood undifferentiated manual actions globally – as chimpanzees still do. But it is most probable that hominids used many more of them. The usefulness of such actions is beyond doubt. Just the directional and person-pointing gestures already alluded to could have led to successful hunting parties, because messages like, 'You go over there; You (pointing to another) stay right here; You (to a third) go that way'; change random activity into well-coordinated efforts.

When such global gestures and meanings had become common usage – and the time scheme must be reckoned in hundreds of thousands of years; the next step could be taken. It would require only that human creatures, *Homo erectus* or an earlier grade, began to see the hand of the gesture standing for something or someone and its movement simultaneously representing (often with geometrical similarity) what happened to that something or what that someone did. At that point, from the perspective taken here, nouns and verbs had crystallized out of the whole as sentence parts. Yet, together in the gesture, they still represented their relationship as well as what individually they denoted.

Such metalinguistic observations were neither possible or necessary for the earliest crystallization of nouns and verbs from the whole gesture. Neither are complex structure-creating rules. Simply associating different ways of holding and presenting the hand with different objects and creatures and associating different ways of moving the hand or hands with various changes and actions would have provided the earliest users of a gesture or sign language as powerful a grammar as the 'pivot-open grammar' stage identified in children's language acquisition by an earlier generation of psycholinguists (e.g., Braine 1963; Bullowa 1977).

This similarity should not be taken too literally. Children at the 'pivot-open' or 'two-word utterance' stage (approximately 18 months of age) are far from being able to survive without the nurturing care of adults. But when early human communication had evolved from the global gesture stage to the hand-is-noun, movement-is-verb stage, these humans were very much in control of their lives and their natural and social environment. Their social structure, their tool manufacture, their building of shelters, their use of fire, their artistic drives expressed in durable materials or on cave walls, their adaptation to other animals sharing their habitat, indeed, their whole existence would have been revolutionized by a simple two-element grammar.

A two-element grammar may be simple, but it is powerful and its acquisition is a giant step toward a fully human mind, because it involves a far from simple system; namely, the vision and coordinated movements and whole brain of genus *Homo*. Nor would this grammar have stayed long at the NP (noun phrase) + VP (verb phrase) stage. A gesture performed by swinging one hand across to grasp a finger held upright on the other, universally recognized in suitable contexts as saying, 'I caught it' or 'I grabbed him', already changes the pattern from intransitive to transitive. A head shake or scowl or some such natural expression along with an imitative gesture meaning 'Hitting it like that', could tell an apprentice working on a tool not to keep on going about the task the wrong way. Facial expressions of approval, amazement, and many other emotions visible while the moving hand is expressing a sentence, all add meanings that hundreds of millennia after the fact have come to be known as adverbial and adjectival.

As the human hand was put to more and more uses, artistic as well as utilitarian and communicative, the various shapes and movement paths it took in such activities would readily become signs representing them. Frank Wilson (1998) has shown how the evolution of the joints in human fingers, hand, arm, and shoulder would have been driven by nothing so much as increasing and increasingly varied hand use. It is economical as well as logical to believe that these uses were representational as well as instrumental.

GESTURE, SIGN AND THE ORIGINS OF LANGUAGE

If the gestures present-day speakers make while narrating a story are vestiges of language as it may have existed in an earlier era, they are, however, equivocal clues. Gestures studied by McNeill, like many commonly seen, may be only dimly in the speaker's awareness if at all. But other common gestures, those used in lieu of speech, e.g., 'good-bye', 'after you', 'OK', 'up yours', etc., are usually made with full awareness and seem to have retained the 'less differentiated whole' from which language may have come. There is no reason that the grammatical use of gestures should have driven out their global uses; the latter often provide economical and instant expression necessary in some situations.

Sign languages of deaf people, already mentioned, provide more clues to be investigated, and their users are aware of using them to express all their thoughts and feelings, but again caution is needed. It would be irresponsible to suggest that modern sign languages are just like the very first languages. However, the opposite view, that deaf people's signing is much younger than and dependent on speech is equally mistaken. Merlin Donald writes: 'The regency of formal sign language, and its resemblance to some forms of writing, argues in favor of its classification with ideograph writing and other modern inventions, rather than with oral narrative skills and speech' (1991, p. 308).

This continues an error made long ago by **Bloomfield** and **Sapir** in their treatises on language. It seems to have arisen because their informants on deaf sign language (oralist educators) had a vested interest in repressing signing at all costs; they were paid to teach deaf children to speak and lip read. It is true that in many countries deaf people do use in addition to their sign language a system of manually represented individual letters. Thus, with fingerspelling, they more or less freely introduce words of the local spoken (and written) language into their sign **discourse**. The two systems – actual sign language, and fingerspelling of written words – may also coalesce, as when a fingerspelled word is shortened and otherwise altered to become an actual sign (Battison 1978).

Donald's error in classifying sign languages should not detract from his diligent tracking of the stages in cultural change from *Australopithicenes* to *Homo sapiens*. Visible expression of grammatically linked concepts cannot be as old as the expression of emotions by animals (Darwin 1998), but gestural expression of directions and identification of persons and objects would certainly have appeared not long after the time at which fossil species can be seen as different enough from the southern apes to be included in genus *Homo*.

EXPRESSION, BODY LANGUAGE AND ALTERNATE SIGN LANGUAGES

More than manual gestures mark the evolutionary track of language. These gestures would surely have been accompanied by varying facial expressions and all the behavior subsumed in the popular phrase 'body language' – quite probably with incidental vocalization as well. The earliest languages would certainly have resembled modern deaf sign languages in one way: when vision is the receiving system for language, and when language signs are made of visible human activity, the whole appearance of the sign maker must be attended to. The modern separation of emotion or affect from thought, is just that – a recent effect of inappropriate analysis. As A. G. Cairns-Smith succinctly puts it, 'Conscious thought *includes* feelings' (1996, p. 154). This takes us back to Kinsbourne's observation: thought, logic, grammar, intellect – these may be precipitated out at various times from the undifferentiated whole of what we call emotion, but all of it is really what the brain is doing.

In addition to common gestures and the signs of sign languages of deaf communities (which may be national and, in North America, virtually continental in scope), vestiges are to be found in alternate sign languages. In *Sign Languages of Aboriginal*

Australia (1988) Adam Kendon reports on his extensive study of the sign languages of the Warlpiri and other tribes in the North Central Desert. He concludes: 'However, as our study of the NCD sign languages clearly shows, a sign language is not compelled by the medium it uses to develop in this way' [i.e., in the way ASL, for example develops]. One paragraph earlier, Kendon mentions some of these grammatical developments: 'space . . . exploited for the expression of grammatical relations, the "layered" inflectional system, and the use of so-called "classifier: forms"'. He adds that such exploitation will take place, 'only if there is no prevailing spoken language, shared by all users as a first language' (ibid., pp. 437–8).

The difference in grammatical structure between an alternate sign language such as the Warlpiri use and deaf sign languages as they have been described by linguists, might indicate (along with Kendon's suggestion that the spoken language determines the structure of the sign language) that the NCD sign languages do not lie on the evolutionary trail from a gestural beginning to modern spoken languages and primary sign languages.

However, other alternate sign languages are still used by members of Native American tribes. They preserve old traditions, but these lead one into the widely described but regrettably misunderstood 'Indian Sign Language', which has been given prominent and often inauthentic display in countless Western films. Garrick Mallery's monumental treatise of 1881, *Sign Language among the North American Indians Compared with that of Other Peoples and Deaf Mutes* is a competent anthropological study for its era. However, it is somewhat ambivalent. At times referring to sign language in the singular and emphasizing its universality, Mallery also lists in an appendix the strikingly different signs used to stand for the same meaning by tribes from widely separated regions.

Laymen still ask if there is but one sign language, universally understood; and the answer is, 'Certainly not.' The prevailing opinion from Mallery's time onward favored the attraction of universality, however, and 'the sign language' was promoted by other writers as a world language to usher in universal peace. These proponents, however, found the vocabulary of the Plains inadequate for translating Robert's *Rules of Order* and formal legislative language, and therefore they imported signs wholesale from the picture books of the time that presented the signs of 'deaf-mutes'. Their assumption that the sign language of the Plains was a visible *lingua franca* implied that it was invented when needed, at the time Indian tribes speaking different languages encountered one another and also white buffalo hunters and homesteaders whose language was English or French or German.

Despite the effect of a polyglot convergence on the range where the buffalo roamed, there are indications that much earlier, especially in the southwest, there were tribes with alternate sign languages. One is Mallery's extensive 1870–80 inventory of signs; another is Brenda Farnell's recent study of the Assiniboine or Nakota people on the Fort Belnap Reservation in Montana (1995). She describes a community with two languages (three if English is included), spoken Nakota and 'Plains Sign Talk', and examines in detail (both in the book and in an available CD-ROM) a noted story-teller's performance. This cannot be understood or translated unless one knows both the language he is speaking and the sign language he is using, because the signs and spoken words are truly complementary, not parallel as in McNeill's gesturing narrators or in Warlpiri women's simultaneously signed and spoken conversations.

What Farnell has found goes deeper than the grammatical structure of the spoken and signed languages. Her in-depth ethnography shows the movements of signing as well as dance and ritual iconically, indexically, and symbolically express the Nakota people's conception, for instance, of the earth. They do not impose N–S and E–W, Cartesian coordinates on space, but sweep an arc to include a whole quadrant of the horizon's circle for each direction. The circle is a prime symbol in this tribe's cosmology and figures in their paintings and carvings and dances as well as their signing. Farnell also notes that a mutually translating single sign and spoken Nakota phrase mean both 'thinks clearly' and 'is generous'. Recalling Cairns-Smith's 'Conscious thought *includes* feeling', this Assiniboine sign is made with the hand moving from the heart region, not from the head. In short, Farnell's ethnography clearly establishes the central role of movement in making meaning; not just word and sentence meaning but a culture's whole view of themselves and the universe around them.

There is no clear evidence in all this, however, only likelihood, that movements became sign languages before there was or could be a spoken language. For the nearest thing to solid evidence of that one must look further west, to the one or two living speakers of Klamath and the reports of current and earlier students of this Penutian language and the related extinct Modoc language. It is also possible that once this verb structure has been pointed out, identical structure may be found in verbs of a number of other indigenous languages.

VOCAL SOUNDS AND VISIBLE SIGNS

The Indian languages, Klamath and Modoc contain verbs with an extremely interesting structure. These verbs are composed, in linguistic terms, of two bound morphemes. That is, neither part, which may be a syllable or only a **consonant**, stands alone, but the two together express a clear verb meaning. What is of special interest here about these Native American verbs is that in many of them the first part is a literal translation of a handshape and the handshape stands for an object whose shape the hand visibly suggests. The second part of such a verb translates a manual movement of the kind that whole class of objects requires. Thus in Klamath, to say that someone threw something, the speaker must know what was thrown to pick the correct verb. The verb for throwing a ball and the verb for throwing a spear are different in two respects. The former has a prefix denoting a compact ball-like missile; its suffix denotes throwing overhand with the hand describing an arc. In the verb meaning to throw a spear, the prefix denotes a graspable shaft held up level pointing forward, and the suffix denotes a movement that does not arc but keeps the hand level as it thrusts forward.

This description is of the physical activities that the two verbs of throwing denote. It is not reversible. There is no way that the particular prefix and suffix sounds of Klamath verbs – or the sounds of any other spoken verbs – could have created, directed, or shaped those particular hand and arm actions. Once the human hand-arm-shoulder had evolved, these two different kinds of throwing – impossible for nonhumans – would have been used, as paleontology attests they were. These would have been very useful activities for a creature smaller and less well equipped than its primate cousins and other potential predators. But these actions would have been in practical use of course before they came to be used as visible representations.

The earliest, most natural representations of these ways of throwing would have been imitative actions with the hand empty. Moreover, these iconic-indexic signs would have looked very much as our present gestures and modern sign language signs for the same actions still do. Such verbs in Klamath and Modoc, and quite possibly in other indigenous languages, preserve the **semantic** nature and the necessary sequence of the gestural parts – a handshape is formed before it is moved. This is evidence as plain as any we are likely to find that a spoken language could develop from associating vocal sounds with visible signs that had already been paired with definite meanings. The nature of sight and sound rules out the converse, that gestures could have begun as translations of these or any other vocables.

There is no firm proof that early human insight into the structure of global gestures initiated language complete with syntactic structure, but entertaining this as a working hypothesis could lead to better understanding of the evolution of brain and mind as well as of language and culture. Recognition of the semiotic power in gestures, which sounds lack, could also improve education and child rearing. It is well documented that meaningful positive interaction in the first three years of a child's life has lasting effect on mental development (Hart and Risley 1995). Incontestable too is that all children, hearing as well as deaf, communicate (use their minds, that is) gesturally for some months before they use the language of their adult caretakers (Volterra and Iverson 1996). Not just deaf children but children generally could benefit from increased scientific and public awareness of the potential in gestures. While many of a speaker's hand and arm movements may be dispensable adjuncts to what is being spoken, gestural representations, because they involve hand and eye and brain coordination, are still powerful stimulants to mind.

FURTHER READING

Armstrong, D. (1999) *Original Signs: Gesture, Signs, and the Sources of Language*, Washington, DC: Gallaudet University Press.

Armstrong, D. *et al.* (1995) *Gesture and the Nature of Language*, Cambridge: Cambridge University Press.

Corballis, M. C. (1999) 'The gestural origins of language', *American Scientist* 87 (2): 8–16.

Stokoe, W. C. (1997) 'Language is natural but not automatic', *Semiotica* 113 (3/4): 369–83.

Wilson, F. R. (1998) *The Hand: How its Use Shapes the Brain, Language, and Human Culture*, New York: Pantheon.

4

LANGUAGE IN THE ECOLOGY OF THE MIND

RAY JACKENDOFF

The relation of language and the mind has been recognized for centuries as one of the most important and most controversial issues in philosophy and psychology. The present article outlines one contemporary position and briefly contrasts it to other current views. However, in that the terms *language* and *mind* are open to a broad range of interpretations, it is necessary to begin by making clear how they are intended here.

WHAT IS MIND?

Traditionally, the mind is understood as the seat of consciousness and volition; the 'mind–body problem' concerns the relation of consciousness and volition to the physical world. Since at least Freud, we have become accustomed to speak also of the *unconscious* mind. Modern cognitive science has come to use the term mind (or mind/brain) for the 'functional activity' of the brain, some of which is conscious and much of which is not.

A standard way to understand functional activity is in terms of the hardware–software distinction in computers: the brain is taken to parallel the hardware, the mind the software. When we speak of a particular computer running, say, Word 97, and speak of it storing certain data structures that enable it to run that program, we are speaking in functional terms – in terms of the logical organization of the task the computer is performing. In physical (hardware) terms, this functional organization is embodied in a collection of electronic components on chips, disks, and so forth, interacting through electrical impulses. Similarly, if we speak of the mind (or mind/brain) determining visual contours or understanding a language, we are speaking in functional terms; this functional organization is embodied in a collection of neurons engaging in electrical and chemical interaction. There is some dispute about how seriously to take the computational analogy (e.g. Searle 1980), but it has proven a robust heuristic for understanding brain processes.

It has become clear that, unlike a standard computer, the brain (and therefore the mind) has no 'executive central processor' that controls all its activities. Rather, the brain comprises a large number of specialized systems that interact in parallel to build up our understanding of the world and to control our goals and actions in the world. Even what seems to be a unified subsystem such as vision has been found to be subdivided into many smaller systems for detecting motion, detecting depth, coordinating reaching movements, recognizing faces, and so forth. Many of these specialized systems have an evolutionary pedigree, being found in primates and more distantly related mammals.

The term *mental representation* is often used to refer to a 'data structure' in the mind; for example, one may speak of the mental representation of shape or of kinship relations. Some researchers reserve this term for 'data structures' that are reflected in *conscious* experience; here, however, the term 'conscious mental representation' will be used for this purpose, admitting the possibility of 'unconscious mental representations' as well.

At present, little is known about how to relate mental representations to their physical embodiment in neurons, other than through relatively gross localization of activity revealed by the exciting new techniques of brain imaging and through more traditional studies of individuals with brain lesions. With few exceptions (primarily in low-level vision, e.g. Hubel and Wiesel 1968), it is far from understood *how* any of these areas do what they do, and what the detailed 'data structures' are that these areas process and store. There is also lively dispute as to how brain activity is related to the traditional problems of consciousness and volition (e.g. Dennett 1991; Crick 1994; Shear 1998).

WHAT IS LANGUAGE?

The term *language* can be understood in a broad sense to encompass almost any structured system, from animal communication systems to computer languages to 'body language' to 'the language of architecture'. Here I wish to understand it in the narrower sense used by linguists, excluding all of the above but including English, Dutch, Chinese, Navajo, and the approximately 6,000 other natural spoken languages of the world (with their **dialect**s). The past 30 years have shown that this class should also include **sign language**s such as American Sign Language (ASL) (Klima and Bellugi 1979; Fischer and Siple 1990).

In an approach to language that links it to properties of the mind, the essence of a language is its pairing of *expressions* and *messages*. **Expression**s are the 'outer' or 'public' aspect of language: the utterances, inscriptions, or **gesture**s created by a speaker that can be physically detected by an addressee. Messages, the 'inner' or 'private' aspect of language, are the thoughts (or concepts or meanings) that the speaker wishes to convey to the addressee by creating the associated expression.

The foregoing paragraph can equally be said of animal communication systems. However, human language goes beyond animal communication in two crucial respects. The first is its range of expression: only human language can speak about objects in the environment, social relations, history, the future, and products of the imagination; only human language can equally convey facts, make requests, and issue orders and instructions. The second is its unlimited productivity: as **Chomsky** (1965, 1972) (following Descartes and **Humboldt**) has emphasized, a human language provides the possibility of an unlimited number of expressions of arbitrary length; moreover, these are associated with correspondingly numerous messages of corresponding complexity. Although some communications are

relatively stereotyped ('How are you feeling?' 'Fine, thanks.'), a substantial proportion of the message–expression pairings that a language user creates and hears are
novel (consider this sentence, for example).

The mental representations involved in language must thus include the messages
(thoughts or concepts) transmitted by means of language; we turn to these shortly.
However, there must also be mental representations of the expressions that serve
as the mode of transmission. These representations must be used both in sending
and in receiving messages. Hence they cannot encode just 'what the expression
sounds like' nor 'how to produce the expression oneself': they must be neutral
between perception and production.

Mentally representing messages and expressions is not sufficient for using
language. A speaker needs a means to map between messages and expressions –
in production, to express a message that one desires to transmit; in perception, to
interpret an expression that one perceives. In addition, since the mental representation of expressions is neutral between perception and production, a speaker
producing an utterance needs to be able to map from mental representations
of expressions to movements of the tongue, lips, etc., which in turn actually make
the noises transmitted through the air; and a speaker hearing an utterance needs
to be able to convert the noises transmitted through the air back into a mental
representation of an expression. We thus arrive at a preliminary architecture of the
system like Figure 4.1. Figure 4.1 is the system for spoken language. Written and
signed language require different mental representations of expressions, and hence
different mappings to messages and to input and output.

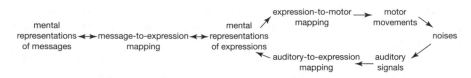

Figure 4.1 System for spoken language

For a good first approximation, the system of mental representations for
messages is the same from one language to the next. Translating from Chinese
into Dutch (for instance) can be thought of as creating Dutch expressions that
express the same messages as the given Chinese expressions. (We will turn to
a second approximation later, concerning the degree to which two languages
may not express the same messages.) On the other hand, since the expressions
of the two languages are different, the system of mapping between messages
and expressions must also be different (see also **translation**). However (again
for a first approximation), the system of mappings between expressions and
their auditory and motor counterparts is essentially independent of what language
is being spoken (and, among signed languages, independent of what language is
being signed).

If the human language faculty is instantiated in the mind as a system along the lines of Figure 4.1, speakers of the same language need to have (essentially) the same system in order to understand one another. Speakers of different languages differ from one another in the system of expressions and in the mapping from messages to expressions; and speakers of different dialects of the *same* language differ in these systems, but to a lesser degree.

Consider now what a word is within this mental system. A word clearly involves a piece of an expression (its pronunciation, and, in a written system, its spelling) – this is its 'outer' aspect. But aside from nonsense words like *brillig* and *tove*, a word also carries with it a concept, a piece of meaning or message – this is its 'inner' aspect. Thus a word must be an association of an outer aspect with a meaning; it is therefore simultaneously part of the system of expressions, of the system of messages, *and* of the system of mapping between the two. A speaker wishing to convey such-and-such a message will use *this* word to map *this* bit of message into this bit of expression, and in turn to map this into motor movements that make a noise. A hearer hearing such-and-such a noise will map the noise into a piece of expression, whereupon it will be possible to use *this* word to map into the intended message. Thus the role of words in the system of language is not just as static bits of data in the mind, but rather as associations that are actively used in mapping back and forth between messages and expressions.

THE COMBINATORIALITY OF LANGUAGE

Much of the neuroscience of language has been concerned with how words stored in long-term memory are activated ('light up') in the course of sentence perception and production (e.g. Caramazza and Miozzo 1997; Pulvermüller 1999). But activation of words alone is not sufficient to account for the understanding of sentences. Consider the sentence in (1).

(1) My brother handed his hat to your sister.

If understanding this sentence consisted only of activating the words, the sentence in (2a), not to mention the complete nonsense in (2b), would 'light up' the same words and hence be understood the same.

(2) a. My sister handed his hat to your brother.
     b. Sister brother hat to handed my his your.

Clearly a sentence is more than a collection of words: the word meanings are structured into the meaning of the sentence by means of **semantic** relations among them. These semantic relations are to some degree signaled by the syntactic structure of the sentence; the 'outer' expression reflects them in terms of word order and (in some languages) inflectional marking such as agreement and case. A sentence thus is a pairing of a message and an expression; its words are combined on the 'message' side through semantic relations, and on the 'expression' side through syntactic structure that signals the semantic relations.

The consequence is that the mind(/brain) must be capable of constructing novel expressions, novel messages, and associations between them 'online', using parts and relations stored in long-term memory. This requires a functional workspace, often called short-term memory or working memory, which is not merely a storage or rehearsal area for information, but rather an active agent in assembling information into structured complexes. As pointed out by Chomsky (1957, 1959; Chomsky and Miller 1963), these complexes cannot be characterized in terms of statistical constructs such as the probability of each word in the sentence occurring in the context of the preceding words: the goal of language understanding is not to predict the next piece of the expression. Rather, the goal is to associate novel expressions as a whole with novel structured messages. Chomsky and Miller's arguments were directed against accounts of language processing in terms of probabilistically sequenced elements (so-called finite state Markov processes), and against behaviorist accounts of learning (e.g. Skinner 1957). But they apply equally to modern-day connectionist treatments of language processing such as those of McClelland and Rumelhart (1986) and Elman (1990), based on learning association strengths among elements of input and output and among the elements of a sequence.

This property of free combinatoriality is not exclusive to the language faculty, of course. It appears for instance in the mental process of understanding the relations among objects in the visual field, which are ever changing and of arbitrary complexity. It appears also in action planning: consider the process of constructing a sequence of motor movements to return a tennis ball, or the process of packing objects optimally into a box. Notably, no mechanism is presently known for instantiating free combinatoriality in a system of neurons; this is a major challenge for the neuroscience of the future (Marcus 2001).

The combinatoriality of language requires us to amplify Figure 4.1: the 'mental representation of expressions' bifurcates into two distinct kinds of information, phonological and syntactic. The former is concerned with the sequence of speech sounds and their rhythmic (prosodic) properties. The latter is concerned with an independent characterization of speech units in terms of parts of speech such as **noun**, **verb**, and adjective, with their grouping into larger phrasal units such as **noun phrase** (a noun and its modifiers) and **verb phrase** (a verb and its arguments and modifiers). The relations among units in **syntax** are notions such as 'syntactic head of a phrase', 'subject of a verb', 'modifier of a noun', 'accusative case', and so forth. These categories and relations are not open to introspection in the way that speech sounds are; they are an 'inner' aspect of the expression, yet distinct from the message.

This bifurcation of the message leads to an organization of the language faculty like Figure 4.2 (the mapping functions are now represented simply by arrows). Words and sentences now have representations in all three of the domains to the left in Figure 4.2.

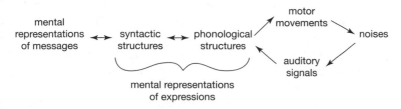

Figure 4.2 Organization of the language faculty

It is worth mentioning that this picture of the language faculty is somewhat different from the standard view within **generative grammar** (Chomsky 1965). There, syntactic structure is taken to be the central generative capacity of language and hence the sole source of free combinatoriality; phonological and semantic organization are derived or interpreted from syntactic structure. Here, free combinatoriality appears in all three components, and the combinations are correlated by the mapping functions (Jackendoff 1997). Syntax, rather than being *the* essence of language, comes to be viewed as an intermediary mechanism that helps map between the 'outer' relations of word order and inflectional **morphology**, visible in phonological structure, and the 'inner' semantic relations that build word meanings into the meanings of phrases and sentences.

Note, however, that such a reorientation of the role of syntax does not represent a rejection of the overall program of Chomskyan generative grammar. It is still necessary to characterize precisely the systems of mental representation that give rise to linguistic experience and behavior, in a way that comports with the free combinatoriality of language; and this is the central goal of generative grammar.

LANGUAGE ACQUISITION AND INNATENESS

The touchstone of Chomsky's approach to language – what brought linguistics into the cognitive sciences – is the problem of language acquisition (see <u>Salkie</u>). In order for a language to be effective for communication, its speakers must have essentially identical systems in their minds, the same mappings between messages and expressions. Yet this system is not present at birth: children obviously learn language on the basis of what they hear in the environment. Nor can the system be *taught* to children explicitly: even if children could understand instruction in the absence of language, most of the system is not open to introspection by the adults who would serve as teachers. Rather, the system must somehow develop in the child's mind in the course of the child's effort to understand and **model** adult linguistic behavior.

The question then arises as to what precursors must be present in the infant's mind in order for the linguistic system to develop in the presence of linguistic input in the environment. In particular, what precursors are present above and beyond general cognitive capacities such as memory and attentional resources, auditory discrimination, motor control of the vocal tract, sociability, the ability to deal with combinatorial structures, and the ability to learn by imitation? That is, what aspects of language learning require of the child a pre-existing cognitive specialization for language? The customary blanket term for these language-specific precursors is **Universal Grammar** (UG) (Chomsky 1965; see also Salkie). So the question can be put this way: how rich is Universal Grammar?

Consider what is at stake in answering this question. Since Universal Grammar is by definition unlearned, it must be transmitted to the infant genetically. Genetic material, of course, cannot directly **code** behavioral or cognitive capacities; it can only direct protein synthesis. Therefore the route from genes to Universal Grammar is necessarily indirect: the genes direct the development of brain structures that are particularly receptive to organizing themselves in certain ways in response to linguistic input. These brain structures *functionally* instantiate UG; their self-organization in response to linguistic input results in the brain functionally instantiating the **grammar** of a language.

Unquestionably, we do not expect the brains of all English speakers to be identical neuron for neuron. Nor do we expect their knowledge of English to be functionally identical, word for word and construction for construction. However, as stressed above, speakers' linguistic systems must be similar enough for effective communication; in fact it is surprising how uniform speakers often are on fine points of linguistic judgment.

In turn, this means that the ability to *learn* language must be relatively uniform from one individual to the next: it is more like learning to walk and run, where individuals differ in details of gait and speed but everyone basically can do it, than it is like learning to play a musical instrument, where individuals differ widely in talent. In fact, learning a second language as an adult is more like the latter: there is far greater variation of aptitude than in the child's learning of a first language. The relative uniformity of first language acquisition, despite wide variation in general intelligence, is indicative of a genetically based brain specialization at work, as observed as early as Lenneberg (1967).

Pushing yet one step further, the presence of a genetic specialization for language acquisition requires a source for the genes in question. The only possibility available is the usual process of genetic variation shaped by natural selection, during the period since the hominid line diverged from the great apes.

On grounds of parsimony, of course, one should estimate the scope of Universal Grammar conservatively, attempting insofar as possible to account for language acquisition by means of more general cognitive capacities. Such a position places less severe demands on brain structure and in turn on evolution. However, the necessity of accounting for the actual details of the language system and its acquisition places a counterpressure on the theory of Universal Grammar: one would like the child's job to be as easy as possible.

This tension between the demands on the child and the demands on genetics and evolution leads to an interesting theoretical dialectic. On one side are the proponents of a relatively rich Universal Grammar, led by Chomsky. In perhaps its clearest version, **principles and parameters theory** (Chomsky 1981), essentially all grammatical properties of all languages are available to the child from the start, rather like a piece of software that comes with all options, requiring only a number of switches to be set to tune it to local conditions. (The child does, however, have to learn the vocabulary (see <u>Salkie</u>).) A similar approach has recently emerged in **phonology** as Optimality Theory (Prince and Smolensky 1993): all phonological constraints are viewed as universal, and the learner needs only to determine which constraints take priority over which others in the local language. When pressed, Chomsky has tended to resolve the tension coming from evolution by denying that evolutionary reasoning is germane to grammatical theory (Newmeyer 1998). Yet, although it is difficult to reason on grounds of evolution to specific detailed properties of language (e.g. the existence of adverbs), the communicative advantages afforded by language more generally bear the marks of natural selection (Pinker and Bloom 1990).

On the other side of the dialectic has been a host of different interest groups, each seeking to minimize or even eliminate Universal Grammar in favor of more domain-general mechanisms.

- Some evolutionary neuropsychologists (e.g. Donald 1991; Deacon 1996), observing that no distinctive neural tissue has been found for the language capacity, and pointing out the evolutionary implausibility of Chomsky's rich and specific UG, simply deny that language could have any significant innate component. However, they offer no account of the extremely elaborate grammatical facts of language that linguists have been at pains to uncover over the past decades.
- Connectionist psychologists and computer modelers (e.g. Elman, *et al.* 1996), asserting that the only mechanisms for innate knowledge could be genetically specified synaptic weights – which are likely impossible – deny therefore that there could be such a thing as a rich innate learning capacity. However, as mentioned above, they propose a model of brain function that is inconsistent with the free combinatoriality of language and other cognitive capacities; and they too ignore virtually all the linguistic phenomena for which a learning theory must account.
- Functionalist grammarians (e.g. Langacker 1987; Givón 1995) attempt to derive grammatical properties of language from more general properties of thought and communicative strategies. This faction does pay considerable attention to the complexity of linguistic structure, often elucidating phenomena to which the Chomskyan school has paid scant attention. Yet there is a residue of grammatical phenomena that functionalist theory rarely attends to, and functionalists have discussed learning theory very little.

Unfortunately, this dialectic has invariably been couched as a choice between, on one side, Chomsky's rich and specific version of Universal Grammar, largely divorced from other cognitive capacities, and, on the other, the total absence of any human specialization for language learning. This polarization has left largely unformulated a range of intermediate hypotheses, in which a somewhat less specific and compartmentalized language specialization is built on top of general capacities and interacts more or less richly with them. The formulation and testing of such hypotheses in future research will depend on a respect for (a) the full complexity of linguistic phenomena and language learning; (b) what little is known about brain instantiation of functional processes; and (c) developmental and evolutionary considerations. In addition, it will require a better characterization of general capacities than we have at present.

The evidence for some degree of unlearned specialization in the language capacity is by now substantial. Here there is room only to list some of the more prominent types of evidence; the reader is referred to such sources as Pinker (1994) and Jackendoff (1994) for details.

- Language universals in phonology, morphology, syntax, and the structure of the **lexicon**.
- The universal time course of child language acquisition, including decay of the capacity for effortless language acquisition around the time of puberty (the 'critical period'). The difficulty of late second language acquisition has been supplemented by evidence from individuals deprived of first language input until past puberty because of social isolation (Curtiss 1977) or deafness (Newport 1990); these individuals also do not acquire full control of grammatical principles.
- The creation of fully grammatical languages by communities of children exposed to degenerate linguistic input. This includes the case of creoles developed from pidgins, for instance in Hawaii early in the twentieth century (Bickerton 1981) and, more recently, the spontaneous emergence of Nicaraguan Sign Language over the ten years following the creation of schools for the deaf in Nicaragua (Kegl *et al.* 1999).
- The attempts to train apes in signed language and various artificial languages (Savage-Rumbaugh *et al.* 1998). My interpretation of the outcome is that the apes do acquire appropriate symbolic use of a limited vocabulary (at most in the hundreds, by contrast with the many thousands achieved already by 6-year-old human children) and possibly very limited principles of symbol combination; however, they never achieve the grammatical complexity (i.e. phrase structure, embedding, and inflection) characteristic of genuine human language (including creoles). Lenneberg (1967) argued that these limitations are not just an issue of brain size, citing what were then termed 'nanocephalic dwarfs' whose brain size was comparable to that of apes; such individuals are deeply retarded but they do learn language.
- The existence of aphasias (specifically linguistic deficits due to brain damage), without damage to other cognitive faculties.
- The impairment of language acquisition by what are evidently genetic defects. These include for instance Specific Language Impairment (Gopnik 1999), in

which regular morphological inflection is particularly affected (this evidence is, however, controversial: Vargha-Khadem *et al*. 1995); and Williams Syndrome, in which general intelligence is impaired, much of language is spared, but *ir*regular morphological inflection is impaired (Clahsen and Almazan 1998).

In addition, it has become abundantly clear that cognitive specialization is hardly restricted to language. As intimated earlier, the brains of humans and all other animals are crowded with innate cognitive specializations. There is therefore no intrinsic reason to disbelieve the claim that the ability to learn language is also a genetically determined specialization, a natural part of the ecology of the human mind. The real issue, still a very open question, is how detailed and extensive it is.

THE RELATION OF LANGUAGE AND THOUGHT

The terms 'language' and 'mind' are conjoined in two major contexts. So far we have been discussing the first: the argument for a genetic basis behind the human language capacity. The second is the relation of language to thought: does one need language to be able to think, and how does one's language affect one's thought?

This second question comes heavily loaded, in that it engages prejudices concerning the relation between humans and other animals. Those who wish to emphasize human uniqueness (going back at least to Descartes) tend to identify language as the source of thought and to think of all animal behavior as brute instinct. Those who wish to emphasize the continuity of humans with animals (including many pet owners) tend to attribute more intelligence to animals than may be warranted. Careful methodology yields a result somewhere in between. Köhler (1927) argued meticulously that his chimpanzees were engaged in creative problem-solving behavior that was not due to any sort of conditioning. On the other hand, their failures at some problems he set them often displayed unexpected limitations in their intelligence. Similarly, Cheney and Seyfarth (1990) observed and performed experiments on vervet monkeys in the wild; they document a high degree of social intelligence, but also demonstrate where the monkeys' power of generalization breaks down.

Still, one might be reluctant to call what nonhuman primates (and dogs and dolphins) do 'thinking'. Thinking, in consonance with Descartes' intuitions, typically is associated with (a) consciousness and (b) verbalizability. Taking these in turn: there is no way to know to what degree animals – and babies – are conscious. Hence one can base no conclusions about their thought on assertions about their consciousness or lack thereof; furthermore, the putative intimacy of the relation between thought and consciousness has not been demonstrated. As for verbalizability: to require that thought be verbalizable, hence denying it to animals, also denies that Mozart and Picasso in their creative moments were thinking. This surely must be the wrong conclusion.

The view of language urged in previous sections provides an alternative (Jackendoff 1996). Verbalization is the linking of an 'outer' or 'public' expression with an 'inner' or 'private' message; the latter, the concept or thought, is what speakers communicate to each other using language. Notice that when one experiences oneself thinking, it is most often in terms of verbal images, 'talking to oneself'. These verbal images have the *form* of public expressions; but they are *not* the 'inner' form in which the actual thought takes place. Moreover, a bilingual can be said to 'think the same thought in different languages'. What makes the two verbal images the 'same thought' is that they are linked to the same 'inner form'.

These observations lead to the rather startling conclusion that 'inner forms', i.e. thoughts, are *never* conscious *per se*. Rather, what appears in consciousness are the 'outer forms' that are linked with thoughts. Most often these are verbal images, but in the case of Mozart and Picasso (and the rest of us on occasion), the outer form linked to the thought is an image in some nonlinguistic modality. This view permits us to attribute thought to animals. It is just that animals cannot be conscious of their thinking in the modality most comfortable to us, namely as verbal imagery.

We have a term for thinking that as it were goes on 'behind the scenes': we call it 'intuition', and find it mysterious and wonderful. The position advocated here is that *all* thinking, by humans and animals, is intuitive, but humans have conscious access to much more of their thinking by virtue of the accompanying verbal images.

This is not to say that human thought is identical to animal thought. There are at least three differences:

- Public linguistic communication allows a far greater degree of interpersonal coordination of thought than is possible among animals, thus making possible history, science, law, and gossip.
- Verbal imagery makes possible a much greater voluntary control of one's own thought processes and therefore richer and more precise reasoning (Dennett 1991).
- Language permits the framing of general concepts and abstract concepts in a way unavailable to other imageable modalities. Hence such concepts can be attended to, examined, and consciously recalled.

Thus although language is not *necessary* for thought, it significantly enhances the character and power of thought – it helps us think *better*. We can grant 'intuitive' thought to animals and babies, and we can grant the possibility of thought, conscious or 'intuitive', in modalities other than language; but at the same time, thought that is linked to overt utterances or verbal imagery through the language capacity is quite different in character.

The view arrived at here runs counter to various influential positions on the relation of language and thought. Perhaps the most extreme are the behaviorists, now mostly extinct, who claimed (e.g. Watson 1913) that thinking is nothing but subvocal speaking, i.e. verbal imagery, and that the idea of a 'concept' behind the language, an 'inner form', is nonsense. However, behaviorism never attempted to explain more than the most trivial of linguistic facts, and those in dubious fashion (Chomsky 1959).

A different sort of argument emerges from some strains of linguistic philosophy, often appealing to **Wittgenstein** (1953). The view is that there is no fixed meaning ('inner form') associated with linguistic expressions; rather, the best one can do is catalog the contextual uses of expressions. There is a germ of insight here, in that the message conveyed by an expression is indeed heavily influenced by one's understanding of the context (Sperber and Wilson 1986; Pustejovsky 1995). But on the other hand, the expression must convey *something* with which the context can interact; if it did not, a hearer could in principle know from the context what message was intended, without the speaker saying anything at all! A great deal of current research in semantics and **pragmatics** is concerned with factoring out the respective contributions to understanding made by linguistic expressions and by context (see Verschueren and **relevance theory**).

A position emerging from linguistics and anthropology, often called the **Sapir-Whorf hypothesis** (Carroll 1956) stresses the dependence of thought on language, claiming that differences among languages strongly affect the thought processes of their speakers. Again there is a certain degree of plausibility to this claim, particularly in the realm of vocabulary. However, in this respect it is unnecessary to look to other languages: we can simply look to technical subvocabularies in our own language (say, chemical, medical, cultural, or religious terms) to see how much greater precision is afforded in discourse and thought by virtue of having a more finely divided vocabulary. (Incidentally, the oft-repeated claim that Eskimo languages have dozens of words for snow can be traced to a far less extreme claim by **Whorf**; the actual range is not that different from English sleet, slush, blizzard, powder, etc. (Pullum 1991).)

Whorf's more radical claim was that grammatical structure fundamentally affects thought. He claimed, for instance, that the Hopi language contains no elements that refer to time, and therefore that monolingual Hopi speakers have no concept of time; both aspects of this claim have been refuted by Malotki (1983). More recently, experiments by Levinson and colleagues (1996) have shown some interesting differences in nonverbal spatial understanding by speakers of certain Australian aboriginal and Mayan languages, compared to speakers of European languages; the differences appear to be related to the way these languages encode spatial relations, thus offering support to a limited version of the Sapir-Whorf hypothesis. (However, Li and Gleitman 2000 dispute even these modest results.)

THE RELATION OF LANGUAGE AND THE WORLD

In the mentalist view of language advanced here, an utterance is seen as linking a conscious mental representation of an externalized expression to an unconscious mental representation that serves as a message. This view is far from universally held. Perhaps the predominant view in the philosophical community, stemming, for example, from Frege (1892), is that language is not a psychological phenomenon at all. Rather, language should be thought of as a relation between expressions, the world (or possible worlds), and truth values. The basic statements of meaning, following Tarski (1956), take the form 'Such-and-such a sentence is true if such-and-such conditions obtain in the world (or in such-and-such a possible world).' Minds play no role in such statements; language is taken to be an objective abstract part of the world, rather like numbers.

One must not discount the advances made by this approach in understanding principles of inference, quantification, anaphora, and so forth (e.g. Chierchia and McConnell-Ginet 1990). But from a mentalist point of view, it is important to realize what it ignores: a psychological account of how humans *grasp* and *acquire* language. In connecting an objective abstract language to these psychological phenomena, all the problems raised in the sections above re-emerge: how are principles of free combinatoriality instantiated in the brain, how does the child construct these instantiations given the input in the environment, and what genetic propensities exist in the species that permit language learning to take place with such uniformity?

The mentalist viewpoint can be pushed still further: to the degree that language permits speakers to make reference to the world, it is the world *as conceptualized* that is relevant, not the objective, 'real real world' (Jackendoff 1983; Lakoff 1987). On the one hand, speakers can make reference to all manner of imaginary entities such as Santa Claus and jabberwocks, so long as there is some conceptualization attached to them. Similarly, language is full of reference to entities that exist only by virtue of human conceptualization, such as marriages, college degrees, and political boundaries. On the other hand, one cannot refer to something one has not conceptualized: to make statements like (3a, b), one requires a conceptualization, no matter how skeletal:

(3) a. I'm thinking about something that I can't describe, kind of a vague directionless feeling.
b. I have no idea what *that* was, but there it goes again!

Thus people's use of language requires linking an expression with a conceptualization, precisely the position sketched in Figures 4.1 and 4.2. Language *not* used by people may well be abstract and objective, but is this of much interest?

Two points must be addressed to complete this answer to objectivist/realist philosophy of language. First, how does language avoid individual differences in conceptualization, such as personal associations (this is Frege's argument against a psychological approach)? The answer is that speakers manage to acquire essentially identical systems by virtue of their innate capacities for language and concept acquisition. Such differences as exist are normally negotiated in the course of conversation, each speaker attempting to make allowances for the other's state of understanding (Clark 1996).

Second, how do humans make contact between the 'real real world' and their conceptualization? The answer is through the perceptual and motor systems, which provide a complex (and still hardly understood) mapping from the external world into thought and from thought into action. In other words, Figure 4.2 can be expanded to make Figure 4.3.

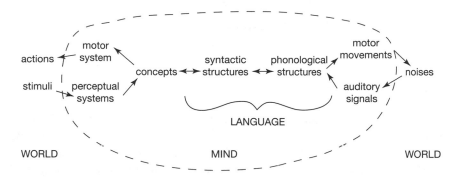

Figure 4.3 Mapping the external world

Concepts expressed in language that are relatively concrete (e.g. 'tree', 'red', 'eat') are to a significant extent mapped from external stimuli through the perceptual systems or through the motor system into actions; those that are relatively abstract (e.g. 'strategy', 'depreciate', 'abstract') are much less directly related to stimuli or actions in the world.

To sum up, we have presented here an approach in which language is firmly embedded in the ecology of the human mind. Humans use language to communicate about states of affairs in the world as they conceptualize it. Language is a cognitively specialized system that links concepts to internal representations of expressions; expressions are in turn linked to noises in the world by further specialized systems of perception and motor control. The child's acquisition of language is guided by a specialized unlearned system, Universal Grammar, which is a product of natural selection. All of these systems are instantiated in the neural organization of the brain. Spelling all their details out in functional, neuropsychological, developmental, and genetic terms is a major challenge for linguistics, psychology, neuroscience, and biology of the twenty-first century.

FURTHER READING

Chomsky, N. (1972) *Language and Mind*, New York: Harcourt, Brace, and World.
Crick, F. (1994) *The Astonishing Hypothesis: The Scientific Search for the Soul*, New York: Charles Scribner's Sons.
Dennett, D. C. (1991) *Consciousness Explained*, New York: Little, Brown.
Jackendoff, R. (1994) *Patterns in the Mind*, New York: Basic Books.
Jackendoff, R. (2001) *Foundations of Language*, Oxford: Oxford University Press.

5

SOCIOLINGUISTICS AND SOCIAL SEMIOTICS

GUNTHER KRESS

A STARTING POINT

The history of linguistic thinking in the twentieth century has to be seen against the background of its concerns in the preceding century with uncovering the histories and relationships of the Indo-European family of languages. It is a story of continuous change, of languages becoming differentiated over time, of connections becoming obscured, yet recoverable through the formulation of 'laws' of linguistic change. It is a story of a journey through time across a large part of Asia and all of Europe. Change is the theme of that journey. Against that concern with history and change, the twentieth century has focused on the *system of language* out of time. The Swiss linguist Ferdinand de **Saussure** is credited with being the originator of this turn. In a series of lectures given at the beginning of that century he formulated a distinction between a concern with language seen in time, a **diachronic** view, and language seen as a system at one moment, a **synchronic** view.

As always, ideas of a foundational kind arise in an environment where such thinking is in any case 'about', and it was that which ensured that of the complex set of ideas which we find in the book produced from lecture notes by some of his students, the *Course in General Linguistics* (1916) those which stressed the synchronic, the system, the autonomy of the system from its environment, were taken up and elaborated. These became the foundation of what has been the mainstream in linguistic thinking through the twentieth century. It led to the position where the centre of linguistic thinking became a concern with form; whether the forms of sound, **phonology**, or the forms of larger level structures, **syntax**.

Of course the mainstream is just that: other streams existed throughout the twentieth century, currents which continued to emphasize the connectedness of language to the social, which stressed the significance of function over form. **Sociolinguistics** constitutes one such current. Its history can be seen as a gradual move away from a position in which language is seen as an autonomous system, discreet from the social (either because 'it just is', by convention for instance, or by virtue of being a mental phenomenon), and an increasing insistence, throughout the latter part of the century particularly, on the shaping significance of the social, and on the close connections of the linguistic and the social.

The concerns of sociolinguistics have been many, and they have reflected the changing social and political concerns of its era. They have ranged from language planning, to the exploration of regional and social **dialect**s, of social **code**s, code switching, language use in interpersonal communication or in communication across cultures, an interest in the languages used in institutions, the variability of language with situation, **politeness** phenomena, the structures of spoken interaction as in **conversation analysis** for instance, the effects of power in language, and the exploration of social issues such as gender, race and other forms of inequity, and many more. Increasingly the focus has moved towards larger level units: whether seen from a more social point of view as **discourse**, or, from a more linguistic point of view as **text**.

Two tendencies are discernible: one is an increasing move away from abstraction and towards a concern with close, fine-grained analysis of what is going on; the second, connected to that, is an increasing tendency to re-integrate the linguistic with the social, a move away from the notion of the autonomous linguistic system. The move towards what is going on is a move away from language seen as an abstract phenomenon, towards language seen as *material* in the literal sense. This may appear in matters such as hesitation phenomena, turn taking in conversation, frequency or length of participation in an interaction, etc. What is revealed in such work is the meaningfulness of all aspects of communication, the fact that *representation*, the making of meaning, happens at all levels and engages very many aspects of linguistic behaviour well beyond those encompassed in 'core linguistics'. As this happens, sociolinguistics is increasingly, if implicitly, constituting a challenge to core linguistics; at the same time it is, even if implicitly, blurring the boundaries between that which is linguistic, that which is social, and that which lies in other semiotic modes.

In the meantime another development is underway. It suggests that the shape and the direction of the current communicational world demand a re-assessment, in which language is just one of a number of modes of communication, all of which are culturally and socially shaped. Verbal language is being displaced as a communicational mode by image, in many sites of public communication: whether in school textbooks, in newspapers, in reports produced in institutions of all kinds, in the electronic media, and in the information and communication technologies in general. Image has ceased to be there as mere illustration; that is, as an embellishment of the central, the written text. Image is now fully communicational in very many forms of text This means that neither linguistics nor sociolinguistics is any longer sufficient as the theoretical enterprise to account fully and plausibly for central aspects of representation and communication. And so the chapter provides arguments for the necessity of a new start in thinking about meaning, one which was promised both by Saussure (1916) and by Charles S. **Peirce** (1935, 1958) at the beginning of the century, in which an all-embracing theory would provide an account of human **semiosis** in all its manifestations. Via the use of examples this chapter argues for a position which can do justice to the requirements of this shift in the current world of representation.

First, then, an argument to establish the concept of *multimodality*, that is, the idea that communication and representation always draw on a multiplicity of semiotic modes of which language may be one; second, to tackle the central issue of the arbitrary or motivated character of **signs**, and to argue for motivation in all sign-making. Third, the chapter argues that in a full account of representation and communication the notion of context will need to be rethought; fourth, that none of this can fruitfully be considered without addressing questions of power, affect and the always transformative work of sign-makers. This can then lead to a satisfactory account of representation and communication in the contemporary world, as well as of the central issue of semiotic change in all semiotic modes

MULTIMODALITY: DECENTRING LANGUAGE

I have in front of me an entirely unremarkable text, a report written by an 11 year old in a science classroom in London. It was handwritten, in a lined copybook. It has a heading, a subheading, eight lines of handwriting, and a drawing at the bottom. It also has her teacher's comment on the bottom left corner. I ask myself what I would need to say, minimally, to convey the meaning of this text . Of course, that immediately opens the door to an impossible undertaking: there are a very large number of things that I can say. And you, the reader of the text in Figure 5.1 could immediately and plausibly add your meanings to my set.

Figure 5.1

So that is not my question really. Rather it is this: what would a theory need to encompass in order to give an understanding of the **meaning** that we might all regard as essential here? My answer, to jump ahead somewhat, is to say that if I were to talk about the written text alone, then you would feel that a crucial aspect of meaning was left out. I will return to the issue of the written part of this text.

Let me provide a brief context. The text had been produced at the end of a series of lessons on plant cells. There had been much talk by the teacher, reference to a textbook and to some worksheets, and much discussion. The teacher asked the class (all girls) to prepare a slide of the epidermis, the bit of slippery skin between the fleshy layers of an onion, and to look at it under a microscope, with four young women working together in each case around the one microscope, with the one slide under it. He then asked them to write a report of what they had done, and to draw a picture of what they had seen. He gave some instructions, such as: put your writing at the top, use black pencil only. Each of the four young women produced their own text.

In as far as the lesson was about what a plant cell is like, it is clear immediately that that information is not contained in the written part of this text: it exists in the drawing. The writing has the function less to give a report of what went on, more to turn that into a procedure to be followed by other experimenters. It is the drawing which gives us information about what the student saw when she looked into the microscope. If as the teacher I want to know what she had seen, what she had learned about the central issue of curriculum here, then it is the image that provides that. And the teacher has responded, by writing his comment, suggesting what else might have been done, in an oblique criticism of what she drew.

Of course, when I say that what she had learned is revealed in the image, that isn't the full story. A science teacher will regard it as essential that the students should learn to write up what they had done in a fashion considered appropriate for science; the procedures to be followed in doing an experiment are at the core of 'doing science'. But the point of this lesson was that of the curricular content, and that doesn't appear in the writing.

There is here a specialization of tasks between image and writing. Writing is used to tell what happened, it informs about the events; image is used to show what there is or was, it informs about content. Language serves one function, image another. Language is not the full carrier of all meaning, nor even of all 'central' or 'essential' meaning. Let me turn now to another text produced by a student from the same group of four (Figure 5.2).

Figure 5.2 is startlingly different. The image is at the top of the page, not as the teacher had requested. It seems to bear no or little relation to that in Figure 5.1. It is hard to imagine that the two young women had looked at the same slide, the same bit of 'reality'. And where the written text of Figure 5.1 is highly procedural as a **genre** (it is close to a 'recipe' indicating literally step by step what needs to be done) the writing here is much more narrative-like: it gives an account of what events happened, in sequence, it tells a story; it is not a procedure, generically speaking. The teacher seems much happier with what this student 'saw' and drew;

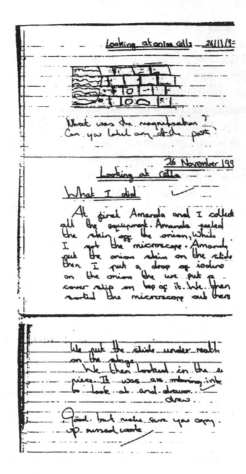

Figure 5.2

his comments do not offer an implied criticism, but offer suggestions. His response shows that he regards the drawing as the core of the text.

There are a number of issues which arise immediately. One is, as I have already indicated, that a theory of representation and communication which focuses on language alone will not suffice, in this instance at any rate. A second one is that of specialization: if other modes take some of the communicational load, then the question of what load language takes arises; and following from that, if there is a functional specialization between the modes – writing doing one kind of job, image another, what effect will that have on language itself? The other issues are to do with representation: how do we make sense of the very different responses of these young people to the same bit of reality, the same teaching, the same textbooks and worksheets? And a further question that can be raised here is: why is writing chosen for the one task, and image for the other?

The teacher's differing response to the two drawings might give us an answer to the first question. The drawing in Figure 5.2 is seemingly (nearer to being) correct, the one in Figure 5.1 is not. Where does the standard for correctness come from? In this case the textbook and one of the worksheets had spoken of cells looking like bricks in a wall, and had suggested that the students should look out for something that looked like a brick wall. Hence the teacher's comment: 'Did what you saw look like my "diagram" in any way?' But neither the textbook, the worksheet, or the teacher's 'diagram' contained any sign of the large or the several smaller airbubbles drawn in Figure 5.2. So that drawing is not a copy, at least not straightforwardly, of either the teacher's diagram or the image in the textbook.

In the teacher's talk preceding this task he had used a different metaphor, that of a honeycomb. The four students had chatted while they were doing the experiment, and they had introduced further metaphors: 'Oh, it looks more like a dry stone wall' and 'It's a bit like a wavy weave.' Whether Figure 5.1 draws more on wavy weave than honeycomb is difficult to say; it is clear that it is not influenced by the metaphor of the brickwall. The teacher's critical comment also indicates that he had not really been aware of the potentially shaping effect of his spoken metaphor, that of the honeycomb; his focus had been on the pedagogic power of the image.

In each case the students have made their selection from meanings which had been made available in the lessons, which had been around, selecting some and ignoring others. The metaphors which had been around guided their seeing, but their seeing also guided their inner representation: 'Oh, it looks more like a drystone wall' is a representation (her drawing in fact represents something that looks like a drystone wall) which both draws on 'brick wall' and modifies it, transforms it, and makes a new representation which is not what was available before and yet is related to it. The children are both embedded in meanings and in the structures of their environment – here the classroom, but not only that, because both 'drystone wall' and 'wavy weave' come from somewhere else – and at the same time they are able to select from that environment according to their *interest* and to transform what they have drawn on in their new representations.

The teacher preferred one image over the other; his authority/power allows him to do so, and it might lead him to insist that the student who drew the honeycomb/ wavy weave change her image (he did not). But both images are transformations of the meaning resources that were available to these young people; and the transformations are expressions of their interest in relation to this domain.

What can we say about the choice of the semiotic **modes** used for representation, writing and image? It would have been possible for the teacher to say: 'Write out for me, in descriptive detail, what it was that you saw when you looked through the microscope.' The children would have obliged, and produced written texts that did that. They would not have represented what they did in their drawings, because the mode of the visual makes possible forms of representing which are not available to the mode of writing, and vice versa. The visual is founded on the *logic of display in space*, on the *simultaneous presence of elements* represented as standing in specific relations to each other. The written (and the spoken much more so) is founded on the *logic of succession in time*, on the *sequential unfolding of events*. A culture can make the decision to work against the logic of each, as Western cultures have done for the past three or four hundred years, or to work with them in any number of ways.

The rise of linguistics in the West needs to be seen in that context; and the emergence of sociolinguistics, in the second half of the twentieth century in particular, must be understood in the context of the constraints on representation produced by that decision. We are now in a period of upheaval in the landscape of communication in which the modes of language as writing, and of image are newly coming into contestation. The texts produced by the young people here are entirely usual in their environment, entirely usual to them, but are also increasingly usual in the communicational practices in the West. This is forcing a deep reassessment not only of the place of modes of representation other than language, but of language itself, whether as speech or as writing

THE MOTIVATED SIGN

In discussing the texts of Figures 5.1 and 5.2 I commented in passing on the different generic forms chosen by the two writers. The teacher had made no stipulation on what genre they should use, so this was a choice more open for them than others here. As no rule, explicit or implicit, seemed to have been at issue, none was there to break; and the question of error or mistake does not therefore arise, as it did with the drawing.

We can ask then what motivated the choice of one genre over another. Was it merely accident? Two of the four chose narrative-like forms, the other two procedure-like ones. Genres bring with them meanings: a procedure has a different meaning to a report; both genres could be used as vehicles for the expression of certain contents, as they are here for instance. The meaning would be significantly changed. Given the existence of a choice or a set of choices we are entitled to attribute *interest* to the choice that is made. Some insight into what the interest might have been is provided by the meanings of the genres. The procedure might have been felt by their choosers to be more scientific; the other two writers might have felt that as well but wished to be more personal. In this instance, genre was available as a **signifier**, and the young makers of signs found their meanings best accommodated in each case by the use of that genre/signifier which proved apt as the vehicle for their **signified**s, their meanings.

In this approach to meaning the overriding concern is the interest of the maker of a sign: what is it that she or he wishes to represent and communicate, and what is the apt form – the form that already, through its histories of use as much as in its material aspects – suggests itself as the best, the apt means, of being the carrier of that which is to be represented and communicated? This is a social semiotic approach to representation, in which *sign* is central, and sign is the result of intent, the sign-makers' intent to represent their meanings in the most plausible, the apt form.

This approach contrasts with that of mainstream linguistics throughout the twentieth century: it has largely been the science of the signifier rather than the science of the sign, that is, the science that dealt with form. Meaning was strictly separated from form, leading to the emergence of subdisciplines to deal with meaning: **semantics**, stylistics, **pragmatics**, and sociolinguistics.

The struggle of sociolinguistics to establish itself can only be understood in the context of its attempt at a mirroring of the central assumption adopted by the mainstream of linguistic theorizing, that is, **American structuralism**, of which Noam **Chomsky** (1957, 1965) is the best-known contemporary exponent.

The question of the motivated sign has not been an issue in mainstream linguistics. Saussure's famous statement (1916) that the relation of signifier and signified is arbitrary and conventional has formed an undisputed common sense in that form of linguistics. One of its corollaries in the field of sociolinguistics has been what can be called 'correlationalism'. This takes the autonomy of form from meaning (and context) for granted, that is, it proceeds on the basis that form is not determined or produced by context, but that it correlates with it. That applies as much to notions of code-switching, as it does to the variability at the micro-level of phonology, as in **Labov**'s (1972a, 1978) well-known writings, where he showed that the pronunciation of certain words (whether, for instance in the word *beard* the *r* is pronounced or not by speakers in New York) varied quite precisely with the social position of the speaker.

In other words, within correlational views the linguistic code is not determined in its characteristics, whether in its syntax, **morphology**, phonology, by contextual factors, but is independent from them. At a second stage, a secondary kind of code can then become established which leads to the existence of correlations: if you are in context X, then code Y will be the appropriate code to use. Of course, here as elsewhere in what I am saying, it is essential to insist that I am talking about the mainstream: whether in linguistics or in sociolinguistics. Other positions existed all along, such as that of British Functionalism (**Halliday** 1978, 1985), European functionalism (**Bühler** 1990) or that of Soviet philosophy and psychology of language (**Bakhtin** 1986; **Vološinov** [1929] 1973; Vygotsky 1978) (see also Coupland and Jaworski).

But it is clear that a direct challenge to the notion of the arbitrary relation of signifier and signified is essential if sociolinguistics, even now, is to free itself from the fetters of the conceptions of the mainstream. Here I will proceed via a discussion of two further examples, one from the field of visual representation, and one from that of language.

My first example, Figure 5.3, is a drawing made by a 3 year old. Sitting on his father's lap he drew a series of circles, and when he had completed the drawing said: 'This is a car.' How is this a car? Clearly enough the meaning that he wished to represent, his signified, was 'car' and he chose what were for him criterial features of 'car', namely wheels, to represent 'car', the object in his mind. Wheels were for him criterial of car. At the age of three it may be that wheels are what the eye falls on most immediately; the family car at the time was a VW Golf, a car with wheels perhaps particularly prominent; wheels might also be that feature of 'car' which most captured his attention, in 'going round and round', etc.

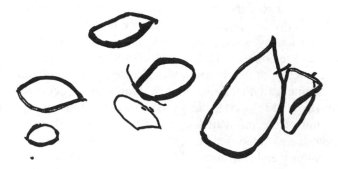

Figure 5.3

Several general points emerge. First, when we represent an object or event we never represent all its features but only ever represent it partially, precisely in relation to our interest at the moment of representation in the phenomenon. The fact that representations are only ever partial is easily missed, as is the fact that their partiality is a reflex of our interest in the phenomenon. Language is particularly likely to obscure this: a word is a word, and seems to fully represent that which it seemingly stands for in our utterances. Second, our representations/signs are always metaphors: 'a car is wheels', and in this instance, a second metaphor, 'a wheel is a circle'. Finally, this process is founded on the assumption that the signifier (circle in one case, wheels in the other) should have in its make-up those features or characteristics which already signal the meanings of the signified; the signifier is 'ready', so to speak, on this occasion to be the carrier of the features of the signified.

My second example here goes the other way around: in the 'car as wheels' example, a meaning was looking for its form, a signified was looking for its apt signifier so to speak. In the next example a signifier is looking for its signified. The example comes from a primary school in London. The class of 8 year olds has been studying the reproductive cycle of frogs (see Figure 5.4). The teacher has asked the class to write about this topic.

James is in the position of all language learners: he meets forms which he does not know, and which he knows are signs; but all he has as 'clues' are the characteristics of the signifiers. He acts on the assumption that the 'shape' of the signifier is a good indication and a reliable guide to the 'shape' of the signified. The meaning of the word which he does not know comes to him in two ways: as a set of words, the lexical form/signifier (as he deduces it) of 'frogs born', and the signified which he does not know but feels that he can infer from the shape of the signifier, namely the abstract word/meaning for the stuff that tadpoles emerge from.

James does not fall prey to the pervasive and persistent idea that the relation of signified to signifier is one from meaning to sound (that the relation is one between 'concept'/ signified on the one hand, and sound sequence/signifier on the other, that is, that he has to somehow find a connection between the sound sequence *f r o g z*

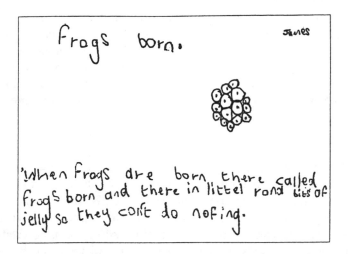

Figure 5.4

b o r n and the concept that corresponds to the jelly-like substance with the eggs inside). He knows that the signifier-stuff in this case is lexical material, 'words'.

James' problem is precisely that of any reader: meeting signifiers and inferring from their shapes the characteristics of the signifieds in order to make a new sign. His approach pays attention both to the shape of the stuff that is read, that is, he treats 'text' as having shape and resistant characteristics, and it shows how the reader is nevertheless forced into processes of deduction from the shape of the signifier to the shape of the signified. The resolution of this process of deduction is the transformative work of reading. Hence no reading is like any other, and yet no reading is arbitrarily arrived at either. This overcomes a problem in theorizings of reading: it acknowledges that texts have real features (reflecting the social histories of their making) which are the prompt for the reader's attempt to find appropriate signifieds for them, so that they can become signs for the reader, and it acknowledges that readers do work which is shaped by their social and individual interests, in making signs from an assemblage of signifiers.

At this point the question of power enters again. James' sign will not stand; the power of the institution in which he is present will assert itself, not to speak of the communities of which he is a member already. A powerful reader can assert her or his right to the legitimacy of their sign-making. In this fashion the ideas of the powerful become the ideas of the group, as **Marx** might have said. It is important to recognize that from the reader's point of view the text is an assemblage of signifiers, of which the reader knows that they were made as signs in the motivated relation of signifiers and signifieds.

For writers as for readers the sign is thus always inescapably an effect of social factors. Their interest in the matching of signified with signifier is the expression of their social histories, their assessment of present social contingencies and of the communicational environment including relations of power or solidarity. All these, as well as matters of affect, find their realization in the always new metaphor of each sign made in writing and in reading. Hence *the social is in the sign*; it is not a question of a correlation between an autonomously existing sign, and an external social reality, of a context around the sign, or around the text as complex sign. The sign is fully social, the work of social/semiotic agents expressing their sense of the social world at a particular moment, and of their affective response in it.

CONTEXT

In a correlational view of language context appears as the other in a pair of terms: language on one side, and all the rest – context – on the other, and the two are brought into some regular relation with each other. Features of the text can be referred to aspects of the context to gain their full sense. In non-correlational theories of language, context forms a kind of backdrop (or has no status at all), brought into play whenever some feature of the text proves resistant to explanation. Here is a piece of text, also from a science classroom , though not the one referred to above. The teacher is talking about blood circulation to a mixed class of 13 to 14 year olds.

Spoken text	Action
now if we look at *that* on *our*	places model on front desk
model you can actually see *here*	stands behind model arms in front
the heart has four main blood vessels	picks up heart points at heart
okay now	puts heart back in model
and if we take *the front* off, you can	takes front panel off heart
see what's going on *inside*,	lifts heart out to in front of him
basically the blood is coming round	sticks out index finger,
loops from *the rest of the body* into *this*	from his head to heart, puts finger in
first chamber *here* . . . okay it goes	chamber moves finger about in
from *this chamber* into *this*	chamber
bottom chamber on *this* side *that's*	moves finger to next chamber
where *the first pump* happens	slowly contracts hand into fist, twice

If we look at speech alone (which has been a traditional way of conducting research on what happens in classrooms), we find many elements of language not fully explicit in their meaning. I have emphasized some of them here. What is *that* in line 1, what does it refer to? Where is *here*, in line 2?; etc. Linguistic theory has produced the category of **deixis** to account for questions such as these: the two elements here are deictic, they point 'outside' of language to aspects of the context; (whereas 'the heart', 'the blood', have been referred to in prior speech so that deixis operates within language). 'Pointing outside language' assumes, however, the view of language as self-contained, as autonomous. We can ask if that corresponds to our experience of communication. Do we experience, in a situation such as this, language as separate, against a backdrop of context?

In the video recording of this lesson the teacher stands behind a bench, behind him a whiteboard with a diagram representing in highly abstract fashion the path of blood in its circulation around the body; in front of him is a three-quarter lifesize model of the upper torso and head of a human body. His **gesture**s integrate action on the model with action on his own body, and they perform other representational tasks – showing regular pumping, contraction and expansion of the heart, etc. It is a communicational event in which a multiplicity of modes are in play – gesture, model and action with the model, image, speech, positioning in the space of the classroom, the teacher's body as semiotic resource – an orchestration of these modes, designed for pedagogic effect.

Not all the modes are employed in the same way, to the same degree, at all times. In the brief extract here speech is prominent; at other times, and for considerable stretches, speech is absent. Not all the modes serve the same function: in this instance I am inclined to say that – as with the onion cells texts – language (here as speech) is not central, but the model is. Speech has a secondary function. Once we see that, the question of deixis becomes quite different: speech is not the central mode referring 'out', but speech acts as a secondary mode supporting the tasks performed by the teacher with the central mode of the model.

In this example we have a multimodal representational ensemble, with different modes performing specific (and continuously varying) functions. This ensemble is treated by the teacher (as designer/rhetor/orchestrator) as a whole, and in his making of signs he establishes links across the modes: the signified of the model has as its signifier an element in speech, *that*; the signifier *here* (in line 2) has as its signified an element in the semiotic mode of the model, the heart; and so on. There is no context as an *outside*: there is an ensemble of semiotic modes brought together into an integrated whole. The idea of 'pointing outside' is replaced by the notion of signs made across semiotic modes, of cohesive ties establishing signs across modes. Many of the central issues of the theoretical area of deixis within linguistics disappear: it can be seen as a problem produced by a view of language as autonomous.

Similarly, the view of language as *correlating* with the social, with contexts of whatever kind, will need to change, whether at the macro level as in code-switching, or at a micro level as in phonological variations in differing social contexts. The small example from the classroom stands for semiosis at all levels. This is not to say that a concept such as code-switching has lost its utility: it may well be the best way to describe what is a real phenomenon at the level of social description. Semiotically however, code-switching is an instance of sign-making as described here, though operating at a larger level.

The question posed earlier about the functional differentiation of modes arises very clearly here. Why does the teacher choose to use this mode for that purpose, and that other mode for that purpose? At a later point he is likely to use yet another mode for a quite similar purpose. For instance, in this small textual sample, he uses speech to do quite a lot of interpersonal communication: 'Now if *we* look at that on *our* model *you* can *actually* see . . . .'. Some of this establishing of solidarity could be done differently: in other classrooms the teacher might come round from behind the bench, standing in front of it, using a spatial mode to establish solidarity. Or, he might not use the model at all, choosing to convey the curricular content via image (in a video or a CD) or via syntactically more formal speech.

The point is that the teacher's role as designer of representation and communication becomes foregrounded: he needs to control, in order to shape an apt communicational ensemble, a whole range of modes which formerly might have been assigned to 'context'. Design works in the service of rhetorical purpose: this mode is chosen for this purpose because now, at this point, with this audience, and with this audience in this state (for instance, fresh in from the playground) this will serve best. At another point, his or her assessment will be: now I must present what we have done in 'canonical' form, and this mode – maybe image as diagram, or language as writing – will serve best to provide both the epistemological possibilities, and the form of authority needed.

These are questions which have been central to sociolinguistics for much of its life, in the second half of the twentieth century at any rate. The social semiotic approach taken here goes well beyond notions of appropriate action in relation to well understood linguistic and social codes. In that conception, the individual simply 'implements' an existing system, she or he has no agency in a real sense. It also goes well beyond the idea that to represent and to communicate is to make choices from a repertoire of available meaning options, as in Halliday's (1978, 1985) systemic functional grammar. In the latter approach *choice* from available resources for meaning-making is the action which the language user can engage in. That is a considerable degree of agency; though it remains limited by the possibilities of the system.

In a social semiotic approach the existence of available resources is acknowledged, as is the fact that their shape is the result of the past actions of semiotic/social agents acting in the constraints of their locations, but acting transformatively, both in choosing the resources (which modes, which elements within each mode to use as signifiers for new signs), and in transforming them in relation to the interests that they have in a particular moment of communication.

CHANGE AND HISTORY IN SEMIOTIC SYSTEMS

All human semiotic systems change, though not at a rate usually noticed by those who are constantly engaged in their 'use'. If the metaphor of 'sign-making' has any plausibility, and if the metaphors/signs constantly newly made do express the assessment of the social situation in which sign-makers find themselves, as well as their own social and cultural histories, and their affective states in the moment of representation, then we have an account both of change (signs are constantly newly made, the resources of representation are constantly remade) and of the directions of change, at least broadly (the sign always embodies the state of the social and the cultural as assessed by the signmaker). And we have a theory that says that it is the individual, engaged in representation and communication who is the agent of that change.

How can such an assumption be justified or documented? The only place to look is of course in the microhistories of sign-making. The evidence is then everywhere once we have decided to look through this lens. It is there in the gradual move by children into the semiotic systems of their cultures, as much as it is in every semiotic interaction. The next recounted example makes this point; it also shows that the process of transformation is at work in language as everywhere else.

The example is now well over twelve years old. It was an interview on a Sydney radio station with a 'youth' appeal. The female interviewer and the two interviewees were in their early twenties. The interviewees were two Australian women who had returned from Tokyo, where they had worked as hostesses in bars. The interview was conducted as part of the International Year of Women.

The interviewer opened this section of the interview with the question/assertion that hostesses were like geisha girls, there to 'entertain men'. The interviewees respond by saying that being a geisha is an art form, and that men often bring women guests; and hostesses don't entertain men, 'they entertain the man', and do so 'with music, with dance', it rests on a skill comparable to others in the entertainment 'sector'; what hostesses do is to 'entertain the male sector'.

The element I have focused on in my summary is the syntax of the **verb** *entertain* and its (micro)history in this interaction. In the interviewer's first use it is used transitively 'they entertain men'. A true transitive verb is one in which the subject **noun** of the verb is the agent responsible for the action, and the action has real, direct effect on some entity. If 'entertain' is taken as a euphemism for sexual intercourse, then the use of the transitive form of the verb constitutes an accusation which the two returnees wish to reject. They both engage in verbal defence, using the resources of syntax to do so. Their first move is to change the object noun from the specific plural 'entertain men' to the abstract generic 'entertain the man'. That diffuses the accusation somewhat: it is difficult to have sex with 'the man'. A similar move is that from transitive to the intransitive 'they entertain with music, with dance', where the direct object has disappeared and in its place there is an instrumental complement: like 'chopping logs with an axe'. While both uses seem slightly odd to me, as transformations they do not unsettle the syntactic system itself: 'entertaining the man' can be seen to be analogous to 'entertaining the public', and similarly for the instrumental use. However, the use 'entertain the male sector' goes beyond the bounds of the syntax of *entertain*. In the usage which I have observed, *entertain* needs to have an animate entity as its object noun. You can entertain a human, an animal (if it is assumed to have intelligence) but you cannot entertain a log, or a plate of chips. *Sector* is not an animate noun, and so the 'selection restriction **rules**' (to borrow a term from older forms of Chomskyan grammar) between transitive verb and direct object have been broken.

Of course, in the approach put forward here there is no 'breaking of rules', there is transformation of available resources. But the grammatical potential of the verb *entertain* is now different, it has been changed, whether we see it as the breaking of rules or as the transformation of linguistic resources. The syntax of the language has been altered. The change here will have repercussions throughout the language.

The motivation for this transformation is entirely clear, and the direction of the change is a result of the social contingencies surrounding the making of the text. This is how the social enters into and shapes the linguistic.

Of course, not too much will happen as a result of this one incident; though the two young women carried the day on that occasion. This is simply one instance, and unless conditions were such that this usage was repeated over and over, it will not have a lasting effect in the language as a whole. It is likely to leave a trace, however slight, in the language history of the three participants. The principle, however, is clear. The social conditions of the day – the state of affairs in feminist politics in Australia, as well as much larger issues such as global economics – why did the young women go to work in Tokyo? – and much more besides, such as the censorious attitude of the interviewer, based on an older set of values, all of these are there as motivation and interest giving rise to this shift. *The social is in the sign*. The sign carries the history of its making, and in that it carries the history and the meanings of the social group in which it was made.

A SEMIOTIC APPROACH TO REPRESENTATION AND COMMUNICATION

In the past hundred years there have been several attempts at a theoretical unification of the different modes of representation. One of the most productive was that of the so-called Paris School semioticians (Barthes 1973c, 1977b) or the work of Thomas A. **Sebeok** (1976a, 1977), or indeed that of Umberto **Eco** (1973, 1976). The work of the Paris School foundered on one issue above all: the mistake of taking language as the privileged mode of communication, and the attempts to use its theoretical and descriptive apparatus to provide accounts of other modes. Roland **Barthes**, whose work stands unrivalled in many respects in providing insight into all aspects of social and cultural life as semiotically organized, had developed the notion of the motivated sign; in his article 'Myth today' (1973a) he gives a very clear account of that; that was not the problematic issue. However, the unity of semiotics is not to be found at the level of the semiotic modes, but at the level of the principles of human semiosis. In the discussion of the *affordances* of modes earlier in this chapter I pointed to the distinct semiotic 'logics' of image and speech, logics which have their foundation in the very materiality of the 'stuff' from which modes are made. Gesture, for instance, combines the logics of space with those of time, of display with those of sequence. There is no plausibility therefore in any attempt to describe (as had been insisted on for most of the past century) gesture in terms of language, whether in its appearance as speech or as writing.

At the level of mode there is difference, of two kinds: one produced by the affordances of the material in which the mode is shaped, and one by the cultural/ social histories of how these affordances have been dealt with in different cultural places, how they have been shaped in the histories of different cultures (one deeply persuasive instance for me are the histories of different writing systems, say, the alphabetic versus the picto/ideographic). At the level of semiotic principle there is no difference. It is absolutely evident therefore that what is the case for language is not the case for other modes (i.e. questions such as: are there nouns, sentences, etc. in the image?); there will be partial congruence only. What is the case, however, is that the principles of human semiosis are at work in the same way in each mode, taking account of the affordances of each mode.

The issue of *materiality* of modes therefore becomes a major one. In the contemporary communicational landscape, which does not just permit but exploits a range of modes (in part, of course, fuelled by the newly opened possibilities of electronic technologies – though in part only) choice from among modes becomes possible. Mode, given the issue of materiality, shapes what representations will be like: what can be represented and how. In the research from science classrooms referred to above, there are some 3D models of plant cells. With three dimensions the possibilities of differentiated representation multiply; and the question of what material to use forces itself into the foreground: is the impermeability of the cell-wall best represented by using stiff cardboard, or by using clingfilm? Each choice has meaning. Is the nucleus best represented by a bit of sponge coloured red (it is like the 'brain' of the cell and therefore spongy, and it is important so that *red* might be the best colour), or is it best represented by a smooth pebble?

But materiality also directly relates to the physiology of human bodies, to the senses through which humans can engage with their world. Different materials engage with different senses: sight with colour, touch with smoothness, hearing with sound. These constitute different routes of perception, different routes for affect, and possibly different psychological/cognitive possibilities (Gardner 1993; Sacks 1984). As the world of representation moves increasingly from communication to use, making the earlier metaphor of the 'consumption of texts' into the commonplace of all cultural activity, the distinction between the significance of writing on the outside of a bottle of mineral water may be no more and may be less than the significance of the shape of the bottle, or its colour, or the images on the label, or the feel of the bottle in the hand when I pour the water, or the taste and texture of the water when I drink it. Meaning resides in all of these.

As the world of those who have a degree of affluence moves from self-definition through a place in the social ('I am an academic', 'I am married', 'I am Australian') to definition through consumption ('I shop at The Gap', 'We buy only French mineral water', 'I prefer living in Europe'), which becomes identity as (life) style, so the boundaries between what was communication and what was economic or other social practice, between text and commodity, between the semiotic and representational and the non-semiotic and non-representational evaporate. The choice of sneakers that I purchase and wear has become an act of communication through which I (re)present myself. *Taste* will become an essential theoretical category in semiotics, as will *aesthetics*, seen as the *politics of style*.

In this environment the distinctions between semiotic modes need to remain, but the functionalities, the significance, of the modes needs to be reassessed. This is not an argument against language, though it is an argument against core linguistics as presently conceived. It is an argument for sociolinguistics, but not as a satellite or subdiscipline of linguistics, but *as* linguistics. The notion of the motivated sign, of *the social in the sign*, makes that possible and necessary. Reconceived in this way, (socio)linguistics will be one of the essential theoretical components of the multimodal communicational world.

ACKNOWLEDGEMENTS

I wish to thank Carey Jewitt both for comments on this chapter, and for her crucial work in the research on science classrooms used here. Many of the ideas on multimodality draw on work by Theo van Leeuwen and myself. This chapter was written while the author held an appointment as Visiting Professor in the Department of English at the City University of Hong Kong.

FURTHER READING

Coulon, R. (1989) 'French and Australian socio-semiotics: worlds apart and yet so close', *International Journal for the Semiotics of Law* II (6): 313–24.
Coupland, N. and Jaworski, A. (eds) (1997) *Sociolinguistics: A Reader and Coursebook*, London: Macmillan.
Downes, W. (1998) *Language and Society*, Cambridge: Cambridge University Press.
Giglioli, P. P. (ed.) (1972) *Language and Social Context: Selected Readings*, Harmondsworth: Penguin Books.
Gumperz, J. (ed.) (1982) *Language and Social Identity*, Cambridge: Cambridge University Press.

6

PRAGMATICS

JEF VERSCHUEREN

STUDYING LANGUAGE USE

Today, the term '**pragmatics**' is most directly associated with the study of language use, though it originated in the context of a more general theory of **semiosis**. For Charles **Morris** (1938a), syntactics was the study of the relationships of signs to other signs, while **semantics** investigated the connections between **sign**s and the **object**s to which the signs are applicable, and pragmatics ought to be devoted to the relationships between signs and their users or interpreters. In other words, pragmatics 'deals with the biotic aspects of semiosis, that is, with all the psychological, biological, and sociological phenomena which occur in the functioning of signs' (ibid., p. 30). Or, 'Any rule when actually in use operates as a type of behavior, and in this sense there is a pragmatical component in all rules' (ibid., p. 35).

After its introduction into linguistics, every effort was made to define pragmatics as a separable *component* of a linguistic theory (for a detailed account, see Levinson 1983). However, the implications of Morris's characterization could have been used to predict the difficulties involved. If it is the case that pragmatics approaches language as a form of behavior, there must indeed be a pragmatic way of looking at any aspect of language at any level of structure. In other words, unlike the traditional components of a linguistic theory, pragmatics does not have its own privileged object of investigation. And if this emphasis on behavior implies psychological, biological, and sociological considerations, pragmatics must by definition be highly interdisciplinary, thus rubbing against the hyphenated disciplines (psycholinguistics, sociolinguistics and the like) while differing from them by its lack of a correlational object of its own (the mind, society, and the like). Such definitional efforts, therefore, have been stranded either on vague and impracticable distinctions (such as semantics studies meaning out of context, while pragmatics studies meaning in context) or on *ad hoc* lists of topics that were supposed to belong to the province of pragmatics (in particular: **deixis**, conversational implicatures, presuppositions, **speech act**s, and conversational structures; some of the classical studies on these topics are, e.g., Fillmore 1975, Grice 1975, Karttunen 1974, Searle 1969, Sacks *et al.* 1974, respectively).

An alternative view, going back radically to Morris and gaining ground slowly, is to treat pragmatics as a specific identifiable *perspective* on language, in particular a functional perspective studying language from the point of view of its usage phenomena and processes (see Verschueren 1999). Since language use involves human beings in all their complexity, the perspective in question is necessarily interdisciplinary, touching on aspects of cognition, society, and culture in a coherent and integrated approach, without privileging any of these specific angles. For the same reason, the perspective in question must pay attention to flexible processes of making linguistic choices, both in production and in interpretation, from a variable (and in principle infinite) range of options, in a manner that is negotiable and dynamic rather than mechanical, thus betraying a high degree of adaptability. It is the purpose of the following pages to translate this theoretical stance into a number of more practical observations.

A WORLD OF COMMUNICATION

The social world is truly a world of communication, **discourse**, or **rhetoric**. The obvious cases are conversations and meetings, advertisements, books and magazines, radio and television. But this general claim is true at a deeper level as well. Just look at an ordinary newspaper. At first sight, it is supposed to tell you about what is really happening out there in the world. Upon closer scrutiny, however, what is 'really happening' and is worth reporting seems to be largely discursive in nature. Taking a random issue of the *International Herald Tribune* in October 1999, we come across the following extremely different articles (identified here by their titles):

(1) In Web Gamble, Venerable Britannica Gives It Away
(2) Lawmakers in Indonesia End Prospects for Habibie
(3) U.S. Stocks Rise on Tame Inflation

Article (1) is directly about types of *media*, and hence obviously about communication. It reports on the struggle for survival of the then 231-year-old Encyclopedia Britannica, traditionally published in book form, in an age increasingly dominated by electronic media and the Internet; the most recent decision in this struggle is to provide free access to the encyclopedia on the Internet, a decision which is described as a gamble. Article (2) reports on *politics*, a domain of human activity which is also predominantly communicative. It reports on the political prospects of Indonesia's president Habibie. This report is based entirely on communicative data:

(4) the newly independent national assembly rejected his recent state-of-the-nation address.

Clearly, a 'rejection' is a verbal act, even if it is based on a vote which requires only 'yes' or 'no' or the pushing of a button that substitutes 'yes' or 'no'. Further, the object of the rejection is a 'state-of-the-nation address', an overall assessment, in words, of the health and prospects of a country. But what about the hardcore *economics* in article (3), a world that is supposed to be governed by facts and figures? The stock market, barometer of economic well-being, is entirely a function of buying and selling, two communicative activities which are themselves directly influenced by other communicative events:

(5) the Commerce Department reported that consumer prices rose only moderately in September, suggesting that inflation was still under control.

In other words, stocks can rise because of a 'report' that 'suggests' that inflation is under control. No doubt, the newspaper's report on this report will generate further effects in the so-called 'real' world of business and finance. Is there no 'news', then, about non-communicative facts or events? To be sure, there is the occasional note on a hurricane or an earthquake. But the note grows into a real report only when there are human, hence social, and hence communicative, implications.

It is the task of pragmatics, as the science of language use, to subject this discursive world to close and systematic scrutiny. Pragmatics, in that sense, differs from communication studies only in that the focus is on language. But the very nature of the enterprise dictates that pragmaticians are not at liberty to abstract from non-linguistic determinants of what language use is all about.

ACTIONS, CONTEXTS, CONSEQUENCES

The basic pragmatic observation about language use is that it is always a form of *action*. This insight gave rise to speech act theory (Austin 1962; Searle 1969). The action concept, however, goes beyond the sentence-size acts usually referred to as speech acts (assertions, commands, questions, promises). In the above examples, only example (4) involves a speech-act-like form of behavior, a 'rejection'. The 'reporting' in (5) almost certainly consists of multiple assertives combined with predictions. The 'gamble' in (1) is a complex strategy involving a variety of action types.

The actions in question have real-world *consequences*. Thus a gamble may be lost or won. The rejection of a state-of-the-nation address may destroy a president's political future and may have consequences for a country and its inhabitants. Reporting on inflation may result in specific patterns of buying and selling. This aspect was referred to as the '**perlocution**ary effects' of a speech act by **Austin** (1962). Because of the unpredictability of such effects they were left out of later theorizing about speech acts on the assumption that they were not essential for an understanding of the language *system*. Yet, whenever actual instances of language *use* are at issue, they cannot simply be left out. Even if a specific effect is rarely clear at any given moment of uttering, the goal-orientedness of verbal behavior is such that the behavior itself is defined by it.

Further, linguistic action is always embedded in a *context*. Whatever segment of the physical world, the social world, or the mental world is within the vision of either the utterer (speaker) or the interpreter (hearer) in the course of producing or interpreting a piece of communication, may serve as relevant context for an understanding of what is happening. And so does any aspect of the linguistic context, including properties of the channel of communication itself. Thus example (1) appeals to knowledge about (i) a series of books called the Enclyclopedia Britannica and the Internet (aspects of a 'physical' context in a very broad sense of the word); (ii) institutionalized carriers of knowledge, sources of information, values of trustworthiness and reputation ('social' context); and (iii) managers' intentions in relation to economical survival and guarding a product's reputation ('mental' context). Example (2) evokes a world characterized by (i) the existence of a group of islands called Indonesia, where many people live (physical); (ii) a set of practices called 'politics' and a specific political tradition called 'democracy' (social); and (iii) love of power and the strategic thinking involved in keeping or getting power (mental). Example (3) makes sense only with reference to (i) objects involved in trade (physical); (ii) the social practice of trade, buying and selling, and the institution of 'money' (social); and (iii) the Commerce Department's desire to preserve stability and just about everybody's wish to make money (mental). All three examples are embedded in a 'linguistic' context consisting in a specific linguistic channel, namely, written newspaper language, a specific **genre** of language use, namely, a news report, and the intertextual links between all the pieces of communication required to produce the reports. (For the notions of genre and intertextuality, see Bakhtin 1986 and Briggs and Bauman 1992.) Context is so essential to the process that changes in contextual ingredients inevitably result in different actions with different consequences. If you, instead of the Indonesian national assembly, were to reject Habibie's state-of-the-nation address, Habibie would hardly be troubled. Or if I, rather than the Commerce Department, were to suggest that inflation was still under control, buying and selling on Wall Street would no doubt ignore my suggestion. This does not mean that context is stable and objectively 'out there'. Rather, since all ingredients of a speech event are potentially relevant aspects of context and their range is so wide that they cannot possibly all be activated, context is effectively generated in the course of any instance of language use as a result of participants' orientations towards a selection of ingredients (Auer and Di Luzio 1992; Duranti and Goodwin 1992), a selection which often leaves clear traces that can be called contextualization cues (Gumperz 1982). Deixis (by means of personal **pronoun**s, adverbs of time and space, and the like) is one of the anchoring devices marking the contextual embeddednesss of language in use, which warrants its prominence as a topic in the pragmatic literature.

MEANING GENERATION – ASSERTED AND IMPLICIT

From a pragmatic perspective, language use is all about **meaning**. In contrast to semantics, which studies the correlations between meanings and forms as part of a language system, pragmatics focuses on processes of meaning generation. The basic goal is to gain insight into the meaningful functioning of language in the life of human beings. Meaning, seen from that angle, is a highly intangible phenomenon. In actual use, strict form-meaning or form-function correlations hardly exist at all. There are two main reasons for this. First, in order to interpret a piece of verbal communication, one must take into account, as should be clear from the above, the action type it belongs to within its proper context. This is, for instance, why the Internet is such an unreliable – albeit useful – source of information. Without assuming that people are liars or that they are intent on misleading – though they may be that, too – the uncontrolled nature of the Internet medium results in a network of communicative fragments originating in very different settings, corresponding to very different goals and ambitions, and requiring very different forms of interpretation in relation to parameters that are not in plain view so that adequate interpretation is often beyond reach. Not everyone posting messages on the Internet wants to provide information; what may be involved may be simply a form of self-expression or self-representation, jokes that are not easy to recognize as such, hidden agendas of various types, commercial considerations, and the like. Without adequate clues as to such contextual ramifications, interpretation becomes very hard – which is why, if the search for information is the main goal, entering the Internet through a controlled and edited medium such as the Encyclopedia Britannica is the sales argument underlying the gamble referred to in example (1).

The second reason why fixed form-function relationships are rare and why meaning is so intangible, lies in the impossibility of saying fully explicitly what one means. There are many types of meaning that are not directly 'visible' or literally 'said': presuppositions, implicatures, indirect speech acts (Searle 1975). In addition to what is literally asserted, *implicit meaning* is so important in language use that it has been identified as the topic *par excellence* of pragmatics (in particular by Östman 1986). In order to illustrate this, let us turn again to the Encyclopedia Britannica, representing a form of communication the identified purpose of which is to give information that is as clear and explicit as possible.

Let us assume that we are interested in learning about the Democratic Republic of the Congo. In the printed version of the Encyclopedia, we may run into trouble immediately, depending on the year of publication, as there was no country by that name until May 1997. Thus, even for a simple search, background information would be required. In that respect the electronic version is easier, though a number of medium-specific communicative skills have to be acquired before we can use it. At least two options are open to us. We may type the name of the country into a search box; alternatively, if we know that the Democratic Republic of the Congo is a country in Africa (note again the need for background knowledge) we can go to a map of the world, click on Africa, click on the Democratic Republic of the Congo, and get access to a concise article that leads us further to more detailed texts with the help of hyperlinks. In the concise article (of the 1999 version) we read:

(6) Zaïre occupies the heart of the Congo River basin, which comprises about three-
    fifths of the country's total area.

A first potential obstacle to the interpretation of this seemingly straightforward sentence presents itself in the name 'Zaïre' (which is also at the top of the article). When interpreting sentence (6) we must assume that there is such a place called Zaïre. In the pragmatic literature this is called an existential presupposition. That this is by no means trivial emerges from the fact that today there is no country anywhere in the world officially known as 'Zaïre'. The encyclopedia article resolves some of the resulting confusion by saying that since May 1997 the official name is 'Democratic Republic of the Congo'. But on those grounds the nomenclature of the entire article would have had to be adapted. The reason why this did not happen is no doubt to be found in material circumstances (complications involved in making systematic changes in a large body of interrelated texts – this takes time), but maybe also in an assessment of the political situation which was judged to be so unstable that a fast change might require a reversal soon afterwards. At any rate, we simply have to allow for the 'misused' existential presupposition, otherwise it would be impossible to make the correct link between article and map.

Second, knowledge of geography is required to understand what 'the Congo River basin' is (an expression to which also an existential presupposition is attached). In particular, when looking at the map, it may seem surprising that this basin occupies only three-fifths of the country's total area, which is covered with waterways most of which ultimately end up in the Congo River.

Further, an understanding of the implicit type of meaning manifested in metaphorical language use is required. The **noun** 'heart' in (6) obviously does not refer to the central muscle of an animal's body, but simple to a more abstract 'center'. This center is indeed abstract, otherwise there would be a contradiction between Zaïre occupying the heart of the Congo River basin and the Congo River basin comprising only part of Zaïre's total land area. How can X be the heart of Y without X belonging completely to Y?

A final interpretive complication resides in the combination between 'heart' and 'occupy'. There is a metaphorical sense in which 'occupying X's heart' is a fixed collocation. But in that case 'heart' belongs to a different metaphorical domain (not the core–periphery domain but the domain of sentiment). As a result, 'occupy' has to be given its literal meaning in this case, though it occurs together with a metaphorically used 'heart' with which it often forms a metaphorical collocation.

One may assume that no-one would interpret a sentence like (6) wrongly in any of the senses I have just suggested. That judgement, however, is based on an assumption of what the British-American philosopher Paul **Grice** would call *cooperativeness* (Grice 1975). For an average interpreter, for instance, a crucial assumption would normally be that the author is trying to be relevant, in which case there would have to be an essential link between 'Zaïre' and the 'Democratic Republic of the Congo'. (An entire theory of pragmatics, *relevance theory*, was based on the notion of relevance; see Sperber and Wilson 1986.)

The notion of cooperativeness was formulated by Grice in relation to conversational practices. According to the theory, whenever a principle of communication (such as 'Be relevant') seems to be broken, the assumption of cooperativeness leads to interpretations involving forms of implicit meaning called *conversational implicatures*. Just look at (7):

(7) A: 'I need information on the Democratic Republic of the Congo'.
     B: 'Have you tried the Encyclopedia Britannica?'

Following the theory, A's utterance, in order to be fully functional in a conversation, implicates that A thinks B can help him or her to get the needed information. In a different theoretical framework, speech act theory, this would be called an *indirect speech act*: what looks like an ordinary statement is in fact a request for help. Further, B's utterance, as a response to a request for help, would be irrelevant if it would be only a question – though it is that, too. It must implicate that B thinks the Encyclopedia Britannica has some decent information to offer on the Democratic Republic of the Congo.

There are also other expectations that shape interpretation. These may be based on conventions of a particular discourse genre – an aspect of what we have called linguistic context. In an encyclopedia-type text on a specific country the most general geographical information is expected to be given first. That expectation immediately rules out any other interpretation than the literal meaning of 'occupy' and a specific locational metaphorical sense of 'heart' in 'occupies the heart'.

Every language contains many devices for coding implicit meaning. Going back to the same article, look at (8):

(8) Zaireans still create such traditional objects as masks, figurines, and stone- and nail-studded statues.

A simple word like 'still' carries clear presuppositions: the presupposition that Zaireans used to make the named objects in the past, and that – maybe – it is a little surprising that they still do so today.

Other implications may be less innocent and they may involve frameworks of socio-cultural and political interpretation which, when inserted by way of a presupposition-carrying construction, are harder to notice and are therefore more easily seen as self-evident. Consider (9):

(9) The Congo, under the inexperienced leadership of Patrice Lumumba, was ill-prepared for self-government.

'Under the inexperienced leadership of Patrice Lumumba', which is inserted in such a way that its underlying assertion is obviously taken for granted, immediately serves as an implicit explanation for at least one major reason why things went wrong with the Congo after its independence in 1960.

These are just some examples of types of unasserted, yet clearly present meaning. Implicit aspects of meaning are responsible for the fact that, in the social world which is predominantly a world of communication, almost nothing is exactly what it looks like.

DYNAMICS AND NEGOTIABILITY

If the relationships between forms and meanings are not fixed because of the contextualized action status of instances of language use and because of the high degree of implicitness, meaning generation must be a quite dynamic and negotiable process. In other words, verbal communication does not just consist in putting pre-existent meaning into form, followed by a process of deciphering. Meanings may emerge that were not there before.

By way of example, let us look at the way in which texts (or other pieces of discourse) interact. Such intertextuality is extremely common in any modern urban environment, which is always a dense semiotic network. Just take a look at the London Underground. The warning 'Mind the gap!' is omnipresent, written on the platform floors and to be heard in announcements at many stations as well. This presents a golden opportunity for advertising for a clothing store chain named 'The Gap', with gigantic billboards saying 'Every gift only GAP'. Another discourse genre prevalent in the same environment is the series of 'Poems on the Underground', poems displayed inside the trains between the commercial ads. Grasping this opportunity in combination with the gap warning, a brand of toothpaste put up advertisements in the form of a poem focusing on a loved one's gap between the otherwise healthy row of teeth. In terms of meaning, one of the consequences is that the Underground warning itself is turned into an indirect ad for a clothing store chain as well as for a brand of toothpaste, and that any poem on the Underground may serve as a reminder of the toothpaste.

In institutional settings (see e.g. Drew and Heritage 1992; Sarangi and Slembrouck 1996) processes of meaning negotiation – not to say meaning con-struction – are often clearly in evidence, as guided by communicative constraints imposed by those settings. One of the best examples in the pragmatic literature may be Goodwin's (1994) analysis of the Rodney King trials in Los Angeles. When stopped for a traffic violation on 3 March 1991, King, an African American, was violently beaten by a group of four police officers. When a tape of this event, recorded by an amateur video photographer, was released, public outrage led to the policemen being put on trial for the excessive use of force. Courtroom proceedings are properly understood in terms of the frame of meaning imposed by the highly institutional activity type. Yet this is itself embedded in a much wider context of communication: for one thing, there might not have been a trial without the public outrage generated by showings of and comments on the video tape; as a result, from the start the trial was part of a general public and political debate, with real involvement on the part of many people; furthermore, the event was highly mediatized throughout. It would be a mistake to ignore the influence of this surrounding layer of communication and social strife. Clearly, whatever is said during the trial will be adapted to various degrees, as to both content and style, to a range of addressees, in particular journalists, media audiences, and political lobbies. To the extent that the event can be seen as self-contained, it still represents a highly complex activity type.

Structurally, the trial consists of a constellation of different types of utterances and utterance clusters: a variety of monologic utterances (the judge giving instructions, the jury summation) and dialogic utterance clusters (witness interrogations), all intertextually linked (as in interrogation sequences, the jury summation summing up what has preceded, etc.). Contextually, participant roles are well defined (the accused, the judge, the prosecutor, defense attorneys, jurors, witnesses, expert witnesses). Those institutional roles are defined in terms of the pre-allocation of turns or turn types (or types of verbal genres) to be used by each of them: judges give instructions, attorneys ask questions (of an institutionally permissible kind) and object to each other's questions, witnesses answer them, jurors mostly listen (acting as side participants throughout most of the proceedings, as direct addressees mainly during the summations, and as collective utterers at the very end). The dynamics of the overall interaction is determined by those structures and roles, which the different participants are quite conscious of, in combination with a clear task to be performed: deciding on the guilt or innocence of the accused.

The resulting process takes the shape of a contest between prosecution and defense, where it is the task of the prosecution to prove guilt, whereas it is enough for the defense if they can cast reasonable doubt on the guilt of the accused. Given the contest nature of the event, participants also know that the main concern of neither prosecution nor defense is necessarily the search for 'truth', but rather the pursuit of strategies to win. In this process, language is the most powerful tool to construct the desired meanings. I will give just one example of how this worked in the first Rodney King trial, following Goodwin's analysis. Apparently, the prosecutor started from the assumption that they had a solid case, with hard and unmistakable evidence in the form of the video tape. However, it was enough for the defense to impose what Goodwin calls a 'professional vision' on what could be seen on the tape to create a frame of interpretation that would at least lead to 'reasonable doubt'. To that end they brought in expert witnesses, whose first task it was to decompose what looked like a massive beating, and to label and categorize the fragments, as in (10) (where numbers between brackets indicate pauses in seconds).

(10) EXPERT: There were,
            ten distinct (1.0) uses of force.

            . . .

            In each of those, uses of force
            there was an escalation and a de-escalation, (0.8)
            an assessment period, (1.5)
            and then an escalation and de-escalation again. (0.7)
            And another assessment period.

                                    (From Goodwin 1994, p. 617)

The categorization is very consciously introduced to provide what is visible with a new meaning. In a context where professional practice allows the use of force when necessary, especially the term *assessment* frames the event as involving rational and completely responsible behavior on the part of the police officers. In the same vein, in a different fragment kicks are defined as tools for policework, on the same level as a side handle baton, a categorization strategy which eliminates the associative link between kicks and anger or malice. This is just one of the devices that were used to create the impression that the police officers were just doing their job. Thus verbal tools can be used to provide the same evidence with completely different meanings.

Such processes are not restricted to institutional contexts. In any ordinary conversation (see e.g. Atkinson and Heritage 1984; Hutchby and Wooffitt 1998), meanings are continuously negotiated guided by some general interactional constraints including affect, involvement, **politeness**, and the like (R. Lakoff 1973; Brown and Levinson 1987). That is, a given utterance does not have a fixed meaning once it has been produced and interpreted. Subsequent conversational moves may necessitate reinterpretation, clarification, renegotiation. Nor does this process necessarily stop when a conversation ends. Just think of an attempt to follow ordinary road instructions, an activity involving a series of consecutive steps confirming earlier interpretations or reinterpreting a preceding form of face-to-face interaction.

METAPRAGMATIC AWARENESS

The contextually situated processes of meaning generation that form the essence of language use are mediated through the human mind. Obviously, perception and representation, planning, and memory are involved. But there is more. Without reflexive or metapragmatic awareness of what one is doing when using language, language use would never be the process of meaning generation that we know. Reflexive awareness is a function of the uniquely human ability to see others as mental being just like the self (see Tomasello 1999). This is what enables language users to design utterances for specific audiences, to anticipate interpretations, to hypothesize about an utterer's intended meaning, and to monitor the extent to which an interpreter understands one's utterances. In Silverstein's terms:

> Without a metapragmatic function simultaneously in play with whatever pragmatic function(s) there may be in discursive interaction, there is no possibility of inter-actional coherence, since there is no framework of structure – here, interactional text structure – in which indexical origins or centerings are relatable one to another as aggregated contributions to some segmentable, accomplishable event(s).
> (1993, pp. 36–7)

All languages contain markers of metapragmatic awareness. They include phenomena such as (i) the self-referential use of phrases such as 'this paper' at the beginning of an academic paper, which does not only refer to the overall activity of which the chosen phrase is itself a constitutive part, but which also categorizes that overall activity as a specific genre of language use, thus providing it with a specific frame of interpretation; (ii) the explicit intertextual links that are introduced by expressions such as 'see . . .', 'the following . . .'; (iii) metapragmatic descriptions of a verbal activity carried out outside of the activity of which the description is a part, as in 'Silverstein *defines* metapragmatics as . . .'; (iv) the choice of a modality as in 'will be' vs. 'can be' vs. 'could be' vs. 'should be' vs. 'might have been', which draws explicit attention to the status of the choice in the utterer's conceptualization of the ideational state of affairs referred to; (v) a wide range of other metapragmatic markers such as the quotation marks surrounding 'pragmatics' at the beginning of this article, which draw attention to the lexical choice-making itself, as a kind of warning against unreflective interpretation. Ultimately, the entire stretch of discourse of which this sentence is part is about properties of language use, formulated at the metalevel of linguistic theory and analysis, and hence it is one long marker of metapragmatic awareness, abounding with categorizations, suggestions, claims, etc.

Metapragmatic awareness may be situated at a very high level of consciousness, as when we write papers on linguistics. On the other hand, processing may also become very automatic. This may take place at the level of grammatical choices. At a higher level of structure, patterns of meaning in discourse may become so habitual that they are taken for granted and are no longer questioned. That is where ideology comes in (sometimes in the form of language ideology; see Schieffelin *et al.* 1998), probably the trickiest domain of meaning at the level of social life. Paying attention to the interaction between explicit and implicit forms of meaning, pragmatics provides excellent tools for discourse-based empirical ideology research (e.g. Blommaert and Verschueren 1998).

CONCLUSION: THE IMPORTANCE OF VARIABILITY

As Hymes said, 'in the study of language as a mode of action, variation is a clue and a key' (1974, p. 75). The choices that language users make in the course of producing and interpreting utterances derive from an infinite and ever-changing range of variable possibilities. Yet, under many circumstances, awareness of variability is as hard to achieve as awareness of ideological patterns. All language users form habits of linking forms with meanings. Some of those habits are idiosyncratic, others are conventional within communities of various shapes and sizes, but they will always serve as the initial guidelines for both production and interpretation. Since there is so much variability, however, different interlocutors' habits will rarely coincide completely. Hence the need for meaning negotiation, a need which is always there, and not only in the most obvious cases such as intercultural communication contexts (again a favorite domain for pragmatic research; see e.g. Gumperz 1982).

FURTHER READING

Clark, H. H. (1996) *Using Language*, Oxford: Oxford University Press.

Davis, S. (ed.) (1991) *Pragmatics: A Reader*, Oxford: Oxford University Press.

Gumperz, J. J. (1982) *Discourse Strategies*, Cambridge: Cambridge Univerity Press.

Verschueren, J. (1999) *Understanding Pragmatics*, London: Edward Arnold and New York: Oxford University Press.

Verschueren, J., Östman, J.-O., Blommaert, J. and Bulcaen, C. (eds) (1995 ff.), *Handbook of Pragmatics* (bound manual in 1995, followed by looseleaf annual instalments), Amsterdam and Philadelphia: John Benjamins.

7

LANGUAGE CHANGE

JEAN AITCHISON

English is slithering away, judging from complaints in books and newpapers. A tradition of worry dates back centuries: 'I do here . . . complain . . . that our Language is extremely imperfect; that its daily Improvements are by no means in proportion to its daily Corruptions' moaned Jonathan Swift in 1712 (Swift 1966, p. 107). Eighteenth-century writers perhaps had some excuse for their pessimism, because relatively little was then known about language change. Swift and his colleagues feared that their own work might not survive unless they could somehow halt English in its tracks.

But language change is as inevitable as the erosion of hills, or the silting up of river estuaries – though unlike disintegrating cliffs, language change is not decay: new vocabulary allows any language to respond to novel situations, while at a deeper level, language maintains its patterns, and preserves efficient linguistic interaction.

Human language is not unique among animal communication systems in its tendency to alter itself continually. Humpback whales change their songs every year, and some birds incorporate novel sounds into their songs: Australian lyre-birds have been heard to imitate kookaburras, chain-saws, and even car alarms.

Yet only in the twentieth century have linguists discovered how and why language change occurs. At one time, a sound or word was assumed to slowly change into another, like a tadpole growing legs and gradually becoming a frog. Yet nobody ever succeeded in identifying the half-way stage, the tadpole with front legs, as it were. This is because the tadpole-to-frog (gradual change) model is a false one. Cuckoos provide a better image than tadpoles (Aitchison 1995). A 'cuckoo' (replacement) model has now supplanted that of slow alteration. A new sound or word creeps in alongside the old, then eventually replaces it, like a young cuckoo getting larger and larger, and finally heaving the original occupant out of the nest. But even the cuckoo image is an oversimplification. In some cases, several possibilities compete, like candidates vying with one another in an election. Eventually one wins out over the others. But the variants may fluctuate for years, even in the speech of a single person.

VARIATION: THE KEY TO UNDERSTANDING CHANGE

Change, we now know, involves variation. Variation can occur without change, but change cannot occur without variation. The American linguist William **Labov** was the first to demonstrate this conclusively. He showed that the systematic study of variation could reveal language change in progress (Labov 1972c).

Everyone had always known that speech varied for several reasons, such as geographical region, social class, age, ethnicity, sex, and formality of the occasion. But in the past, the variation had been regarded as too much of a random mish-mash to be worth studying in any depth. Labov's contribution was to show that variation could be reliably charted.

Language, of course, covers a range of phenomena: sounds (**phonetics** and **phonology**), word formation and word endings (**morphology**), word combinations (**syntax**), **meaning** (**semantics**), and language use (**pragmatics**). Labov started with sounds. He demonstrated that phonetic variation could reveal how sound change spreads.

The first task, he suggested, was to identify sounds which might be fluctuating. These he called 'variables'. Some variables were 'discrete' (either present or absent), as with New York *r*, which was sometimes pronounced in a word such as *cart*, sometimes not. Others were continuous, as with the first **vowel** in the word *coffee*, which slid across a range of different pronunciations.

Having decided on his variables, Labov then interviewed a random sample of speakers from different social classes, and both sexes, eliciting a spectrum of styles: reading word pairs, reading a passage, formal spoken speech and informal spoken. Labov and his co-workers were unknown to the informants, so it was relatively easy to elicit a fairly formal spoken style. It was more difficult to obtain samples of casual speech, though this was accomplished to some extent by allowing old folk to reminisce, and by asking younger ones if they had ever been in danger of death: as the informants remembered near-death incidents, their speech style became agitated and colloquial. Labov also noted down how an informant's style sometimes changed, when he or she spoke to their children, or answered the telephone.

Labov plotted his findings on graphs, which revealed, first, that the probable number of examples of a variable at any level of formality could be reliably quantified with regard to any one sociolinguistic factor, such as socio-economic class. Second, the way changes happened was revealed: speakers gradually increased or decreased the proportion of a variable in a particular style, or styles.

At a superficial level, *how* changes occurred was closely linked to *why*. Within any community, language change is related to prestige: people speak in the way they want to speak, sometimes consciously, at other times without realising it.

Some changes have overt prestige: speakers regard certain pronunciations as 'classy', and they want to talk that way themselves, as with New York *r*. People felt it was 'better' to insert *r*. This positive attitude was shown by the fact that *r* was used more often in formal, careful, speech, than in casual informal chat. This is also true of *h* in British English. Speakers assume they 'should' say *h*, and sometimes even insert it in places where it never was, as shown by the gardener buying parts for a fence who asked for a *Harris rail* for what is technically an *arras rail*. Such overt 'hypercorrection' tends to occur in fairly formal styles, when people are trying to speak in a careful way, especially if they are insecure, and want to impress those around.

In such cases, a significant difference is sometimes found between conscious, careful speech, and ordinary casual conversation. This was particularly true of lower middle-class women, Labov and others found. Perhaps such women want their children to speak 'nicely', or perhaps they themselves wished to be judged by their behaviour, which they thought should be 'ladylike'.

But sometimes the changes were covert. The speakers were not necessarily aware of the change, they just wanted to sound like their friends, or the people they admired. Teenagers in Detroit, according to one study, were divided into two types: 'Jocks' on the one hand, and 'Burnouts' on the other (Eckert 1989). Jocks were those who wanted to follow a conventional lifestyle. They pronounced the first vowel in words such as *mother*, *supper*, much as their parents did. Burnouts, on the other hand, took drugs and were regarded as potential 'drop-outs'. Their conversation contained a greater proportion of non-standard vowels, and they were moving away from the type of speech adopted by the more conventional Jocks. These Detroit teenagers were not necessarily aware of what they were doing when they talked, they just wanted to sound like their friends. Similar work on teenage gangs in Reading, England, showed that the ringleaders tended to have fairly extreme speech, and other gang members imitated them, often without realising it (Cheshire 1982): one '**marker**' (significant speech characteristic) was the addition of a non-standard -*s* to present-tense **verb**s, often idiosyncratic ones, as 'we legs it', meaning 'we ran away'.

Small-scale studies such as that of Reading -*s* were not undertaken via Labov-type social surveys, but by more informal methods: researchers were able to infiltrate gangs and networks of acquaintances by being introduced as the 'friend of a friend'. This technique was pioneered in Belfast in Northern Ireland by Jim and Lesley Milroy (L. Milroy 1987; J. Milroy 1992). Such small-scale, careful investigations therefore complement larger, more impersonal surveys.

These studies, all of which were carried out in the second half of the twentieth century, have revealed how and why language change spreads from speaker to speaker. In a group of friends, or other social group, key members of a group exaggerate some marker. Other group members copy this: they want to 'belong' and be fashionable, much as teenagers copy fashions in clothes from one another. Sometimes they are aware of doing this, but not always.

Changes spread beyond the original group via 'weak links', group members who belong to more than one language network, and routinely come into contact with people outside their local clique. Accommodation then occurs, that is, speakers consciously or subconsciously shift their speech in the direction of those they are talking to. Humans are friendly animals who do this naturally, often without realising it. Usually, both speakers in a conversation adjust the way they talk, but in some cases, one side accommodates more than the other. Accommodation is particularly common in the case of shop assistants, who try to sound like their customers, as Labov noted in New York, and Lesley Milroy in Belfast.

Belfast, in Northern Ireland, was for a long time split into two parts, east and west, often with open hostility between the halves. Yet some changes spread across the east–west divide via shop assistants: in one city-centre store, women from poorer west Belfast subconsciously imitated the speech of the better-off male customers from east Belfast, and eventually spread elements of their speech to their own west Belfast pals (Milroy and Milroy 1985).

Changes happen via face-to-face contact, as these studies indicate. Parents often worry that television is wrecking their youngsters' speech. But television has relatively little effect. At the most, it can send across the message that it is acceptable to speak in different ways.

Certain key factors have therefore emerged about the spread of language change: first, change occurs when one variant gets used more widely, and gradually ousts the previous norm. Second, change happens via person to person contact. Third, changes may be overt (noticed) or covert (unnoticed), but in both cases those adopting the change want to speak like the people they are imitating, even though they may not realise this.

DEEPER CAUSES

At first sight, these language changes may give the impression of being swayed by fashion or of being due to simple sloppiness: 'There is no more reason for language to change than there is for jackets to have three buttons one year and two the next', claimed the linguist Paul Postal (Postal 1968). 'We are out of the habit of caring for our language . . . Oh, please, English-lovers everywhere, do your bit for the language. Let's stop this slide down the slippery slope', urged a letter to a Sunday newspaper in 1981. Yet these views are false. Language change is not random, nor can it be halted. At any given time, only certain parts of the language are likely to change. A more sophisticated look at linguistic change views it as the interaction of various levels.

A social trigger is needed to ignite a change. This may set off a linguistic tendency which is waiting, ready to go, like a ripe apple about to fall, which is nudged to the ground by a sudden gust of wind. The social trigger may pick on a sound, as with New York *r*. Or it may select a word ending, as with the Reading teenagers. It could single out an aspect of syntax, such as questions or negatives: speakers of Indian English tend to place negatives towards the end of sentences, as: 'All of these pens don't work', where in British English one would be more likely to say: 'None of these pens work': the English of these Indian speakers has been influenced by Hindi, which places its negatives towards the ends of sentences. Or word meaning could be affected: 'I was absolutely devastated' said someone who had spilled wine on a friend's carpet, when originally *devastate* was used of laying waste a country in war.

These changes may seem bizarre and disparate. But changes do not happen chaotically and randomly. Deeper causes underlie the social triggers. These less obvious causes of change fall into one of two broad categories: natural tendencies on the one hand, and therapeutic changes, those which mend any broken patterns, on the other (Aitchison 2001).

Natural tendencies are phenomena which happen again and again in the languages of the world. It is normal to lose final **consonant**s on words, for example. It has happened in French, in Italian, and in Polynesian languages. It is underway in some Chinese dialects, and also in English. Sounds at the ends of words are relatively weak: try saying *pip, tit, kick*, and notice how strong the initial consonants sound, compared with the final ones (those at the ends of words). Final consonants are sometimes left unexploded: the breath which has built up behind the closure in the mouth is not let out, especially if the word is followed by another consonant, as with *kick* in 'Kick the door down'. Then, as a next stage, a 'glottal stop' (a stoppage of breath deep in the throat) replaces the final consonant, before its eventual disappearance.

Judging from letters to newspapers, a number of people are concerned about this process. Oddly, those who condemn these fading consonants in English often regard languages such as Italian which do not have many final consonants as 'beautiful', apparently forgetting that an Italian word such as *vino* 'wine' is derived from a Latin one with a final consonant, *vinum*.

Yet weakening affects more than a few word endings. **Morpheme**s (minimal meaningful units), words and even phrases can be eroded over time: the phrase *mea domina* 'my lady' became *ma dame*, then *madam*, then *ma'am*, and finally even just *m*, as in *yes, m* (Hopper 1994, p. 29). The loss of morphemes is comparable to the lives of civil servants, according to the nineteenth-century German linguist Georg von der Gabelentz (1891; see Hopper 1994). They are hired, they work for most of their lives, they are sent into semi-retirement, and finally retire fully, while new applicants line up to be hired. When these employees die, they do not necessarily disappear, he suggested, but may be 'mummified' and remain around as lifeless forms.

In modern terminology, the process is known as grammaticalization, or grammaticization, a term coined by Antoine Meillet, who defined it as 'the attribution of a grammatical character to a previously autonomous word'. Tok Pisin, spoken in Papua New Guinea, provides a good example in its word *save* 'know' (Aitchison 1996). Variants of this word occur around the world in **pidgin**s (restricted languages used for communication between people with no common language). These forms are thought to have their origin in a Portuguese word *saber* 'know', a remnant from the widely used nautical jargon of the fifteenth and sixteenth century, when Portugal was a major sea-faring nation.

In Tok Pisin, the word is sometimes found meaning 'to know', as in *God i save olgeta samting* 'God knows everything'. But alongside its use as a main verb on its own, *save* became used before another verb, in a so-called 'serial verb' construction. In this case, the verb originally meant 'know how to', as in: *mi save kukim kaukau* 'I know how to cook sweet potato'.

But the meaning 'know how to' gradually merged with, and changed into 'be skilled at', and eventually into 'be accustomed to'. It is not always easy to decide which of these overlapping meanings is intended, as in a newspaper advertisement for toothpaste: *Planti switpela kaikai i save bagarapim tit bilong yu hariap* 'Lots of sweet foods [*i* untranslatable particle] know how to/are skilled at/are accustomed to wreck teeth of you fast' (*bagarapim* is a normal word meaning 'wreck' borrowed from Australian English. It is used for everything from an air crash to tooth decay, with no obscene overtones.)

In spoken speech, *save* before another verb has now been shortened to *sa* and standardly means 'be accustomed to, habitually': *mi sa kirap long moning long hapas siks* 'I habitually get up in the morning at half-past six'. Tok Pisin *save* has therefore split into two. The original full form *save* retains its meaning 'know', but the shortened *sa* has become a verbal particle meaning 'habitually'.

Around the world, meaning shifts associated with grammaticalization tend to follow similar, though not necessarily identical routes. Words meaning 'know' often get weakened, for example. The English word *can* once meant 'know', as its German relative *können* still does, as in *ich kann ein wenig Deutsch* 'I know a little German'.

Parallel pathways occur in numerous, unnconnected changes. Similar social and **discourse** effects are found the world over. Negatives are routinely doubled or tripled to make them stronger. In Chaucer's *Canterbury Tales* (fourteenth century), the knight was always courteous: *He nevere yet no vileyne ne sayde* 'he never said no bad thing' (Prologue l.70). And in some non-standard varieties of British English, this heaping up is still found: 'I don't know nothing 'bout no bag!' asserted a London teenager accused of bag-snatching.

In New York, Labov recorded a sentence: 'When it rained, nobody don't know it didn't' (Labov 1972c, p. 150). This seemingly bizarre sentence was due to the heaping up of negatives to make them more emphatic. It in fact meant: 'Nobody knew that it rained when it did'. Or, to take another New York example: 'Back in them times, there ain't no kid around that ain't – wasn't even thinkin' about smokin' no reefers.' The speaker – a 29-year-old male – meant that no kid was even contemplating smoking reefers at that time.

French shows a different pattern of negative strengthening. Its original negative was *ne* (from Latin *non*). But various strengthening words were added: 'not a jot', 'not a straw', 'not a dot' (Ashby 1981). One of these, *ne . . . pas*, originally 'not a step', has won out as the normal negative, as in *je ne sais pas* 'I do not know' – though increasingly, *ne* is being dropped, and *pas* regarded as the 'real' negative: *je sais pas*, so the whole process may start over again.

Politeness also has a role to play. Humans everywhere try to avoid confrontation (Brown and Levinson 1987). In many languages, direct commands are rare, except when addressing children. In English, a request for payment is likely to say: 'Prompt payment would be appreciated', rather than 'You must pay now'. In some languages, direct address to another person is considered less polite than a more indirect approach, as in French. A French speaker would be more likely to say: *On y va* 'one goes there' rather than the French equivalent of 'we are going'.

In the long run, switched-around sentences may lead to more permanent alteration, as has already happened with the words meaning 'you' in several languages. In French, the polite *vous* has for some time been more usual than the intimate *tu*. The result is that French *vous*, once the plural, is now the singular form also for all but intimate friends and family.

So-called 'afterthought' is another recurring discourse factor. In Old English, verbs were usually placed at the end of sentences. But this final verb could be displaced, if the sentence contained an 'afterthought', a phrase seemingly added on afterwards (Stockwell 1977):

> *On thaem waeron eac tha men ofslaegene buton fifum*
> On that were also the men slain, except five.

Afterthought was therefore one factor which led speakers to feel that it was normal to place verbs in the middle of sentences.

Numerous other social and discourse factors may play a role. For example, in languages in general, shared information is often placed first in a sentence, and newer information at the end (Tomlin 1986). Known information tends to be preceded by the definite article *the* and fresh facts by the indefinite article *a*:

> The boy in the blue shirt ate a banana

In some languages, such as Indonesian, this has resulted in changed rules of grammar: it is impossible to put an indefinite article at the beginning of a sentence. Social and discourse factors are therefore important in language change. All those mentioned so far have been identified across numerous cultures, and have sometimes disrupted existing norms.

PATTERN NEATENING

But the human mind cannot remember a junk heap of random elements. It deals best with organised patterns. Neatening up these patterns is therefore a standard procedure, even though humans do it subconsciously, and are not usually aware that it is happening.

Take the past tense *girded* in place of older *girt*. This regularised past tense can be regarded as an attempt by English to tidy itself up. Most past tenses end in -*d*, and this is also the ending put onto any new verbs, as *she grumped* 'she said grumpily'. It is also the suffix attached to compounds, as in *greenlighted* 'gave permission to proceed', even though *lit* is still the normal past tense of the verb *light*. *Girded* has therefore joined the predominant pattern.

Neatening of syntax happens in much the same way. At one time, the word *chance* was a so-called impersonal verb, as in:

> *Him chaunst to meete upon the way a faithlesse sarazin . . .*
> It chanced that he met on his way a faithless Saracen.

101

But then **noun**s lost their endings. Take the sentence:

Achilles chaunced to sle Philles (*c*.1400)
Achilles happened to slay Philles.

Nobody could tell that *Achilles* once had an accusative ending, like the **pronoun** him. English speakers therefore re-analysed the construction in accordance with the predominant sentence pattern, subject–verb–object (Denison 1993). In twentieth-century English, impersonal verbs have continued to drop out, and only a few still remain, mainly weather verbs, as in *it's raining, it's snowing*. Syntactic changes therefore creep into a language, often without being noticed. Yet in many cases, these creeping changes are therapeutic: they can iron out discrepancies, and help to preserve patterns.

Speakers are even less aware of pattern neatening at the level of sounds. Consonants tend to come in pairs, one with vibration of the vocal cords (voiced) as in *b*, and the other with late onset of the vibration (voiceless) as in *p*, with both members of the pair being produced in the same part of the mouth: *b* and *p* are bilabial, articulated with both lips. But occasionally, one of a pair is missing. At one time, [phonetic ʃ] as at the beginning of *ship* did not have a partner. But over the years, a partner has developed the sound [phonetic ʒ] as at the end of *rouge, beige*. This sound came from two sources: first, French borrowings, as in the examples given, second, from the fast pronunciation of [*z*]+ [*j*] (*y*), as in *leisure, pleasure*. But, *h*, on the other hand, has remained alone, without a partner. Partly because *h* is a weak sound, and partly because it is on its own, it is in danger of fading from the language. It probably would have disappeared, as it already has in some varieties of English. But strong social pressure has maintained it: 'First and foremost, let me notice that worst of all faults, the leaving out of the aspirate where it ought to be and putting it where it ought not to be,' said Henry Alford (1864, p. 40).

Vowels also remain patterned in a way which is normally hidden from speakers. Front vowels (those produced with the tongue fairly far foward, such as *i, e*) tend to run in parallel with back vowels (those produced with the tongue fairly far back, such as *u, o*). English vowels are changing rapidly, but are doing so in an orderly way. Young Londoners saying the word *beat* may sound to older speakers as if they are saying *bite*, with the first part of the dipththong or gliding vowel pronounced with the mouth wider open than in the past. Similarly, with the comparable back vowels, the pronunciation of *boot* may sound like *boat*. The front and back vowels are moving along parallel tracks. Any language therefore swings about, following the needs of its speakers, who are often unaware of what is happening. But it inevitably retains its patterned nature.

DYING LANGUAGES

But if languages are so clever at adapting to their speakers' requirements, and at maintaining themselves, how do they ever die? The languages of the world are decaying at a phenomenal rate. Around 6,000 languages are currently spoken, according to our best guesstimates (Hale *et al*. 1992). Yet in a century's time, only about 10 per cent of the current total may still survive, it has been estimated.

Languages die because their speakers no longer want to speak them. Or, more accurately, they die because their speakers want to learn the languages of power, of which English is currently predominant. In a worldwide survey carried out by the British Council, 95 per cent of respondents agreed with the statement that: 'English is essential for progress as it will provide the main means of access to high-tech communication and information over the next twenty-five years' (British Council 1995). People want to learn English both for their own sake, and for that of their children. And as they acquire English, their own language, or that of their parents, decays.

The death of Gaelic is one of the best studied cases of how it all happens. Gaelic has a complex noun pluralisation system. Older fluent speakers have eleven different methods of plural formation, according to Nancy Dorian, who studied East Sutherland Gaelic (Dorian 1981). The four basic devices were suffixation, vowel change, final consonant change, and final consonant lengthening. The younger speakers could handle mainly suffixation, the device prominent in English. The forms which were unique to Gaelic were rarely used by the young, less fluent speakers.

But the languages – Gaelic and English – were not always used one at a time. In language death, the languages involved are not necessarily kept apart. The speakers know both languages, to some extent, and language mixing is widespread. Shared structures are given a high priority. But the language with high prestige gradually encroaches on the other, and the low prestige variety fades away.

This can happen to the language of whole communities, as with Gaelic. But the process can be seen in the speech of immigrants who move to a new country, and forget their original language, retaining in the end only a few vocabulary items. A child whose family moved from Israel to America wanted to talk like her new friends. She could speak both English and Hebrew, but turned more and more to English (Myers-Scotton 1998). Eventually, only a few Hebrew vocabulary items remained in her speech, inserted into an English frame:

I'm menageving myself. I want to inagev myself.
I'm drying myself. I want to dry myself.

Language death, then, is an extreme form of language change, but ultimately, it is based not on any defect in the dying language, but on the prestige of the 'takeover' language. The speakers may end up talking a language different from that of their parents, but it will have triumphed because it is prestigious, and not because it is in any way flawed.

To summarise, language change is inevitable. It takes place partly at a surface, social level, because people want to sound like those they admire, and also to fulfil cultural requirements, such as politeness norms. But although social desires and cultural needs may trigger change, the changes triggered are ready to happen at a deeper level. Only certain changes are likely to occur.

Changes may superficially upset the equilibrium of a language. But ultimately, language will adjust its patterns. Like a thermostat, it is self-regulating. A language, if used continually, never collapses. Language loss is due to the wish of the speakers, when they no longer want to talk their language.

Human beings all speak. No human culture has been found without a language. The rise and fall of languages is due to the rise and fall of prestige of those who speak those languages. The current worry is that there will be fewer and fewer languages which future generations will want to speak.

FURTHER READING

Aitchison, J. (2001) *Language Change: Progress or Decay?*, 3rd edn, Cambridge: Cambridge University Press.

Campbell, L. (1998) *Historical Linguistics*, Edinburgh: Edinburgh University Press.

Crowley, T. (1997) *An Introduction to Historical Linguistics*, 3rd edn, Oxford: Oxford University Press.

McMahon, A. (1994) *Understanding Language Change*, Cambridge: Cambridge University Press.

Trask, R. L. (1996) *Historical Linguistics*, London: Arnold.

8

THE CHOMSKYAN REVOLUTIONS

RAPHAEL SALKIE

MYTHS

Noam **Chomsky** is one of the best known names in modern linguistics. He is also one of the most misunderstood. To get a sound grasp on Chomsky's work, it is vital to strip away the myths and illusions that surround it and to focus on the core questions that he tries to address.

One of the many myths surrounding Chomsky is the belief that his approach to the study of language has been enormously influential: it is said that he has been cited in research papers more often than any other living person. The reality is that only a small proportion of research into language is carried out in the Chomskyan framework: far more linguistic research looks at the social aspects of language, the history of languages, how to learn and teach languages, how to use computers to process language, and other areas where Chomsky's influence has been negligible. As for the citations of Chomsky's work, the crude statistic does not tell us how many of the people who refer to Chomsky actually understand him correctly. Of those that do, the majority of citations are probably hostile or dismissive. Chomsky himself says that his work has always been a minority interest in the field, and this is not modesty but the truth.

Another myth is that Chomsky's linguistics has something to do with his political activity. Chomsky is famous as a left-wing critic of American foreign policy: he denounced the American invasion of Indochina in the 1960s, and three decades later he has been equally scathing about the American-led attack on Yugoslavia in 1999. In both these cases – and many others in between – Chomsky has argued forcefully that the reasons given to justify military action by the USA are a tissue of hypocrisy and lies. Sometimes his arguments involve exposing the misleading use of expressions like 'terrorism' or 'the peace process' by his political opponents. This looks like linguistic analysis, but there is no significant link between this kind of critical examination of language and the highly specialised and technical work that Chomsky has undertaken in linguistics. Chomsky is always cautious on the question of links between his linguistics and his politics: he never raises the matter himself, and when he is asked – as he often is – about the two sides of his work, he usually restricts himself to general points about human nature. Sometimes he also makes what he himself describes as banal points about his obstinate refusal to accept claims which are not supported by evidence, whether they are from politicians or scientists. Chomsky's political writings are well worth reading, but it is not necessary to study them if you are trying to understand what Chomsky has to say about language.

A third myth has to do with the 'Language Acquisition Device': Chomsky is supposed to believe that we all have such a device (affectionately shortened to LAD) in our heads, and that we use this device when we learn our first language as children. It would follow from this that Chomsky does research into how children learn to speak and understand language, and that he supports his theory of the LAD on the basis of this research. It therefore comes as a surprise to find that Chomsky has never done any research of this kind. He has not used the term 'Language Acquisition Device' for many years (partly because it has been persistently misunderstood), and when he did use the term he did not want to imply that we have some kind of machine in our brains which learns languages for us. It would be more accurate to say that Chomsky was proposing some abstract analyses of the human mind.

PHILOSOPHY

People who discuss the human mind in an abstract way are called philosophers: indeed, Chomsky was once described by a leading language scholar as a 'neo-medieval philosopher'. The description is interesting for two reasons. First, it illustrates the hostility – often amounting to personal abuse – that Chomsky's work has regularly provoked. Second, although intended as a criticism, that is not how Chomsky would take it: he would probably accept the description as basically accurate, with the proviso that he understands 'philosophy' rather differently from his accuser. For Chomsky, the study of language is worthwhile precisely because it enables us to shed light on some of the fundamental questions of philosophy. A good way to approach his linguistics is to start with these questions.

First, then, how does Chomsky approach philosophy? When Chomsky talks about 'philosophy' he means something different from what most people have in mind. More precisely, he has a different attitude to the questions that philosophers deal with. A central question of philosophy is whether there are things that we can know for sure, and if so, how these things are different from things that we are less sure about and others that we can know nothing about (see Russell 1948, for an elegant discussion of this question). Put like this, the question sounds abstract and probably irrelevant to most people: it is reasonable to ask what difference the answer might make to our daily lives. One reason for this is that philosophers often talk at a high level of generality instead of examining the world in detail. In other words, they engage in philosophy rather than in the activity that we have come to call 'science'.

Chomsky rejects this distinction between philosophy and science, which he sees as harmful and of recent origin. In medieval times, he points out, science and philosophy were part of the same enterprise of understanding the world: science was the part which used observation and measurement, while philosophy was the part which considered the right questions to ask, the best methods to employ for answering them, and what the answers might tell us in a broader picture (see Chomsky 1988, p. 2 and 1996, pp. 31–54). Crucially, science and philosophy tried to be consistent with each other: if the general principles suggested that certain lines of inquiry would be fruitful, then inquiry would proceed accordingly. If certain observations cast doubt on general principles, then the principles would be reconsidered.

If science and philosophy are closely linked, then the philosophical question of what we can know for sure takes on a new dimension. Science is all about reliable knowledge: that is why scientists make careful observations, conduct controlled experiments which can be replicated by other researchers, are cautious in not extending their findings beyond limited areas, and in general behave like scientists rather than trusting feelings, myths or prejudices. If the best scientists available agree about the facts, then a rational person will take that as the most solid starting point for further investigation. Anyone who wants to think about the issue of certain knowledge will note those areas where science has made the most progress, and will try to use similar methods and principles in other domains of inquiry.

LINGUISTICS AS A SCIENCE

For anyone engaging in linguistics, the specific question is how we can achieve the most certain knowledge about language. Linguists before Chomsky modelled themselves on biology. During the nineteenth century, biology and linguistics both made enormous – and similar – strides. The biologist Charles Darwin, for example, travelled to distant parts of the globe, collected many specimens of plants and animals, observed them closely in order to note their differences and similarities, and put forward the bold and exciting hypothesis that many were descended from a common ancestor. Darwin's hypothesis incorporated a new interpretation of how different species evolved: the theory of natural selection.

At around the same time scholars of language collected data about languages in many parts of the world, examined them closely for differences and similarities, and put forward the bold hypothesis that many of them derived from a common ancestor called Indo-European. (Subsequently similar common ancestors were proposed for many of the languages of Africa and America.) The hypothesis was bold because there are no written records of Indo-European, and no archeological or historical evidence of the people who spoke the language. The hypothesis was based on certain conceptions about how languages evolved, just like the theory of natural selection in biology.

By the time Chomsky began to study linguistics, the field was less concerned with the history of languages and more with examining languages closely for differences and similarities. The division of languages into genetic groups like Indo-European was still taken for granted, but more attention was devoted to classifications based on the properties of languages, particularly their phonological (sounds; see **phonology**) and morphological (word structure; see **morphology**) properties. Just as biologists spent a great deal of time cataloguing plants and animals, so linguists regarded their field as mainly about cataloguing the languages of the world. Techniques for collecting reliable data about a wide range of languages were developed. This was a vast and complex intellectual achievement, one that is sometimes unjustifiably belittled in histories of linguistics.

Chomsky was convinced, however, that biology was the wrong model for linguistics. He thought that physics was the science which had achieved the best results, and he resolved to try the methods of physics, rather than biology, in the study of language. What Chomsky admires about physics is its breadth and depth. The theories of Galileo and Newton, for instance, are so broad that they apply to tiny objects as well as the planets and the stars. The depth of their theories comes from a particular kind of abstract reasoning. Objects on the earth move in almost straight lines, while planetary motion is almost circular. Building on Galileo's work, Newton proposed a mysterious force called gravity which operates in perfectly straight lines – unlike anything we see in nature. He showed that certain mathematical assumptions about gravity could explain the motion that we actually witness around us. The explanation required a complex framework of assumptions and reasoning, and there were things that it failed to explain, but within this framework it succeeding in explaining many things.

Here is how Chomsky describes the methods used in physics:

> The 'Galilean style' in physics is 'making abstract mathematical models of the universe to which at least the physicists give a higher degree of reality than they accord the ordinary world of sensation' . . . We have no present alternative to pursuing the 'Galilean style' in the natural sciences at least.
>
> Some might argue . . . that we can do still better in the 'human sciences' by pursuing a different path. I do not mean to disparage such possibilities. It is not unlikely, for example, that literature will forever give far deeper insight into what is sometimes called 'the full human person' than any mode of scientific inquiry can hope to do. But I am interested here in a different question: to what extent and in what ways can inquiry in something like the 'Galilean style' yield insight and understanding of the roots of human nature in the cognitive domain? Can we hope to move beyond superficiality by a readiness to undertake perhaps far-reaching idealisation and to construct abstract models that are accorded more significance than the ordinary world of sensation, and correspondingly, by readiness to tolerate unexplained phenomena or even as yet unexplained counterevidence to theoretical constructions that have achieved a certain degree of explanatory adequacy in some limited domain, much as Galileo did not abandon his enterprise because he was unable to give a coherent explanation for the fact that objects do not fly off the earth's surface.
>
> (Chomsky 1980, pp. 8–10)

Chomsky thus proposed to use the methods of physics rather than biology in his approach to language: he aimed to build abstract theories which might only explain part of the data rather than attempting to classify observable phenomena exhaustively. But so far we have only seen how his *methods* were inspired by physics. What about his *questions* about language: where did they come from?

KNOWLEDGE OF LANGUAGE

Here we need to return to our philosophical question about certain knowledge from a different angle. Someone who can speak a language has 'certain knowledge' of a special sort. For instance, anyone who is proficient in English knows that example (1) is an acceptable English sentence:

(1) One day even the state of Mississippi, a state sweltering with the heat of injustice, sweltering with the heat of oppression, will be transformed into an oasis of freedom and justice.

Speakers of English also know that (2) is not a possible English sentence:

(2) Justice and freedom of oasis an into transformed be will, oppression of heat the with sweltering, injustice of heat the with sweltering state a, Mississippi of state the even day one.

Whether a person recognises (1) as part of Martin Luther King's 'I have a dream' speech depends on their individual experience, but no speaker of the language will doubt that (1) is a well-formed sentence of English while (2) is not. Where does this certainty come from? Chomsky gives the obvious answer, which is that a speaker of English has a 'system of knowledge' in her or his head, and it is this system of knowledge which constitutes 'the English language' in the only intelligible sense of that term.

It is worth elaborating this point a little, not only because it is central to Chomsky's whole enterprise, but also because it has often been bitterly attacked. One dictionary defines *English* as follows:

The official language of Britain, the U.S., most parts of the Commonwealth and certain other countries. It is the native language of over 280 million people . . . It is an Indo-European language belonging to the West Germanic branch.

(Collins 1994, p. 516)

This is a *geographical* conception of the English language, and it is accurate as far as it goes, but it does not get to the heart of the matter. If English was only spoken by two people living on a desert island somewhere, it would still be the same language, but what is it that would make it the same language? The answer has to be the one that Chomsky gave: the system of knowledge in their heads is what defines English. The geography of the language is secondary.

In a famous passage written in 1965, Chomsky stated his position like this:

Linguistic theory is concerned primarily with an ideal speaker–listener, in a completely homogeneous speech community, who knows its language perfectly, and is unaffected by such grammatically irrelevant conditions as memory limitations, distractions, shifts of attention and interest and errors (random or characteristic) in applying his knowledge of language in actual performance . . .

> We thus make a fundamental distinction between competence (the speaker–hearer's knowledge of his language) and performance (the actual use of language in concrete situations).
>
> (Chomsky 1965, p. 3)

Opponents of Chomsky have attacked this statement on the grounds that performance is tangible, observable and measurable, whereas knowledge cannot be directly observed. You cannot open up a person's head and find 'knowledge of a language'. The critics therefore claim that linguistic knowledge is mysterious and metaphysical, whereas linguistic behaviour is concrete and real: how, they ask, can the scientific study of language rest on such a shaky foundation?

Chomsky's reply to these objections has two parts, a practical one and a philosophical one. First, he argues that the idealisations and abstractions set out in his 1965 statement simply describe what all linguists do. I have on my shelf an introductory book about Welsh, not intended to be Chomskyan in any sense. The book lists various rules which are claimed to be part of the **grammar** of that language. If I were to make a tape recording of natural Welsh speech, I would certainly find 'shifts of attention and interest and errors' on the tape. Clearly, though, it would be ridiculous to expect my textbook to say anything about such matters. The perfect Welsh described in the book is an idealisation of what actually happens: it describes the knowledge that Welsh speakers have of their language, not the quirks of individual speakers.

The philosophical answer is about scientific method. If we investigate a physical system, we expect that the internal properties of the system will be relevant to its behaviour: indeed, it would be stupid to think otherwise. The engine of a car behaves the way it does because it is made mainly of metal: if it were made of chocolate it would behave differently. Chomsky argues that we should take the same attitude to mental phenomena. The regular patterns of behaviour that we find in linguistic performance presumably do not come from nowhere: they reflect systems of knowledge in the minds of speakers of a language. When we describe a language we are therefore describing part of the minds of these speakers.

Chomsky refers to the shift in thinking about language in the 1950s – for which he was largely responsible – as 'the cognitive revolution'. Instead of taking a language as a collection of sounds and marks on paper made by a geographically defined group of people, he argued that a language is a system of knowledge in the mind of – at the limit – a single speaker. The system of knowledge cannot be directly observed, but in that respect it is like the inside of the sun, which is also inaccessible for practical reasons. Astronomers nonetheless propose theories about the inside of the sun based on observations about the behaviour of the sun; linguistics can do the same about the inside of our heads. Presumably knowledge of language has a physical correlate: it must be stored in our brain in some concrete form, just like any knowledge. Brain scientists may one day be able to identify the physical correlates of linguistic knowledge: in the meantime, linguists can propose theories about the structure of this knowledge, and these theories can be further investigated by brain scientists (cf. <u>Jackendoff</u>, this volume).

FROM KNOWLEDGE OF LANGUAGE TO THE LANGUAGE FACULTY

Given a system of knowledge, there are four basic questions that one can ask about it:

1 What is the system of knowledge?
2 How does it come to be in a person's mind?
3 How is it stored physically in the brain?
4 How is it put to use in behaviour?

For the study of language, we can put aside question 3, which as we have just seen is a matter for brain researchers, and question 4, about which Chomsky says that little of any consequence can be said, despite its intrinsic interest. The answer to the first question is given by proposing a grammar of a particular language – more specifically, a **generative grammar**. The term *generative* has two senses: first, it means 'explicit, comprehensive, and not dependent on the linguistic knowledge of the scientist who writes or reads it'. In the second place, *generative* has a mathematical sense: it refers to a formal system which can build an infinite set of structures using finite means. Our knowledge of a language can encompass an infinite number of sentences, most of which we have never used or heard before. The words in the sentences may not be new, but the combination of words often is. There is no limit to the set of English sentences, so the system of knowledge must be capable of building an infinite set of structures: at the same time, our heads are finite in size, so the system must be finite.

The answer to the second question comes in several parts. If a person has some knowledge in their head, then logically that knowledge may have one of three sources:

1 It may be in the brain at birth – in other words, it may be transmitted via our genes.
2 It may develop in the brain as the person grows, analogous to the growth of teeth. We are not born with teeth, but pathological cases apart, our genes determine that we will develop a first incomplete set and a second complete set of teeth by certain ages. In the same way, we may not have linguistic knowledge in our mind at birth, but our genes may cause the development of this knowledge by a certain age, independent of any experience that we may have.
3 The knowledge may be learned from experience.

Clearly, the words of a particular language are learned from experience: no one has ever claimed that the vocabulary of English or any other language is programmed into our genes at birth. It may be, however, that parts of the structure of languages

111

are genetically transmitted. Whether that is the case or not is a matter for empirical investigation.

If parts of our linguistic knowledge are genetic, then these parts must be universal: they must apply to all human languages. This follows from the fact that we do not seem to be genetically predisposed to learn any particular human language: the same infant will acquire English if surrounded by English input, or any other language if the relevant input is available. Chomsky therefore refers to these parts of our linguistic knowledge – assuming they exist – as **Universal Grammar** (UG) (see Jackendoff, this volume).

Are there any reasons to think that, in fact rather than as a matter of logic, parts of our linguistic knowledge are genetic? Chomsky argues that there are several. First, the acquisition of language by young people takes place within certain ages, and follows regular sequences. Particular sentences and rules are normally learned before others, with variation only to a limited extent between individuals. In this respect, acquiring a language is like learning to walk: apart from people with mental or physical disabilities, all young people learn to walk by a certain age and in a certain sequence, with only minor variation. We commonly presume that learning to walk is genetically determined, and it is sensible to conclude that the development of language is too.

The second argument is that all languages have features in common. To take a simple example, all languages seem to distinguish **vowel** and **consonant** sounds, and for every language so far investigated it is possible to distinguish grammatically between **noun**s and **verb**s. There are languages which are 'atypical' in various respects: for instance, English has an unusually large inventory of vowel sounds (nearly twenty) compared with most languages. But there are no known languages which are wildly different from all the others: all the English vowel sounds also occur in many other languages, and in other respects there are no 'unique' languages. Claims to the contrary do not stand up to investigation: for instance, the commonly held belief that the Basque language is different in its grammar from every other language in the world is untrue. Languages do differ, of course, but not in unlimited ways. When we learn a new language we are immediately struck by the obvious differences; but from a detached scientific viewpoint it is possible to argue that it is the similarities between languages which are more significant.

The third argument is based on work in generative grammar. Research has, Chomsky claims, indicated **rule**s and principles in particular languages which go far beyond the evidence available to young people who are acquiring a language. It is not simply that young people generalise beyond the evidence, for instance in putting plural endings on nouns which they have only ever heard in the singular. Chomsky's point is that the same rules and principles are regularly acquired by different people, despite cases where the evidence for them is not available at all. It is difficult to illustrate this point without being very technical, but a simple example might make it clearer (see Salkie 1990, pp. 28–51 for a more detailed discussion). Suppose a young person hears this sentence:

(3) Mississippi will be transformed into an oasis of freedom and justice.

Based on other sentences that the person has heard, she or he may be able to turn it into a question like this:

(4) Will Mississippi be transformed into an oasis of freedom and justice?

If we want to describe the young person's knowledge at this stage in the form of a rule for turning a statement into a question, a first attempt might be:

(5) Swap the first two words, putting the second one first and the first one second.

If this simple rule, which is adequate for examples (3) and (4), were the correct rule for English questions, then young people acquiring English would hear sentences like (6) and attempt to make them into questions like (7):

(6) The State of Mississippi will be transformed into an oasis of freedom and justice.

(7) *State the of Mississippi will be transformed into an oasis of freedom and justice.

(The asterisk before (7) indicates that this sentence is ill-formed in some way.)
    In fact, young people NEVER make mistakes like (7). This suggests that instead of using a simple rule like (5), they use a more complex rule like (8):

(8) Swap the first **noun phrase** and the first **auxiliary** verb.

This is a *structure-dependent* rule: instead of using simple notions like *first word* and *second word*, it depends on more complex structural notions like *noun phrase*. No language has a rule like (5), and the fact that young people acquiring a language never try to use rules like (5) goes beyond the evidence available to them. This suggests that structure-dependence is part of UG.
    If these arguments are correct, then UG is a reasonable theoretical construct. Universal features of language are, Chomsky argues, hardwired into our genes and we do not 'learn' them any more than we learn to grow teeth. By studying the grammars of particular languages, linguists who share Chomsky's goals and methods are thus able to investigate a fundamental property of the human mind, namely the *language faculty* as modelled by theories of UG. We can now see what Chomsky was referring to in the passage cited above when he proposed to search for 'insight and understanding of the roots of human nature in the cognitive domain'. Any universal feature of the human mind is by definition part of what makes us human, our 'human nature'. A feature as important as the language faculty – perhaps the single feature that distinguishes us most sharply from other animals – is central to being human: it is part of 'the roots of human nature'. It may sound like a giant leap to move from grammar to the roots of human nature, but

Chomsky argues that the leap is a legitimate one: for him, this is what makes linguistics interesting and important.

BACK TO PHILOSOPHY

Chomsky's use of terms like 'human nature' is anathema to some philosophers, in particular those who believe strongly that the human mind is a blank sheet at birth, and that knowledge cannot be transmitted through our genes. This point of view is called *empiricism*, and it is associated in particular with philosophers such as Hume and **Locke**. Empiricists deny that there is such a thing as 'human nature', claiming that all our knowledge and our personality are derived from experience. Their arguments are opposed by other philosophers like Descartes and Leibniz who maintained that we are born with innate knowledge, a position called *rationalism* (see Cottingham 1988; Woolhouse 1988). Until quite recently, rationalism had something of a bad press: it was associated with mystical concepts such as 'the eternal realm of ideas' in Plato's writings. Before the development of modern genetics, it was difficult for rationalists to explain exactly how knowledge could be passed on to new humans prior to any experience of the world.

Chomsky has no patience with empiricism. He argues not just that empiricism is wrong, but that it amounts to an obstinate refusal to face reality, and is thus more akin to a mental aberration than a coherent intellectual stance. Whether a piece of knowledge is innate or learned through experience is a factual question: it is a question that can be investigated by observation and analysis, rather than by ruling out one of the answers in advance of investigation, which is what empiricists do. In the case of language there are good reasons for supposing that there is innate knowledge, as we have seen, along with knowledge that is learned from experience. In other words, Chomsky gives factual, evidence-based arguments that empiricism is wrong, and has developed a scientific research programme based on rationalist principles. As we noted above, he sees philosophy and science as part of the same enterprise of understanding the world and our place in it. The study of language is one area where scientific progress has direct implications for philosophy, to the benefit of both.

Where does this leave us on the question of certain knowledge? Chomsky's reasoning leaves us with an apparent paradox, though it is one that all scientists face. Scientific knowledge, based on careful observation of the facts, the selection of certain facts as susceptible to analysis, and the formulation of abstract theories to explain only these facts, seems to be the most secure knowledge that we can arrive at. Such knowledge is limited and partial; furthermore, it is almost sure to be wrong, in the sense that new scientific research will probably come up with different theories which may have significant implications for philosophy, forcing us to question some of the beliefs that we currently hold. Scientific knowledge is thus the most certain, but at the same time fundamentally unstable and uncertain. This, in Chomsky's opinion, is simply the way the world is: instead of making us uncomfortable it should make us excited because there is so much still to learn.

DEVELOPMENTS IN LINGUISTICS

Nowhere has this instability been more evident, and arguably more productive, than in the linguistic research carried out by Chomsky and his associates. We turn now to some of the most important advances, though we can only sketch them here.

Early work by Chomsky and his colleagues (from the mid-1950s to the mid-1960s) was sometimes labelled **transformational grammar**, because much attention was devoted to grammatical rules called *transformations*. A simple example of such a rule would be the one for forming questions that we formulated as (8) above: the rule takes a statement and 'transforms' it into a question according to a formal procedure. In fact, transformations were conceived by Chomsky as operating not on sentences but on abstract analyses which were intended to represent some of the properties of sentences. These abstract analyses were known as **deep structure**s, and though the word 'deep' was used here in a strictly technical sense it was mistakenly assumed by some commentators that deep structures had something to do with hidden layers of the human personality, perhaps similar to Freud's unconscious mind (cf. Harris, this volume, for some critical discussion).

Not only was this interpretation of Chomsky a long way off target, but the idea that transformations are central to his work is also unhelpful. For one thing, transformational rules are just one of many formal devices that grammarians have proposed, and they have no special status. Second, even linguists who rejected or misunderstood Chomsky's broader aims were often happy to adopt transformations, because they are a convenient descriptive device and can be adapted to make exercises for language learners. For Chomsky, however, transformational rules were part of a formal apparatus intended to be used in generative grammars of individual languages and in hypotheses about the nature of Universal Grammar, a quite different enterprise. This leads us to the third reason why transformations should not be seen as vital: from the mid-1960s, Chomsky and his colleagues devoted considerable effort to *reducing* the power and scope of transformations. A look at why this was thought necessary may bring Chomsky's work into clearer focus.

If UG plays a role in first language acquisition, then powerful rules like transformations are not the sort that we should be looking for. Young people acquire their first language quite easily, in the sense that they do not appear to consider a wide range of grammars but only a small number. The evidence for this comes from the kind of 'mistakes' that they make: as we saw earlier, many possible errors are simply not found. Transformations, on the other hand, can be used to construct a huge range of grammars, most of which do not exist. What we need, then, are principles of UG which constrain transformations and only allow a limited number of possibilities. The principle of structure-dependence that we outlined above is one such principle. In recent work, many other principles have been proposed to limit UG in this way.

The basic idea is that from a small amount of random, scattered and degenerate input (the speech that she or he hears nearby) a young person should be able to use the principles of UG to construct a grammar of any human language. The principles need to be tight enough so that they only cover human languages, but flexible enough to account for all human languages. Research in the 1980s and early 1990s tried to meet these requirements by using the notion of *parameter*. A simple example is word order: in languages like English the order of words is severely restricted, whereas in languages like Russian there is much more freedom to use a variety of different word orders. This difference is called a parameter of variation between languages, and in this particular case it is a very salient one which a young person acquiring either type of language can become aware of easily.

The proposal is that UG makes available a number of such parameters, which have to be 'fixed' one way or the other by the young person on the basis of the evidence around them. Once the parameter has been fixed either in the 'English' way or the 'Russian' way, this will have consequences for other rules in the grammar of these languages. The young person will not have to learn these consequences: they will follow automatically once the parameter of UG has been fixed correctly. UG, seen as a system of **principles and parameters**, thus makes the process of language acquisition easy. As well as being an interesting theory of how languages are acquired, this framework is a good one for making scientific progress. If a grammarian suggests that the principles and parameters should be formulated differently from previous proposals, this will have major empirical consequences throughout the grammars of particular languages. Such a suggestion is thus a strong hypothesis, which can be readily tested against a large amount of data (see Culicover 1997 for an introduction to this area).

The most recent work in Chomsky's framework proposes even stricter limits and constraints on possible grammars (cf. Chomsky 1995). Known as *minimalism*, this line of work tries to formulate a small number of extremely general principles of UG which interact in complex ways to get the right results. Many of the specific rules, principles and parameters which held centre stage in earlier work have been discarded or subsumed under these general principles. The notion of deep structure has been abandoned, and indeed so has surface structure. The details are complex and cannot be elaborated here, but the motivation remains the same: to construct a theory of UG that accounts for the widest possible range of human languages while being compatible with the facts about language acquisition.

CONCLUSION

Chomsky's linguistics continues to flourish and develop, suggesting that Chomsky's original questions about language were useful and productive ones. Chomsky has often been criticised for changing his theories, but the criticism is ridiculous: science is all about refining and occasionally discarding theories as new evidence and new analysis come to light. Many people liked deep structure and transformations and have been reluctant to accept Chomsky's more recent work:

such people are like the Catholic Church in the seventeenth century, which refused to accept the theories of Galileo and Newton because they conflicted with religious beliefs. It is to Chomsky's credit that the study of Universal Grammar continues to move forward, overturning old assumptions and throwing up new problems.

We started by saying that Chomsky's influence has been small, if influence is measured by counting the people who are actively involved in his research programme. Whether his linguistics is nevertheless important is a matter of opinion. Quite apart from its intrinsic merits, however, Chomsky's achievement as an intellectual is outstanding. Despite bitter hostility and misapprehension he has persevered with his research into language, responding to his opponents with rational argument and honest debate. His political activities have provoked similar animosity and misunderstanding, to which he has responded in the same way. This is a remarkable record, and one which will certainly stand the test of time.

FURTHER READING

Barsky, R. (1997) *Noam Chomsky: A Life of Dissent*, Cambridge, MA: MIT Press.
Chomsky, N. (1982) *The Generative Enterprise: A Discussion with Riny Huybregts and Henk van Riemsdijk*, Dordrecht: Foris.
Cook, V. and Newson, M. (1996) *Chomsky's Universal Grammar: An Introduction*, 2nd edn, Oxford: Blackwell.
Newmeyer, F. (1986) *Linguistic Theory in America*, 2nd edn, London: Academic Press.
Smith, N. (1999) *Chomsky: Ideas and Ideals*, Cambridge: Cambridge University Press.

9

LINGUISTICS AFTER SAUSSURE

ROY HARRIS

INTRODUCTION

Linguistics is a term of no great antiquity. It came into fashion in the nineteenth century when scholars began to distinguish between various possible approaches to the study of language and languages. Many, including **Saussure**, insisted on a distinction between traditional **philology**, focused on the study of literary and other texts (particularly those of earlier periods) and a more general form of inquiry which sought to study languages themselves, irrespective of whether they had produced texts of literary or cultural importance, or of whether they had produced any texts at all. Linguistics eventually emerged as the preferred term for this more general form of inquiry, of which the prospectus and methods were set out in Saussure's posthumously published *Cours de linguistique générale* (*Course in General Linguistics*). This key treatise appeared in 1916, having been compiled from the notes taken by Saussure's students at courses of lectures that he gave at the University of Geneva in the years 1907–11.

In the present chapter, 'after Saussure' will be taken to mean 'after the publication of the *Cours*' and accordingly the name 'Saussure' will be taken to designate for convenience the putative author of that treatise, even though we know that the published text was a work of reconstruction by various hands, in particular those of Charles Bally and Albert Sechehaye (Godel 1957).

Within five years of its publication Saussure's *Cours* had become widely read in linguistic circles (De Mauro 1972, p. 366). Translations into various languages followed. An initially critical reception gradually yielded to acceptance. By 1957 (centenary year of the eponymous Saussure's birth) it was possible for a professional academic linguist to write: 'We are all Saussureans now' (Spence 1957). But whether they all were – and, if so, to what extent – are tricky questions.

LINGUISTICS AS A SCIENCE

Linguistics, as envisaged in Saussure's *Cours*, was to be a 'science'. That idea has certainly survived down to the present day. (For discussion, see Crystal 1985, pp. 76ff.; Harris 1992.) Not many academics currently holding posts in linguistics will define their subject without invoking the term *science*, and some departments of linguistics even incorporate that term into their title (as if officially calling their subject a science automatically made 'scientists' of them). But the survival of the notion that linguistics should be a science has little to do with Saussure. *Science* is one of the most popular and vacuous buzzwords in modern academic culture, particularly in those areas where the 'scientific' status of a subject is in doubt. Every discipline wants to get in on the act (partly because the funding for 'scientific' projects and departments is far more generous than for 'non-scientific' enterprises). During the latter part of the nineteenth century, various fringe subjects were queueing up and vying for official recognition as 'sciences'. Apart from linguistics, those in the academic queue included anthropology, psychology and sociology. Saussure was by no means the first to champion the 'scientific' status of linguistics. What he did, which others had failed to do, was set out a comprehensive case for what could be included in this domain and why.

Saussure defined linguistics by reference to three aims: (i) to describe all known languages and record their history; (ii) to determine the forces operating permanently and universally in all languages and formulate general laws accounting for all attested linguistic phenomena; and (iii) to delimit and define linguistics itself (Saussure 1916, p. 20). If he were alive today he would doubtless be struck by the disparity of achievement in attaining these specific goals.

Documenting the languages of the world

Progress in describing all known languages and recording their history has not been spectacular. However one decides to count the number of languages in the world (a permanently contentious issue), the majority have still not been studied in any depth. A few, on the other hand, are disproportionately well documented. These tend to be languages with the greatest number of speakers and high cultural prestige, where practical demand for teaching materials is considerable. At the other end of the scale, however, 'endangered' languages also tend nowadays to be a focus of attention, the objective being to record them before they become extinct (Robins and Uhlenbeck 1991; see also Aitchison, this volume). An even more quixotic type of enterprise seeks proactively to resuscitate dying languages by teaching them to new generations of speakers as part of the 'cultural heritage' they are in danger of losing. There is no evidence of any such conservationist zeal on the part of Saussure.

Language universals

The search for language universals has attracted much interest but met with mixed fortunes (Greenberg 1966; Bach and Harms 1968; Payne 1994; Croft 1994). Its problematic aspects are in part related to (i), since if there are large numbers of languages which have not been adequately investigated, it is difficult to have confidence in claims to the effect that certain features are found in *all* languages. There are other sources of scepticism too, which concern the *a priori* assumptions on which claims to universality are based, together with the difficulty of deciding whether features apparently present in more than one language are really 'the same'. Thus, for instance, it might at first sight seem a trivially simple matter to determine whether a particular language has words for 'Yes' and 'No'. But on closer inspection it becomes apparent that in English the words *yes* and *no* contrast and complement each other in a variety of quite subtle ways, which are certainly not matched by, for instance, the French pair *oui* and *non*. Once this is realized, it becomes obvious that even to pose the question in terms of having words for 'Yes' and 'No' is to pose it in a way that begs the question by assuming that English sets the standard of comparison for other languages. It is one thing to see the difficulty: quite another is to propose some non-question-begging way of reformulating the question.

Partly in response to these problems, distinctions are now drawn which would have been unfamiliar to linguists of Saussure's generation. For example, in addition to 'absolute' universals (which supposedly all languages share), there are 'statistical' universals ('In any language x is always more frequent than y') and 'implicational' universals ('If a language has x then it will also have y').

The most ambitious claim in this domain is the so-called 'universal base hypothesis', which claims that all languages can be reduced to the same set of basic rules. The author of the *Cours* would have been unimpressed by this, since in effect it reintroduces the kind of '**Universal Grammar**' that was already current in the Middle Ages, where the assumption was that Latin offered a perspicuous example of the structure common (with only minor variations of detail) to all languages. In the thirteenth century Roger Bacon – who was certainly acquainted with far fewer languages than Saussure – had claimed that the basic **grammar** of all languages is identical (*grammatica una et eadem est secundum substantiam in omnibus linguis*). The trouble is that, given a set of units, categories and rules defined at a high enough level of abstraction, it will always be possible to 'find' them exemplified in any particular language under investigation. Do all languages have **noun**s? Do all languages have **vowel**s? The answers to such questions depend on how terms such as 'noun' and 'vowel' are defined. The definitions can always be made to 'fit the facts' and the 'facts' can always be interpreted so as to 'fit the definitions'. When the search for universals is conducted in this way it soon becomes self-stultifying.

Subfields of linguistics

What would probably have surprised Saussure more than anything else is the degree of fragmentation and specialization now evident in what was in his day a relatively homogeneous field of inquiry. Linguistics as a self-defining discipline has defined itself into a diversity of inquiries that often have little in common but the appeal to the term *linguistics*. A glance at any current glossary reveals such branches as: anthropological linguistics, applied linguistics, biolinguistics, clinical linguistics, computational linguistics, critical linguistics, educational linguistics, ethnolinguistics, **neurolinguistics**, pragmalinguistics, **psycholinguistics**, **sociolinguistics** and many more.

Now whereas Saussure was acquainted, for example, with the work of Broca on the language centres of the brain, he would not have called that kind of investigation *neurolinguistique* or have regarded it as a legitimate subfield of linguistics proper. Similarly, he would not have regarded the study of doctor–patient dialogue or classroom interactions between teacher and pupils as falling within the confines of the discipline whose boundaries he was attempting to define. Nor would he have seen the relevance to linguistics of experiments in teaching language to apes. **Phonetics** is a grey area in Saussure's *Cours* and has remained so ever since. Some theorists are adamant that phonetics is not a part of linguistics, which they regard as starting with **phonology**. But how one can do any phonological analysis without phonetics is something of a mystery. (For Saussure, actual sounds uttered were not constituent parts of the linguistic sign, and yet he called one of its components the *image acoustique*.)

In short, one might say that linguistics has done the opposite of what Saussure hoped: it has *failed* to define itself. Instead, what has happened is that research which has anything to do with language at all now finds itself labelled by some compound term of which the second element is *linguistics*. Furthermore, the boundaries between these various branches of inquiry are often unclear.

LANGUE AND *PAROLE*

The state of affairs summarized under (i), (ii) and (iii) above may be regarded as due, at least in part, to the failure by linguists to deal with some of the practical and theoretical difficulties that Saussure left unresolved. In that sense, contemporary linguistics is still trying – not very successfully – to cope with the Saussurean legacy. Some of these problems will be examined below.

Saussure distinguished, consistently and emphatically, between *langue* and *langage*. This distinction is not altogether easy to render into English for want of a corresponding pair of words. For Saussure, *langage* includes both *langue* and *parole* (Saussure 1916, p. 38). The latter is the implementation in speech of the system (*langue*) which the language-user brings into play in any given act of linguistic communication (*parole*). The priority of *langue* as far as (Saussurean) linguistics is concerned can be boiled down to the proposition that if any episode of human speech is to be the subject of serious scientific inquiry it must be related in the first instance to a system which must be presupposed as underlying it.

A later generation of linguists rebaptized Saussure's distinction between *langue* and *parole* as 'linguistic **competence**' versus 'linguistic **performance**' (Fromkin and Rodman 1978, pp. 6–9 *et passim*). For a sceptical view, see Lakoff 1973a. But this terminological innovation makes no headway in resolving the difficulties attaching to the distinction itself. Matters are not helped by the lack of consistency between different theorists (or even sometimes in the same theorist on different occasions) regarding the way the distinction is to be drawn. Exactly what belongs to *parole* (performance) and what to *langue* (competence) remains in doubt.

Saussure hesitates over where to draw the line, presumably because he sees that individual speakers can exercise great freedom over how to combine linguistic signs into **syntagmatic** sequences (of which an infinite number are possible in any given language). So it becomes unclear after a certain point whether particular combinations are authorized by 'the language system' or whether they are in fact individual innovations. For this reason he hedges his bets on the status of the sentence (*phrase*) as a unit of *langue*.

> Where syntagmas are concerned . . . one must recognize that there is no clear boundary separating the language (*langue*), as confirmed by communal usage, from speech (*parole*), marked by freedom of the individual. In many cases it is difficult to assign a combination of units to one or the other. Many combinations are the product of both, in proportions which cannot be accurately measured.
>
> (Saussure 1916, p. 179)

What Saussure does not explain, however, is how in such cases the investigating linguist is to decide what to include in a description of the language system (*la langue*) and what to leave out.

Linguists of the American generativist school who later proposed the distinction between 'competence' and 'performance' naïvely supposed that any language *L* could be *defined* as a set of sentences (Chomsky 1957, p. 13), and proposed that a linguistic description was a set of rules that distinguished the sentences of *L* from the non-sentences (i.e. the ungrammatical sequences of forms of *L*). Accompanying this was a heavy emphasis on quasi-mathematical formalization, reflecting an underlying assumption that languages like English and French could be treated in the same way as the artificial 'languages' of formal logic, with their 'well-formed formulae'. The term *generate*, introduced by **Chomsky** in 1957 and borrowed from mathematics, refers specifically to the assumption that a grammar consists of a finite set of **rule**s for specifying an infinite set of strings of symbols by explicit **algorithmic** operations. An important set of these were termed 'transformations' (a term borrowed from mathematical logic): hence this approach was commonly referred to as 'transformational-generative' grammar (see **transformational grammar** and **generative grammar**). Generativists subsequently embarked on lengthy debates about how many transformations had to be postulated for any given language and what their hypothetical properties were. The upshot was to make linguistics 'look like our conception of physics or of chemistry', as one linguist put it (Matthews 1979, p. 14), turning grammar into an arcane algebra whose formulae – unlike the 'traditional' rules of the school grammar book – were inaccessible save to specialists and beyond lay comprehension altogether. It was thus, unlike Saussurean linguistics, pedagogically useless into the bargain.

The notion that a language could be treated as just a set of sentences would doubtless have amused Saussure considerably. The theoretical embarrassment was made more acute by the generativists' assumption that the concrete evidence for sentencehood consisted *not* in actual performance (*parole*) but in the so-called 'intuitions' of 'native speakers'. Generativists thus generated for themselves a double dilemma as linguists. One was how to access the so-called 'intuitions' and distinguish these from mere opinions (which might be based on all kinds of educationally inculcated or socially motivated views of linguistic 'correctness'). The other was how to determine the qualifications for being a 'native speaker'. It soon emerged that apparently well-qualified 'native speakers' were by no means all in agreement about the 'sentences' of their native language. So either some members of the community (but which ones?) were presumably not genuine 'native speakers' after all, or else, worse still, what had originally been assumed to be language *L* now turned out to be more than one language (but how many?).

LANGUAGE AND DISCOURSE

Generativists spent what in retrospect seems decades of wasted effort in the jejune attempt to formalize the concept of 'linguistic competence' in terms of sentence-rules, having failed to pay sufficient attention to the basic problem that Saussure had drawn attention to years earlier. Linguists who realized that **discourse** is in any case not just a succession of sentences, but exhibits structural coherence over a far wider syntagmatic span, sidestepped the generative framework and developed what is variously known today as **'discourse analysis'**, 'discourse linguistics' or 'text linguistics' (van Dijk 1985; Beaugrande 1994). This pays particular attention to such properties as **'cohesion'** and 'narrativity', examining how sequences of events and other kinds of information are reported over longer stretches of talk or writing, up to and including book-length presentation. This movement is in effect a development of Saussurean syntagmatics (not of sentence-based grammar), and it is authentically Saussurean in the sense that Saussure placed no upper bound on the linearity of syntagmatic relations.

LANGUAGES AND LANGUAGE-NAMES

Once the simplistic notion that a language is just a set of sentences is abandoned, the problem remains of where to locate, within the observably diverse totality of language use, the kind of system that Saussure called *langue*, as distinct from *langage*. The obvious difficulty (both for Saussure and for his successors) was that such systems do not unambiguously correspond to the commonly accepted language-names (such as 'English', 'French', 'Latin', etc.). So there is no guarantee that everything called, say, 'English' belongs to the same linguistic system (*langue*). Nor is there any guarantee that a person who claims to be speaking a certain language (e.g. 'English') is actually conforming consistently to the requirements of one particular system.

The problem cannot be circumvented, as is sometimes supposed, by appeal to the linguistic community's sense of its own identity. Thus, for example, it has been claimed that 'English' is the language defined by reference to the collectivity of speakers who believe of themselves and of one another that they are speakers of English (Pateman 1983, p. 120). Quite apart from the circularity of this theoretical manoeuvre, and the problem of languages that go under various language-names, such a criterion automatically excludes any speaker whose membership of the linguistic community is marginal or in dispute. This would inevitably leave the linguist with a residue of speakers languishing in linguistic limbo. Does general linguistics require the assumption that everyone speaks at least one identifiable language? If so, what are the criteria for an 'identifiable language'? If not, how does general linguistics deal with the case of speakers who somehow manage to slip through the net?

SYNCHRONIC AND DIACHRONIC LINGUISTICS

Saussure was clearly aware of most of the problems mentioned above, and they were inherited by those who followed his attempt to establish linguistics as an independent academic discipline. The majority of his successors followed Saussure's lead in at least one respect. They accepted Saussure's narrowing down of the concept of *langue* in a way that relates to the passage of time. Saussure drew a basic distinction between what he called **synchronic** and **diachronic** linguistics and gave priority to the former. He would doubtless be gratified today to observe that the study of linguistic change occupies a far less prominent place in the activities of linguists than it did in the nineteenth century.

Phenomena pertaining to *langue* are synchronic phenomena; that is to say, we do not have to consider them as subject to change. They exist at a certain point in time and are systematically related to one another at that point. These 'static' relations in part define what Saussure regarded as *langue*. Diachronic linguistics, on the other hand, is concerned with relations between entities changing over time. It examines, for example, how, why – and in what sense – Latin gradually 'turned into' French. The 'survival' of the Latin word *mare* as French *mer* ('sea') is a typical diachronic phenomenon; or, more exactly, one exemplification of a whole series of diachronic phenomena. For, according to Saussure, Latin *mare* and French *mer* are in no sense 'the same word', even though they may appear under the same rubric in etymological dictionaries.

Most of Saussure's successors accepted the 'synchronic–diachronic' distinction, which still survives robustly in early twenty-first-century linguistics. In practice, what this means is that it is accounted a violation of principle or linguistic method to include in the same synchronic analysis evidence relating to diachronically different states. So, for example, citing Shakespearean forms would be regarded as inadmissible in support of, say, an analysis of the grammar of Dickens. Saussure is particularly severe in his strictures upon linguists who conflate synchronic and diachronic facts.

However, setting up the 'synchronic–diachronic' distinction does not automatically solve the problem of how to distinguish one *état de langue* from another. Saussure himself shows signs of worrying about whether temporal succession is a reliable criterion. If different states merge chronologically into one another, it would seem that some other basis must be sought for identifying the linguistic 'system' that synchronic linguistics places at the forefront of its inquiry.

Thus any linguist who sets out to describe a single linguistic system *L* (one *langue* in the Saussurean sense) immediately has to confront the problem of how to locate and recognize it. For observable linguistic usage is characterized above all by its apparent heterogeneity. Unless this diversity can be 'reduced' in some way, there is little hope of identifying a coherent system.

LINGUISTIC HETEROGENEITY

How has post-Saussurean linguistics tried to deal with this problem? One move has been to relocate the linguistic system not at the level identified by such blunt labels as 'English', 'French', etc. but at the level of '**dialects**' or 'varieties'. In the *Cours* we find the suggestion – but it is hardly more than that (Saussure 1916, p. 132) – that in order to find synchronic systematicity it will be necessary to consider 'dialects and sub-dialects'. This move corresponds to the lay perception that people who may be speaking, say, 'English' – and would describe themselves as 'English' speakers – nevertheless are not necessarily all speaking *the same* English. They may differ noticeably one from another in features of pronunciation, grammar and vocabulary. How can a 'synchronic' linguistic description accommodate this amount of variation?

Dialects and isoglosses

In the first place the linguist may try to narrow down the scope of linguistic description geographically. Thus if informants are chosen from particular regions, 'English' may be subdivided into American English, Australian English, Welsh English, Scottish English, etc., each being treated as a separate variety (Trudgill and Hannah 1982). But this strategy brings problems in its turn. Within such broad groupings there are still geographically distinct variations (e.g. between New York and New Orleans, or between Bristol and Liverpool). Furthermore, although both in Saussure's day and since then the practitioners of so-called 'dialect geography' have tried to delimit linguistic areas by such techniques as plotting 'isoglosses' (lines on maps which supposedly mark the boundaries of the geo-graphical spread of particular linguistic features) modern transport conditions and population movements increasingly make such attempts seem futile. Languages do not 'stay in one place' because their speakers do not stay in one place either.

A further weakness in attempts to pin down linguistic variation geographically arises from the fact that even when a very precise location is pinpointed for investigation it is commonly found that speech in the local community is far from uniform, varying according to such factors as the age, sex and social strata of the speakers. 'Sociolinguistics' is the general term now employed to designate linguistic investigations with this kind of diversity as the focus of attention. As a subdiscipline of linguistics it barely existed in Saussure's day, but in recent decades probably more work has been done in sociolinguistics than in any other field of language studies (Coulmas 1997). The socially defined variety of a language spoken by a certain social group within a community is sometimes called a 'sociolect' (in order to distinguish it from the 'dialect', based on geographical criteria).

Idiolects

A quite different strategy for trying to identify the synchronic language 'system' as a viable object of linguistic description has been to restrict attention to the speech of a single speaker. Each individual is envisaged as having a personal variety of speech, and this personal variety is known technically as the 'idiolect'. Thus, in the final analysis, what is nowadays spoken as 'English' can be broken down, according to this view, into as many different idiolects as there are speakers (i.e. millions). Whether any two such idiolects are *exactly* alike is a moot point: the usual assumption is that they will be found to differ in certain features, however minimally.

At first sight it might seem that getting down to the level of the individual speaker is a neat way round the problem of how to decide whether the language of a group of speakers is sufficiently uniform for this variety to be considered a single 'dialect' or 'sociolect'. But the strategy is flawed for a variety of reasons. Linguists have been unable to agree on how an idiolect is to be defined. One famous definition, dating from the 1940s, was: 'the totality of the possible utterances of one speaker at one time in using a language to interact with one other speaker' (Bloch 1948). This definition already tries to forestall two objections. One is that the characteristic way an individual speaks may vary over the course of a lifetime. The other is that an individual may speak differently to different addressees in different circumstances. This is a linguistic phenomenon now known as 'accommodation' (Giles 1994). But the attempts to circumvent these objections still leave the linguist short of the desired objective, i.e. isolating a stable, consistent form of speech to investigate. For even in the course of a single conversation with the same interlocutor it is possible for a speaker to introduce noticeable variations of pronunciation, grammar, vocabulary, etc. Furthermore, it is hard to know how to make sense in practical terms of a 'totality of possible utterances' directed to a single interlocutor 'at one time'. And this, in any case, seems to give us in the end not a definition of an idiolect but what other theorists call a 'style' or **'register'**. The more narrowly one tries to restrict the scope of a linguistic description, the more elusive the notion of *langue* becomes.

Here Saussure set his successors a problem which has still not been solved. It is, indeed, the foundational problem of **'descriptive' linguistics** – a weasel word (*descriptive*) if ever there was one. For however much the linguist exercises a right to restrict the enterprise (i.e. to exclude this, that and the other from consideration), there is still no guarantee that the underlying 'system' can be captured by the resources of the descriptive apparatus available. One of the things Saussure never quite managed to deal with satisfactorily – or, some would say, deal with at all

– was the linguistic status of his own descriptive metalanguage. But nor have his successors fared any better, at least in the mainstream of modern linguistics. Linguists are still in the awkward position of trying to achieve levitation by tugging at their own metalinguistic shoelaces. And this is because the reflexivity of language on which linguistics relies cannot in the end be reconciled with the crude (positivist) notion of 'description' that linguists needed (still need?) in order to make their academic discipline appear to qualify as a 'science'.

IDEAL SPEAKER–LISTENERS AND FIXED CODES

A related problem concerns the status that 'the language system' (*langue*) is deemed to have in relation to the individual speaker. According to Saussure, a language belongs not to the individual but to the community. The language itself is not complete in any one speaker, but only in the collectivity. This doctrine posed problems for later generations of linguists, who found it difficult to accept the metaphysics of collectivization. So they finessed it by referring to an 'ideal speaker–listener'. This fictitious character was supposed to be (i) an individual, but also (ii) an individual who possessed a 'perfect' (synchronic) knowledge of the language L (being, of course, *ex hypothesi* a 'native speaker' of L). It was obvious from the start that this ideal speaker–listener talk was a theoretical subterfuge for evading the problem to which Saussure had drawn attention. A feeble attempt to justify it was made by invoking the 'scientific' comparison between the observation of actual gases in the laboratory and the behaviour of an 'ideal' gas (under stated conditions of temperature, pressure, etc.). That such justifications were invoked at all indicates the extent to which post-Saussurean linguistics was still seeking – and still is seeking – parity of status with the 'sciences'. What the comparison overlooks is that the study of language, unlike the study of gases, is in no way beholden to mathematics and mathematical models.

The notion that each language (*langue*) can be thought of as represented by an 'ideal' speaker–listener is another way of conceptualizing languages as fixed codes. For it is hard to see how an ideal speaker–listener could be ideal without an infallible judgment as to whether a proposed form of expression were correct or not. In other words, this hypothetical figure is posited *ab initio* as one who already 'knows' whether such-and-such a construction is acceptable, whether such-and-such a word is admissible, whether such-and-such a pronunciation is authentic, whether a given sentence means such-and-such or not. If the 'ideal' speaker–listener's views of those matters varied from one occasion to the next, that would automatically be a disqualification for the theoretical role that such a personage is called upon to perform. It is important here to note the difference (often blurred) between ideality and typicality. A typical speaker–listener is not – and could hardly be – an 'ideal' speaker–listener in the sense theoretically required, although these notions are commonly conflated. (To see the difference, consider the claim that George is a *typical* gardener. It does not follow from this that George is an *ideal* gardener: far from it.)

DEEP STRUCTURE AND SURFACE STRUCTURE

The postulation of an 'ideal speaker–listener' for every language tended in the 1960s and 1970s to go along with acceptance of a dogmatic distinction between the **'surface structure'** of a language and its **'deep structure'**. Thus, for example, *The dog bit the postman* and *The postman was bitten by the dog*, although different on the 'surface', were seen as 'deeply' identical (i.e. in some – allegedly intuitive but not very clearly explicated – sense, as one and the same sentence). This is a kind of distinction Saussure never drew, and his 'failure' to draw it was seen by generativists as a basic inadequacy in Saussurean linguistics. They were the prime promoters of the 'surface' versus 'deep' dichotomy, since their model of sentence 'generation' logically required an underlying set of units on which combinatorial algorithms could operate. In terms of their model, Saussure could be criticized for simplistically supposing that the linguistic sign was a 'surface' unit, thereby insisting on criteria for delimiting one syntagmatic unit from the next.

Here again, however, generativists embarked on an enterprise of hoisting themselves with their own theoretical petard. Once the 'surface' of Saussurean sign-delimitation is abandoned, the depths of possible underlying structures become unfathomable. Is there a 'deep' linguistic level at which active sentences are identical with their passive correlates? Or verbs with corresponding adjectives? And how would we ever know?

Fairly recently, generativists have begun to admit that perhaps the 'deep structure' hypothesis should be abandoned, or at least demoted to the status of a 'prosaic technical gadget' (Pinker 1994, p. 120). But such admissions are rarely accompanied by granting that Saussure may have been right after all.

GLOSSEMATICS

If the language of the 'ideal speaker–listener' is an unconvincing extrapolation, it is at least no more unconvincing than the language conceived as a system independent of any concrete realization at all. This was the outcome of Louis **Hjelmslev**'s interpretation of Saussure, which laid the foundation for the Danish linguistic school of glossematics. Glossematicians took the Saussurean dictum that *langue* is 'form not substance' (Saussure 1916, p. 163) to its logical conclusion, and argued that the languages now in existence and available to observation are merely historical realizations of certain systems which could equally well exist in other manifestations (not necessarily spoken and not necessarily written either). Thus 'the task of the linguistic theoretician is not merely that of describing the actually present expression system, but of calculating what expression systems in general are possible as expression for a given content system, and vice versa' (Hjelmslev 1961, p. 105).

BEHAVIOURISM AND PSYCHOLOGICAL REALITY

Both glossematics and generativism, although claiming to improve on Saussure, are manifestly at odds with Saussure's stipulation that the linguist, in describing *la langue* in any given case, should set up no more and no less categories and distinctions than those already recognized 'consciously or unconsciously' by its speakers (Saussure 1916, p. 195). This was the first formulation of the goal of 'psychological reality' in descriptive linguistics. It has proved to be a nightmare for linguists ever since.

Why? In the first place because the whole notion of the Saussurean linguistic sign seemed too 'psychologistic' to those linguists (particularly in the USA) who had been won over to the cause of behaviourism. A sign which consisted of a 'concept' linked to an 'acoustic image' in the mind of the speaker struck them as altogether too mysterious and invisible as a basis for an 'empirical' science of the kind linguistics was supposed to be. As far as they were concerned, a 'science' had to deal with observables, not with what might – or might not – be going on somewhere inside the head. An immediate consequence of this was that the Saussurean sign had to be replaced by something more tangible – an audible linguistic form and its connections with 'the real world'. But this shift in outlook brought problems in its wake, since linguists were not expected to be experts in analysing 'the real world', that being the province of the various physical and biological sciences. The conclusion drawn was that linguistics could not deal with the 'meanings' of words except, to quote one leading behaviourist of the 1930s, in cases involving 'some matter of which we possess scientific knowledge' (Bloomfield 1935, p. 139). So whereas it was all right to define the meaning of the English word *salt* as 'sodium chloride (NaCl)', since science told linguists that that was what the substance called *salt* 'really' was, no such information was available for defining words like *love* and *hate*, not to mention all the other aspects of 'the real world' that science had not yet investigated.

This was a notable step backwards for linguistics, not only because it meant an admission that there were important aspects of language that linguists were incompetent to deal with, but also because it reverted to a notion of 'meaning' which Saussure had already castigated as inadequate for the discipline. This was the ancient idea that words were just vocal labels attached to 'things' already existing. (Here we have the substance sodium chloride and there we have the word *salt*. The former is the meaning of the latter.) The traditional model for this nomenclaturist account was the biblical story of Adam naming the animals in the Garden of Eden. Saussure anticipated **Wittgenstein** in explicitly rejecting this crude theory as totally incapable of providing a satisfactory account of linguistic **semantics**.

Only when the star of behaviourism had waned somewhat in academic psychology did it become 'respectable' once again for linguists to discuss meaning in Saussurean or neo-Saussurean terms. But this did not actually solve the problem either. The fly in the linguistic ointment of 'psychological reality' is apparent when we consider Saussure's proviso 'conscious or unconscious'. How, in practice, can any 'scientist' hope to probe in detail the depths of the speaker's linguistic unconscious? Certainly not by going around with questionnaires asking whether certain combinations of forms are 'good' English sentences or whether dictionary definitions of words like *salt* are 'correct'. A more refined version of the same mistake was made by those 'psychological realists' who proposed to test the 'reality' of grammatical rules in the laboratory by determining how long it took informants to come up with the 'passive' version of an 'active' sentence ('The postman was bitten by the dog' vs. 'The dog bit the postman'). The error there consisted in supposing that the 'rules' of the language are invariant procedures by which the human brain 'converts' one syntagmatic combination into another. Saussure, again, would have been laughing at the naïvety of any such assumption.

LINGUISTIC METHODOLOGY

The problem of 'psychological reality' in linguistics tended to merge with two related issues, both of them controversial in their own right. If linguistics was to be a science, it was argued, linguists must develop a methodology comparable to those of the natural sciences. Thus bias and introspection by the linguist must be banned and only objective, verifiable methods employed. This led to much argument about which so-called 'discovery procedures' the linguist should in practice adopt when facing a corpus of evidence to analyse. In the second place, there arose doubts not merely about whether the goal of 'psychological reality' was realistically attainable, but about whether linguistic descriptions described anything 'real' at all. Those who believed in the objective existence of linguistic structure were called 'God's truth' linguists. Those who believed, on the contrary, that linguistic structure was an artefact of the linguist's analytic methods were known as 'hocus-pocus' linguists. Although these terms are no longer much used, the underlying debate continues to surface in a variety of ways. Thus one reason for rejecting the 'rule systems' approach to linguistic description is that the rules themselves are invented to meet the requirements of the systematization chosen, and have no independently verifiable correlates either in the speaker's mind or in the speaker's utterances.

CONTEXT

In Saussure's programme for linguistics there is no provision for the study of the actual contexts in which speakers communicate to one another. In other words, the assumption is that a language system (*langue*) remains invariant across all contexts. It makes no difference who the actual speakers are or in what circumstances they are speaking. This somewhat implausible assumption is today championed only by partisans of what is now called 'autonomous linguistics', to which a majority of surviving generativists belong (Newmeyer 1994). Others, however, have realized that it makes little sense (and serves no purpose) to insist on treating languages as self-contained mental systems which bear no relation at all – except externally and fortuitously – to the lives of their speakers and the communicational purposes to which they are constantly being put.

Thus between 'autonomists' and 'non-autonomists' the divisive issue concerns the role of communication. For the former, communication is simply a set of uses to which, as it happens, the verbal tools available can be put; whereas for the latter language *is* a form of communication and we cannot seriously account for the existence of the 'verbal tools' unless we see them as serving communicational ends.

INTEGRATIONISM, FUNCTIONALISM AND PRAGMATICS

In the non-autonomist camp, the most radical position is that taken by 'integrationists', who deny that linguistic signs can be defined except by reference to the actual communication situations in which they occur (Harris 1998). A less radical position is that of 'functionalists' (Dik 1994; Martinet 1994). Functionalism is a theoretical hat with very wide brims, broad enough to shelter all those who see linguistic structure as being moulded in response to communicational demands and to biomechanical factors. Thus, for instance, certain features of phonological systems would be explained by reference to properties of the human vocal tract and the communicational need to clarify auditory distinctions. The term 'functional' is in particular associated with the so-called '**Prague School**', a group of neo-Saussurean linguists who in 1926 founded the Linguistic Circle of Prague and included among their members Vilém Mathesius, Roman **Jakobson** and Nikolai **Trubetzkoy** (Vachek 1964; Fried 1972). '**Pragmatics**' is the term that has now become general for a broad variety of studies – whether overtly functionalist or not – that place emphasis on the need to study language in relation to the actual circumstances of its use (Mey 1994). Some pragmaticians even refer to the 'pragmatic competence', as distinct from the 'linguistic competence', of speakers; but exactly how pragmatic competence can be defined, other than by reference to the specifics of particular communication situations, it is difficult to see. In that respect, contextualized pragmatics leads to a position which coincides with that taken by integrationists.

LANGUAGE AND WRITING

Finally, Saussure's programme for linguistics was based on a fundamental assumption about the relationship between speech and writing. In identifying *la langue* as the system which was the object of investigation in linguistics, Saussure made it quite clear that writing was not part of it (Saussure 1916, p. 46). In effect, he equated language with spoken language. The majority of academic linguists throughout the twentieth century followed this lead. Statements to the effect that 'writing is not language' are commonplace.

But this raises a variety of problems in applied linguistics and psycholinguistics, particularly in the educational sphere, where learning to read and write early assumes paramount importance in linguistic education. So dogmatic adherence to the view that linguistics is concerned only with speech threatens to cut the discipline off from having anything relevant to say about the situation obtaining in most literate communities.

Why did Saussure take this line? And why was it followed by most of his successors? Doubtless because admitting writing to parity of linguistic status with speech would have caused enormous theoretical problems for a discipline that wanted to maintain its own academic independence. As mentioned in the opening paragraph of this chapter, linguistics originally sought to distinguish itself from 'philology', which had established a monopoly of the study of literary texts. But perhaps more important than this was the consideration that if writing were admitted as 'language' there would in effect have been straightaway a need to set up two branches of linguistics; one dealing with language in pre-literate communities and the other dealing with language in literate communities. By insisting on the doctrine of the 'primacy of speech' linguists guaranteed the unity and independence of their own academic subject.

Nevertheless, writing could not be rejected out of hand, because the main source of information that linguists had available about languages of the past consisted of written texts. Saussure thus found himself in an awkward situation. Either linguistics had to say nothing at all about languages having no live speakers to provide evidence for the linguist (which would have been the more honest approach), or else a compromise had to be reached which would allow the linguist 'indirect' access to dead languages. Saussure opted for the latter. He was thus obliged to claim that although writing had no linguistic status, it was nevertheless a separate system of signs which had as its sole purpose the 'representation' of speech.

This compromise was always a fudge. Furthermore, it obliged both Saussure and those of his successors who followed this line to go to extraordinary lengths to explain why in fact so few writing systems actually 'represented' speech in any straightforward or internally consistent manner. Nor were linguists able to give any convincing explanation of why it should be that the writing system could actually influence the spoken system, as it apparently does in cases of 'spelling pronunciations'. (Saussure had to dismiss these as 'monstrosities'.) In short, the attempt to deal with writing revealed the limitations of the doctrine of the 'primacy of speech' and exposed modern linguistics to the charge, laid by **Derrida** (1967) and others, of 'phonocentrism'.

Current reactions by linguists to the problem of writing fall into three general classes. (1) Say nothing about it. This seems to be characteristic of most generativists, who have no discernible theory of writing at all. (2) Treat speech and writing as separate autonomous systems. This is typically the position adopted by glossematicians (Uldall 1944) and Prague-school theorists (Barnet 1972). (3) Treat speech and writing as integrated systems of communication in all literate societies. This is the position adopted by integrationists (Harris 1995).

CONCLUSION

To sum up, linguistics after Saussure expanded and diversified in ways that Saussure shows no sign of anticipating. But in so doing it lost any theoretical consensus or coherence as regards the objectives of linguistic inquiry or the methods to be pursued in attaining them. As one contemporary linguist has put it: 'If asked point blank what the object of their science is, I assume that few professional linguists would hesitate to answer that it is "language". But if asked what they mean by "language" serious divergences would soon appear' (Martinet 1984). That observation is itself a comment on the extent to which linguistics has proved unable to resolve the problems that were part and parcel of the Saussurean legacy. The opening chapter of the *Cours* concludes with the statement that 'the fundamental problems of general linguistics still await a solution'. It is ironic how apposite that statement still is today.

FURTHER READING

There are no satisfactory 'histories' of modern linguistics. Current issues can perhaps best be followed by consulting the successive volumes of *Proceedings* of the International Congress of Linguists (held every five years). The best encyclopedia covering all branches of the subject is *The Encyclopedia of Language and Linguistics*, edited by R.E. Asher, Oxford, Pergamon, 1994, (10 vols), entries in which have been referred to on various occasions in this chapter. The publication *Saussure and Linguistics Today*, edited by Tullio De Mauro and Shigeaki Sugeta, Rome, Bulzoni, 1995, addresses a variety of issues concerning Saussure's continuing relevance to contemporary linguistics and contains contributions by leading Saussurean scholars.

10

DISCOURSE

NIKOLAS COUPLAND AND ADAM JAWORSKI

CONTRASTING DEFINITIONS OF 'DISCOURSE'

Discourse is sometimes defined in disarmingly simple terms. For Stubbs, discourse is 'language above the sentence or above the clause' (Stubbs 1983, p. 1). By this definition, all language in use, but not curses, shopping lists and road signs, for example, is discourse. In much more abstract terms, reflecting on his own theoretical writings on discourse, Foucault suggests that he has widened the scope of the term discourse, 'treating it sometimes as the general domain of all statements, sometimes as an individualizable group of statements, and sometimes as a regulated practice that accounts for a number of statements' (Foucault 1972, p. 80, cited in Mills 1997, p. 6).

These definitions seem very distant from each other. The first makes discourse seem entirely unexceptional and neutral, while Foucault's phrase 'regulated practice' hints at issues of power and conflict. Stubbs points us to the local instance (because discourse is any instance of language involving more than just a sentence), while Foucault entertains huge generalities (e.g. 'the general domain of all statements'). In this chapter, which adopts a more *functional* approach, we want to show that discourse does indeed require us to look at language in both its local and its global dimensions, and that both definitions above are therefore relevant. Local instances of language-in-use are rich in socio-cultural significance; large-scale norms, values and ideologies are inscribed in discourse patterns. The most incisive approaches to discourse are those that combine the detailed analysis of language, in particular instances of its use, with the analysis of social structure and cultural practice.

Nowadays, discourse is a core concept across the humanities and social sciences, well beyond the disciplines of linguistics and **semiotics** themselves. The origins of **discourse analysis** are to be found in linguistics, linguistic philosophy, social anthropology and theoretical sociology. We will not try to trace the history of discourse analysis here in detail (see Jaworski and Coupland, 1999, for a selection of influential writings on discourse and demonstrating discourse analysis, historical and contemporary). But the unifying insight that discourse analysis offers is that important aspects of our social lives are constructed in and through language, whether in the moment-to-moment social interchanges of everyday talk or in the beliefs, understandings and principles that structure our lives. Discourse analysis is therefore the attempt to observe, unravel and critique these acts of construction. The theoretical position it adopts can itself be called 'constructivist' because it makes the radical claim that the realities we take to define our social circumstances, and our selves within them, are to a large extent socially constructed (Shotter and Gergen 1989; Shotter 1993).

This constructivist (or constructionist) view of identity can be traced back to the work of Goffman and his notions of 'self-presentation' and 'interaction order' (1959, 1967). Goffman argued that interactants engage in conversation as a form of social action which, to use his (1974) favourite theatrical metaphor, is used to create a specific 'dramatic effect' (Goffman 1959, pp. 252–3). Communication is, then, a ritualised process that allows its participants to construct and project desirable versions of their identities, enacted in a succession of performances targeted at specific audiences. Because social actors in conversation are inter-dependent, the behaviour of one participant defines and constructs social relations and the identities of other members of the group. Thus, social **meaning** is emergent in interaction and the identities of social actors are multiple and dynamic (change-able in the course of interaction). A lot of discourse analytic research has examined various aspects of how identities are constructed, for example, in relation to gender (e.g. Coates 1996; Cameron 1999), ethnicity (Tannen 1999), age (e.g. Coupland *et al*. 1991; papers in Coupland and Nussbaum 1993), public image (Jaworski and Galasiński 1998), or health (Young 1999).

Two textual instances

In Stubbs's sense, Text 1 is a pretty routine instance of talk, and of discourse.

Text 1

Two thirteen year-olds discussing a schoolteacher.

David: He's a real dickhead he just bawls you out without listening at all.
Oliver: Yeah what an asshole (.) I can't stand him he's always raving raving on.
(adapted from Holmes 1999, p. 336)

(The symbol (.) marks a brief pause during Oliver's turn at talk.) We would in fact prefer to call this fragment of represented talk a '**text**', because it is a record of what has been said between David and Oliver, over one short sequence of verbal interchange. What we can record and print as a text was produced and experienced in quite a different way by David and Oliver themselves. To them, their talk was not a pre-formed text. It was a cumulative process of using language, socially, that ended up generating what we see as text. Treating language-in-use as discourse means trying to account for the social nature of communication as it is enacted, and how people make and interpret meanings in specific social circumstances. Text 1, however routine it seems, can therefore be seen as the product of a complex interweaving of personal, social and cultural processes, for which the term discourse stands as shorthand.

When words are spoken (or written), it is rather difficult to separate them from their context of use, which includes the purposes speakers have, the identities of the speakers and what has been said previously. Connections between the social and linguistic elements of interaction have to be made by speakers (or writers), in planning their contributions to discourse events, and for recipients to interpret spoken utterances or written sentences. Non-participating observers, such as discourse analysts scrutinising instances like Text 1, have to reconstruct as much as they can of the interplay of social and linguistic processes.

Let's look more closely at Text 1. Minimally, we need to know who is talked about in order to identify the **referent** of the pronoun 'He', David's first word and the subject of his abuse. The meaning and social implications of this exchange would have been completely different if the referent of 'He' was another schoolboy rather than the boys' teacher. Similarly, it is rather important for us to know that the speakers *are* schoolboys rather than teachers (talking about one of their colleagues) for example. So it is not sufficient for the interpretation of discourse to know the meanings of individual words arranged in a particular way in actual utterances, spoken or written. We need to draw on additional knowledge about the world in which these utterances are produced in order to build interpretations of them, and different people may come up with different interpretations of the same stretch of discourse depending on their particular knowledge and experience of the world. For example, as overhearers, the teachers of the two boys might interpret their discussion as 'rudely insulting', while the boys' friends might call it 'just chatting'.

We could then ask about the purpose and function of the exchange. What pay-offs can it offer to those who undertake it? Tracy and Coupland (1990) overview the literature on communication goals and introduce a distinction between 'task' or 'instrumental' goals (e.g. talking to exchange factual information) and 'identity' and 'relational' goals (e.g. in asserting group membership and solidarity). Generally, instrumental goals relate to the referential meaning of utterances (what is talked about, what attributes are linked to subjects, etc.), whereas identity and relational goals relate to how speakers present themselves (Goffman 1959), manage their own and their interactants' 'face-wants' (Brown and Levinson 1987) and negotiate power and social distance through talk. Although utterances are typically multi-functional, i.e. they perform both task and identity/relational goals (and others) at the same time, one set of goals may be dominant in any one utterance. If we assume that this isn't the first time that the two boys have talked about their teacher, we have to rule out the primacy of *information exchange* in this case. It is likely that the dire opinion of the teacher that the boys are sharing is already well established, and both participants need no convincing on that point. So if the boys are not saying anything new to each other, why are they saying it? They are presumably invoking their mutual relationship as mates, and their in-group identity as pupils (in contrast to teachers as an out-group). They are performing their shared social position discursively, and this perhaps includes their shared gender and age identities.

The local design of the boys' exchange plays a part in expressing in-group solidarity. Like many two-party talk exchanges, this one is based on a first utterance inviting a response. Spoken exchanges are routinely two-part structures (e.g. reciprocated greetings, or a compliment followed by compliment responses). In **conversation analysis** these are known as 'adjacency pairs' (Schegloff and Sacks 1999). But Text 1 is not a typical adjacency pair because its second element (Oliver's response to David's utterance) is optional, or at least not required by the design of the preceding turn at talk. Oliver chooses to say something in response to David's complaint about the teacher, and, more importantly, he chooses to agree with him in a way that mimics David's original utterance. David's 'dickhead' is echoed by Oliver's 'asshole' – words drawn from the same language style or **'register'**, which we might call in-group slang. Oliver's 'Yeah' is of course an expression of assent, and 'I can't stand him' picks out and reinforces the evaluative force of David's original characterisation of the teacher. David's comment 'he just bawls you out without listening at all' is directly matched by Oliver's 'he's always raving raving on'. This is a meta-discursive comment (discourse about discourse, see Jaworski *et al.* 2000) which also shows how people base some of their social evaluations of others on how they use language.

In sum, the interpersonal function of discourse in Text 1 is realised at a number of different levels: topic gossip about an out-group member reinforces feeling of in-groupness (Coates 1989; J. Coupland 2000); vocabulary – use of slang and taboo words invokes a shared male identity (Kuiper 1991); response strategy – Oliver's agreement is supportive of David (Holmes 1999) and positively polite (Brown and Levinson 1987; <u>Verschueren</u>, this volume); and structural parallelism across utterances – Oliver's mirroring of David's utterance adds to the sense of supportiveness.

Text 2 illustrates how discourse allows participants to claim and establish power relations, which we define here as a degree of interpersonal influence, authority and control. It is an extract from a phone-in programme on a British radio talk show. The topic of the programme is 'telethons', and the caller widens the remit of the discussion to requests for charitable donations, which she receives by post.

Text 2

CALLER: I have got three appeals letters here this week. (.) all askin' for donations.
   (.) two: from those that I always contribute to anyway.
HOST: Yes?
CALLER: But I expect to get a lot more.
HOST: So?
CALLER: Now the point is there is a limit to . . .
                                    [
HOST: What's that got to do what's that got to do with telethons though?
CALLER: Because telethons . . . (Continues)

(adapted from Hutchby 1999, p. 581)

(In this transcript, (.) again indicates a brief pause and [indicates overlapping speech; we have omitted all other transcribing conventions used in the original.) In his analysis of this text, Hutchby (1999) argues that the caller is invited to set his/her agenda for the discussion. This unspoken entitlement seems to be ensured by the caller's privileged opening position in discourse. However, the host can exert control over the agenda set by the caller by making a 'second-position challenge'. For example in Text 2, the second turn by the Host consists of a single-word question 'So?', which introduces an element of authority and control over the caller, in at least two ways. First, it challenges the legitimacy of the caller's agenda; second, it requires the caller to give an account of her agenda-setting. The controlling aspect of 'So?' is clear after the caller fails to provide an explanation of the relevance of her agenda in response to it, and she is interrupted by the host (another discursive strategy for claiming interactional power – Zimmerman and West 1975) with a direct request for an account of her agenda-setting: 'What's that got to do what's that got to do with telethons though?'. The host's previous question ('Yes?') seems not so much a challenge but rather fulfils the task-oriented function of eliciting more information from the caller. It is only when enough information has been gathered by the host that his challenge is directed at the caller's intervention on the grounds of its relevance and validity.

DISCOURSE COMMUNITIES AND DISCOURSE GENRES

Our commentaries on these brief sequences of talk try to illuminate the discourse events which have generated them. There is a sense in which we can never access those events and their sub-components and processes fully. Even the participants themselves, and even if we were able to replay their talk to them and question them about it, would probably be unable to provide definitive analyses. In fact, it is not clear that there can ever be a definitive analysis of any one sequence of discourse. One of the fundamental principles of discourse analysis is that there are no definitive readings of social and sociolinguistic events. Indeed, much of the impetus for a discourse approach has come as a critical response to research traditions which have assumed that they do have methods for producing definitive analyses, and, in making this assumption, have closed off discussion of the social effects of language prematurely (e.g. Potter and Wetherell 1987). Discourse analysis is more comfortable with the notion of interpretive ambiguity and polyvalency than most classically empiricist research traditions (such as hypothesis testing in experimental research). Discourse analysts have insisted that academic research is itself a set of discourses, and that we need to examine how research serves particular interests and constructs its meanings and values, reflected in its own texts, accordingly (Gilbert and Mulkay 1984; see also a recent debate in the journal *Discourse & Society* 1999 for discussion of these issues).

Even so, discourse analysis can achieve a form of reliability and generalisability – which are two requirements of classical research methods. In the two texts we have examined, the discourse processes at work are by no means unique to the particular moments recorded. As we suggested, David and Oliver seem to be articulating an identity shared by many other people than themselves – schoolkids or perhaps schoolboys. Their language, while it is of course 'their own' language individually, is an instance of a group or community language. And it is not only so by virtue of its linguistic forms (e.g. the slang items, which we could label part of a youth dialect). It is a form of socio-cultural *practice*, a 'way of meaning' (Halliday 1978) which goes beyond language style itself. This brief, local instance is 'linked through' to a set of values and stances that are familiar in the culture. This is the perspective that Fairclough adopts when he writes that '"Discourse" is for me more than *just* language use: it is language use, whether speech or writing, seen as a type of social practice' (Fairclough, 1992, p. 28).

Discourse practices are structured in two general dimensions, by the groups or 'members' that perform or control them and by the social circumstances of their use. Therefore we can identify *communities of practice*, like those coalescing around motherhood, or shopping, or body culture (Holmes and Meyerhoff 1999; Coupland and Coupland 2000). Simultaneously, discourse practices will be structured as a set of **genre**s (Bakhtin 1981; 1986). The concept of 'genre' was originally a literary one, referring to conventionalised types of literary texts, such as ballads, novels or sonnets. Non-literary discourse genres include gossiping, speech-making, narratives, or general conversation. **Bakhtin** argued that we must expect language to show a rich mixing of genres or what he called 'voices', so that many or most language texts will be multiply voiced or *heteroglossic* (see **heteroglossia**). Graddol's (1996) study of a wine label illustrates how different parts of the label, as a semiotic space, draw from different genres – for example, a description of the type of wine and its qualities, a health warning, and a bar and numerical code. Many different voices are realised – consumerist, legal, commercial – addressing potentially different audiences – consumers, health promoters, retailers – and for different reasons.

THE LATE-MODERN WORLD OF DISCOURSE

There are many reasons to believe that 'the turn to discourse' is more than an academic fashion, and may be linked to a radical re-shaping of social life. Contemporary life, at least in the world's most affluent and 'developed' societies, has qualities which distinguish it quite markedly from the 'Modern' industrial, pre-World War II period. One of the most obvious manifestations of what Giddens (1991) has called 'Late' or 'High Modernity', and what is more generally referred to as *postmodernity*, is the shift in advanced capitalist economies from manu-facturing to service industries.

Fairclough (1992, 1995b) refers to one part of this phenomenon as the *technologization* of discourse in post-Fordist societies, i.e. those in which the economic core is no longer associated with mass production of motor cars and similar industrial developments but with high-tech industries and a large service sector. Thus, manufacturing and assembly workers working on production lines, isolated from consumers of the items they are producing, have been largely replaced by teams of workers networked together on communication tasks of different sorts or representing their companies in different kinds of service encounters with clients. In a rather literal sense, language takes on greater significance in the world of providing and consuming services, even if only in the promotional language of selling services in the competitive environment of banking, insurance companies or telephone-sales warehouses.

Rapid growth in communications media, such as satellite and digital television and radio, desktop publishing, telecommunications (mobile phone networks, video-conferencing), email, Internet-mediated sales and services, information provision and entertainment, has created new media for language use (alongside traditional ones). It is not surprising that language is being more and more closely scrutinised, for example within school curricula and by self-styled experts and guardians of so-called 'linguistic standards' – see Milroy and Milroy 1998; Cameron 1995; <u>Aitchison</u>, this volume). It is simultaneously being shaped and honed by advertisers, journalists and broadcasters in a drive to generate ever-more attention and persuasive impact. Under these circumstances, language itself becomes marketable and a sort of commodity, and its purveyors can market themselves through their skills of linguistic and textual manipulation (Bourdieu 1991).

The two social theorists who have had the greatest influence in the development of postmodern thought on discourse are Pierre Bourdieu and Michel Foucault. Their interest in discourse is not so much in empirical examination of actual, interactional data, but in discourse as an abstract vehicle for social and political processes. Language in Bourdieu's (1991) theory of social practice is related to his notion of 'habitus', i.e. internalised group norms or dispositions whose task is to regulate and generate the actions (practices), perceptions and representations of individuals, and to mediate the social structures which they inhabit. Two important and interrelated aspects of habitus are that it reflects the social structures in which it was acquired, and reproduces these structures. Thus, a person who was brought up in a working-class background will manifest a set of dispositions which are different from those acquired by a person from a middle-class background and these differences will, in turn, reproduce the class divisions between both individuals (and their groups).

For Bourdieu, language is a locus of struggle for power and authority in that some types of language (styles, **accent**s, **dialect**s, **code**s, and so on) are presupposed to be 'correct', 'distinguished' or 'legitimate' in opposition to those which are 'incorrect' or 'vulgar'. Those who use (in speaking or writing) the varieties ranked as acceptable, exert a degree of control over those with the dominated linguistic habitus (Bourdieu, 1991, p. 60). The field of linguistic production, however, can be manipulated: the symbolic capital claimed by the authority of 'legitimate' language may be reclaimed in the process of negotiation 'by a metadiscourse concerning the conditions of use of discourse' (Bourdieu 1991, p. 71; see also Bourdieu 1999, p. 505). In sum:

The habitus . . . provides individuals with a sense of how to act and respond in the course of their daily lives. It 'orients' their actions and inclinations without strictly determining them. It gives them a 'feel for the game', a sense of what is appropriate in the circumstances and what is not, a 'practical sense'.

(Thompson, 1991, p. 13)

Foucault's (1979) primary concern with discourse is as a vehicle for the (re)production of power relations. For him, power is dispersed throughout all social relations and as a force which prevents some actions but enables others. However, power is not confined to large-scale, macro processes of politics and society. It is a potential present in all everyday exchanges and social encounters (cf. Hutchby 1999; see also our analysis of Text 2 above). In Foucault's system, power relations are enacted through the discursive practices of such institutions as schools, medical clinics, prisons, and so on, which exert a degree of control and scrutiny over individuals, their practices and their identities. For example, Foucault (1999) argues that the proliferation of discourse about sex and sexuality at the beginning of the Modern era, has not 'simply' led to the suppression of children's sexuality, but acted as a vehicle for the construction of an acceptable version of their sexuality. In our own studies of how discourse constructs identities for people of different ages, we argued that 'Tracking the social construction and reproduction of old age through talk seems an effective research orientation for demonstrating that "elderliness" is a collective subjectivity as much as a biological or biographical end-point' (Coupland *et al*. 1991, p. 207).

Another important aspect of Foucault's (1977) view of power is that it is explicitly linked to *knowledge*. Mills illustrates this point as follows:

[W]hat is studied in schools and universities is the result of struggles over whose version of events is sanctioned. Knowledge is often the product of the subjugation of objects, or perhaps it can be seen as the process through which subjects are constituted as subjugated; for example, when consulting a university library catalogue, if you search under the term 'women', you will find a vast selection of books and articles discussing the oppression of women, the psychology of women, the physical ailments that women suffer from, and so on. If you search under the term 'men' you will not find the same wealth of information.

(1997, p. 21)

The idea of knowledge as power is related to Foucault's (1977) notion of the 'regimes of truth' which facilitate the reproduction of patterns of power, dominance and control. It is through such regimes of truth which find pronouncement in 'expert discourse' on such social issues as parenthood ('single mothers'), addiction, sexuality, criminality, youth culture, and so on, that individuals in postmodern societies are controlled and scrutinised (cf. Cameron *et al*. 1999).

Similarly, discourse ceases to be 'merely' a function of work; it becomes work, just as it defines various forms of leisure and, for that matter, academic study. The analysis of discourse becomes correspondingly more important – in the first instance for those with direct commercial involvement in the language economies, and second, for those who need to deconstruct these new trends, to understand their force and even to oppose them.

As has been argued by social semioticians (see <u>Kress</u>, this volume), representation is a process subject to regimes of production and reception, which in turn are reflective of the ideological complexes present in the society. Practices of representation, resting on more or less uncontested sets of classification of people and circumstances, are always part of a communicative situation, which, in turn, is marked by and indicative of the power differentials between communicators as well as those who are the object of representation (see e.g. Hodge and Kress 1988; Kress and van Leeuwen 1996).

Following this tradition of research, Galasiński and Jaworski (forthcoming) demonstrate how travel stories in the British press represent locals to the tourist in ways which are indicative of the hegemonic positions from which the travel stories are written. The locals are typically depicted as members of relatively homogenised, undifferentiated ethnic or social groups, or tokenised individuals who are more or less prototypical bearers of the 'national', 'ethnic' or other group characteristics. Alternatively, the local 'Other' is a largely 'featureless' individual, whose sole task appears to aid the author in his/her journey through a strange, exotic land. In those writings, the local communities are represented as part of the general characterisation of the country/region/island that the author has travelled to. The local people are nothing more than part of the 'landscape' of the target destination. In his study of travel agency marketing, Silver (1993, p. 305) goes as far as proposing that touristic representations not only reinforce stereotypes, but also imply that natives exist predominantly for consumption by Western tourists (and even, just like nature, can be photographed without permission). Consider the following example:

Text 3

What I recall about Taranto is strolling among children, lovers and old people in the sunshine in the public gardens above the Mare Piccolo, the inland sea where the Italian naval ships are berthed, and then night in the dense crowd of the Via d'Aquino, gradually losing in the hubbub the angry voice of the young woman shouting.

(*The Guardian*, 27 September 1997; quoted in Galasiński and Jaworski, forthcoming)

The author invokes several groups of locals, but they remain anonymous and undifferentiated. Moreover, they form part of a longer *list* of the elements making up the scenery of a town. The locals provide mere background for the author's stroll, in the same way as the 'sunshine', 'public gardens' and the 'inland sea'. This visual setting is complemented by the acoustic landscape. This is often presented as being as exotic and incomprehensible as the rest of the foreign environment. The example juxtaposes the anonymity of 'the dense crowd' with such sound characterisation as 'hubbub', 'angry voice', 'woman shouting', all suggesting a degree of deviance from orderly and rational talk.

Such 'Othering' processes allow travelogue writers to distance themselves from the locals and to legitimise their usually disadvantaged position (see Coupland 2001). By creating specific versions of discursive representations of the local Other, travelling journalists create in their arrogance a self-serving and self-gratifying environment for casting themselves in the role of heroes who have ventured into the great unknown, faced all possible dangers and came back triumphantly to tell the story (and cash the cheque).

IDEOLOGICAL CONTESTS

The theoretical work of Foucault (see above) and that of Michel Pêcheux (1982) has been very influential in introducing the link between discourse and ideology. Pêcheux stresses how any one particular discourse or 'discursive formation' stands, at the level of social organisation, in conflict with other discourses. He gives us a theory of how societies are organised through their ideological struggles, and how particular groups (e.g. social class groups or gender groups) will be either more or less privileged in their access to particular discourse networks. Local and global perspectives come together when some type of discourse analysis can show how the pressure of broad social or institutional norms are brought to bear on the identity and classification of individuals.

An excellent example is Mehan's (1999) analysis of a psychiatric interview in which the doctors are to assess the mental health of a patient before deciding whether he can be released from the psychiatric hospital (and re-admitted to prison). Mehan demonstrates how the patient and the doctors construct totally opposite views of the patient's mental state; the patient claiming 'normalcy' and the doctors refuting his claims re-interpreting all he says as symptoms of mental instability. Interestingly, during the interview, the doctors ask the questions and let the patient answer them in some detail, even though they are phrased as yes/no questions (see Text 4). This serves the purpose of examining or scrutinising the patient (cf. Foucault, referred to above). Their evaluation, however, takes place after the patient has been removed. It is then that his responses are 'strategically decontextualised' (Mehan 1999, p. 569; see Text 5). Consider the following examples:

Text 4

DOCTOR: Are you in any group therapy here?
PATIENT: No! There is no group, obviously I do not need group therapy, I need peace and quiet. See me. This place is disturbing me! It's harming me . . . I'm losing weight. Every, everything that's been happening to me is bad. And all I got, all I get is: 'well, why don't you take medication?' Medication is disagreeable to me. There are people to whom you may not

give medication. Obviously, and the medication that I got is hurting me, it's harming me!

(adapted from Mehan, 1999, p. 567)

Text 5

One of the doctors commenting on the patient's expressed emotion.
The louder he shouts about going back the more frightened he indicates that he probably is.

In his study, Mehan (1999) demonstrates how both sides (the patient and the doctors) come to the examination totally unprepared to accept the opposite (and conflicting) views of the other party; the patient claims he is ready to be released from the hospital and the panel sees him as totally unfit to be released. Both sides engage in an argument trying to sanction their version of reality but in the end it is the party that can command greater power, i.e. the panel, whose version of the 'truth' about the patient becomes dominant. As Mehan puts it: 'All people define situations as real; but when powerful people define situations as real, then they are real *for everybody involved* in their consequences' (ibid., p. 573).

The Mehan study clearly illustrates how discourse can be a site of conflict between competing ideologies. Ideology has been a notion central to other analysts working with discourse from slightly different angles, e.g. Billig (1990, 1991) in rhetoric and van Dijk (1998) in Critical Discourse Analysis (see below). It is demonstrably the case that ideology, not unlike social categories in general (see above), is intimately related to situated practices of day-to-day interaction. In fact, van Dijk argues that it is through discourse and other semiotic practices that ideologies are formulated, reproduced and reinforced. Accomplishing ideology is an important end in political (both with capital and small 'p') discourse because its acceptance by the audience, especially mass media audiences, ensures the establishment of group rapport. As Fowler (1985, p. 66) puts it, through the emergence of a 'community of ideology, a shared system of beliefs about reality' creates group identity.

We understand the term ideology as a set of social (general and abstract) representations shared by members of a group and used by them to accomplish everyday social practices: acting and communicating (e.g. van Dijk 1998; Billig *et al*. 1988; Fowler 1985). These representations are organised into systems which are deployed by social classes and other groups 'in order to make sense of, figure out and render intelligible the way society works' (Hall 1996, p. 26).

Billig *et al*. (1988) make a distinction between 'lived' and 'intellectual' ideology. The former term is close to the way ideology was defined in the preceding paragraph, as illustrated in Mehan's example of doctors deploying certain shared beliefs and representations of the patient in order to make sense out of the examining process, and reaching their preferred conclusion. 'Intellectual' ideology is understood as an overall, coherent system of thought: political programmes or manifestos, philosophical orientations or religious codes. This distinction is useful because it shows ideology working at two levels: the participants' coherent, formal systems of belief (i.e. their intellectual ideologies), and their objectives in self- and other-presentation, in expressions of opinions which represent and satisfy their and their groups' preferred views of reality, constructed to suit local goals of interaction (see Jaworski and Galasiński 1998). One of the ideologically relevant discourse structures pointed to by van Dijk (1998, p. 209) is interaction, and, more specifically, the realm of interactional control or ideological legitimation (see Jaworski and Galasiński 1999). Who starts the exchange, who ends it, who initiates new topics, who interrupts whom, and which address forms are used in the course of interaction, may all be indicative of the interlocutor's power and as such are ideologically charged. To use van Dijk's (1998, p. 209) term, social interaction has an 'ideological dimension'.

CRITICAL DISCOURSE ANALYSIS

As the previous examples show, discourse analysis offers a means of exposing or deconstructing the social practices which constitute '**social structure**' and what we might call the conventional meaning structures of social life. It is a sort of forensic activity, with a libertarian political slant. The motivation for doing discourse analysis is very often a concern about the opaque patterns of social inequality and the perpetuation of power relationships, either between individuals or between social groups, impossible though it is to pre-judge moral correctness in many cases (Fairclough 1995a).

In all but its blandest forms, such as when it remains at the level of language description, discourse analysis adopts a 'critical' perspective on language in use. Fowler is explicit about what 'critical' means for his own research, much of it related to literary texts. He says it does *not* mean 'the flood of writings about texts and authors which calls itself literary criticism', nor the sense of 'intolerant fault-finding':

> I mean a careful analytic interrogation of the ideological categories, and the roles and institutions and so on, through which a society constitutes and maintains itself and the consciousness of its members . . . All knowledge, all objects, are constructs: criticism analyses the processes of construction and, acknowledging the artificial quality of the categories concerned, offers the possibility that we might profitably conceive the world in some alternative way.
>
> (Fowler, 1981, p. 25)

There are many elements in Fowler's definition of critical analysis that we have already met as hallmarks of discourse analysis, notably its questioning of objectivity and its interest in the practices which produce apparent objectivity, normality and factuality.

Language, as a social phenomenon, is both a product and a reflection of the values and beliefs of the society that employs it. Thus, the construction of any message designed to represent some reality necessarily entails decisions as to which aspects of that reality to include, and then decisions as to how to arrange those aspects. Each of the selections made in the construction of a message carries its share of these ingrained values, so that the reality represented is simultaneously socially constructed (Hodge and Kress 1993, p. 5; see also Fowler *et al.* 1979; Fairclough 1992; van Dijk 1993; Chouliaraki and Fairclough 1999). In this sense, Critical Discourse Analysis follows, broadly, the **Whorf**ian position on the influence of language on thought and perception of reality (see Whorf 1997).

What we called the forensic goals of discourse analysis re-surface in Fowler's definition, probing texts and discourse practices in order to discover hidden meaning- and value-structures. His view of society as a set of groups and institutions structured through discourse is closely reminiscent of Foucault's and Pêcheux's theoretical writings (see above).

But if Fowler's critical perspective is established in all or most discourse analysis, why does critical discourse analysis need to be distinguished as a separate tradition? One reason is historical. Several early approaches to discourse, such as the work of the Birmingham school linguists who developed analyses of classroom discourse (Sinclair and Coulthard 1976), had mainly descriptive aims. They introduced an elaborate hierarchical framework for coding teachers' and pupils' discourse 'acts', 'moves' and 'transactions' in classroom talk. The intention was to provide an exhaustive structural model of discourse organisation, from the (highest) category, 'the lesson', down to the (lowest) category of individual speech acts. A critical approach to discourse distances itself from descriptivism of this sort. It foregrounds its concern with social constructionism and with the construction of ideology in particular. As Van Leeuwen says, 'Critical discourse analysis is, or should be, concerned with . . . discourse as the instrument of the social construction of reality' (1993, p. 193). Ideological structures are necessarily concerned with the analysis of power relations and social discrimination, for example through demonstrating differential access to discourse networks.

Fairclough gives the clearest account of Critical Discourse Analysis as ideological analysis:

> I view social institutions as containing diverse 'ideological-discursive formations' (IDFs) associated with different groups within the institution. There is usually one IDF which is clearly dominant . . . Institutional subjects are constructed, in accordance with the norms of an IDF, in subject positions whose ideological underpinnings they may be unaware of. A characteristic of a dominant IDF is the capacity to 'naturalise' ideologies, i.e. to win acceptance for them as non-ideological 'common sense'. It is argued that the orderliness of interactions depends in part upon such naturalised ideologies. To 'denaturalise' them is the objective of a discourse analysis which adopts 'critical' goals. I suggest that denaturalisation involves showing how social structures determine properties of discourse, and how discourse in turn determines social structures.

> (Fairclough, 1995a, p. 27)

The important point about concepts such as 'naturalisation' and 'denaturalisation' is that they are dynamic processes. They imply a continuing struggle over social arrangements and acts of imposition and resistance. In fact, the critical perspective is oriented to social change, in two different senses. First, Critical Discourse Analysis, particularly in Fairclough's work, sets out to understand social changes in the ideological use of language. We have briefly mentioned Fairclough's arguments about 'technologisation'. Under this heading, he identifies an on-going cultural 'process of redesigning existing discursive practices and training institutional personnel in the redesigned practices' (ibid., p. 102), brought about partly through so-called 'social skills training'. Fairclough suggests that social skills training is marked by the emergence of 'discourse technologists', the policing of discourse practices, designing context-free discourse techniques and attempts to standardise them (ibid., p. 103). He finds examples in the instituting of 'staff development' and 'staff appraisal' schemes in British universities (and of course elsewhere). New forms of discourse (e.g. learning terminology which will impress supervisors or assessors, or learning how to appear efficient, friendly or resourceful) are normalised (made to appear unexceptional) and policed or monitored, with a system of status-related and financial rewards and penalties following on from them. Other discursive shifts that Fairclough has investigated are the conversationalisation of public discourse and the marketisation of public institutions (again, in particular, universities).

The second aspect of change is the critic's own attempt to resist social changes held to curtail liberty. Ideological critique is often characterised by some form of intervention. Notice how Fowler (in the quotation on p. 145) mentions 'profitably conceiv[ing] the world in some alternative way'. A critical orientation is not merely 'deconstructive'; it may aim to be 'reconstructive', reconstructing social arrangements. Fowler's use of the term 'profitable' is perhaps unfortunate, although he seems to mean 'more justifiable' or 'more fair'. Fairclough also writes that:

> the problematic of language and power is fundamentally a question of democracy. Those affected need to take it on board as a political issue, as feminists have around the issue of language and gender . . . Critical linguists and discourse analysts have an important auxiliary role to play here [i.e. secondary to the role of people directly affected] in providing analyses and, importantly, in providing critical educators with resources of what I and my colleagues have called 'critical language awareness'.
>
> (ibid., p. 221).

(A range of perspectives on critical language awareness is provided in Fairclough 1992.)

Critical Discourse Analysis in this view is a democratic resource to be made available through the education system. Critical Discourse Analysts need to see themselves as politically engaged, working alongside disenfranchised social groups (see also Cameron *et al.* 1999).

CONCLUSION

We started this chapter with two contrasting definitions of 'discourse' and we suggested that our own approach to discourse needs to incorporate both approaches, the 'textual' and the 'abstract'. It is perhaps useful to conclude with another definition, which attempts a more comprehensive view of discourse:

> 'Discourse' . . . refers to language in use, as a process which is socially situated. However . . . we may go on to discuss the constructive and dynamic role of either spoken or written discourse in structuring areas of knowledge and the social and institutional practices which are associated with them. In this sense, discourse is a means of talking and writing about and acting upon worlds, a means which both constructs and is constructed by a set of social practices within these worlds, and in so doing both reproduces and constructs afresh particular social-discursive practices, constrained or encouraged by more macro movements in the overarching social formation.
>
> (Candlin, 1997, p. ix)

The above definition, and the two quoted at the beginning of this chapter, combine two fundamental approaches to discourse: as language-in-use and language-use relative to social, political and cultural formations, i.e., language reflecting social order but also language shaping social order, and shaping individuals' interaction with society. This is the key factor explaining why so many academic disciplines entertain the notion of discourse with such commitment. Discourse falls squarely within the interests not only of linguists, literary critics, critical theorists and communication scientists, but also of geographers, philosophers, political scientists, sociologists, anthropologists, social psychologists, and many others. Despite important differences of emphasis, discourse is an inescapably important concept for understanding society and human responses to it, as well as for understanding language itself.

FURTHER READING

Brown, G. and Yule, G. (1983) *Discourse Analysis*, Cambridge: Cambridge University Press.

Cobley, P. (ed.) (1996) *The Communication Theory Reader*, London: Routledge.

Coupland, N. and Jaworski, A. (forthcoming, 2002) *Key Concepts in Language and Society*, London: Routledge.

Drew, P. and Heritage, J. (eds) (1992) *Talk at Work: Interaction in Institutional Settings*, Cambridge: Cambridge University Press.

Gumperz, J. J. (1982) *Discourse Strategies*, Cambridge: Cambridge University Press.

Part II
KEY THEMES AND MAJOR FIGURES IN SEMIOTICS AND LINGUISTICS

A

ABDUCTION Abduction is the inferential process by which hypotheses are framed. It is the process of inference by which the rule that explains the fact is hypothesized through a relation of similarity (**icon**ic relation) to that fact. This rule that acts as the general premise may be taken from a field of **discourse** that is close to or distant from that to which the fact belongs, or it may be invented *ex novo*. If the conclusion is confirmed it retroacts on the rule and convalidates it (ab- or retro-duction). Such retroactive procedure makes abductive inference risky, exposing it to the possibility of error. At the same time, however, if the hypothesis is correct the abduction is innovative, inventive and sometimes even surprising (cf. Bonfantini 1987).

According to Peirce:

Abduction is the process of forming an explanatory hypothesis. It is the only logical operation which introduces any new idea; for induction does nothing but determine a value, and deduction merely evolves the necessary consequences of a pure hypothesis.

Deduction proves that something *must* be; Induction shows that something *actually is* operative; Abduction merely suggests that something *may be*.

(*CP* 5.172)

The relation between the premises and the conclusion may be considered in terms of the relation between what we may call, respectively, interpreted **sign**s and **interpretant** signs. In induction, the relation between premises and conclusion is determined by **habit** and is of the **symbol**ic type. In deduction it is **index**ical, the conclusion being a necessary derivation from the premises. In abduction, the relation between premises and conclusion is iconic, that is, it is a relation of reciprocal autonomy. This makes for a high degree of inventiveness together with a high risk margin for error. Abductive processes are highly dialogic and generate responses of the most risky, inventive and creative order. To claim that abductive argumentative procedures are risky is to say that they are mainly tentative and hypothetical leaving only a minimal margin to convention (symbolicity) and mechanical necessity (indexicality). Abductive inferential processes engender sign processes at the highest levels of otherness and dialogicality.

The degree of dialogicality (cf. Ponzio 1985, 1990a) in the relation between interpreted and interpretant is minimal in deduction: here, once the premises are accepted the conclusion is obligatory. Induction is also characterized by unilinear inferential processes: identity and repetition dominate, though the relation between the premises and the conclusion is no longer obligatory. In contrast, the relationship in abduction between the argumentative parts is dialogic in a substantial sense. In fact, very high degrees of dialogicality are attained and the higher, the more inventive becomes reasoning.

Abductions are empowered by metaphors in simulation processes used to produce models, inferences, inventions, and projects. The close relationship between abductive inference and verisimilitude is determined

151

by the fact that, as demonstrated by **Welby**, 'one of the most splendid of all our intellectual instruments' is the 'image or the figure' (Welby [1911] 1985a, pp. 13; cf. also Petrilli 1986; Petrilli 1995b, 1998b). Given the close relationship among abduction, icon and simulation, the problem is not to eliminate figurative or metaphorical discourse to the advantage of so-called literal discourse, but to identify and eliminate inadequate images that mystify relations among things and distort our reasoning. As Welby states, 'We need a linguistic oculist to restore lost focussing power, to bring our images back to reality by some normalizing kind of lens' (Welby [1911] 1985a, p. 16). (**SP**)

See also DIALOGUE.

Further Reading

Peirce, C. S. (1955) 'Abduction and induction', in J. Buchler (ed.) *Philosophical Writings of Peirce*, New York: Dover.

Peirce, C. S. (1992) 'Types of reasoning', in K. L. Ketner (ed.), *Reasoning and the Logic of Things: The Cambridge Conferences Lectures of 1898*, Cambridge, MA: Harvard University Press.

Sebeok, T. A. and Umiker-Sebeok, J. (1980) *'You Know My Method': A Juxtaposition of Charles S. Peirce and Sherlock Holmes*, Bloomington: Gaslight.

ACCENT From a semiotic viewpoint, the concept of accent is particularly relevant not as a graphic signal to denote a stress, a stressed syllable, nor as pronunciation, as in the expression 'he speaks with an American accent', nor as a tone of voice, e.g an angry tone. Considered semiotically, the accent is not merely a graphic or acoustic device, nor does it solely concern verbal signs. Insofar as it is engendered among individuals and is created within a social milieu, the accent refers to the evaluative accentuation present in human verbal and nonverbal **sign**s. The verbal sign, both oral and written, is a sign in a strong sense, not just a signal, but is endowed with plasticity of **meaning** which enables it to respond to different ideological perspectives and different senses. By virtue of such qualities, the verbal sign above all not only has a **theme** and meaning in the referential, or content, sense of these words, but also a value judgment, a specific evaluative accent. There is no such thing as a word, especially a word used in actual speech, whether written or oral, which does not have an accent in terms of evaluative intonation (cf. Ponzio 1980a, 1992a). Through a passage from Dostoevsky's *Diary of a Writer*, which analyses the conversation of a band of six tipsy artisans, **Vološinov** (1973, p. 103) shows how evaluations, thoughts, feelings, and even trains of reasoning can be expressed merely by using the same noun with an accent that is different each time. (**AP**)

ALGORITHM **Lacan** extends this mathematical notion to the fields of language and unconscious structure. The mathematical algorithm is an effective procedure which produces a solution to a query about a part of a structure in a finite number of steps. What Lacan calls the '**Saussure**an algorithm' insists on the movement to another **signifier** in order to develop the **meaning** of a first. In Lacan's usage an algorithm can produce, rather than a solution, a procedure for analysis. (**BB**)

ALTERITY Alterity (or otherness) indicates the existence of something on its own account, autonomously, independent of the I's initiative, volition, consciousness, recognition. Alterity is a synonym of materiality understood as objectivity. The world of physical objects is other with respect to the I. One's own body, the body of each and every one of us, is other in its autonomy from volition and consciousness.

But the most other of all is the other person in his/her irreducibility, refractoriness to the I. Assassination is proof of the other's resistance and of the I's checkmate, his/her powerlessness. Of course we also have 'relative alterity' which **Peirce** classifies as **secondness**, but this is the alterity of the I, in one's roles (of a father relative to his child, a student relative to his teacher, a husband relative to his wife, etc.). But the alterity of the other as other is 'absolute alterity'.

Consequently, when a question of absolute and non-relative alterity arises (cf. Levinas 1961, 1974; Ponzio 1996; Ponzio 1998c), the otherness of the other person can neither be reduced to the communitary 'We' of Heidegger's *Mitsein* (*being-with*), nor to the Subject–Object relation of Sartre's *being-for*. Alterity is located inside the subject, the I, in the heart itself of the subject, without being englobed by the latter. For this reason the subject cannot become a closed totality but is continually exposed to **dialogue**, is itself a dialogue, a relation between self and other. Contrary to Sartre and Hegel, the self of 'being conscious of oneself' does not coincide with consciousness nor does it presuppose it; rather, it is pre-existent to consciousness and is connected to it by a relation of alterity. The other is inseparable from the ego, the I, the Self (*Même* as intended by Emmanuel **Levinas**), but cannot be included within the totality of the ego. The other is necessary to the constitution of the ego and its world, but at the same time it is a constitutive impediment to the integrity and definitive closure of the I and of the world.

The relation to the other – as authors like Charles S. Peirce, Victoria **Welby**, Mikhail **Bakhtin**, Charles **Morris**, and Levinas teach us – is a relation of excess, surplus, of escape from objectivating thought, it is release from the subject–object relation; on a linguistic level it produces internal dialogization of the word, the impossibility of ever being an integral word (cf. Bakhtin 1929, 1963; Vološinov [1929] 1973). (**AP**)

Further Reading

Levinas, E. (1989) 'Time and the other', in S. Hand (ed.), *The Levinas Reader*, Oxford: Blackwell.

AMERICAN STRUCTURALISM Linguistics in America developed in a distinctive way in the late nineteenth and early twentieth centuries. A great deal of energy was spent on recording and classifying the indigenous languages of America, and linguists therefore looked for rigorous methods of collecting and analysing data. This involved a deliberate effort to break away from preconceptions based on European languages, and to treat each language in its own terms. The focus was on the sounds and the word structure of each language, as these were regarded as concrete and replicable; information about sentence structure was felt to be less dependable, and the **meaning** and use of language were seen as hard to catalogue reliably and were often given less attention.

Although it would be misleading to talk of a 'school', an emphasis on observable elements of structure underpinned much of the work during this period. It has been fashionable for many years to highlight the theoretical inadequacy of structuralist linguistics, but its descriptive achievements were enormous and reflect the great intellectual labour and pioneering dedication that gave rise to them. (**RS**)

See also BLOOMFIELD, SAPIR and HARRIS.

Further Reading

Fought, J.G. (1994) 'American structuralism', in R. Asher and J. Simpson (eds) *The Encylopedia of Language and Linguistics*, vol. 1, Oxford: Pergamon Press, pp. 97–106.

ANTHROPOSEMIOTICS 'Anthropo-semiotics' is a name for the study of the human use of **sign**s. It is one of the recent branches on the tree of terms that has grown out of Charles S. **Peirce**'s original coinage of the term '**semiosis**' to name the action of signs. This usage was suggested to Peirce (Fisch 1986b) by reading Philodemus (i.54–40bc). Thus, the study of semiosis gives rise to the branch of knowledge that Peirce followed **Locke** in calling '**semiotics**', or 'the doctrine of signs'. So, just as semiotics is the name for the general study of the action of signs (or semiosis), so anthroposemiotics is the name for the specific study of the human use of signs (or anthroposemiosis). The other main branches on this tree of terms, to wit, **zoö-semiotics** (the study of the communicative behavior of animals that do not have language), phytosemiotics (the study of communicative behaviors in plants), and physiosemiotics (study of communicative behaviors in the physical universe at large), have all been tied to specific authors of the twentieth century (see Deely 2000, Ch. 15); but precise authorship of the term 'anthroposemiotics' has, curiously, so far not been identified.

The first work devoted exclusively to the subject of anthroposemiotics (Deely 1994c) concentrated on the species-specifically distinctive features of anthroposemiosis. But the field is actually much broader than such a study would suggest, inasmuch as all the other systems of signs that are found outside the human species are also found at play, in one manner or another, within the human species, and so form a part, even if not the species-specifically distinctive part, of anthroposemiosis. In this way 'anthroposemiotics' may be said to revive within the doctrine of signs the ancient Stoic notion of the human being ('anthropos') as the microcosm wherein is summarized and concentrated all that is to be found in the cosmos or universe at large. So the field opened up under the

designation of anthroposemiotics actually is vast, subsuming all the traditional studies of human life and culture but under a new focus or perspective, namely, the attempt to appreciate the role of the sign in making possible all that is distinctively human in the realms of life, action, and knowledge. The traditional humanities, art, medicine, technology – all can be grouped under the heading of 'anthroposemiotics'.

The reworking of traditional ideas of the human being under this perspective will eventually require nothing less than an encyclopedia wherein the traditional materials of the human sciences can be presented as they have been rethought in the perspective proper to the doctrine of signs. Such an enterprise will have the advantage from the outset of overcoming the split between 'human' and 'natural' sciences (*Naturwissenschaften* und *Geisteswissenschaften*) by virtue of the perspective proper to the sign, recognized to be, from its earliest systematization (Poinsot 1632), superior to the division between nature and culture, because inclusive of both. From the standpoint of anthroposemiotics, culture itself is a part of nature, albeit a species-specifically distinctive part, every bit as much as the human body. **(JD)**

See also BIOSEMIOTICS and STOICS AND EPICUREANS.

Further Reading

Deely, J. (1990) *Basics of Semiotics*, Bloomington: Indiana University Press.
Nöth, W. (1990) *A Handbook of Semiotics*, Bloomington: Indiana University Press.
Sebeok, T. A. (1985) *Contributions to the Doctrine of Signs*, with Foreword by B. Williams, Lanham, MD: University Press of America.

ARGUMENT A set of interdependent statements or beliefs where some, the premisses, support a conclusion. In **Peirce**'s semeiotic an argument is a sign of a lawful relation between premisses and conclusion. There are three types of inference, or passage from premisses to conclusion, depending on the argument form: deduction, or certain reasoning, induction, where general conclusions are drawn from select cases, and abduction, or intelligent guessing. **(NH)**

See also RHEME and DICENT.

ARISTOTLE Greek philosopher (384–322 BC), one of the most respected authorities of the ancient world, and often referred to throughout the European Middle Ages simply as 'the philosopher'. A pupil of Plato, he lectured on topics ranging from metaphysics and poetics to politics and biology. Although he left no work specifically devoted to the study of languages or **grammar** or etymology (as modern scholars understand those subjects), he laid the foundations of Western logic. Logic is arguably what he saw as the analysis of language at the level of abstraction necessary to make tenable generalizations about it. It is sometimes said that Western logic would have taken quite a different shape if Aristotle had spoken some other language than Greek. **(RH)**

AUGUSTINE Christian saint and theologian (354–430), bishop of Hippo in North Africa. He is generally regarded as perpetuating the Stoic theory of **sign**s, and in particular as championing the distinction between natural and conventional signs, but his interest in these matters was dictated by his religious convictions and problems involving interpretation of the sacraments and the scriptures rather than by anything else. The same is true of Augustine's pronouncements on translation, where his underlying motivation was to justify the early Church's use of Latin versions of the Bible. He held that it was possible for words to share the same **meaning** in spite of belonging to different languages. Augustine's account of how he learned his native language as a child was taken by **Wittgenstein** as typifying a common but extremely naïve view of how language works. **(RH)**

See also STOICS AND EPICUREANS.

AUSTIN John Langshaw Austin (1911–60) was Professor of Philosophy at Oxford University, where he was one of the prominent figures in a tradition known as the Oxford school of '**ordinary language philosophy**'. The tenets of this tradition, as well as Austin's personal style, are captured nicely in the formulation of his philosophical goal as an attempt to discover

the distinctions men [*sic*] have found worth drawing, and the connections they have found worth making, in the lifetimes of many generations: these surely are likely to be more numerous, more sound, since they have stood up to the long test of the survival of the fittest, and more subtle, at least in all ordinary and reasonably practical matters, than any of you and I are likely to think up in our armchairs of an afternoon – the most favoured alternative method.

(1957, p. 24)

It is from this angle that Austin approached a wide range of traditional philosophical topics, such as the problem of **truth**, knowledge and **meaning**, or the problem of free will. His language-based philosophical method was presented as an antidote against a more popular logical empiricism.

His most influential and lasting contribution was made in the philosophy of language, where, not surprisingly, his method and object are made to merge. In *How To Do Things With Words*, the William James Lectures delivered at Harvard University in 1955, published posthumously in 1962, Austin dwells on the observation of language as a form of action. Whenever something is *said*, something is *done by* or *in* saying it. From this point of view he questions the distinction between **constative** utterances such as 'It is raining outside' (in which something is *said*, and which are either true or false) and **performative**s such as 'I name this ship the Queen Elizabeth' or 'I apologize' (in which something is *done*, and which may be happy or unhappy depending on whether a number of conditions are fulfilled, e.g. in relation to the identity of the speaker who may or may not be the appointed person to christen the ship or his/her intentions which may or may not be appropriate to the act of apologizing). He observes that also constatives are subject to criteria of felicity unrelated to truth or falsity (e.g. 'All John's children are bald' is neither true nor false in a context in which John does not have any children). Conversely, performatives are liable to a dimension of criticism closely related to truth and falsity (e.g. 'I declare you guilty' may be a verdict that was reached properly and in good faith; yet it matters whether the verdict was just or not). Thus rejecting the distinction, Austin then introduced a three-fold conceptual framework to capture different aspects involved in every type of utterance: the **locution** (the act *of* say-ing something with a specific phonetic and grammatical form and with a specific meaning), the **illocution** (the act performed *in* saying something, such as asserting, promising, or ordering), and the **perlocution** (the act performed *by* saying something, such as persuading, deceiving, or frightening). This framework became the basis of **speech act** theory, as developed further by John Searle and as adopted by numerous linguists from the 1960s onwards. (**JV**)

Further Reading

Austin, J. L. (1961) *Philosophical Papers*, Oxford: Oxford University Press.

Austin, J. L. (1962) *How To Do Things With Words*, (ed.) J. O. Urmson, Oxford: Oxford University Press. (2nd revised edition, 1975, (eds) J. O. Urmson and M. Sbisà, Cambridge, MA: Harvard University Press.)

Warnock, G. J. (1989) *J. L. Austin*, London: Routledge and Kegan Paul.

AUXILIARY A **verb** which helps another verb rather than itself referring to an action or event. In the sentence *Susie will reach the top*, the main verb is *reach*: the auxiliary *will* helps to express the time of reaching. Auxiliaries are important in many areas of English **grammar**. (**RS**)

See also SYNTAX.

B

BAKHTIN Mikhail Mikhailovich Bakhtin (Örel 1895–Moscow 1975), a Russian philosopher. He met Pavel N. Medvedev (1891–1938) and Valentin N. **Vološinov** (1884/5–1936) in Vitebsk in 1920 and established relations of friendship and collaboration with them. Together they formed the 'Bakhtin Circle' with the participation of the musicologist I. I. Sollertinskij, the biologist I. I. Kanaev, the writers K. K. Vaginov and D. I. Kharms, the Indologist M. I. Tubianskij, and the poet N. A. Kljuev. Even if only on an ideal level, Bakhtin's brother Nikolaj (1894–1950) may also be considered as a member of the 'Circle' (cf. Ponzio, 'Presentazione. Un autore dalla parte dell'eroe', in N. Bakhtin 1998, pp. 7–13). Having left Russia in 1918 N. Bakhtin eventually settled in Birmingham, where at the University he founded the Department of Linguistics in 1946. He died there four years later.

During the 1920s Bakhtin's work interconnected so closely with that of his collaborators that it is difficult to distinguish between them. This would seem to confirm his thesis of the 'semi-other' character of 'one's own word', in spite of the critics who insist on establishing ownership and authorship. Bakhtin played a significant role in writing Vološinov's two books, *Freudianism: A Critical Sketch* (1927) and *Marxism and the Philosophy of Language* (1929) as well as *The Formal Method in Literary Scholarship* (1928), signed by P. N. Medvedev. He also contributed to various articles published by the same 'authors' between 1925 and 1930, as well as to Kanaev's article 'Contemporary Vitalism' (1926). And even when the 'Circle' broke down under Stalinist oppression, with Medvedev's assassination and Vološinov's death, the 'voices' of its various members were still heard in uninterrupted **dialogue** with Bakhtin who persevered in his research until his death in 1975.

Problems of Dostoevsky's Art was published in 1929, followed by a long silence broken only in 1963 when at last a much expanded edition appeared under the title *Problems of Dostoevsky's Poetics*. With Stalinism at its worst, in fact, Bakhtin had been banished from official culture and exiled to Kustanaj. In 1965 he published his monograph *Rabelais and His World*. A collection of his writings in Russian originally appeared in 1975 and another in 1979, followed by editions of his unpublished writings or re-editions of published works by himself and his circle (cf. in English, Bakhtin 1981, 1986, 1990). Since then numerous monographs have been dedicated to his thought (Clark and Holquist 1984; Holquist 1990; Morson and Emerson 1989, 1990; Ponzio 1980a, 1992a, 1998a; Todorov 1981).

Evaluated as 'critique', in a literary as well as philosophical sense after **Kant** and **Marx**, Bakhtin's fundamental contribution to 'philosophy of language' or 'metalinguistics' consists in his *critique of dialogic reason*. He privileged the term 'metalinguistics' for his particular approach to the study of **sign**, utterance, **text**, **discourse**, **genre**, and relations between literary writing and nonverbal expressions in popular culture, as in the signs of carnival. Bakhtin's critique of dialogic reason focuses on the concept of *responsibility without alibis*, a non conventional responsibility, but which concerns existential 'architectonics' in its relation with the I, with the world and with others and which as such cannot be transferred. Dialogue is for Bakhtin an embodied, intercorporeal, expression of the involvement of one's body, which is only illusorily individual, separate, and autonomous. The adequate image of the body is that of the 'grotesque body' (see Bakhtin 1965) which finds expression in popular culture, in the vulgar language of the public place and above all in the masks of carnival. This is the body *in its vital and indissoluble relation with the world and with the body of others*. With the shift in focus from identity (whether individual, as in the case of consciousness or self, or collective, as in a community, historical language, or cultural system at large) to **alterity** – a sort of Copernican revolution – Bakhtinian critique of dialogic reason not only questions the general orientation of Western philosophy, but also the tendencies dominating over the culture engendering it. (**AP**)

Further Reading

Bakhtin, M. M. (1981) *The Dialogic Imagination: Four Essays*, trans. C. Emerson and M. Holquist, Austin, TX: University of Texas Press.

Bakhtin, M. M. (1984a) *Rabelais and His World*, trans. H. Iswolsky, Bloomington: Indiana University Press.

Bakhtin, M. M. (1984b) *Problems of Dostoevsky's Poetics*, trans. C. Emerson, Minneapolis: University of Minnesota Press.

BARTHES Roland Barthes (Cherbourg 1915–Paris 1980), French semiotician, literary theorist, critic of the mediocrity of literary criticism and of ideology, writer and painter. In 1947 he began publishing an analysis of Albert Camus's 'Blank writing' ('*écriture blanche*') in the journal *Combat*. As a French language teacher in Alexandria (Egypt), he met **Greimas** and took an interest in **Saussure**, **Hjelmslev** and **Jakobson** while continuing his studies in literature and theatre, focusing especially on Brecht and the historian Michelet.

He settled in Paris in 1950, after which *Le degré zéro de l'écriture*, was published in 1953, followed by *Michelet par lui-même* in 1954. His interest in semiology, literature and the *nouveau roman* (Robbe-Grillet, Butor, etc.) dovetails with his critique of mass culture ideology. *Mythologies* (1957) testifies to such interests: Barthes focuses on 'everyday objects', from automobiles to products in plastic, detergents and potato chips, considered through categories taken from authoritative authors such as Saussure, Hjelmslev, and **Marx**. *Système de la Mode* (1967, written between 1957–63) belongs to the same context. It studies the relation between verbal and nonverbal semiotic systems in women's attire as illustrated in fashion magazines, which also led his attention to fashion as spoken (as a mode of speaking) (*la mode parlée*), without which images are nothing.

In *Eléments de sémiologie* (1964) the relation between verbal signs and nonverbal signs is central. The linguistics of the linguists must be abandoned, he argues, to employ a far broader concept of language as a practice that models and organizes **discourse** fields. On leaving aside the limited view of linguistics as conceived by the linguist (an analogous critique was conducted by Morris 1946), it becomes evident that 'human language is more than the pattern of **signification**: it is its very foundation' and that it is necessary 'to reverse Saussure's formula and assert that semiology is a part of linguistics' (Barthes 1967a, p. 8). Another 'shift' produced by this essay is the transition from a *sémiologie de communication* (Saussure, Buyssens, Prieto, Mounin) to a *semiotics of signification*, according to which signs are not only those produced intentionally to communicate (but also, for example, symptoms in medical semiotics, or 'dreaming' according to Freud). These studies in general semiotics, which have concrete application, include 'L'introduction à l'analyse structurale des récits' (1966b).

The 'transgressive character of semiotics' is also present in Barthes' contributions to literary analysis such as *Sur Racine* (1963), *Essais critiques* (1964), *Critique et vérité* (1966), *S/Z* (1970), *Sade, Fourier, Loyola* (1971), *Le plaisir du texte* (1973), *L'Empire des signes* (1970) and *Fragments d'un discours amoureux* (1977). Here his interest in literature goes together with his interest in signification and for what, in an essay of 1975 ('L'obvie et l'obtus', now in Barthes 1982) he calls the 'third sense', *the semiotics of significance*, whose object is not the message (semiotics of communication), nor the symbol in the Freudian sense (semiotics of signification), but the *text* or *writing*, that is, the maximum opening of sense which characterizes especially literary writing (cf. Ponzio 1995b; Marrone, 'Introduzione', in Barthes 1998: ix–xxxv). But the filmic, the pictorial, the musical (*Image-Music-Text*, 1977b), the photographic (cf. *La chambre claire*, 1980) also achieve significance. Owing to the interdependency between the readerly (*lisible*) text and the writerly (*scriptible*) text of the writer (*scripteur*, *écrivant*), which instead is present to a lesser degree in the text of the *non-literary author* (*écrivant*), the reader assumes a role of co-authorship and therefore participates dialogically in the constitution of sense.

From 1962 to 1967 Barthes taught sociology of signs, symbols and representations at the École Pratique des Hautes Etudes en Sciences Sociales. In 1967 he was called to the Collège de France. His inaugural *Leçon* at the Collège (1977) attributes to literary writing a subversive character thanks to the shift operated by significance: it enables the *écrivant* to say without identifying with the subject-author and therefore to escape the order of discourse which the speaker reproduces when he obeys *langue*. (**AP**)

Further Reading

Barthes, R. (1967) *Elements of Semiology*, trans. A. Lavers, London: Cape.
Barthes, R. (1974) *S/Z*, trans. R. Howard, New York: Hill and Wang.
Barthes, R. (1977) *Image-Music-Text*, ed. and trans. S. Heath, London: Collins.

BAUDRILLARD Jean Baudrillard (b. 1929), French social theorist. The early Baudrillard saw society as organized around conspicuous consumption and the lavish display of commodities by means of which one could acquire identity, prestige, and status in the community. Baudrillard made efforts to combine Saussurean semiological theory in terms of a 'critique of the political economy of the sign' with a **Marx**ist critique of capitalism (Baudrillard 1975, 1981). For the later Baudrillard, labor is no longer a force of production but has itself become just another **sign** among signs. Production is nothing more than the consumerist system of signs referring to themselves (Baudrillard 1983a, 1983b, 1988, 1995).

Baudrillard's mass media have generated an inundation of images and signs the consequence of which is a 'simulation world', which erases the age-old distinction between the 'real' and the 'imaginary'. The privileged domains of modernity – science, philosophy, labor, private enterprise, social programs, and above all, theory – are sucked up by a whirlwind of vacuous **signifier**s and into a 'black hole'. The age-old cherished illusions of the referential sign vanish, as signs and their objects implode into mere disembodied signs. Consequently, the commodities of contemporary 'postmodern' culture organized around conspicuous consumption have lost their value as material goods. Like signs in **Saussure**'s differential system of language, they take on **value** according to their relations with all other sign-commodities in the entire system. Everything is flattened to the same level, that of signifiers existing in contiguous relationship with other signifiers, the totality of which composes a vast tautological system. Individuals become nothing more than socially invented agents of needs. Each individual becomes tantamount to any and all individuals. The individual, like any given sign-commodity, is equal to no more than any and all other sign-commodities of the same name and value.

Three 'orders of simulation', Baudrillard writes, have culminated in our mind-numbing, complex, 'postmodern' social life: (1) the order of the counterfeit (the natural law of value) which coincides with the rise of modernity, when *simulacra* implied power and social relations; (2) the final stage of the industrial revolution, when serial production and automation (based on the commercial law of value), opened the door to infinite reproducibility, and machines began to take their place alongside humans; and (3) our present cybernetic society, when models began to take precedence over things, and since models are signs, signs now began to exercise the full force of their hegemony. This third order simulation is obsessively binary or dyadic in nature – which is to be expected, for after all, Baudrillard's own model is indelibly Saussurean. Language, genetics, and social organization are analogous and governed by a binary logic underlying social models and **code**s controlling institutional and everyday life. In contrast to classical theories of social control, Baudrillard's theory *prima facie* appears radically indeterminate: everything resembles 'a Brownian movement of particles or the calculation of probabilities'. Signs and modes of representation rather than representation itself come to constitute 'reality'. Signs become mere atoms: lonely, hermetic signs making up a new type of

social order. They become charged with **meaning** only in relation to, and take their rightful place in the language of, the media with respect merely to other signs in the entire interwoven, variegated, labyrinthine tapestry. Signs have no destiny other than that of floating in an undefinable, referenceless space of their own making. (**FM**)

See also BINARISM.

Further Reading

Baudrillard, J. (1975) *The Mirror of Production*, trans. M. Poster, St. Louis: Telos.

Baudrillard, J. (1981) *For a Critique of the Political Economy of the Sign*, trans. C. Levin, St. Louis: Telos.

Gane, M. (ed.) (1993) *Baudrillard Live: Selected Interviews*, London: Routledge.

BENVENISTE Emile Benveniste (Cairo 1902–Paris 1976) was a French linguist and defining figure in the thought of postwar France and beyond. Educated at the Sorbonne by **Saussure**'s student, Antoine Meillet, Benveniste went on to teach at the Collège de France from 1937 until 1969. Although Benveniste was never granted the celebrity afforded to many of his contemporaries, he was still a major force across disciplines in academic circles. J. G. Merquior reports 'I still recall how we were awestruck as we passed by the door of his office on the way to **Lévi-Strauss**'s crowded seminar' (1986, p. 15). Furthermore, it is clear that Benveniste is the father of **poststructuralism**, his work from the late 1930s onwards paving the way for the critiques of **structuralism** offered by the likes of **Derrida**, **Lacan**, **Kristeva**, the later **Barthes**, **Baudrillard** and assorted Anglo-American theorists in studies of film, literature and philosophy (see Easthope 1988).

Benveniste's work mainly took place within the field of Indo-European languages, but it was probably the collection of his essays, *Problèmes de linguistique générale* (1966, translated into English in 1971), which lent his insights greater currency. The essays in the volume were short, highly focused and closely argued. They ranged from a penetrating critique of Saussure's principle of arbitrariness in the **sign**, 'The nature of the linguistic sign', through a consideration of the general role of prepositions, 'The sublogical system of prepositions in Latin', to his essay on the 'third person' as a 'non-person', 'The nature of pronouns'. Despite the minute reasoning behind each of these essays, they all ask the larger questions which force a fundamental re-orientation of post-Saussurean general linguistics. Even more than the work of **Jakobson**, these essays are concerned with the consequences of the phenomenon known as 'Subjectivity in language' (the title of essay number 21 in the volume).

In this light, it is easy to see how Benveniste so influenced poststructuralists. 'It is in and through language that man constitutes himself as *subject*,' he writes, 'because language alone establishes the concept of "ego" in reality, in *its* reality which is that of being' (1971, p. 224). For Benveniste, the separation of *I* and *you* in **dialogue** was crucial to the category of *person* because it is the means by which the individual sets him/herself up as a subject in **discourse**. The personal **pronoun**s are just one, albeit most important, means by which each speaker appropriates a language; **deixis** is another means, demanding that **meaning** can only be realized with reference to the instance of discourse in which the deictic category appears. As such, language creates the designation of person; but it also contributes to the human understanding of such supposedly autonomous phenomena as time and space.

Yet the subject is not only made possible by language in Benveniste's theory; in a development which makes his work congenial to some variants of psychoanalysis,

the subject is fundamentally split in relation to the linguistic capacity. Benveniste identifies two sides of any use of language: he calls these *énoncé* and *énonciation*. The *énoncé* is simple enough: it is the statement or content of the particular instance of language, what is being said. The *énonciation*, on the other hand, is the *act* of utterance and presupposes a speaker and a listener. The two can be recognized when separated in this abstract way but, in practice, they are always entangled. In a room containing a large group of people, one person might whisper to those within earshot that one of the group who is out of earshot has very bad body odour. The *énoncé* will be about a person who smells, but the *énonciation* will be a whisper. Yet the one is caught up in and necessitated by the other: the personal remark is made all the more personal by the *sotto voce* rendering of it.

The subject of this dynamic in language cannot help being pulled in two ways. There will be the rendering of him/herself as a subject represented in the use of pronouns such as *I* (*énoncé*); but there will also be that other 'I' who does the rendering (*énonciation*). The dilemma, here, is made clear in such paradoxical constructions as 'I am lying', in which the subject speaking *must* be separate from the subject represented in the instance of discourse.

Benveniste's writings on subjectivity and language found a ready welcome in post-structuralist and psychoanalytical circles. However, his work is more wide-ranging than this fact allows and his essays in general linguistics are worth repeated readings, especially as they so frequently coincide with **ordinary language philosophy**, **pragmatics**, the work of **Morris** and **semiotics**. Benveniste's contribution to international semiotics is now well known. After retiring from the Collège de France he became President of the **IASS**, an organization that, with others, he had initiated. He died in tragic circumstances in 1976. (**PC**)

Further Reading

Benveniste, E. (1971) *Problems in General Linguistics*, trans. M. E. Meek, Coral Gables: University of Miami Press.

Benveniste, E. (1973) *Indo-European Language and Society*, trans. E. Palmer, London: Faber.

Lotringer, S. and Gora, T. (eds) (1981) *Polyphonic Linguistics: The Many Voices of Emile Benveniste, Semiotica* (Special Supplement).

BERKELEY George Berkeley (1685–1753). Second of the three most influential British empiricists: **Locke**, Berkeley, and Hume. On the assumption that only sensations can be experienced, and that nothing can be sensed but ideas, Berkeley concluded that only mind and ideas exist. He claimed that we can only have ideas of ideas, not of objects out of mind, and he denied that we can have abstract general ideas. We can distinguish real experience from imagination by its greater vividness and by the continuity that characterizes reality. But Berkeley held that 'to be is to be perceived', so the connectedness of the ideas that constitutes reality depends on continual perception. This Berkeley attributed to God. So Berkeley accepted the reality of ordinary experience but denied that there is an external world that causes sensations and is the source of the continuity we experience. Charles S. **Peirce** argued that this was a sham **realism**, and that Berkeley belongs in the **nominalist** tradition. However, Peirce was impressed with Berkeley's proto-pragmatic idea that thoughts are **signs** and his rejection of material objects that can have no sensible effects. Hume, a more skeptical empiricist, denied mind along with matter and admitted only impressions and ideas. (**NH**)

See also Jackendoff (this volume).

Further Reading

Warnock, G. J. (1953) *Berkeley*, Harmondsworth: Penguin.

BERNSTEIN Basil Bernard Bernstein (b. 1924), British sociologist, is known for his work on linguistic factors in the sociology of education. After the Second World War he spent three years running boys' clubs in the working-class East End of London where he found himself negotiating the differences between Reform and Orthodox Judaism in the local population. In 1947 he enrolled at the London School of Economics and, after changing from a Diploma in Social Science, took a BSc. Econ. degree. Like so many figures of the period who were to become influential in British intellectual life, especially in cultural studies and sociology (e.g. Richard Hoggart, Raymond Williams, Stuart Hall), he then spent a period teaching in adult education. Until 1960, he taught full-time industrial workers on 'day release' at the City Day College. Following this there was a period as a research assistant at the Department of Phonetics, University College, London; here he became influenced by the work of **Sapir**, **Whorf**, Cassirer, Vygotsky and Luria. Later, he joined the University of London Institute of Education and came into contact with intellectual currents such as **structuralism**, and individuals such as Ruquaia Hasan, Michael **Halliday** and Mary **Douglas**.

Bernstein's own work developed within the Sociological Research Unit of the Institute of Education were he later became Professor. In an early paper (1962) he had focused on hesitation phenomena among school pupils and introduced the notion of 'codes' in his analysis. Subsequent papers expanded on this and generated the concepts with which he became most associated: the **elaborated** and **restricted** codes. Because of the currency of these specific ideas and the popular fixation on them to the detriment of other areas of his work, Bernstein became a figure of controversy. Bernstein himself sums up the matter fairly when he says that the political Left initially liked his ideas because they indicted inequality; but later, especially with the new Left, he was castigated for omitting discussion of poverty and other material factors and simply reproducing inequality in an attempt to impose middle-class norms; the Right, on the other hand, were happy that Bernstein had 'proved' that high culture was beyond the reach of the working classes. All these views were oversimplified and, as Bernstein states, all insisted on the idea of linguistic 'deficit' (1971, p. 19).

For some, Bernstein remains 'one of the most original and creative of modern British sociologists' (Atkinson 1985, p. 7). Halliday (1973, p. xvi) succinctly emphasizes the benefits of Bernstein's work when he says that rather than remaining blind to the consequences of language for its users it focuses on language's very sociality, an apprehension of 'language as meaning rather than language as structure'. At the very least, Bernstein's work is a precursor of contemporary post-Foucauldian investigations of **discourse** in education. (**PC**)

Further Reading

Bernstein, B. (1971) *Class, Codes and Control vol. 1: Theoretical Studies Towards a Sociology of Language*, London: Routledge and Kegan Paul.

BINARISM In linguistics, the assumption is that contrasts may be analysed in terms of binary oppositions or choices. Thus, in **phonology**, for example, **consonants** may be classified in terms of the opposition between 'voiced' and 'voiceless'; or in **grammar**, number specified by reference to the opposition between 'singular' and 'plural'. The logical basis of binarism is negation, i.e. the proposition 'not *p*' as opposed to '*p*'. thus binarism is often associated with the assumption that one member of the pair is 'marked' (i.e. plus or positive) and the other 'unmarked' (i.e. negative or lacking the feature in question). Binary analyses may be controversial for at least two reasons. One is that they tend to provide a straitjacket into which more subtle and elaborate kinds of linguistic contrast have to be forced. The other is that although binarism poses as an analytic methodology it is in effect an *a priori* theory about universals of linguistic structure and lacks any well-argued foundation.

In **semiotics** and cultural studies generally binarism has had a bad press because the insistence on such oppositions ('good' vs. 'bad', 'scientific' vs. 'unscientific', 'democratic' vs. 'undemocratic', etc.) is seen as a way of inculcating those values favoured by current establishments and suppressing dissidence or alternative views. (**RH**)

See also *DIFFÉRANCE*.

BIOSEMIOTICS Throughout Western history, most semiotic theories and their applications have focused on messages, whether verbal or not, in circulation among human beings, generally within their cultural setting. This kind of semiotic inquiry – characterized as anthropocentric and **logocentric** – has been the rule since ancient times, with the partial exception of iatric semiotics (symptomatology, diagnostics, or the like), practiced and written about by physicians such as Hippocrates of Cos (*c.* 430 BCE) or Galen of Pergamon (129–*c.*200), as well as their innumerable modern successors, notably Thure von Uexküll, MD (b. 1908), who regards biosemiotics as an underlying exemplar for all psychosomatic medicine. Indeed, the ultimate cradle of biosemiotics rests, if tacitly, in antique medicine.

Step by hesitant step, the scope of traditional semiotics has immensely widened after the 1920s, or, to put it the other way around, 'normal' **semiotics** gradually became embedded and submerged in the far vaster domain of what the Italian medical oncologist, Giorgio Prodi (1928–87), came to denominate 'nature semiotics' (1988). The study of biological codes is nowadays more commonly designated *Biosemiotics* – a term independently coined in recent decades in the USA and elsewhere – which harks back to the work of Jakob von **Uexküll**'s (1864–1944) now classic work, *Theoretische Biologie* (1920, et seq.). Biosemiotics presupposes the axiomatic identity of the semiosphere with the biosphere.

Uexküll called his subject matter *Umweltlehre*, the study of phenomenal self-worlds, perhaps best rendered as unique models of each subject's universe. Every subject is the constructor of its 'significant surround', each wrapped according to its equipment of perceptual organs – which order perceptual **sign**s into perceptual cues; and effector organs – which are parts of the operational world of the subject, signs for the changes which the effector evokes in the object through which the perceptual cue is extinguished. A so-called functional cycle links parts of the environment with the internal model of a living being via its perceptual organs and effector organs, coordinated with the medium in which the animal maneuvers (e.g., fin/water, wing/air, foot/path, mouth/food, weapon/enemy, or the like). Such networks are made up of signs accessible only to the encoding subject; they remain 'noise' for all others.

The Swiss psychologist and founder of zoo biology, Heini Hediger (1908–92), influenced by J. von Uexküll's theories, studied animal flight responses, the precepts of taming and training of captive animals in the wild as well as in zoo and circus environments, and the domestication of household pets and farm animals. He was chiefly responsible for working out, by strictly empirical biosemiotic routines, concepts of individual and social space in applications to animals of many kinds.

These were later applied by others to humans and further developed under such labels as 'proxemics'.

While Uexküll tested various animal species singly, say, the tick in search of mammalian blood, Hediger often investigated them in their dyadic interdependence with other species, signally so with *Homo sapiens* (famously including interactions of the 'Clever Hans phenomenon' kind). Later, reflections on animal semiosis (dubbed '**zoosemiotics**') were extended by other scholars to plants ('phytosemiotics'), fungi ('mycosemiotics'), and, importantly, to the global prokaryotic communication network within and between different bacterial cells evolved three and a half billion years ago ('microsemiotics, cytosemiotics').

The body of any living entity consists of an intricate web of semioses; the term 'endosemiosis' refers to trains of sign transmission inside the organism. The messages that are transmitted include information about the **meaning** of processes in one system of the body (cells, tissues, organs, or organ systems) for other systems as well as for the integrative regulation devices (especially the brain) and such control systems as the immune **code** (crucially capable of distinguishing self from non-self). Among the other fundamental endosemiotic codes are the genetic code, the metabolic code, and the neural code. **(TAS)**

See also ANTHROPOSEMIOTICS.

Further Reading

Hoffmeyer, J. (1993) *Signs of Meaning*, Bloomington: Indiana University Press.

Kull, K. (2001) *Jakob von Uexküll, Semiotica*, forthcoming [Special issue].

Merrell, F. (1996) *Signs Grow: Semiosis and Life Processes*, London: University of Toronto Press.

BIRDWHISTELL Ray Lee Birdwhistell (1918–94) introduced '**kinesics**', the study of body motion as a communication system in human interaction. Born in Cincinnati, Ohio, he remained deeply attached to Kentucky, his parental home. He gained a PhD in anthropology from the University of Chicago in 1951 for a study of socialization in rural Kentucky. While at Chicago he became acquainted with Margaret Mead and Gregory Bateson. Their influence on one another was mutual and considerable. In 1956 he was involved with Bateson in the 'Natural History of an Interview' project at the Center for Advanced Study in the Behavioral Sciences in Palo Alto. Begun on the initiative of linguists and psychiatrists, this was the first attempt ever to examine face-to-face interaction as a multimodal communication process in which micro-analyses of sound-synchronized films of interactions were undertaken. It laid the foundations for Birdwhistell's fundamental ideas about the nature of kinesics and communication. Birdwhistell taught at the University of Toronto, the University of Louisville, Kentucky, and the University of Buffalo, New York. He directed the Project on Human Communication at the Eastern Pennsylvania Psychiatric Institute in Philadelphia, and was Professor in the Annenberg School of Communications, University of Pennsylvania. He was a charismatic teacher and had a wide influence on several generations of students. (**AK**)

Further Reading

Kendon, A. and Sigman, S. J. (1996) 'Ray L. Birdwhistell (1918–1994): Commemorative essay', *Semiotica*, 112: 231–61.

BLOOMFIELD Leonard Bloomfield (1887 –1949) was a major pioneer in modern linguistics, and a leading figure in **American structuralism**. After doctoral research on the history of the Germanic languages, he went on to do important work on native American and Austronesian languages. His book *Language* (1933) expertly synthesized much of what was known in linguistics at the time, and is still well worth reading. Bloomfield worked hard to establish linguistics as an independent subject and played a prominent role in setting up the Linguistic Society of America in 1924. He wrote introductory textbooks on Dutch and Russian as well as many academic papers.

The epitome of the cautious scholar, Bloomfield refused to make claims that were not backed up by painstaking observation and analysis. He was unwilling to use the **meaning** of words and sentences as the basis for grammatical analysis, as he was not convinced that meaning could be described scientifically. He did not, however, ignore meaning altogether: the later chapters of *Language* discuss meaning and change of meaning extensively. (**RS**)

See also SAPIR.

Further Reading

Hall, R. (1987) *Leonard Bloomfield: Essays on His Life and Work*, Amsterdam: John Benjamins.

BOAS Franz Boas (1858–1942), born in Germany of Jewish parentage, first studied physics and geography there before turning to anthropology. Following his first Arctic expeditions, he relocated to the United States in 1887. He became involved with the Chicago World's Fair 1892–1894, the Jessup North Pacific Expedition 1897–1902, and major museums. Between 1896–1936 he taught anthropology at Columbia University, training the first generation of professionals. His ethnographic research focused on the North West coast of North America.

Boas' integrated time (historicity) and space (context) in language, culture, and biology, thus contesting the then deterministic, reductionistic conflation of race and culture (Williams 1996). He distrusted the presumption of 'progress' and the unilineal, orthogenetic cultural evolutionism of his day (Boas [1911] 1963). Boas' 'culture' was a loose conjunction of relationships (Stocking 1966). The **Sapir-Whorf hypothesis** – concerning interplay between language, culture, and cognition – was co-formulated by one of his students. Boas' recognition of oral language as both means for data collection and as substance for analysis itself contributed to the mission of structural linguistics.

Boas' innovative commitment to intensive ethnographic data collection rather than nomothetic generalizations, to longitudinal studies, and to training of native investigators, set the stage for substantive theory-building in later twentieth-century anthropology (Goldschmidt 1959; Stocking 1996). (**MA**)

See also AMERICAN STRUCTURALISM.

Further Reading

Stocking, Jr., G. W. (ed.) (1996) Volksgeist *as Method and Ethic: Essays on Boasian Ethnography and the German Anthropological Tradition* (History of Anthropology, Vol. 8) Madison, WI: University of Wisconsin Press.

BRÉAL Michel Bréal (1832–1915) introduced historical comparative **grammar** in France. Having studied with Franz Bopp, his initial inspiration was the German tradition. However, from the very beginning Bréal stressed that the approach to linguistic evolution as a 'natural' science should be enriched with reference to a human and cultural dimension. In his seminal work, *Essai de sémantique* (1897) he moves from linguistic form to function and **meaning**, intrigued in particular by functional distinctions that are not given directly by the form and by the role of human intelligence in filling those gaps in the process of interpretation. Bréal thus became one of the founding fathers of present-day **semantics** (and maybe a cognitive linguist *avant la lettre*), defined in his words as 'a science of **signification**'. He believed firmly in the complementarity between the science of language and philology as an ingredient of historical research. In his meaning-oriented approach to language change and development, or the evolution of signification, the concept of human volition is the key. (**JV**)

Further Reading

Bréal, M. (1995) *De la grammaire comparée à la sémantique: Textes de Michel Bréal publiés entre 1864 et 1898*, ed. P. Desmet and P. Swiggers, Leuven: Peeters.

BRØNDAL Viggo Brøndal (1887–1942), Danish linguist and language philosopher, Professor of Romance Philology at the University of Copenhagen (1928–42). His studies in Paris (1912–13) with Antoine Meillet and his reading of Ferdinand de **Saussure**'s *Cours de linguistique générale* (1916) immediately after its publication made structural linguistics his main field. His philosophical training with Harald Høffding gave his **structuralism** a philosophical and historical perspective and opened his eyes to phenomenology, especially Edmund Husserl's *Logische Untersuchungen* (1900–1), and formal logic. Together with Louis **Hjelmslev** he founded the Cercle Linguistique de Copenhague in 1931 and the journal *Acta Linguistica Hafniensia* (1939–).

The double perspectives of formalism and phenomenology and of linguistics and philosophy shaped his contribution to linguistics and **semiotics** as outlined in the programmatic essays 'Langage et logique' (1937) and 'Linguistique structurale'

(1939) as well as in other essays reprinted in *Essais de linguistique générale* (1943). His project was to articulate the relation between language and thought in such a way that it became methodologically applicable to the analysis of language on all levels from **phoneme**s to **discourse**. This project was carried out as a **Universal Grammar** constituted by a limited number of logical categories and a series of structural principles for the combination and interrelation of the basic logical elements. In Brøndal's theory, the Universal Grammar as well as the language-specific **grammars** contain four dimensions that all articulate the thought–language relation in a particular way: **morphology** and **syntax**, the symbolic dimension and the logical dimension (to be compared with, respectively, expression and content).

Brøndal's work on a Universal Grammar concentrates on morphology in *Ordklasserne* (1928; French translation 1948), while he only outlines semantics in *Præpositionernes Theori* (1940; French translation 1950) and syntax in *Morfologi og Syntax* (1932). He deals only sporadically with **phonology** and **phonetics**. The core of his theory is a reinterpretation of **Aristotle**'s philosophical categories in a phenomenological perspective. From the outset Brøndal's theory constitutes a synthesis of classical and modern linguistics in an ambitious attempt to comprehend human reality on the basis of language universals, also integrating the concepts of the logic and the linguistic philosophy of scholasticism, **Port-Royal**, Leibniz, and **Humboldt** as well as Husserl's phenomenology and the relational logic of logical positivism.

Although an ardent structural linguist, Brøndal never defended the idea of language as a purely immanent structure. His favorite image of language is a geometry by which we turn the world into **meaning**, and in doing so we can move both the structure of the world and our own position in it.

To Brøndal, language is first of all intentional in the phenomenological sense of Brentano and Husserl: language is object-oriented and constitutive for the human relation to the world. Brøndal applies the reinterpreted Aristotelian categories: substance, quantity, quality, and relation to build a grammar from this basic assumption.

The requirements of structural linguistics helped Brøndal to define the categories for morphological and syntactical purposes in necessary and sufficient interrelationship. But he also develops a set of specific relative categorics, especially Symmetry, Transitivity, and Connectivity, from the logical relations of formal logic, mainly for semantic purposes.

Like his concept of Universal Grammar and the concept of intentionality, Brøndal's idea of structural laws is influenced by Husserl's *Logische Untersuchungen* (1900–1), an influence stimulated by Brøndal's discussions with Roman **Jakobson** on Husserl's concept of founding (*Fundierung*), i.e. the hierarchical relationship between elements of a totality. Although the basic notions of Brøndal's doctrine cover the area which in other theories is defined by notions originating in the sign, Brøndal most often focuses on the word as his structural and semiotic key concept.

Brøndal's main contributions to semiotics (Barthes 1953; Greimas 1966, 1970) are his analyses of the structural laws of language and his constant effort to synthesize linguistics and philosophy, methodology and epistemology in refusing the doctrine of language as a purely immanent structure. (**SEL**)

See also HJELMSLEV and BARTHES.

Further Reading

Brandt, P. A. (ed.) (1989) *Linguistique et Sémiotique, Travaux du Cercle Linguistique de Copenhague* XXII.

Larsen, S. E. (1987a) 'A semiotician in disguise', *The Semiotic Web '86* (1987), 47–102.

Larsen, S. E. (ed.) (1987b) *Actualité de Brøndal, Langages 86*.

BÜHLER Karl Bühler (1879–1963), a German psychologist and linguist, was the founder and director of the Institute of Psychology at the University of Vienna (1922–38). Bühler's term for **semiotics** was 'sematology'. He is best known as a pioneering advocate of the **sign** character of language. The focal point of all linguistic analysis is the speech event (*Sprechereignis*) which takes place in two fields: an **index** field (*Zeigfeld*), constituted by **deixis**, and a **symbol** field (*Symbolfeld*), constituted by signs with conceptual content. Language signs have three functions: as symptoms they express inner states of speakers, as signals they give directions to hearers, and as symbols they represent states of affairs in the world. Following **Humboldt**, Bühler believed that each language had its own world view (*Weltansicht*). Like Mead, he was a strong advocate of the social matrix of **meaning** and the primacy of action. His theory of metaphor paved the way to developments in **cognitive linguistics**. With his organon model of language as communication between senders and receivers he anticipated **biosemiotic** studies of cell and animal communication through effector signs and receptor signs. Major works are *Ausdruckstheorie* (1933) and *Sprachtheorie* (1934). The latter has been translated into English (Bühler 1990). (**EB**)

Further Reading

Innis, R. (1982) *Karl Bühler: Semiotic Foundations of Language Theory*, New York: Plenum Press.

C

CHOMSKY Noam Chomsky (b. 1928) is an American linguist and political campaigner. Born in Philadelphia, Chomsky had nearly dropped out of university when he met Zellig **Harris** through a shared interest in left-libertarian Jewish politics. Harris encouraged Chomsky to study linguistics, and soon Chomsky won a fellowship at Harvard University. In 1955 he moved to the Massachusetts Institute of Technology (MIT) in Boston, where he has been based ever since.

Chomsky put forward a new approach to the study of language, though he has often said that his work is a development of ideas that were commonplace in the Renaissance and the Enlightenment. His starting point was profound dissatisfaction with the structuralist linguistics (see **American structuralism**) that flourished in America in the first half of this century. His forceful critiques of structuralism (Chomsky 1964a) and the behaviourist psychology with which it was linked (Chomsky 1964b) helped to build his reputation, though they also aroused enormous hostility which has continued to this day.

The structuralists' emphasis on observable data had led them to regard a language as a set of utterances: thus the English language was everything that speakers of English said and wrote, taken as a whole. Chomsky had two practical objections to this view of language. First, this set is potentially infinite, and therefore although it can be specified mathematically, it does not exist in the real world (in the same way that the set of positive integers does not exist in the real world). Second, this set includes errors, repetitions, false starts, and similar things that linguists typically ignore when they describe a language.

A more fundamental objection to structuralism, in Chomsky's view, was that it failed to capture the common-sense view of a language, which is tacitly assumed by all linguists. What speakers of a language have in common (and what a **grammar** of that language tries to describe) is a system of knowledge in their minds. Chomsky dismissed arguments by philosophers that knowledge is not something that can be investigated scientifically: on the contrary, he argued, if this knowledge exists in our minds, it must have a more tangible reality than a 'language' in the structuralist sense. In some way, the knowledge must have a physical existence in the neural circuits of the human brain. The term 'knowledge' is just an abstract way of referring to this part of our brains. This abstraction is just as legitimate as any abstract procedure in science: physicists, for instance, constantly use abstract models of the universe (involving perfectly straight lines, notions like 'points' which have location but no magnitude, and so on). The question is whether insight and understanding can be gained by using abstract models: condemning all abstraction out of hand is simply unscientific dogma.

Chomsky went on to argue that some aspects of this linguistic knowledge are innate, that is, they result from human genetic programming rather than being learned from experience. The main aim of his research programme is to specify these genetic properties of language, which he calls **Universal Grammar**. (RS)

See also COMPETENCE, DEEP STRUCTURE, GENERATIVE GRAMMAR, PRINCIPLES AND PARAMETERS THEORY, TRANSFORMATIONAL GRAMMAR and Jackendoff (this volume). **(RS)**

Further Reading

Chomsky, N. (1996) *Powers and Prospects*, London: Pluto Press.
Cook, V. and Newson, M. (1996) *Chomsky's Universal Grammar: An Introduction*, 2nd edn, Oxford: Blackwell.
Salkie, R. (1990) *The Chomsky Update: Linguistics and Politics*, London: Unwin Hyman.

CLAUSE A group of words including, as a minimum, a subject and a finite **verb**. We distinguish clauses from sentences because some sentences contain more than one clause. The sentence *I love you because you are kind-hearted* contains two clauses: *I love you* (subject *I*, finite verb *love*) and *you are kind-hearted* (subject *you*, finite verb *are*). **(RS)**

CLOSED TEXT Before the appearance of Umberto **Eco**'s essays on the aesthetics of the open work (*Opera aperta* 1962; *The Open Work* 1989), it was generally assumed that there are no such things as completely open or closed **texts** (especially literary ones). Such a distinction today takes into consideration Eco's definition of what constitutes openness and consequently considers as closed any text that sets clear constraints on the reader's possible interpretations. In short, the author has intentionally constructed (if it is possible) a text as a fixed system, completed, with no ambiguities or implications, and with no operative choices or open-ended possible readings.

This must not be confused with the notions of 'limits' that are outlined in Eco's *The Limits of Interpretation* (1990), where the same author who with his notions of 'open work' may have been partly responsible for having shifted the authority on the possible **meaning**s foreseen by an author, first to the text and then to the reader (as we see with deconstructionists), nearly three decades later insists that even though there may not be a set number of possible interpretations of a text, most certainly one cannot make a text say what it has no intention of saying.

Unlike scientific texts, it is difficult to conceive that literary works could have only one possible level of reading/ interpretation. By closed texts it is assumed that we are referring to a text structured in such a way that not only does it not elicit a reader's inventiveness or his free play of interpretive cooperation in finding possible meanings/conclusions, but that it actually regulates our reading by pointing to specific messages, or pieces of information, that the author wishes to convey. A closed text is exhausted by its reading because it does not call for mental or psychological interaction with the author. In general, closed texts are associated with conveying information and messages rather than meaning and cultural awareness. **(RC)**

See also OPEN TEXT.

Further Reading

Eco. U. (1979) *The Role of the Reader: Explorations in the Semiotics of Texts*, Bloomington. Indiana University Press.

CODE Communication is classically described as an exchange of **meaning**s that are represented by **sign**s. Coding is the process of representing meanings systematically. Communicators can be said to encode their meanings into particular sequences of signs (e.g. strings of sounds, marks on paper, or visible gestures); recipients can be said to decode such meanings from the sign sequences they receive.

A code itself is therefore the set or system of rules and correspondences which link signs to meanings. Potentially, any one meaning can be represented by any sign, arbitrarily chosen. As **Saussure** indicated, there is no inherent link between the meaning of the word 'ox' and the shape of that word (phonetic or graphic) in English, or between that meaning and the French word 'bœuf'. The only general requirement is that the coding rules are known and followed by the relevant community of code users.

The coding of meaning in human languages is multi-dimensional. **Jakobson** distinguished **paradigmatic** from **syntagmatic** dimensions of linguistic organisation, as underlying coding principles. That is, the coding conventions of any human language need to specify paradigms from which meaningful signs have to be chosen, to fill our specific 'slots' in a sequence of signs. An example is choosing a **noun** from a set of possible nouns, to convey a selected meaning. The conventions also require language users to build chains of 'syntagms', according to specified combination rules. For example, some types of modifiers must appear before others in English ('large' must appear before 'steel' in 'a large steel bridge'). At the level of word **morphology** (the construction of words out of meaningful parts), adjectives are quite regularly formed by adding certain suffixes to **verb**s in English – 'watch-able', 'believe-able'. Similarly, verbs are formed by adding suffixes to nouns or adjectives – 'item-ise', 'regular-ise'. But grammatical and lexical coding rules of this sort must be accompanied by further rules for representing grammatical sequences in speech, writing or some other medium. For example, in standard English pronunciation the suffix morpheme '-able' is coded as the neutral vowel called 'schwa' plus 'b' plus 'l'. The suffix '-ise' is coded as the sound sequence 'ai' (the diphthong) plus 'z' (the voiced sibilant).

Coded realisations of meanings can themselves be re-coded. For example, speech is often seen as the primary code for a human language, with conventional written (orthographic) forms as secondary or overlaid representations. In turn, written forms of a language can be re-coded into binary digital strings to be stored and exchanged in computing applications. Earlier technology allowed written languages to be re-coded and transmitted as Morse code. Morse code or digitised written English can be further re-coded by rules that encrypt it – that is, render it unintelligible to everyone who doesn't have access to the decoding rules.

Non-linguistic representation also involves coding. Music and pictures, for example, have their own means of representing **semantic** information and semantic relations. **Kress** and Van Leeuwen give the example that some meanings conveyed by locative prepositions in English are realised in pictures by the formal characteristics that create the contrast between foreground and background (1996, p. 44). Gestural communication is coded, although for most people, only a relatively small range of **gesture** signs will have firmly agreed, specific significance within a community. Sticking out one's tongue might denote mild deprecation of a target person, whereas distending one's cheek with one's tongue might have no codified meaning. It might signify that the speaker has a particle of food lodged between two teeth, but nothing of focused, interactional significance. Turning the palms of one's hands upwards while speaking might suggest that the speaker is dismayed, or uncertain, but these meanings are not strictly codified. A clear exception is gestural signing among hard-of-hearing users, where the level of formal specification is the same as with spoken or written codes. We must therefore distinguish between formal and informal coding, and degrees of codification.

Socio-cultural norms and conventions can, rather generally, be thought of as codes, such as dress codes, politeness codes, and institutional codes of practice. Once again the implication is that communities of people will agree on rules prescribing (and outlawing) sets of behaviours in specific circumstances, such as revealing more of their bodies on beaches than in churches. Codes of etiquette can prescribe event sequences (syntagms) too, such as what one eats first at a formal dinner, or the co-ordinated timing of drinking a toast. Cultural and sub-cultural groups may in fact be defined by their shared adherence to codes of this sort. Outside of anthropological analyses, or reflexive commentaries in cultural narratives, cultural codes will generally be tacit understandings rather than explicitly codified rules, but no less influential and constraining for that.

While the notion of coding is therefore a core one for **semiotics**, it nevertheless risks oversimplifying some facets of communication. Culturally endorsed associations between forms or **signifier**s and **signified** meanings are rarely as neat as the coding model implies they are. In the case of human language, meanings can rarely be defined as the precise denotata of specific words or expressions. Certainly across cultural groups, there can be a significant variation between the meanings of apparently equivalent forms. Even in Saussure's example of 'ox' and 'bœuf', this is clearly the case. These words do not encode identical meanings in English and French. Benjamin Lee **Whorf**'s principle of linguistic relativity points out how social realities are categorised differently by different communities. The implication is that coding, even linguistic coding, is a more active and variable process than is often assumed.

A further, fundamental point is that we should not overstate the extent to which human communication is accurately to be described as a sequence of encoding and decoding operations. Studies of discourse processing, such as Sperber and Wilson in their work on **relevance theory**, argue convincingly that meaning making is more of an inferential process than a coding process. That is, speakers do not simply encode meanings which listeners, who share an understanding of the code, can directly recover. Rather, speakers deploy signs on the understanding that listeners will find them relevant. The precise relevance, however, remains to be established through the active search procedures listeners activate. The direction and result of inference cannot be guaranteed by speakers in advance. Meanings are not 'there to be discovered', coded into utterances, as much as they are actively constructed by listeners on every occasion of social interaction. (**NC** and **AJ**)

See also <u>Sebeok</u> (this volume), GESTURE and SPEECH COMMUNITY.

Further Reading

Geertz, C. (1993) 'Thick description', in *The Interpretation of Cultures*, London: HarperCollins.

Kress, G. R. and van Leeuwen, T. (1996) *Reading Images: The Grammar of Visual Design*, London: Routledge.

Sperber, D. and Wilson, D. (1995) *Relevance: Communication and Cognition*, 2nd edn, Oxford: Blackwell.

COGNITIVE LINGUISTICS The word 'cognitive' means 'having to do with thinking', so cognitive linguistics can be understood broadly as the study of language in connection with thought. This connection can, however, be understood in several different ways.

Chomsky describes his approach to linguistics as forming part of what he calls the 'cognitive revolution' which took place around the middle of this century. For Chomsky, the central feature of this revolution was a new belief that knowledge was amenable to scientific investigation. Linguistic knowledge is only one type of knowledge, but it can be studied empirically and hypotheses can be formulated about the structure of linguistic knowledge in the human mind. Chomsky distinguishes knowledge of a particular language, which is described by a **generative grammar** of that language, from knowledge of language in general, which is covered by **Universal Grammar**.

Linguistics is thus in Chomsky's view part of cognitive psychology, but it employs methods which look very different from those usually used by psychologists. Despite its cognitive foundations Chomsky's methods are strictly linguistic, though the hypotheses put forward are influenced by their cognitive foundations: the development known as **principles and parameters theory** is a clear example. Chomsky has nothing to say about how linguistic knowledge is used: in other words, he does not try to link language with the active process of thinking.

Other linguists have tried to explore the relationship between thinking and language, and would see their work as part of cognitive science. The assumption behind this work is that human beings are essentially machines, and that the functioning of the human mind can be described in the same way as the functioning of a computer (note that Chomsky is not committed to this assumption, which he explicitly rejects). Computers are machines that process information, and cognitive scientists have tried to analyse language in the same way. One aim has been to program computers to understand and use language, an aim that has had only partial success up to now.

A third strand of research is called cognitive grammar, and is committed to the view that the structure of language is strongly influenced by the way the mind works (another assumption that Chomsky rejects). The key names in cognitive grammar include Ronald Langacker and George Lakoff, and they regard grammar as essentially 'symbolic', its role being to structure and symbolise the conceptual content of language. Unlike Chomsky, cognitive grammarians refuse to make a sharp distinction between linguistic knowledge and other types of knowledge. Their work in semantics tries to look at **meaning** in a broad perspective, going beyond simple dictionary-type definitions of words and attempting to identify the whole range of mental experience associated with words and sentences when they are used in specific contexts.

Cognitive linguistics thus covers a number of frameworks, with radically different assumptions about the relationship between language and the mind. What they have in common is the belief that an exclusive concern with language is less useful than research which links language and other aspects of human experience: but the nature of that link remains contentious. (**RS**)

See also Jackendoff (this volume).

Further Reading

Johnson-Laird, P. (1993) *The Computer and the Mind: An Introduction to Cognitive Science*, 2nd edn, London: Collins.

Langacker, R. (1986) 'An introduction to cognitive grammar', *Cognitive Science* 10: 1–40.

Salkie, R. (1990) *The Chomsky Update: Linguistics and Politics*, London: Unwin Hyman.

COHESION The category of 'cohesion' deals with the formal elements and principles which make a collection of sentences into a **text**. These range from **pro(noun** or sentence) forms such as 'these' (at the beginning of this sentence), 'this' (as in the preceding two words), 'therefore'; text-organizing elements such as 'however'; to the repetition and/or substitution of lexical elements to form lexical chains; to the uses of **syntax** to fit a sentence (or part of a sentence – as in this parenthesis just now) to its specific place in the unfolding text. (**GRK**)

COMPETENCE A person's knowledge of a particular language, as opposed to **performance**, the actual use of a language in concrete situations. Someone who is competent in a language can normally speak and understand the language, but disability such as deafness may permanently impair or prevent some aspects of performance, and other factors (emotion, background noise, food in the mouth, etc.) may temporarily obstruct performance. It is a person's competence in a language which makes their use of that language possible, and which is fundamental in linguistics.

When we say 'the English language', then, we normally mean 'the particular system of linguistic knowledge that certain people have acquired, called English'. Dictionaries and **grammar**s of English aim to describe this competence accurately and explicitly, leaving aside performance factors as irrelevant. The distinction between competence and performance is very similar to **Saussure**'s separation of *langue* and *parole*, though Saussure puts more emphasis on the shared, social aspects of *langue*. It has sometimes been said that competence is mysterious and that only performance is concrete and observable: **Chomsky** argues, however, that competence is a straightforward notion and that explaining performance may be impossible in principle. (**RS**)

See also Salkie and Jackendoff (this volume).

Further Reading

Chomsky, N. (1965) *Aspects of the Theory of Syntax*, Cambridge, MA: MIT Press.

COMPONENT A **generative grammar** must have several components, notably a set of words (**lexicon**) and rules for combining them (**syntax**), pronouncing them (**phonology**) and interpreting them (**semantics**). A central research task for linguistics is to specify the division of labour between the different components. Different researchers have made the division in different places, with important empirical and theoretical consequences, leading to much productive debate. (**RS**)

CONATIVE One of the six fundamental functions given in the **Jakobson**ian **speech act**, determined by the addressee factor of the speech act. When the focus of the utterance is on the addressee, more salient forms of the conative function occur phonemically, grammatically or syntactically. Examples include vocative case and the imperative mood. (**EA**)

CONNOTATION A putative 'second-order meaning', often a 'cultural' one, complementing **denotation**. An apple is called 'green' because that is its colour when it is unripe. When 'green' is used of a person because he or she is unripe/immature, it has been used as a metaphor; it has been extended beyond its core meaning. Such uses lead to a 'penumbra' around the word, indicating its connotations. The distinction between denotation and connotation is especially associated with the work of **Barthes** and **Hjelmslev**. (**GRK**)

CONSONANT A speech sound in which the breath is obstructed, usually by the tongue, lips or teeth. The term is also used for letters which represent consonant sounds, but alphabets are unfortunately not always consistent: the word *law*, for instance, contains a consonant sound followed by a vowel sound, but is written with a final consonant letter *w* as if it contained three sounds. (**RS**)

See also VOWEL.

CONSTATIVE In the contrast constative–**performative**, the term 'constative' is used

174

to describe declarative utterances or statements, which can be said to be true or false. It was because of their dimension of truth or falsity that constatives formed the focus of attention for most philosophers of language before the advent of **speech act** theory. J. L. **Austin** showed, however, that just like performatives a constative or statement of fact can also be 'infelicitous' in ways unrelated to truth. For instance, 'All John's children are bald' violates the presupposition that John has children if pronounced in a context where John does not, in fact, have children. Similarly, 'The cat is on the mat' violates the implication that the speaker believes the cat to be on the mat if stated by someone who does not in fact hold such a belief. Finally, 'All the guests are French' entails that it is not the case that 'Some of the guests are not French' and would violate this entailment if followed by that second statement. (**JV**)

Further Reading

Austin, J. L. (1963) 'Performative-constative' (1958) in *Philosophy and Ordinary Language*, ed. C. E. Caton, Urbana, IL: University of Illinois Press, pp. 22–54.

CONVERSATION ANALYSIS The origins and much of current practice in Conversation Analysis (CA) reside in the sociological approach to language and communication known as ethnomethodology (Garfinkel 1974). Ethnomethodology means studying the link between what social actors 'do' in interaction and what they 'know' about interaction. **Social structure** is a form of order, and that order is partly achieved through talk, which is itself structured and orderly. Social actors have common-sense knowledge about what it is they are doing interactionally in performing specific activities and in jointly achieving communicative coherence. Making this knowledge about ordinary, everyday affairs explicit, and in this way finding an understanding of how society is organised and how it functions, is ethnomethodology's main concern (Garfinkel 1967; Turner 1974; Heritage 1984b).

Following this line of inquiry, CA views language as a form of social action and aims, in particular, to discover and describe how the organisation of social interaction makes manifest and reinforces the structures of social organisation and social institutions (see, e.g. Boden and Zimmerman 1991; Drew and Heritage 1992).

Hutchby and Wooffit, who point out that 'talk in interaction' is now commonly preferred to the designation 'conversation', define CA as follows:

> CA is the study of recorded, naturally occurring talk-in-interaction . . . Principally it is to discover how participants understand and respond to one another in their turns at talk, with a central focus being on how sequences of interaction are generated. To put it another way, the objective of CA is to uncover the tacit reasoning procedures and sociolinguistic competencies underlying the production and interpretation of talk in organized sequences of interaction.
>
> (1998, p. 14)

As this statement implies, the emphasis in CA, in contrast to earlier ethnomethodological concerns, has shifted away from the patterns of 'knowing' *per se* towards discovering the structures of talk which produce and reproduce patterns of social action. At least, structures of talk are studied as the best evidence of social actors' practical knowledge about them.

One central CA concept is preference, the idea that, at specific points in conversation, certain types of utterances will be more favoured than others (e.g. the socially preferred response to an invitation is acceptance, not rejection). Other conversational features which CA has focused on include: openings and closings of conversations; adjacency pairs (i.e. paired utterances of the type summons–answer, greeting–greeting, compliment–compliment response, etc.); topic management and topic shift; conversational repairs; showing agreement and disagreement; introducing bad news and processes of troubles-telling; (probably most centrally) mechanisms of turn-taking.

In their seminal paper, Sacks, Schegloff and Jefferson (1974) suggested a list of guiding principles for the organisation of turn-taking in conversation (in English). They observed that the central principle which speakers follow in taking turns is to avoid gaps and overlaps in conversation. Although gaps do of course occur, they are brief. Another common feature of conversational turns is that, usually, one party speaks at a time. In order to facilitate turn-taking, which usually takes place in 'the transition relevance places' (Sacks *et al.* 1974), speakers observe a number of conventionalised principles. For example, speakers follow well-established scripts, as in service encounters, in which speaker roles are clearly delineated. They fill in appropriate 'slots' in discourse structure, e.g. second part utterances in adjacency pairs, and they anticipate completion of an utterance on the basis of a perceived completion of a grammatical unit (a **clause** or a sentence). Speakers themselves may signal their willingness to give up the floor in favour of another speaker (who can be 'nominated' by current speaker only). They can do this by directing their gaze towards the next speaker and employing characteristic gesturing patterns synchronising with the final words. They may alter pitch, speak more softly, lengthen the last syllable or use stereotyped discourse **marker**s (e.g. *you know* or *that's it*). (**NC and AJ**)

Further Reading

Hutchby, I. and Wooffitt, R. (1998) *Conversation Analysis*, Cambridge: Polity Press.

Schegloff, E. A., Ochs, E. and Thompson, S. A. (1996) 'Introduction', in E. Ochs *et al.* (eds) *Interaction and Grammar*, Cambridge: Cambridge University Press.

Ten Have, P. (1999) *How to Do Conversation Analysis*, London: Sage.

CREOLE A language which results from extended contact between two languages, incorporating features from each and used as a native language. One of the languages involved is often a European colonial language (English, French, Portuguese, etc.), but this is not always the case. Many creoles have similarities, and experts disagree about why this is: some argue that different creoles have influenced each other, while others maintain that properties of Universal Grammar are responsible. (**RS**)

See also PIDGIN.

CYBERSPACE The term, cyberspace, was created by William Gibson in his 1984 novel, *Neuromancer*. It is a combination of two words: cybernetic and space. 'Space' is an extremely nebulous word with multiple significations best understood by reference to the concepts of **semiosis** and the semiotic web – the latter being an image coming from a spider's web which predates the Internet. Yet the very difficulty of grasping the **meaning**s of the word 'space' makes it ideal for the complex notion of cyberspace. The other component of the term cyberspace, 'cybernetics', comes from the Greek for navigating and controlling a vessel, especially a ship. In the mid-twentieth century it became associated with machines which can control themselves in some fashion, such as autopilots, robots, and computers. Thus by this derivation cyberspace is automated, automatic space which can direct and control itself.

Gibson did not intend this exact meaning, however. What he invented in his novel was a space computer 'hackers' traveled when they had connected their minds directly into a computer network. The virtual reality they lived in was rich enough and developed enough to be equivalent to 'real', sensory, reality. For Gibson and his hackers cyberspace is a 'space' which is the domain of (human/computer network-created) virtual reality. Yet by having his human characters link directly with this new space he bridged the gap between real and virtual so that they overlap. For some critics the concept of 'mind' best describes the consciousness humans apply to both virtual and non-virtual realities.

John Perry Barlow (1996) even goes so far as to describe cyberspace as the new home of Mind (his capitalization). He further describes it as 'an act of nature' and says that 'it grows itself through our collective actions'. For him 'Cyberspace consists of transactions, relationships, and thought itself, arrayed like a standing wave in the web of our communications. Ours is a world that is both everywhere and nowhere, but it is not where bodies live.'

Although Barlow defines cyberspace as a world and Mind, others define it as a community. In fact, the concept of a human community sharing a 'space' determined by computers and their networks is one which influences many critics of cyberspace. Mitch Kapor, founder of the Electronic Frontier Foundation, argues that virtual communities hold utopian possibilities when he says that 'life in cyberspace . . . at its best is more egalitarian than elitist, and more decentered than hierarchical'. Others are less sanguine. Sherry Turkle (1995) gives many negative descriptions of individuals' relationships to cyberspace while Ledgerwood (1995, 1997, 1998a, 1998b, 1999) has described how individuals relate to aspects and genres of this community/communal space which most feel to be at once intimate and distancing.

Thus to summarize, cyberspace is a semiotically understood series of **interpretants** which are created and received by humans communicating with each other and their computers via networks which combine to create a 'mind' and a 'community' not creatable in other ways. (**MDL**)

Further Reading

Ludlow, P. (ed.) (1996) *High Noon on the Electronic Frontier: Conceptual Issues in Cyberspace*, Cambridge, MA: MIT Press.

Rheingold, H. (1993) *The Virtual Community: Homesteading on the Electronic Frontier*, Reading, MA: Addison-Wesley Publishing Company.

Turkle, S. (1995) *Life on the Screen: Identity in the Age of the Internet*, New York: Simon & Schuster.

D

DEEP STRUCTURE In early versions of **generative grammar** the level of analysis before any transformations have applied. It was argued that the semantic **component** operated on deep structures. For instance, a sentence like *Ruby hopes to arrive on time* would have a deep structure of the form *Ruby hopes [Ruby arrives on time]*. This analysis makes it clear that it is Ruby who will arrive, even though *to arrive* has no subject next to it as **verb**s normally do. A transformation called Equivalent **Noun Phrase** Deletion (*equi*) deleted the second occurrence of *Ruby*, and changed *arrives* into *to arrive*.

Although popular outside mainstream generative grammar, this conception of deep structure was quickly abandoned by specialists, for various empirical and theoretical reasons. What remains is the notion that a sentence can be represented in a series of abstract ways, with rules linking the different levels of representation. **(RS)**

See also SURFACE STRUCTURE.

Further Reading

Chomsky, N. (1965) *Aspects of the Theory of Syntax*, Cambridge, MA: MIT Press.

DEIXIS Words which pick out features of the speech situation are called deictic words or are said to have the property of deixis, a Greek word for 'pointing'. They include *I* and *you* (referring to the speaker and hearer), *here* and *this* (referring to the place where the speaking occurs) and *now* (referring to the time of speaking). Deictic words are sometimes called 'shifters' (especially after **Jespersen** and **Jakobson**). **(RS)**

DENOTATION The term rests on a theory of language in which words are the names of phenomena in the world, and language is stable, so that relations of word to object are fixed. If **connotation** is the realm of cultural **meaning**s, then denotation is the phenomenon of 'pure' naming, theoretically devoid of culture's influence. Denotation names the appropriate relation of word to phenomenon; 'green', for example, names a specific area of the colour spectrum. **(GRK)**

See also CONNOTATION.

DENOTATUM 'Where what is referred to actually exists as referred to the object of reference is a denotatum' (Morris 1938, p. 5). For example, if the **sign** 'unicorn' refers to what it designates considering it as existent in the world of mythology, that sign has a denotatum since it exists in that world. If, on the other hand, the sign 'unicorn' refers to what it designates considering it as existent in the world of zoology, that sign does not have a denotatum since it does not exist in that world. In this case the sign has a designatum (ibid.) or a **significatum**, as **Morris** (1946) was later to call it, but it does not have a denotatum. 'It thus becomes clear that, while every sign has a designatum, not every sign has a denotatum.' Morris's distinction between designatum and denotatum avoids misunderstandings as regards the **referent**. In the triangular diagram of the sign proposed by **Ogden** and **Richards** (1923) the referent is always foreseen and forms one of the three apexes. On the contrary, in other **semantic** theories (cf. Eco 1975, 1984), the referent is eliminated given that what the sign refers to does not always exist as referred to by the sign in which case the desigatum is not taken into account.

As demonstrated by Augusto Ponzio (1981a, 1990b, 1997b; Ponzio *et al.* 1985), the sign always has a referent, or in Morris's terminology, a designatum, and if this referent exists as referred to by the sign, it also has a denotatum: the referent of 'Cheshire cat' in Lewis Carroll's *Alice in Wonderland* is a designatum as well as a denotatum; 'God' has a referent both as a designatum and denotatum for the believer, whereas in the proposition 'God does not exist', 'God' has a referent (otherwise the proposition would not make sense), but only as a designatum and not as a denotatum. (**SP**)

DERRIDA Jacques Derrida was born in Algeria in 1930, and studied philosophy at the École Normale Supérieure in Paris, where he has taught for many years. He first came to prominence in 1967 with the publication of *Writing and Difference* and *Of Grammatology*. These were followed by *Margins of Philosophy* and *Positions* (1972), *Glas* (1974) and *The Post Card* (1980). At the heart of Derrida's work is the analytic procedure known as deconstruction, which involves taking an opposition such as internal/external and turning it on its head in order to subvert the opposition. This procedure has been applied to two figures prominent in the field of linguistics, Ferdinand de **Saussure** and J. L. **Austin**.

Thus in 'Linguistics and grammatology' (1976), Derrida deconstructs Saussure's opposition between speech and writing. Saussure claimed that the object of the linguist's study should be spoken language, since writing exists for the sole purpose of representing language and, as such, is 'unrelated to [the] inner system' of language (Saussure [1916] 1974, p. 3). Here, says Derrida, Saussure is speaking for an entire metaphysical system going back to Plato, who privileged speech and *mneme*

(living memory) over writing and *hypomnesis* (the auxiliary aide-mémoire). What Saussure and this whole tradition refuse to recognise, says Derrida, is that it was only with the advent of phonetic writing that the concept of **sign** became thinkable (see also Ong 1982, p. 61), and that in fact all instituted **signifier**s, whether 'graphic' or phonic, are *written* signifiers. In this way Derrida overturns the opposition speech/writing by installing writing as the privileged term.

In 'Signature event context' Derrida (1982) deconstructs Austin's opposition between serious and non-serious **speech act**s. The deconstruction of Austin revolves round the philosopher's claim that a **performative** utterance can only be felicitous if the speaker intends to carry it out, and will be 'hollow or void if said by an actor on the stage', where language is not being used 'seriously' (Austin 1962, p. 22). Starting off with the premise that speech acts must necessarily be iterable (repeatable), Derrida goes on to claim that all speech acts are in a sense 'quotations' and therefore non-serious. He thereby subverts the opposition serious/non-serious by installing non-serious (that is, quoted) as the privileged term. He also challenges the role assigned by Austin to intentionality: if speech acts are quotations, then 'the intention which animates utterance will never be completely present in itself and in its content', given that the 'iteration which structures it introduces an essential dehiscence' (Derrida 1982, p. 326). Dehiscence is a botanical term meaning 'the bursting open of fruits in order to discharge their mature contents': for Derrida it is a metaphor for the process of making and interpreting **meaning**, since dehiscence leads to reproduction but 'limits what it makes possible', in a 'law of undecidable contamination' (1977, p. 197).

Derrida's deconstruction of Saussure finds echoes in the work of linguists who reject Saussurean dualisms; and his insistence that the making and interpreting of meaning are subject to a 'law of undecidable contamination' links him to those who seek to capture indeterminate aspects of language (see Firth 1957, p. 227; Halliday 1978, p. 51, 139; Lemke 1995, p. 180). (**RM**)

See also BINARISM.

Further Reading

Derrida, J. (1976) *Of Grammatology*, trans. G. C. Spivak, Baltimore and London: Johns Hopkins University Press.

Derrida, J. (1981) *Positions*, trans. A. Bass, Chicago: University of Chicago Press.

Derrida, J. (1982) *Margins of Philosophy*, trans. A. Bass, Chicago: University of Chicago Press.

DESCRIPTIVE LINGUISTICS The activity of recording the properties of languages accurately and concisely. Descriptive linguistics may be concerned with an individual language, or with a wide range of languages; in the latter case it is called typological linguistics. Contrastive linguistics, dealing with two or a small number of languages, falls in between.

Descriptive linguistics is often opposed to prescriptive linguistics, which tries to say how people *should* speak and write, rather than recording objectively how they *do* speak and write.

Another comparison is with theoretical linguistics, since descriptive linguists try to use only concepts that all linguists recognise, rather than concepts or rules which are only employed within a particular theory. Sometimes the distinction is hard to apply, since any piece of research in linguistics will have descriptive and theoretical content. Linguists who are interested in description will tend to present more data, often authentic examples of language use taken from tape recordings or from large samples of written texts. Linguists who are more theoretically inclined will be less interested in data collection for its own

sake, and more in finding evidence for the particular theory that they support.

Sometimes a contrast is made between descriptive and applied linguistics, which is the attempt to use insights from linguistics to improve language learning and teaching. (**RS**)

DESIGNATUM See **DENOTATUM** and **SIGNIFICATUM**.

DIACHRONIC, DIACHRONY The mainstream of linguistic thinking in the twentieth century was dominated by attempts to understand the interrelations of elements in a system, the relation of elements in structures and the relation between the system and the structures. It might be said to be **synchronic** in its orientation. Linguistic work in the preceeding century, by contrast, had been concerned with changes in systems (in languages, in 'families' of languages), the tracing of such changes, and the establishing of 'laws' that might be discovered underlying such changes. 'Grimm's Law', for instance, explained the link between voiceless plosive sounds – /p/, /t/, /k/ – and their equivalent fricatives, showing the relation between English *nut* and German *Nuss*. This was typical of a diachronic approach.

Major effort had gone into two areas in particular, the sound systems of (families of) languages, and the semantic changes of words. This work established beyond question the relatedness of groups of languages across Europe, the Middle East and the Indian sub-continent both over time and at particular periods (the relatedness of languages such as Italian, Portuguese, Spanish, Catalan, langue d'oc, Rumanian, and their common derivation from Latin).

One of the central issues for **semiotics** in the coming decades will be to simultaneously consider diachrony and synchrony: to connect the micro-histories of social interactions with the relative stabilities of representational systems, so that history is always seen as present in structure. (**GRK**)

DIALECT The term names systematic differences within one language in words and sounds, with less emphasis on **syntax**. In work deriving from nineteenth-century historical linguistics, dialect boundaries were established, as lines that can be drawn on a map showing the distribution of criterial words (e.g. 'the weakest member in a litter': 'runt'; or, in one German dialect, *Wurnagei*). On one side of the line the word is used, on the other it is not. Similar lines can be drawn for the sound systems of dialects (north of a line in England *France* is pronounced with a vowel sound as in *mat*, south of it with a sound as in *car*).

The distinction between what is a language and what is a dialect is always a political one (Fishman's dictum, for instance, that 'a language is a dialect with an army and a navy'). It rests on the state of affairs deriving from relative geographical stability of populations. Increasing mobility corrodes the integrity of (geographical and social) dialects. The mobility produced by the media and the advent of mass-literacy accelerates and deepens this process. Political power is often used to attempt to control, channel, and direct these processes, suppressing dialects, or even promoting dialects to languages. (**GRK**)

See also Harris (this volume) and SOCIOLINGUISTICS.

Further Reading

Chambers, J. K. and Trudgill, P. (1980) *Dialectology*, Cambridge: Cambridge University Press.

DIALOGUE External or internal **discourse** in which the word of the other, not necessarily in the second person, interferes with one's own word. It is also a discourse **genre**. Philosophers like Charles S. **Peirce** and Mikhail **Bakhtin** consider it as the modality itself of thought. For this reason, a distinction must be drawn between *substantial dialogicality* and purely formal *dialogicality*. Substantial dialogicality is not determined by the dialogic form of the text, *formal dialogicality*, but by the *degree of dialogicality* in that text which may or may not take the form of a dialogue. In other words, as shown by Augusto Ponzio (1994), substantial dialogicality is determined by the higher or lower degree of opening towards **alterity**.

Another distinction concerns verbal action, dialogue included, which from a pragmatic viewpoint may be considered as an end in itself, as carrying out an instrumental function, in which case it is a means to an end, or as determining and evaluating ends and means. On the basis of both distinctions, Bonfantini and Ponzio (1986) propose the following tripartite typology of dialogue:

(1) *Dialogue as an end in itself*, in other words, conversation or entertainment dialogue. This type of dialogue refers to talking for the sake of talking, to dialogue with a **phatic** function and may in turn be divided into

(1.1) *conformative-repetitive dialogue*; and

(1.2) *di-verting dialogue*.

An example of variant (1.1) is offered by certain forms of television communication which tends to be repetitive, obeying hyperdetermined compositional-instructional rules and just as hyperdetermined decoding processes.

(2) *Dialogue functional to attainment*, which may in turn be divided into: (2.1) *exchange dialogue*; and (2.2) *competition dialogue*.

(3) *Cooperative or reflective or investigative dialogue*. Using the

degree of substantial dialogicality as the criterion for differentiation, this type of dialogue may be classified (on an increasing scale in the degree of dialogicality) as:

(3.1) *re-discovery and revelation dialogue*;

(3.2) *research and construction dialogue*;

(3.3) *exploration and problematization dialogue* (on the relation between dialogue and truth, cf. Bonfantini, Ponzio and Petrilli 1996).

Dialogue may be tied to the logic of identity or open to displacement towards alterity. The second case moves away from what has been classified as attainment dialogue, where interlocutors aim at achieving an end, therefore, at maintaining and reconfirming identity. Dialogue is of central importance in argumentative reasoning, which is reasoning that is not fixed in terms of defense and reproduction of identity but rather is open and available to otherness. Mikhail Bakhtin has highlighted how unilaterality, ossification, rectilinear dialectics derives from sclerotized dialogue. Monological, unilinear and totalizing dialectics is oriented towards a given synthesis and conclusion and as such calls for, as demonstrated by Ponzio (1993), a critique of dialogic reason. That is critique of the category of Identity which dominates over Western thought and praxis today. (**AP**)

Further Reading

Bakhtin, M. M. (1981) *The Dialogic Imagination: Four Essays*, trans. C. Emerson and M. Holquist, Austin, TX: University of Texas Press.

DICENT A word introduced by Charles S. **Peirce** for the second division of his trichotomy of **signs** that concerns how they are interpreted. A dicent sign (or dicisign) is, or tends to be, interpreted as a sign of fact or actual existence. One of several kinds of dicent signs is the **proposition**, which combines a dicent element, tending to indicate the fact of the matter (subject), and a rhematic element, tending to describe it (predicate). (**NH**)

See also RHEME and ARGUMENT.

DIFFÉRANCE A term coined by the French philosopher Jacques **Derrida**, in his deconstruction of the linguist Ferdinand de **Saussure**. In his *Course in General Linguistics*, Saussure proposed that a basic principle in the study of language was the principle of difference, which states that 'concepts are purely differential and defined . . . by their relations with other terms of the systems' (Saussure [1916] 1974, p. 117). Derrida sees difference as static, and he seeks to transform it by introducing the term *différance* (in French both the act-of-differing and the act-of-deferring). Claiming that all **signifier**s are 'written' (even if they are spoken), Derrida uses the spacing between words in the written language as a metaphor for the process of making **meaning**: the spacing, he says, means that meaning is always deferred, by virtue of 'the very principle of difference which holds that an element functions or signifies . . . only by referring to another past or future element' (1981, pp. 28–9). *Différance* therefore is the 'systematic play of differences', which are 'neither fallen from the sky nor inscribed once and for all in a closed system' (ibid., p. 27). (**RM**)

Further Reading

Derrida, J. (1981) *Positions*, trans. A. Bass, Chicago: University of Chicago Press.

DIGLOSSIA The use of two languages within a community. Many communities use two (or more) languages in their everyday interactions. Monolingualism is the exception throughout the world (by something like 75:25 per cent). Where diglossia (or tri-glossia) exists, a 'high' and a 'low' form is often available, through switching between the two, to signal social **meaning**s of status and formality. (**GRK**)

DISCOURSE The word is used in two distinct though connected senses. One points to a **meaning** such as 'extended stretch of language'; the other points to the social organization of contents in use. The former is characteristic of linguistically oriented work; the latter of socially focused approaches. There is often considerable overlap between the two.

The linguistic approach focuses on formal properties of stretches of language *above* the level of the sentence, for instance, establishing frequencies of word use; of syntactic structures; of lexical collocations; of regularities of structures of the **text** itself; of above-sentence level units in the text (topic structures; paragraphs; (elements of) scripts; **genre**s; turn-taking structures in spoken interactions, etc.).

The linguistically focused approach goes back to work by Zellig **Harris** who realized that certain problems of structuralist linguistics could not be solved by reference to the sentence alone, but had to be explained by relations across sentence-boundaries. Inevitably this involved considerations of meaning, as well as the development by him of the formal concept of *transformation*.

In the socially focused approaches text (whether spoken or written) is the material site where socially produced meaning emerges. *Text* is the means of realizing non-material social meanings, in language or in other representational modes. *Discourse* is social; and text need not be linguistic.

In such approaches the social can be known only through its appearance in the text, the focus is on the social-discursive construction of the world. Broadly speaking, the aim is to discern and describe textual elements as indicators of social or social psychological entities such as *identity* and formations of identity (e.g. gendered identity); or *subjectivity*. The attempt is to uncover how discursive organization makes available – and suggests – particular 'inner' configurations which can form the basis of outwardly apparent entities such as what it is to be a 'proper' father, daughter, citizen, etc., and how it produces behaviours and structures which follow from such (inner) structures.

This work itself is influenced by the theories of Louis Althusser, for whom ideologies make appeals to individuals to assume certain positions; and to the theories of Michel Foucault, whose work showed the discursive constructions of potent social/historical categories. For Foucault such larger level constructs were produced in 'institutions' such as the legal system, the medical profession, the Church, Western science, which produced and projected statements which regulated the domain of their power.

One of the most extensive applications of this approach has been in the work of Edward Said, in particular in his book *Orientalism* (1995). Said shows how 'the West' has produced an all-encompassing discourse about 'the East', namely what it means to be 'oriental'. Work in a similar vein deals with issues of nationalism and racism. Approaches in which the linguistic/ textual and the social/ideological are brought closely together are those of 'Critical Discourse Analysis', in which linguistic and textual realization are seen as direct indicators of social/ideological organizations beyond them. (**GRK**)

See <u>Coupland and Jaworski</u> (this volume), DISCOURSE ANALYSIS and MEDIA DISCOURSE.

Further Reading

Schiffrin, D. (1994) *Approaches to Discourse*, Oxford: Blackwell.

DISCOURSE ANALYSIS With the emergence of the term **discourse** as a major explanatory category in the humanities and social sciences from the 1970s onward (Foucault's inaugural lecture 'Orders of discourse' was delivered in 1959), discourse analysis became a term often fashionably used for any work that concerned itself with **text**s in any form. It may be best to reserve the term for accounts of regularities of various kinds which can be made to be apparent in texts, as signs of social (or social-psychologial) organizations which are manifest in the text. These can be referred 'back' to institutions in which they originate. The approaches range from those which place more emphasis on linguistic/textual form to uncover the realization of social entities in discourse, to those which place emphasis on larger level structures of content often lexically manifested in a text. Discourse analysis is concerned equally with establishing the internal characteristics and constitutions of discourses; the relation of discourses with each other; and their social and psychological effects – in the constitution of subjectivities, identities, social orders, behaviours and practices. (**GRK**)

See Coupland and Jaworski (this volume), DISCOURSE, CONVERSATION ANALYSIS and HARRIS.

Further Reading

Gumperz, J. J. (ed.) (1982) *Language and Social Identity*, Cambridge: Cambridge University Press.

Jaworski, A. and Coupland, N. (eds) (1999) *The Discourse Reader*, London: Routledge.

Lee, D. (1992) *Competing Discourses*, London: Longman.

DISTINCTIVE FEATURE Technical term in linguistics for a property which serves to distinguish one unit from another of the same kind. In **phonology**, distinctive features are often said to be those in respect of which one **phoneme** differs from another phoneme of the same language. (**RH**)

DOUGLAS One of the most prolific of twentieth-century anthropologists, Mary Tew Douglas (b. 1921) was trained at Oxford University and did ethnography among the Lele of (the present) Zaire. The titles of just a few of her (sometimes co-authored) books index the range of her contributions to British **structuralism**: *Purity and Danger* (1966); *Natural Symbols* (introducing group/grid analysis) (1970); *The World of Goods* (1979); and *Risk and Culture* (1982). (**MA**)

E

Eco The international scholar of **semiotics**, expert on aesthetics, sharp observer of mass media and cultural phenomena, and best-selling novelist (*The Name of the Rose*, 1980; *Foucault's Pendulum*, 1988; *The Island of the Day Before*, 1994), Umberto Eco was born in Alessandria in 1932. He has attracted readers and critics around the world with every publication since his first polemical and innovative essay *The Open Work* (1989; *Opera aperta*, 1962).

Semioticians began to pay attention to Umberto Eco at the first international conference on semiotics, the **IASS** Congress in Milan, June 1974, where he was elected secretary of the association. In the preface to the Proceedings (*A Semiotic Landscape*, 1979), commenting on Roman **Jakobson**'s lecture Eco suggests that the history of philosophy could be read in terms of semiotics. He pursued this suggestion at the second congress of the IASS, in Vienna (1979), with a lecture on 'Historiography of semiotics'. This remains a fundamental axiom that can be traced throughout Eco's writings from *A Theory of Semiotics* (1975), and *Semiotics and the Philosophy of Language* (1984), to *The Search for the Perfect Language* (1997), and *Kant e l'ornitorinco* (1998; *Kant and the Platypus* 2000).

A student of philosophy and aesthetics under the guidance of L. Pareyson at the University of Turin, Eco's initial concerns with the production of signs and communication can be traced to his studies on media and popular culture in the early 1960s. His readings of Charles S. **Peirce** and Charles **Morris**, his collaboration with the eminent semiotician Thomas A.

Sebeok, and his enthusiasm for **Lotman**'s socio-semiotics, fueled his new concerns with **Barthes**' chains of **signifier**s, Peircean triadic relations between **sign** (**repre-sentamen**), **interpretant** and **object**, encyclopedia, **paradigmatic** structures, mechanisms of **abduction**, and the universe of intertextuality. This distancing from Saussurean **semiology**, Claude **Lévi-Strauss**' ontological **structuralism** (see in *The Open Work*, 'Series and Structure'), and, in general, from binary relations between signifier and **signified**, or between sign, **code** and dictionary **semantics**, leads Eco to embrace the notion of a theoretically infinite semiosic process of interpretation of signs and **text**s.

Eco's notion of encyclopedia slowly becomes a reformulation of the spectrum of code in terms of Peirce's notion of **unlimited semiosis**. And like Peirce's view that 'a sign is something by knowing which we know something more' (*CP* 8.332), Eco places less importance on the **referent** and more on the mental processes that follow in the dynamics of our perception of all signs demonstrating that indeed a sign stands for another sign. From the late 1960s onwards Eco, convinced that cultural phenomena are systems of signs, switched his focus from semiotics of communication to semiotics of **signification**, and from sign production and signification to inferential processes in the mechanisms of semiosis.

La struttura assente (1968, 'The absent structure'), documents this transition as it also deals with code, structure and aesthetics, and it lies at the foundation of *A Theory of Semiotics* ([1975] 1976). In *Semiotics and the Philosophy of Language* (1984)

Eco combines his observations on general theories with history of semiotics as he continues to discuss sign, metaphor, symbol, frames, **denotation** vs **connotation**, and encyclopedia. In *Kant and the Platypus*, referring mainly to the works of **Kant** and Peirce, as he elaborates on semiotic issues of perception, categories, awareness, cultural experience, mental associations, and interpretation, Eco revises some of his own earlier theoretical formulations stressing that abduction is the key inferential process that regulates our activities of cognition, logic and interpretation.

Beginning with the essay 'Segno' (1973, 'Sign') Eco investigates the history of philosophy of language as he reconstructs the science of signs and the relationships between sign and thought from ancient writers (from Plato to St **Augustine**), to medieval times (**Ockham** and Bacon), through the seventeenth century (Hume, Wilkins and **Locke**), and to modern thinkers like Kant, Peirce and **Wittgenstein**. His historical research follows his belief that our perception and interpretation of signs are based on a series of inferences (abductions) which go beyond the linear relation of signifier and signified and that a sign does not follow the equation 'a = b' but rather the relation 'a' stands for '_' (Eco 1984).

Throughout his work Eco shows that semiotics, rather than a discipline or a theory, is an interdisciplinary field and an ongoing process of cognition based on the active intervention of our experience and encyclopedic competence (our overall culture). He also maintains that we often rely on ready-made 'frames' (scenes and fragments of our encyclopedia) for our inferences. In his essays, as in his fiction, readers can appreciate how Eco combines linguistics and cognitive sciences, and philosophy and literary theories in order to demonstrate the interrelation of all signs. In so doing he adopts metaphors of libraries, labyrinths, rhizomes, and of the encyclopedia for the interpretation of signs, texts, and cultural events in general.

Eco's overwhelming interdisciplinary competence combined with his talent for making witty observations and analogies, for recalling fascinating anecdotes, and for exploiting intertextual echoes, make his theoretical and scientific essays always informative and entertaining at the same time, as is his fiction. (**RC**)

See also OPEN TEXT and CLOSED TEXT.

Further Reading

Caesar, M. (1999) *Umberto Eco: Philosophy, Semiotics and the Work of Fiction*, Oxford: Polity Press.

Capozzi, R. (ed.) (1997) *Reading Eco: An Anthology*, Bloomington: Indiana University Press.

Eco, U. (1986) *Semiotics and the Philosophy of Language*, Bloomington: Indiana University Press.

ELABORATED CODE The terms elaborated and **restricted code** were developed by Basil **Bernstein** in the late 1950s and 1960s. They point to two central phenomena: one is that the characteristics of the social environment of speakers lead to particular orientations towards their language. The second is that the relative stability of the characteristics of the social environment tends to habitual uses which become settled as **code**. Bernstein, in somewhat later work, spoke of the *coding-orientation* of language users, a particular stance towards the resources of the linguistic system overall.

The code-user is therefore not excluded from other uses of the linguistic system but is seen to have a disposition towards the resources overall, which leads to strongly preferred selections. The social environment of users of the elaborated code is such that addressees of writing or speech cannot be relied upon to share the knowledge of the writer/speaker, so that more knowledge needs to be made explicit in the utterance than it might be for members of groups who share more of the relevant knowledge. Expression of more knowledge and therefore more complex structures requires greater 'elaboration' in the use of language – more elaborate **syntax**, and more elaborate lexis: an elaborated code. (**GRK**)

Further Reading

Bernstein, B. (1970) *Class, Codes and Control*, vol. 1, London: Routledge and Kegan Paul.

EMBEDDING When one **clause** forms part of another clause it is said to be embedded in the larger clause. For instance, in the sentence *I know that you are my friend*, the clause *that you are my friend* is the object of the **verb** *know*, and is thus embedded in the larger clause. (**RS**)

EMPTY SPEECH According to Freud (1905), the existence of a number of 'full' or 'empty' senses of a word is a philological effect. The 'emptiness' of a word can be countermanded by giving it access to a new, or surprising, associative connection: there are contexts in which words lose their 'full **meaning**', only to regain it by being provided with other connections. 'Take a bath', says Freud, has both a full meaning, and an empty one. The movement from one meaning to the other gives access to the unconscious, via the functioning of a joke – 'Have you taken a bath?' 'Why, is there one missing?'. Freud claims that customary or fixed opinions or meanings can be shifted so as to acquire a fuller sense

by techniques equivalent to those used in joking: an equivocation or a play on words then constitutes an effective form of psychoanalytical technique.

Like Freud, **Lacan** considers empty speech (*la parole vide*) in its relation to a deeper speech, which is 'fuller'. He equates the movements from empty to **full speech** with the 'psychoanalytic realisation of the subject'. For most of the 1950s, the terms 'realisation of full speech' and 'realisation of subjectivity' were interchangeable elements of his theory of psychoanalytical technique. (**BB**)

See also LOCUTION and POLYSEMY.

Further Reading

Freud, S. (1960) *Jokes and their Relation to the Unconscious* (1905) in *The Standard Edition of the Complete Psychological Works of Sigmund Freud*, vol. VIII, London: Hogarth Press.

EPICUREANS See **STOICS** and **EPICUREANS**.

EXPRESSION Expressions are the linguistic forms uttered in the performance of propositional acts (proper names, **pronoun**s, **noun**s and **noun phrase**s for referring, and grammatical predicates for predicating) or in the performance of **illocution**ary acts (typically complete sentences). It is in relation to these forms that '**meaning**' can be defined. Often (e.g. in Searle 1969) the link between expressions and meaning is formulated in a 'principle of expressibility' which holds that whatever can be meant can be said. (**JV**)

See also PROPOSITIONS.

FIELD One of three linked terms (the other being **mode** and **tenor**) in the theory of **register**. Field describes the social practices which are the focus of a linguistic (inter)action, spoken or written: on what is, on who acts, who is involved, and on the attendant relevant circumstances. **(GRK)**

FIRSTNESS Firstness is the name given to one of the three categories of phenomena in the universe identified by Charles S. **Peirce**, the other two being **secondness** and **thirdness** (see <u>Merrell</u>, this volume). Firstness helps to explain logico-cognitive processes and therefore, at once, the formation of **sign**s. Analysed in terms of Peirce's typology of signs, firstness coincides with the sphere of **icon**icity. Something which presents itself as firstness, presence, 'suchness', pure quality is characterised by the relation of similarity (cf. *CP* 1.356–358). As demonstrated by Petrilli (1999), firstness is also foreseen by Edmund Husserl's phenomenology of perception and predicative judgment, though his terminology is different.

In *Erfahrung und Urteil* Husserl analyses 'passive predata' as they originally present themselves to perception by abstracting from all qualifications of the known, of familiarity with what affects us. His analyses reveal that similarity plays an important role at the level of indeterminate perception as well. In fact, if, by way of abstraction, we leave aside reference to the already known **object** which produces the sensation (secondness, **index**icality), and from familiarity through **habit** and convention, where what affects us exists as

already given (thirdness, conventionality, **symbol**icity) and as already known in some respect even though it is unknown to us, we end up in pure chaos, as says Husserl, in a mere confusion of data. When colour is not perceived as the colour of a thing, of a surface, as a spot on an object, etc., but as pure quality, or, in Peirce's terminology, when we are in the sphere of firstness where something refers to nothing but itself and is significant in itself, this something eventually emerges as a unit through processes of *homogeneity*. As such it contrasts with something else, that is, with the heterogeneity of other data, for example, red on white. Similarity at the level of primary iconism, that is, of the original, primitive phase in the formation of the sign as an icon, determines homogeneity which stands out against heterogeneity: 'homogeneity or similarity', says Husserl, is achieved to varying degrees through to complete homogeneity, to equality without differences. We could state that similarity is what makes the synthetic unification of firstness or primary iconism possible.

Primary association has nothing psychological about it. Here Husserl's antipsychologism encounters Peirce's. Transcendental primary association is a condition of possibility for the constitution of the **sign**.

By virtue of the dimension of firstness, the dynamical object is not exhausted in the identity of the immediate object, but, as the **ground**, that is as the primary icon, it imposes itself on the **interpretant** over and over again (*immer wieder*, Husserl would say), as its irreducible otherness.

We may only reach this original level of firstness, of primary iconism, by way of abstraction. This involves either a *phenomenological reduction* of the *epoché*, according to Husserl; that is, bracketing the already given world and relative interpretive habits, or an artistic vision. As Maurice Merleau-Ponty shows in relation to Cézanne, painting is the search for the other constrasting habitual attitudes towards familiar objects and conventions.

The painting of Cézanne returns to a perceptual relation where the category of firstness, as understood by Peirce, dominates almost completely, 'à donner l'impression d'un ordre naissant, d'un objet en train d'apparaître, en train de s'agglomérer sous nos yeux' (Merleau-Ponty 1966, p. 25). And agglomeration occurs through associative processes based on similarity. (**SP**)

See also REPRESENTAMEN.

Further Reading

Peirce, C. S. (1955) 'The principles of phenomenology', in J. Buchler (ed.) *Philosophical Writings of Peirce*, New York: Dover.

Peirce, C. S. (1958) 'Letter to Lady Welby, 12 October 1904', in P. Wiener (ed.) *Charles S. Peirce: Selected Writings*, New York: Dover.

Petrilli, S. (1999d) 'About and beyond Peirce', *Semiotica*, 124 (3/4), 299–376.

FIRTH John Rupert Firth (1890–1960), English linguist. Like **Halliday**, **Bernstein** and, later, **Kress**, he was to become associated with the colleges comprising the University of London, first at University College and then at the School of Oriental and African Studies where he was Professor of General Linguistics. He also spent nine years as a professor of English at the University of Punjab. Scrutiny of his later papers from the 1950s in particular, will reveal convincing reasons for his influence on the British tradition of **sociolinguistics**. While, as a linguist, he took the abstract nature of **synchrony** very seriously, he was most concerned with the **meaning** and import of utterances for languages' users. In this, his work follows a similar path to that of his student, Halliday, and that of the Russian theorist, **Vološinov**. Even more pointedly, however, he pursued his studies through examples of language use or text varieties specific to given situations, that is to say through **registers**. His focus on speech events was guided by many principles which have become virtually axiomatic of post-Hallidayan approaches to language and communication. One example of this might be Firth's particularly prescient formulations regarding the status of 'context' in relation to language use, made prior to the crystallization of both **pragmatics** and sociolinguistics (cf. Kress, this volume). (**PC**)

Further Reading

Firth, J. R. (1968) *Selected Papers of J. R. Firth, 1952–1959*, ed. F. R. Palmer, London: Routledge and Kegan Paul.

FULL SPEECH The movement from empty to full speech for **Lacan** gives access to the dependency of the child on the **discourse** of the other. In analytical treatment the subject is directed towards full speech. The aim of interpretation is to outwit the ego, to sidestep its imposition of a more stereotypical speech by means of equivocations, allusiveness, and effects of surprise – to obtain a response that contains full speech. Lacan assumes that full speech is not easily acquired. Being able to recognise what is wanting in relation to the mother, the assumption of full speech is an experience of pain.

Lacan distinguishes two directions: the first is that of the ego-to-ego (or imaginary relationship) – a field of empty speech and its misrecognitions of being. The other is that of 'the direction of the treatment': it aims to bring into play and analyse the broken and lost love relations of childhood. The movement towards full speech is able to take on this assumption of loss in relation to the most cherished love object: it therefore includes within it the structure of these Oedipal relationships, and the consequences of the loss of the primary object of love. **(BB)**

See also EMPTY SPEECH and ILLOCUTION.

Further Reading

Lacan, J. (1977) 'The function and field of speech in psychoanalysis' (1953), in *Écrits: A Selection*, trans. A. Sheridan, London: Tavistock, pp. 30–113.

G

GENERATIVE GRAMMAR A description of a language which is formal and explicit: one which does not rely on the linguistic knowledge of the human being who reads or writes the **grammar**. Generative rules are a convenient notation for writing grammars. In mathematics a sct is said to be generated by the rules which specify it: for instance, the rule 'include months of the year which end in *-ember*' generates the set {September, November, December}. In the same way, the rule 'Put adjectives in front of nouns' generates a set of expressions including *nice meal*, *happy hour*, *fervent believer* and many others in English. For **Chomsky**, a generative grammar of a particular language is interesting if it is a step towards a theory of **Universal Grammar** for all languages. **(RS)**

GENERATIVE SEMANTICS A controversial tendency in linguistics which flourished in the USA in the late 1960s but gradually declined in influence. The disagreement began with a technical dispute about the nature of **deep structure**, which some linguists thought was unnecessary because it was simply the same as **meaning**. As the issues broadened, the emphasis in generative semantics was increasingly on questions of meaning rather than **syntax**, with many arguments put forward that meaning influenced grammatical form. Some generative semanticists claimed that the beliefs and presuppositions of speakers also had a role in **grammar**. Generative semantics was strongly opposed by **Chomsky** and led to a great deal of angry controversy, most of it now of purely historical interest. **(RS)**

Further Reading

Harris, R.A. (1993) *The Linguistic Wars*, New York: Oxford University Press.

GENRE The term has a history reaching back to **Aristotle**, who named prominent literary forms and their textual characteristics. This usage has informed much of the debate in the intervening centuries, establishing the salient textual forms of literary production. Since the 1970s the term has enjoyed an enormous resurgence, in two distinct directions: in the description and naming of new and largely 'popular' forms (popular print fiction, and filmic texts, for instance, the 'Western'), and in the description of all textual production as conforming to regularities. In part, the popularity of the term is a recognition of the social and cultural origin of textual form, as a 'realization' of the features of the social environment in which it has been produced.

The theoretical interest dates back to the late 1970s and the early 1980s. Two strands are discernible: one in which the term genre is used as a near synonym for **text**, that is, genre describes all the relevant features which characterize text. The other treats genre as one of the constitutive categories of text, that is, it sees the text as the product of several distinct social factors.

Genre work of both kinds has been developed in Australia, in Canada and in the USA. Where genre is taken to equal text, emphasis tends to be placed on the overall shape and structure of the text. The narrative is a well-known instance. Or, in a job interview for instance, there are the opening welcoming remarks by the chair of the meeting; the introduction of members of the panel; the thanks to the applicant for attending the interview; the series of questions/answers in turn; the invitation by the chairing member to the interviewee to put questions to the panel, and the concluding remarks. These constitute a relatively stable structure, so much so that it is possible to prepare for, and to provide training in 'interview techniques'. The structures are of relative stability only: job interviews in 2001 are very different from those in 1981.

Genre responds to the changing social structures, of which it is a realization. In genres power is not evenly or equitably distributed, so that the means for alteration are unequal and attended by unequal risk of sanctions. Genres make available specific 'positions' for its participants (e.g. the interviewer, the interviewee), which they may – given the constraints of power – simply adopt, may attempt to change, or may reject entirely.

There is some irony in the fact that the newly intense interest in genre comes at a time when the very constitution and stability of genres have come under the severest pressure. The current period is characterized much more by blurring of generic boundaries, by the dissolution and corrosion of stable types (the interview which becomes a 'chat', the advertisement which has become indistinguishably blended with the feature article) than by the (relative) stability of genres which had characterized the immediately preceding period. This is a reflection of the questions posed by new distributions of power in the contemporary period. (**GRK**)

Further Reading

Altman, R. (1999) *Film/Genre*, London: BFI.

Bakhtin, M. M. (1986) *Speech Genres and Other Late Essays*, trans. by V. McGee, ed. C. Emerson and M. Holquist, Austin, TX: University of Texas Press.

Kress, G. and van Leeuwen, T. (1996) *Reading Images: The Grammar of Visual Design*, London: Routledge.

GESTURE 'Gesture' usually refers to any visible bodily action expressing thought or feeling or that plays a role in symbolic action. Although it cannot be precisely defined, actions considered as 'gesture' are commonly regarded as 'voluntary,' at least to a degree. Such actions range from the informal to the highly formalized. Included are the hand, head and face movements that often accompany speech; bodily actions employed to convey something when speech is impossible; codified forms such as the 'OK' gesture, 'thumbs up' and 'V for victory' gesture; handshakes, embraces, and the like, that play a role in greeting and other interaction rituals. The manual and facial actions of **sign language**s such as those found in communities of the deaf (primary sign languages) (e.g. Klima and Bellugi 1979) or in tribal communities such as certain groups of Australian Aborigines (Kendon 1988) or of Native Americans (alternate sign languages) (Mallery [1881] 1972; Farnell 1995) are also part of 'gesture' but today often receive separate, specialized treatments. Also to be included are the complex gestural systems found in some dance traditions, especially in India; actions in religious ritual such as those performed by priests in celebrating mass or the mudras used in prayer in Tantric Buddhism.

The earliest systematic treatment of gesture in the West is by Quintilian (1924) who discussed it in his treatise on **rhetoric** from the first century. Gesture is discussed in books on courtly etiquette in the sixteenth century. In the seventeenth century many books on the art of gesture in rhetoric and in acting were published (Barnett 1987). Representative are Bonifacio's *L'arte dei cenni (Art of Signs)* (1616),

Bulwer's *Chirologia* and *Chironomia* (1644), Austin's *Chironomia* (1806), J. J. Engel's *Ideen zu einer Mimik* (1756). Gesture was of great interest to the philosophers of the French Enlightenment for what it might reveal about the original nature of language (Seigel 1969; Wells 1987). It was also seen as a possible basis for a universal language (Knowlsen 1965). In the nineteenth century, anthropologists such as Edward Tylor (1865) and Garrick Mallery ([1881] 1972) considered inquiries into gesture important for questions about language evolution.

Today, students of cognition and language examine the relationship between gesture and speech for what may be learned about the thought processes underlying the production of utterances. Gestures used simultaneously with speech are deemed to express aspects of **meaning** not manifest in words and reveal a fuller view of a speaker's concpetualizations (McNeill 1992). The study of the processes by which gestures can become conventionalized and systematized when used apart from speech, as in the elaborate gesture vocabularies found in some cultures (e.g. southern Italy) or in language systems fashioned in gesture such as sign languages, provides insight into the origins and development of symbol formation and the organization and origin of language (Armstrong *et al.* 1995). Gesture is also of interest to students of the history of the culture of everyday life, who study gestures and bodily expression in sculptures, paintings, prints, and the like, for the clues this can provide for an understanding of the expressive practices of the past (Bremmer and Roodenberg 1992). There is also interest in gesture in computer science, both in relation to attempts to develop computers that can respond to the gestures of users and in relation to the development of animated robots. (**AK**)

See also <u>Sebeok</u> (this volume) and KINESICS.

Further Reading

Calbris, G. (1990) *Semiotics of French Gesture*, Bloomington: Indiana University Press.
Kendon, A. (1997) 'Gesture', *Annual Review of Anthropology* 26: 109–28.
McNeill, D. (1992) *Hand and Mind*, Chicago: Chicago University Press.

GRAM See *DIFFÉRANCE.*

GRAMMAR The term 'grammar' has a range of definitions, all of which revolve around the process of systematization in language. Generally, grammar means the rules which are employed in the construction of language structures such as words (see **morphology**) or sentences (see **syntax**). These rules can, on the one hand, be the precise systems which have to be learnt as a child at school and which have been the subject of prescriptions since the teachings of the classical period, and through the 'general' grammar provided during the Enlightenment by the **Port-Royal** scholars. On the other hand, and increasingly following the work of **Chomsky**, the rules have been understood to constitute an 'internalised' capacity for language in humans. In this formulation, the capacity to observe certain syntactical rules is thought to be innate or contained within the genetic **code** passed down to successive generations of humans as a **Universal Grammar**. However, it should be remembered that post-Chomskyan linguistics also identifies rules in languages which are not innate but are sufficiently systematic to allow prescriptions to invariably be effective. Such **generative grammar**s make it possible to write textbooks describing the rules of national languages. Somewhat confusingly, such accounts are often themselves called a 'grammar'. (**PC**)

Further Reading

Crystal, D. (1996) *Rediscover Grammar*, 2nd edn, Harlow: Longman.

GREIMAS Algirdas Julien Greimas (1917–92) was a French semanticist and semiotician. Born in Russia, A. J. Greimas studied law in Kaunas (Lithuania) before enrolling at the University of Grenoble, France, where, before the Second World War, he focused on the language and literature of the Middle Ages. He obtained a first university degree with a specialization in Franco-Provencal dialectology. He enrolled for his military service in Lithuania in 1939 and escaped to France in 1944 when his country was invaded and occupied by the Soviets for the second time, after three years of German occupation (1941–44). He enrolled at the Sorbonne University in Paris. There he obtained his State Doctorate in 1948 with a primary thesis on fashion in France in 1830, a lexicological study of the vocabulary of dress as depicted in the journals of the times, and a secondary thesis, based on the analysis of the various aspects of social life of this same period. Greimas taught the history of the French language at the University of Alexandria, Egypt, where he met Roland **Barthes**, before taking up appointments at the Universities of Ankara and Istanbul, Turkey and Poitiers, France. He was elected to the École Pratique des Hautes Études in Paris in 1965, where he directed a yearly seminar in **semiotics** that attracted a large number of graduate students and professors from France and abroad. This seminar, which continues to be held today by his students and colleagues, subsequently evolved into the Paris School of Semiotics.

Greimas proposed an original method for **discourse analysis** that evolved over a thirty-year period. His starting point began with a profound dissatisfaction with the structural linguistics of the mid-century that studied only **phonemes** (minimal sound units of every language) and **morphemes** (grammatical units that occur in the combination of phonemes). These grammatical units could generate an infinite number of sentences, the sentence remaining the largest unit of analysis. Such a molecular model did not permit the analysis of units beyond the sentence.

Greimas begins by positing the existence of a **semantic** universe that he defined as the sum of all possible **meanings** that can be produced by the value systems of the entire culture of an ethno-linguistic community. As the semantic universe cannot possibly be conceived of in its entirety, Greimas was led to introduce the notion of semantic micro universe and discourse universe, as actualized in written, spoken or **icon**ic texts. To come to grips with the problem of **signification** or the production of meaning, Greimas had to transpose one level of language (the **text**) into another level of language (the metalanguage) and work out adequate techniques of transposition (Greimas 1987).

The descriptive procedures of narratology and the notion of narrativity are at the very base of Greimassian semiotics. His initial hypothesis is that meaning is only apprehensible if it is articulated or narrativized. Second, for him narrative structures can be perceived in other systems not necessarily dependent upon natural languages. This leads him to posit the existence of two levels of analysis and representation: a surface and a deep level, which forms a common trunk where narrativity is situated and organized anterior to its manifestation. The signification of a phenomenon does not therefore depend on the mode of its manifestation, but since it originates at the deep level it cuts through all forms of linguistic and non-linguistic manifestation. Greimas' semiotics, which is generative and transformational, goes through three phases of development. He begins by working out semiotics of action where subjects are defined in terms of their quest for objects, following a canonical narrative schema, which is a formal framework made up of three successive sequences: a mandate, an action and an evaluation. He then constructs a narrative grammar and works out a syntax of narrative programs in which subjects are joined up with or separated from objects of value. In the second phase he works out a cognitive semiotics, where in order to perform, subjects must be competent to do so. The subjects' competence is organized by means of a modal **grammar** that accounts for their existence and performance. This modal semiotics opens the way to the final phase that studies how passions modify actional and cognitive performance of subjects and how belief and knowledge modify the competence and performance of these very same subjects. The challenge ahead lies in working out adequate and necessary descriptive procedures not only of the modal but also of the aspectual features of cognitive and passional discourse: for example, aspects such as inchoativity (the beginning of an action), durativity (the unravelling of an action) and terminativity (the end of an action) that allow for the description of temporality as processes in texts. (**PP**)

Further Reading

Greimas, A. J. (1987) *On Meaning: Selected Writings in Semiotic Theory*, trans. and ed. P. Perron and F. Collins, Minneapolis: University of Minnesota Press.

Perron, P. and Collins, F. (eds) (1989) *Greimassian Semiotics*, *New Literary History*, 20.3 [Speical Issue].

Schleifer, R. (1987) *A. J. Greimas and the Nature of Meaning*, Lincoln, NB: University of Nebraska Press.

GRICE A philosopher of language, H. Paul Grice (1926–85) started his career in the tradition of **ordinary language** **philosophy** while working with **Austin** at Oxford in the 1940s and 1950s. With relatively few publications during his lifetime, he exerted an unparalleled influence on the theory of **meaning**. He introduced a distinction between 'natural' meaning (as in 'Clouds mean rain') and 'non-natural' meaning (or linguistic meaning). Though allowing for the existence of conventional meaning associated with linguistic expressions (some of which may be implicit rather than explicit, as when the expression 'the US President' logically implies that we are talking about 'a US President'), Grice devoted most of his attention to those types of non-natural meaning dependent on the utterer rather than on the structure of words and sentences; hence the term 'utterer's meaning' in contrast to 'sentence meaning' and 'word meaning' (Grice 1957, 1968, 1969). Utterer's meaning, which is occasion-specific in contrast to the 'timeless' sentence and word meaning, is further defined in terms of the speaker's intentions (without denying that some forms of meaning are simply expressed without being intended): utterer meaning is the speaker's intention in the making of an utterance to produce an effect in the hearer by means of the hearer's recognition of the intention to produce that effect.

Observing that utterances, more often than not, mean more than what is literally said, Grice probes into implicit meaning beyond the realm of logical implications (Grice 1975, 1978, 1981). According to Grice, conversations are typically governed by a 'co-operative principle' which says: 'Make your conversational contribution such as is required, at the stage at which it occurs, by the accepted purpose and direction of the talk exchange in which you are engaged' (1975, p. 45). In keeping with this principle, a number of 'maxims of conversation' guide conversational interaction:

1   *The maxim of quantity*: (i) Make your contribution as informative as is

required for the current purposes of the exchange; (ii) Do not make your contribution more informative than is required.

2 *The maxim of quality*: Try to make your contribution one that is true: (i) Do not say what you believe to be false; (ii) Do not say that for which you lack adequate evidence.

3 *The maxim of relation* (later called *relevance*): Be relevant.

4 *The maxim of manner*: Be perspicuous:
   (i) Avoid obscurity of expression;
   (ii) Avoid ambiguity; (iii) Be brief;
   (iv) Be orderly.

Assuming that these maxims are normally adhered to, utterances give rise to conventional or standard conversational implicatures: thus the statement 'It is raining outside' implicates, on the basis of the maxim of quality, that the speaker believes that it is raining outside (an implicature that reflects the sincerity condition of an assertive **speech act**). Often, however, the maxims are obviously broken. But since interlocutors are supposed to be co-operative, any obvious breach of a maxim will lead to further (non-conventional) conversational implicatures. Thus, in Grice's classical example, the response 'There's a garage round the corner' in response to 'I am out of petrol', because it does not adhere to the maxim of quantity, but because co-operativity is assumed, will implicate that the garage has petrol for sale and is open. (**JV**)

See also RULES and SEMANTICS.

Further Reading

Grice, H. P. (1989) *Studies in the Way of Words*, Cambridge, MA: Harvard University Press.

Leech, G. N. (1983) *Principles of Pragmatics*, London: Longman.

Levinson, S. C. (1983) *Pragmatics*, Cambridge: Cambridge University Press.

GROUND A term introduced by Charles S. **Peirce** to denote 'some respect or capacity' on the basis of which something becomes a **sign** or **representamen** (in other words, stands for something else, an object), thanks to another sign which serves as **interpretant**. In fact, the something which serves as a sign does not stand for the object in all respects but in reference to a particular respect or capacity or, as Peirce also says, 'in reference to a sort of idea' (*CP* 2.228). This is the fundamental idea that forms the ground of the representamen. Therefore, this something in its indeterminacy is gradually determined under a certain respect, thanks to which it becomes a sign for an interpretant. If, to recall an example made by Peirce, I say 'This stove is black', the immediate **object** 'stove' is assumed in a certain respect, its 'blackness', which is the ground of the interpretant (cf. *CP* 1.551). From the point of view of the phenomenology of perception (Husserl, Merleau-Ponty) the ground is something which was undifferentiated and is now differentiated in a certain respect, thereby becoming a sign for an interpretant. (**SP**)

H

HABIT An acquired propensity or disposition to act in a regular way in familiar circumstances. Generally the result of repeated uniform reactions or responses, whether physical or intellectual, to events or experiences of the same kind. Instincts may be regarded as natural habits and in the cosmology of Charles S. **Peirce** and others even laws of nature are said to be habits. Habitual responses are usually made involuntarily, without reflection or conscious decision-making, and thus are not subject to immediate self-control; but habits can be intentionally changed by a controlled regimen of behavior repatterning. The role of habit is of key importance in Peirce's philosophy. According to Peirce, beliefs are habits of action produced by inferential processes. He also held that the final effect of **semiosis**, which he called the final **interpretant**, is an intellectual habit, which, although not itself a sign, culminates a process of intellectual refinement through adjustment to experience. This is a central tenet of Peirce's **pragmaticism**. (**NH**)

See GROUND, ICON, INDEX, SYMBOL.

Further Reading

Peirce, C. S. (1905a) 'What pragmatism is,' and (1907) 'Pragmatism', in C. S. Peirce (1998) *The Essential Peirce: Selected Philosophical Writings*, vol. 2, (ed.) Peirce Edition Project, Bloomington: Indiana University Press, pp. 331–45 and pp. 398–433.

HALLE Morris Halle (b. 1923), Professor of Slavic and general linguistics at the Massachusetts Institute of Technology (MIT). Best known as one of the founders of generative **phonology**, he co-authored with **Jakobson** *Fundamentals of Language* (1956) in which their celebrated discussion of **phoneme**s, **distinctive feature**s, aphasia, similarity disorder, contiguity disorder, metaphor and **metonymy** appears. His other works include *The Sound Pattern of Russian* (1959) and *The Sound Pattern of English* (1968 with Noam **Chomsky**). (**EA**)

HALLIDAY The work of Michael Halliday (b. 1925) is the major contemporary alternative to the domination of linguistic thinking by **structuralist** approaches. While structuralists have focused on the **syntagmatic** plane, Halliday focuses predominantly on the **paradigmatic**. 'Meaning is choice in context' is his restatement of a major tenet of **Saussure**. It shapes the impact of his thinking: placing emphasis equally on the actor who makes choices from the resources of the linguistic system, and does so in palpably present contexts. In this there is more than an echo of **Marx** and Engels' 'Men make their own history but not in conditions of their own choosing.'

The system-structure theory of J. R. **Firth**, his teacher, shaped his early work, as in the seminal 'Categories of the theory of grammar' (1961), as have the functionalist approaches to language of the anthropologist Bronislaw Malinowski. The three functions which Halliday posits as inhering in every fully functioning semiotic system – the function to represent events and states of affairs in the world (the **ideational** function), the function to represent the social relations between participants in an interaction (the **interpersonal** function), and the function to represent a coherent account of the world of the message (the **textual** function) – are close echoes of Malinowski. His work is equally influenced by his close knowledge of Chinese gained during a stay in Beijing (1949–51) as a student at that university. The notions of *theme*, of *mood*, and of *transitivity*, as much as his work on the organization of (English) speech, in particular the place of intonation in English (as grammatical and textual), owe most to a perspective from within Chinese.

Three articles published between 1967 and 1969 (in the new *Journal of Linguistics*) 'Transitivity and theme in English' marked a decisive move from the earlier equal emphasis on system and structure and their interrelation, to an emphasis on function: transitivity in the clause as the core of the *ideational function*; mood as the core of the *interpersonal function*; and theme as the core of the *textual function*. This also led to the description of the distinction, grammatically and textually, between language in its spoken and written forms. This is now a common-place in most linguistic thinking, and has begun to replace the abstraction of *language-as-such*. A focus on the significance of the materiality of language (as of other representational systems) is a consequence of this move, and is likely to be one of the major developments in semiotic work in the coming decades.

Halliday's linguistic work has culminated in his extensive description of English in functional terms (1985). In this work the slogan of 'grammar as a resource for meaning' is documented, both in outlining the systems of choices available to members of the culture, and in the potential for the constant remaking of this resource through the normal use of (grammatical) metaphor. The **grammar** has had the most widespread application, whether in the development of parsing programmes in the new information technologies, or in the development of descriptions that enter into language and literacy curricula at any level. **(GRK)**

Further Reading

Halliday, M. A. K. (1976) *System and Function in Language*, ed. G. Kress, Oxford: Oxford University Press.

Halliday, M. A. K. (1978) *Language as Social Semiotic*, London: Arnold.

Halliday, M. A. K. (1985) *Introduction to Functional Grammar*, London: Arnold.

HARRIS Zellig Harris (1915–92) was a leading exponent of structuralist linguistics (see **American structuralism**). Born in the Ukraine, he lived in Philadelphia for most of his life, where he taught linguistics at the University of Pennsylvania. Harris also spent much of his time at Mishmar Ha-emek, a kibbutz in Israel.

Harris is usually remembered nowadays for three things. First, his 1951 book *Methods in Structural Linguistics* is seen as the brilliant final statement of structuralism, just before **Chomsky**'s theories replaced it to become the dominant tendency in American linguistics. Leonard **Bloomfield** had allowed tests of sameness or difference in **meaning** to be used as a basis for grammatical statements, but Harris was committed to the principle that the distribution of linguistic elements was the only sound basis for grammatical analysis. The distribution of an element such as a **morpheme** or a word is simply the sum of the environments in which the element occurs (cf. Fought 1994, p. 103).

An example is the treatment of expressions like *give a damn* or *take no for an answer*, both of which normally only occur in the negative:

(1) Frankly, my dear, I don't give a damn.

(2) You don't take no for an answer
when you've nothing to lose.

Rhett Butler could not have said *I give a damn*, and nor could Tom Robinson have sung *You take no for an answer* (the asterisk indicates that the sentence is not possible in English). Such expressions are found after *don't* in these examples, but they also occur after *hardly* (*I hardly give a damn*), and *never* (*You never take no for an answer*). Bloomfield would have said that these are all negative expression, but for Harris it is the fact that the items occur nearby, not their meaning, which is the determining factor.

This method is sometimes dismissed as a convoluted way of arriving at grammatical analysis, since starting with meaning seems much simpler. Recent work in corpus linguistics by John Sinclair and others (cf. Sinclair 1991), however, is equally consistent in stressing distribution rather than meaning as a more reliable starting point for analysis.

Harris's second contribution is his influence on Chomsky: it was he who introduced Chomsky to linguistics, and his use of the term *transformation* (see **transformational grammar**) foreshadows its later use in Chomsky's work.

Third, Harris coined the term '**discourse analysis**' and tried to extend structuralist methods to texts rather than just isolated sentences.

Harris continued to produce important and original work until late in his life (cf. Harris 1991), but his work was largely ignored except by a small group of close colleagues. This is a great pity: one only needs to read Harris's masterly paper on **Sapir** (Harris [1951] 1984) to see that he had an outstanding mind. (**RS**)

Further Reading

Harris, Z. (1951/1984) 'Review of *Selected Writings* by Edward Sapir (Berkeley,

Univ of California Press, 1949)', *Language* 27.3: 228–333. (Reprinted in K. Koerner (ed.) *Edward Sapir: Appraisals of His Life and Work*, Amsterdam: John Benjamins, 1984, 69–114).

Harris, Z. (1991) *A Theory of Language and Information*, Oxford: Clarendon Press.

Hiz, H. (1994). 'Harris, Zellig S.', in R. Asher and J. Simpson (eds) *The Encyclopedia of Language and Linguistics*, vol. 2, Oxford: Pergamon Press, 1523–4.

HEGEL Georg Wilhelm Friedrich Hegel (1770–1831), German idealist and one of the greatest systematic philosophers known especially for his triadic dialectic method (thesis giving rise to antithesis and resolved in synthesis, which becomes thesis for new antithesis, and so on) and view that history embodies this dialectic as it evolves rationally toward an 'absolute idea'. Hegel's philosophy has been important in the development of Marxism and other European philosophies and influenced some of the classic American philosophers, especially Royce, Dewey, and **Peirce** (in his later years). (**NH**)

HERMENEUTICS Initially 'hermeneutics' appeared as a method of interpretation in the historical and philological science of the eighteenth century but acquired the status of a separate discipline with the works of Schleiermacher and Dilthey. These are characterized by the centrality of the notion of 'understanding' (as a 'hermeneutic circle'), as well as the opposition between interpretation and explanation, typically corresponding to the sciences of man and natural science. Hermeneutics therefore became a fundamental philosophic method based on understanding the imperatives involved in the interpretation of phenomena. With phenomenology hermeneutics entered a new phase, although the father of phenomenology, Husserl, did not emphasize interpretation as heavily as other hermeneutic thinkers. The major twentieth-century phenomenologist, Heidegger, on the other hand, did: for him the methodology of hermeneutics became an ontology of understanding. This perspective was also adopted by Gadamer who, in his landmark work 'Truth and Method' (1975) outlined a philosophical hermeneutics, insisting on the linguistic nature of being and tradition as the horizon of any understanding and experience. This work has had an enormous resonance in contemporary thinking and almost all authors who consider hermeneutics take it as their point of departure.

Another fundamental representative of philosophical hermeneutics is Paul Ricoeur. His main contribution is the reconsideration of the whole structural paradigm and the semiotic approach from the viewpoint of a philosophy of interpretation. Others involved in developing hermeneutics are Gianni Vattimo, who considers the fate of interpretation in postmodernity with reference to nihilism; and Richard Rorty, who asserts that the philosophy of the future, free of any possible prejudice, should be an 'edifying hermeneutics'. Authors like Apel and Habermas have also made considerable contributions, although they are generally opposed to the universality of hermeneutics as an all-embracing approach to philosophical questions. (**KB**)

Further Reading

Palmer, R. E. (1969) *Hermeneutics*, Evanston, ILL: Northwestern University Press.

HETEROGLOSSIA For Mikhail **Bakhtin** the term 'heteroglossia' captured the fact that any society consists of groups of diverse constitution and interests. Their diversity gives rise to difference in language (-use) so that members of any society always speak with many diverse 'voices', which are in contestation in any utterance. Bakhtin's arguments about heteroglossia were demonstrated most spectacularly with reference to the novel form of narrative. (**GRK**)

HISTORICAL LINGUISTICS The study of how languages change over time, sometimes called *philology*. Some historical linguists study a single language in detail, looking at early texts and other evidence of changes in vocabulary, **grammar** and pronunciation. Others look at a group of languages which have similarities and try to reconstruct the original language which gave rise to them. In certain cases we have written records: Latin, for instance, later developed into Italian, Spanish, Rumanian, French, and other modern languages. In many cases, however, we have no written evidence: it is apparent, for instance, that English, German, Swedish and Icelandic can all be traced back to an original language (often called Proto-Germanic), but this language has vanished almost without trace. Proto-Germanic and Latin can also be traced back even further to a common source language.

A broader concern of historical linguists is the mechanisms by which languages change, and the reasons for change. Sometimes one language influences another, as happened when the Normans invaded Britain and many French words were adopted into English. On other occasions a language changes for internal reasons: the letters *gh* in words like *night* were originally pronounced like the *ch* in Scottish *loch*, but this sound eventually disappeared from most types of English. (**RS**)

See also <u>Aitchison</u> (this volume), DIACHRONIC and SYNCHRONIC.

Further Reading

Trask, R. L. (1996) *Historical Linguistics*, London: Arnold.

HJELMSLEV Louis Hjelmslev (1899–1965), Danish linguist and semiotician, Professor of Comparative Philology in Copenhagen (1937–65), founder of the linguistic theory called glossematics. The glossematic project is an attempt to radicalize Ferdinand de **Saussure**'s claim (1916) that language is form not substance. This theoretical approach has been the emblem of the Copenhagen School of linguistics.

The essence of glossematics is contained in *Omkring sprogteoriens grundlæggelse* (1943, English translation, *Prolegomena to a Theory of Language*, 1953) and *Résumé of a Theory of Language* (1975). *Prolegomena* was intended to be the popular version of the theory, *Résumé* the strictly scientific presentation. Both were prepared simultaneously during the 1930s in collaboration with Hans-Jørgen Uldall (1907–57), although his *Outline of Glossematics* (1957) shows essential differences to glossematics in its almost phenomenological approach. A series of Hjelmslev's seminal articles from the 1930s are reprinted in *Essais Linguistiques* (1959) and *Essais Linguistiques II* (1973). With Viggo **Brøndal** he founded the Cercle Linguistique de Copenhague (1931) as well as *Acta Linguistica Hafniensia* (1939–).

Hjelmslev's early work, *Principes de grammaire générale* (1928), *Études Baltiques* (1932), and the *La catégorie des cas* (1935–37) are examples of a structural linguistics prior to glossematics. Here Hjelmslev, like the members of the **Prague School**, defined linguistic units from **distinctive feature**s, i.e. elements bound by formal properties. Glossematics, however, sets up definitions based solely on functions, i.e. element independent relations. All linguistic elements are to be defined, and only to be defined, by their mutual relations, called their functions. The aim of the linguistic analysis is to transform features (like case, syntactical position, glottal stop, etc.) to functions.

Therefore, the linguistic object will be constituted by the method through which the rigorously immanent analysis is carried out: a procedure of dichotomic partitions of the material **text**. The units isolated in each step of the analysis are defined by its relation to other units, the units having no properties beyond this functional definition. The ultimate goal is to turn all linguistically relevant aspects of a text into constants, i.e. the two units in an interdependent relation or one of the units in a unilateral dependence. The structure of a given language phenomenon is the system of relations between the constants. The other units have a unilateral dependence and the simply co-occurrent units are the variables.

The basic linguistic units are called figurae. As they have no content except their function, it is an arbitrary choice what we call expression and what we call content. Together with the rigid immanency of the linguistic structure this radical consequence is the basis of the general semiotic influence of glossematics.

The **sign** is defined as a mutual interdependence between two planes, the expression plane and the content plane. The two interrelated forms, called the expression form and the content form, are the constants of the two planes. The variables of the two planes are the so-called expression substance and the content substance (the last one characterized only vaguely by Hjelmslev). These two substances are articulated by the respective forms so as to bring about a manifested sign in a specific expression substance (for example, the acoustic material of a natural language) and in a specific content substance (for example, the psychological content of a text). The variables have to be studied by other sciences than linguistics in order to aquire a formal status as constants if, and only if, these sciences follow the glossematic procedures, thereby becoming semiotic sciences.

The formal definition of the sign allows for an analysis of the content plane of the sign following the same basic principles as the analysis of the expression plane. This is the basis of structural semantics as carried out on glossematic grounds in most detail by Algirdas J. **Greimas** (1917–92). The emphasis on pure form also implies that the expression substance is irrelevant for the principles of the analysis: glossematics is applicable to any sign system, also non-linguistic systems. The same goes for the content substance: any ideological or psychological contents are secondary to the formal principles that make them accessible as contents. Without the formal articulation they would not exist as contents, but as a chaotic unspecifiable substratum, called the purport, if they existed at all. Any formal sign system articulating substance on the two planes is called a semiotic.

As the sign is a formal unit, the sign itself as a whole can be a content form or an expression form. Thus, the signs of a given sign system may have the signs of another sign system, a so-called denotative semiotic, as their content plane, itself being a meta-semiotic (for instance, linguistics *vis-à-vis* **natural language**s). Or, they may have the signs of another sign system as their expression plane and thereby constituting a connotative semiotic (for instance, the symbols and metaphors of literary language). Hence, natural language only becomes the basic sign system when seen as a denotative semiotic, i.e. only when it

is embedded in a hierarchy of semiotics. The ultimate goal for this progressive hierarchical stratification is to make a meta-semiotic on a higher level transform the variables of the semiotics on the lower levels into constants. This perspective is the most wide-ranging semiotic perspective of glossematics. (**SEL**)

See also BARTHES, DENOTATION and CONNOTATION.

Further Reading

Caputo, C. and Galassi, R. (eds) (1985) *Louis Hjelmslev: Linguistica, Semiotica, Epistemologia, Il Protagora* IV, 7–8.

Rasmussen, M. (ed.) (1993) *Louis Hjelmslev et la Sémiotique Contemporaine: Travaux du Cercle Linguistique de Copenhague* XXIV, Copenhagen: Munksgaard.

Siertsema, B. (1954) *A Study of Glossematics*, The Hague: Martinus Nijhoff.

HUMBOLDT Wilhelm von Humboldt (1767–1835), Prussian diplomat and scholar, saw language as the key to understanding the human mind. He was acknowledged by many later linguists as an important influence. His magnum opus, *On the Kawi Language of the Island of Java*, was published posthumously (1836–9). (**RH**)

I

IASS IASS is the acronym now most commonly used for the International Association for Semiotic Studies (a learned society alternatively identified as AIS, for Association Internationale de Semiotique). This organization, bilingual by constitutional provision, was created on 21–2 January, 1969, by a group of like-minded individuals convened in Paris at the initiative of Emile **Benveniste**, of the Collège de France. Since its foundation, the Association has proclaimed and has endeavored to adhere to three principal aims: to promote semiotic researches in a scientific spirit; to advance global co-operation in this field; and to promote collaboration with local organizations world-wide.

The day-by-day governing body of the IASS is led by its officers each of whom (excepting one, whose term is unlimited) may serve for up to two terms, usually of five years each. Emile Benveniste was elected as the first President in 1969, holding that office until his death in 1976. He was succeeded by Cesare Segre (Italy), then by Jerzy Pelc (Poland); then by Roland Posner (Germany), serving out his first term in 1999 and embarking on his second in the same year. There are currently five Vice-Presidents: John Deely (USA), Gerard Deledalle (France), Adrián Gimate-Welsh (Mexico), Alexandros Ph. Lagopoulos (Greece), and Eero Tarasti (Finland). (Earlier Vice-Presidents included Roman **Jakobson** and Yuri M. **Lotman**.) The first Secretary General was Julia **Kristeva** (France), succeeded upon her resignation by Umberto **Eco** (Italy); this position is presently held by Jeff Bernard (Austria).

The first Treasurer was Jacques Geninasca (Switzerland), succeeded by Gloria Withalm (Austria), a position now occupied by Magdolna Orosz (Hungary). A ninth officer is Thomas A. **Sebeok** (USA), Editor-in-Chief of *Semiotica*.

The officers report to, and are in turn elected once every five years or so by, the members of the General Assembly with an Executive Committee, chosen from among (currently) thirty-eight different countries.

One of the Association's principal responsibilities has been the organization of periodic International Congresses, usually at five-year intervals: the First Congress, convened by Umberto Eco in Milano, was held in 1974, followed by others in Vienna (1979), Palermo (1984), Barcelona/Perpignan (1989), Berkeley (1994), Guadalajara (1997), and Dresden (1999).

The other paramount IASS activity is the co-sponsorship with Mouton (formerly of The Hague, now Mouton de Gruyter, Berlin) of the 'flagship' publication of the IASS, *Semiotica*, established in 1969, now published in 2000 pages annually. By the end of 1999, this journal will have appeared in 127 volumes; an 800-page Index of Vols. 1–100 was published in 1994, supplemented by a Finder List up to date through mid-1999. In addition, the Vienna Secretariat publishes informative Bulletins and Newsletters about IASS business at regular intervals. (**TAS**)

Further Reading

Website of the IASS-AIS: http://vhf.msh-paris.fr/escom/AIS/sem-www/w3-1-assoc.html

ICON One of three types of signs identified by Charles S. **Peirce**, the other two being **index** and **symbol**. The icon is characterized by a relation of similarity between the **sign** and its **object**. However, similarity alone will not suffice to determine an iconic sign. Twins look similar but are not signs of each other. My reflection in the mirror looks like me but is not an iconic sign. For iconic signs to obtain the effect of convention or **habit**, social practices or special functions must be added to similarity. Iconic similarity is a special kind of similarity: it is an abstraction on the basis of a convention, for it privileges given traits of similarity and not others. Similarity between one banknote and another worth $50 is no doubt a sign that the first banknote too is worth $50. But if similarity is complete to the point that the serial numbers of both banknotes are identical, we have a false banknote that cannot carry out a legitimate function as an iconic sign on the money market. All the same, as Peirce states, the icon is the most independent sign from both convention and causality/contiguity: 'An *icon* is a sign which would possess the character which renders it significant, even though its object had no existence; such as a lead-pencil streak as representing a geometrical line' (*CP* 2.304). (**SP**)

IDEATIONAL A term in Systemic Functional Grammar, which assumes that any semiotic system must have the facility to communicate about states of affairs and events in the world. The ideational function indicates the salient participants, and the processes which relate them, usually seen as the 'content' of a sentence. (**GRK**)

See INTERPERSONAL and TEXTUAL.

IDIOM An expression which has come to have a **meaning** that is not simply the sum of its parts. The sentence *We went up the mountain* has a meaning which is a simple function of the meaning of the words in it. The sentence *We are up the creek*, in contrast, does not merely express what its individual words mean: the combination of these words has a special meaning, in this case because *up the creek* is an idiom meaning 'in difficulties'. (**RS**)

ILLOCUTION, ILLOCUTIONARY In the terminological framework introduced by **Austin** (1962) to cope with the multifunctionality of all utterances (**locution**-illocution-**perlocution**), illocution refers to a type of act performed *in* saying something: asking or answering a question, giving a command or a warning, making a promise or a statement, and the like. The basic question is: in what way is a locution uttered on a given occasion of use? The answer to that question is an assessment of the function of what is said or its illocutionary force. Though the illocution is basically a functional category, it is not unrelated to aspects of form. Often there are clear **marker**s of illocutionary force called illocutionary force indicating devices such as **performative verb**s used in explicit performatives (e.g. *I promise to come tomorrow*), or the interrogative form marking a question, or a negation (e.g. 'not' turning a promise into the refusal *I do not promise to come tomorrow*). In later versions of **speech act** theory (Searle 1976 onwards), the notion illocutionary point is introduced as one of the parameters along which classes of illocutionary acts can be distinguished: the point of an assertive is to represent a state of affairs; the point of a directive is to make the hearer do something; the point of a commissive is that the speaker commits him/herself to doing something; the point of an expressive is to express a psychological state; and the point of a declaration is to bring something about in the world. (**JV**)

Further Reading

Austin, J. L. (1962) *How to Do Things with Words*, ed. J. O. Urmson, Oxford: Oxford University Press. (2nd rev. edn, 1975, eds J. O. Urmson and M. Sbisà, Cambridge, MA: Harvard University Press.)

INDEX One of three types of sign identified by Charles S. **Peirce**, the other two being **icon** and **symbol**. The index is a sign that signifies its object by a relation of contiguity, causality or by some other physical connection. However, this relation also depends on a **habit** or convention. For example, the relation between hearing a knock at the door and someone on the other side of the door who wants to enter. Here convention plays its part in relating the knocking and the knocker, but contiguity/causality predominates to the point that we are surprised if we open the door and no-one is there. Types of index include:

1 *symptoms*, medical, psychological, of natural phenomena (actual contiguity + actual causality;
2 *clues*, natural phenomena, attitudes and inclinations (presumed contiguity + non actual causality);
3 *traces*, physical or mental (non actual contiguity + presumed causality).

'An *index*', says Peirce, 'is a sign which would, at once, lose the character which makes it a sign if its object were removed, but would not lose that character if there were no interpretant' (*CP* 2.304). (**SP**)

INTERPERSONAL The interpersonal function deals with the organization and shape of (the **clause** in) language as a means of expressing the social relations between those engaged in communication. It is concerned with expression of both power and solidarity in social relations. (**GRK**)

See IDEATIONAL and TEXTUAL.

INTERPRETANT The interpretant is a concept introduced by Charles S. **Peirce**'s **semiotics**. According to Peirce, **semiosis** is a triadic process whose components include **sign** (or **representamen**), **object** and interpretant.

A *Sign*, or *Representamen*, is a First which stands in such a genuine triadic relation to a Second, called its Object, as to be capable of determining a Third, called its Interpretant, to assume the same triadic relation to its Object in which it stands itself to the same Object.

(CP 2.274)

Therefore, the sign stands for something, its object, by which it is 'mediately determined' (ibid. 8.343), 'not in all respects, but in reference to a sort of idea' (ibid. 2.228). However, a sign can only do this if it determines the interpretant which is 'mediately determined by that object' (ibid. 8.343). 'A sign mediates between the *interpretant* sign and its object' insofar as the first is determined by its object under a certain respect or idea, or **ground**, and determines the interpretant 'in such a way as to bring the interpretant into a relation to the object, corresponding to its own relation to the object' (ibid. 8.332).

The interpretant of a sign is another sign which the first creates in the interpreter. This is 'an equivalent sign, or perhaps a more developed sign' (ibid. 2.228). Therefore the interpretant sign cannot be identical to the interpreted sign, it cannot be a repetition, precisely because it is *mediated*, interpretive and therefore always something new. With respect to the first sign, the interpretant is a *response*, and as such it inaugurates a new sign process, a new semiosis. In this sense it is a more developed sign. As a sign the interpretant determines another sign which acts, in turn, as an interpretant: therefore, the interpretant opens to new semioses, it develops the sign process, it is a new sign occurrence. Indeed, we may state that every time there is a sign occurrence, including the 'First Sign', we have a 'Third', something mediated, a response, an interpretive novelty, an interpretant. Consequently, a sign is constitutively an interpretant (cf. Petrilli 1998d, I.1). The fact that the interpretant (Third) is in turn a sign (First), and that the sign (First) is in turn an interpretant (is already a Third) places the sign in an open network of interpretants: this is the Peircean principle of infinite semiosis or endless series of interpretants (cf. *CP* 1.339).

Therefore the **meaning** of a sign is a response, an interpretant that calls for another response, another interpretant. This implies the dialogical nature of the sign and semiosis. A sign has its meaning in another sign which responds to it and which in turn is a sign if there is another sign to respond and interpret it, and so forth ad infinitum. In Augusto Ponzio's terminology (1985, 1990b) the 'First Sign' in the triadic relation of semiosis, the object that receives meaning, is the *interpreted*, and what confers meaning is the interpretant, which may be of two main types. The interpretant which enables recognition of the sign is an *interpretant of identification*, it is connected to the signal, **code** and sign system. The specific interpretant of a sign, that which interprets sense or actual meaning, is the *interpretant of answering comprehension*. This second type of interpretant does not limit itself to identifying the interpreted, but rather expresses its properly pragmatic meaning, installing with it a relation of involvement and participation: the interpretant responds to the interpreted and takes a stand towards it.

This dual conception of the interpretant is in line with Peirce's semiotics, which is inseparable from his **pragmatism**. In a letter of 1904 to Victoria **Welby**, Peirce wrote that if we take a sign in a very broad sense, its interpretant is not necessarily a sign, since it might be an action or experience, or even just a feeling (cf. *CP*

8.332). Here sign is understood in a strict sense given that the interpretant as a response that signifies, that renders something significant and which therefore becomes a sign cannot, in turn, be anything other than a sign occurrence, a semiosic act, even if an action or feeling. In any case, we are dealing with what we are calling an 'interpretant of answering comprehension', and therefore a sign. In line with his triadomania, instead, Peirce on classifying interpretants distinguishes among feelings, exertions and signs (ibid. 4.536). And in one of his manuscripts (*MS* 318), a part of which is published in *CP* 5.464–496 (cf. Short 1998), he also distinguishes among the emotional, the energetic, and the logical interpretant. The latter together with the triad consisting of the 'immediate', 'dynamical' and 'final interpretant' are perhaps the two most famous triads among the many described by Peirce to classify the various aspects of the interpretant.

The relation between the sign and interpretant has consequences of a semiotic order for the typology of signs and of a logical order for the typology of inference and argument. Whether we have an **icon**, **index** or **symbol** depends on the way this relation is organized. And given that the relation between premises and conclusion is also understood in terms of the relation among sign and interpretant, the triad **abduction**, induction, deduction also depends on it. **(SP)**

See also DIALOGUE, UNLIMITED SEMIOSIS, FIRSTNESS, SECONDNESS and THIRDNESS.

Further Reading

Merrell, F. (1993) 'Is meaning possible within indefinite semiosis?', *American Journal of Semiotics* 10 (3/4): 167–96.

Peirce, C. S. (1955) 'Logic as semiotic: the theory of signs', in J. Buchler (ed.) *Philosophical Writings of Peirce*, New York: Dover.

Peirce, C. S. (1992) 'Some consequences of four incapacities', in N. Houser and C. Kloesel (eds) *The Essential Peirce: Selected Philosophical Writings*, vol. 1, Bloomington, IND: Indiana University Press, pp. 83–105.

IPRA Acronym for International Pragmatics Association, an international scientific organization devoted to the study of **pragmatics** in its widest sense as an interdisciplinary cognitive, social, and cultural perspective on language and language use. Established in 1986, IPrA has roughly 1,500 members in over 60 countries worldwide; it organizes the International Pragmatics Conferences, and publishes *Pragmatics: Quarterly Publication of the International Pragmatics Association*; research activities are co-ordinated at the IPrA Research Center, hosted by the University of Antwerp, Belgium. (**JV**)

Further Reading

Website of the IPrA:
http://ipra-www.uia.ac.be/ipra/

J

JAKOBSON Roman Osipovič Jakobson (1896–1982). One of the most important contributors of the twentieth century to a scientific theory of language as a semiotic system. Graduate of the Lazarev Institute in 1914, Jakobson then enrolled in Moscow University. Co-founder of the Moscow Linguistics Circle in 1915, the St Petersburg's OPOJAZ (Society for the Study of Poetic Language), and the Prague Linguistics Circle in 1926. His scholarship can be divided into his Moscow period (1915–26), his Czechoslovak period (1926–39) and his American period (1949–82). Originally known as a representative of **Russian Formalism**, Jakobson became one of its major critics and, subsequently, a primary contributor to the **structuralist** paradigm. By 1957 Jakobson had become the first scholar to hold simultaneous chairs at both Harvard (specifically the Samuel Hazzard Cross Professor of Slavic Languages and Literatures) and the Massachusetts Institute of Technology. Other American affiliations include the Salk Institute for Biological Studies and a term as president of the Linguistic Society of America.

Jakobson was a major force in bringing Mikhail **Bakhtin** and Charles S. **Peirce** to the forefront of the American scholarly community devoted to literary studies and linguistics respectively. His theoretical contributions include a developed theory of invariance in the study of human language and semiotic systems, a re-evaluation of the Saussurean view of language, a sophisticated notion of relative autonomy, asymmetrical markedness relations, and a multifaceted speech act model that continues to play a profound role in the **modelling** of human language. Some of Jakobson's most profound published contributions include *Remarques sur l'évolution phonologique du russe comparée à celle des autres langues slaves* (1929), 'Musikwissenschaft und Linguistic' (1932), 'Beitrag zur allgemeinen Kasuslehre' (1936), 'Signe zéro' (1939), *Preliminaries to Speech Analysis* (1952), 'Morfologičeskie nabljudenija nad slavjanskim skloneniem' (1958), 'Linguistics and Poetics' (1960), 'Poetry of Grammar and Grammar of Poetry' (1961). (**EA**)

See also SAUSSURE and PRAGUE SCHOOL.

Further Reading

Jakobson, R. (1987) *Language in Literature*, ed. K. Pomorska and S. Rudy, Cambridge, MA: Belknap Press.

Jakobson, R. (1995) *On Language*, ed. L. R. Waugh and M. Monville-Burston, Cambridge, MA: Harvard University Press.

Waugh, L. R. (1998) 'Semiotics and language: the work of Roman Jakobson', in R. Kevelson (ed.) *Hi-Fives: A Trip to Semiotics*, New York: Peter Lang.

JESPERSEN Jens Otto Harry Jespersen (1860–1943), Danish philologist, Professor of English at the University of Copenhagen (1893–1925). Jespersen was a brilliant and hugely productive reformer whose interests spanned almost every area of the study and teaching of languages, and whose radically new ideas in most of these areas came to have an important influence on the direction of linguistics and language teaching methodology. In an age when modern languages were considered inferior to Latin and Greek as objects of scholarly attention, when the categories of Latin grammar were superimposed on the description of other languages as a matter of course, and when the only way of teaching a foreign language was through translation and rote-learning of grammatical paradigms, Jespersen was campaigning to enhance the status of modern languages as autonomous objects of study, and to improve modern language teaching through the application of his own ground-breaking research in **phonetics**.

His best-known work is undoubtedly his monumental *Modern English Grammar on Historical Principles*, I–VII (1909–49), which is one of the great 'traditional' **grammar**s of the English language. However, in setting up the categories of rank and nexus, and explicitly linking active and passive as related constructions – in this and other works such as *The Philosophy of Grammar* (1924) – Jespersen provided fruitful suggestions for later grammarians of various schools of thought. Though his 'notional' approach was condemned by the **American structuralist** movement, it was in turn invoked by **Chomsky** and other Transformational Grammarians in their attacks on the **structuralists**, just as, ironically, it was influential in the origins of Functionalist movements away from **transformational grammar**.

Jespersen was an original thinker, whose acute observations and reflections on language were often way ahead of his times. His study of child language, *Nutidssprog hos börn og voxne* (1916), was inspired by the realization that:

one can read page after page, indeed volume after volume, by most modern linguistic scholars without anywhere coming across the word child (or for that matter the word woman) in

attempts to explain the development of languages.

(Juul *et al.* 1995, p. 120)

And, as has recently been pointed out (Bull 1996), even though Jespersen's often quoted linguistic characterization of 'the woman' (cf. the chapter with this title in *Language: Its Nature, Development and Origin* [1922]) has generally been seen merely as a curious reflection of the prejudices of his time, it is not essentially different from Robin Lakoff's (1975) description – in feminist terms – of 'women's language'. Yet he was also a keen proponent of a linguistic Darwinism according to which linguistic change could be seen as evolution and progress, e.g. in *Efficiency in Linguistic Change* (1941), himself lending evolution a helping hand through his involvement in efforts to construct an international auxiliary language.

In fact, much of Jespersen's work was of a practical orientation. He followed up his idea of teaching English on the basis of the spoken language by employing phonetic transcription alongside text in normal orthography, in his textbooks for learners, which for years were used in the Danish schools. He also wrote one of the most widely used textbooks on the history of the English language in this century, *Growth and Structure of the English Language* (1905). Several of his works in Danish have been translated into other languages. (**BP**)

Further Reading

Jespersen, O. (1922) *Language: Its Nature, Development and Origin*, London: Allen and Unwin.

Jespersen, O. (1924) *The Philosophy of Grammar*, London: Allen and Unwin.

Juul, A. *et al.* (eds) (1995) *A Linguist's Life: An English Translation of Otto Jespersen's Autobiography with Notes, Photos and a Bibliography*, trans. D. Stoner, Odense: Odense University Press.

K

KANT Immanuel Kant (1724–1804), philosophical giant who changed the course of modern philosophy by asking the revolutionary question: 'How is synthetic *a priori* knowledge possible?' Kant answered that we should not presuppose that all knowledge arises from and conforms to objects of thought but, rather, that objects of thought conform to capacities for knowing or conditions of experience. This shift of view is known as Kant's Copernican revolution in philosophy. Since, according to Kant, space and time are forms of human sensibility and, therefore, necessary conditions of human experience, it follows *a priori* that all objects of possible experience will be situated in space and time. This is a transcendental deduction. A consequence of Kant's **metaphysics** is that we can only know objects as they appear (phenomena) not as they are in themselves (noumena or *Ding an sich*). This is Kant's transcendental idealism.

Kant also argued that human understanding presupposes, as a regulative principle, that nature is purposive. In his moral philosophy, Kant distinguishes between hypothetical imperatives, where action can only be understood in relation to human purposes, and categorical imperatives, where commands to action appeal to duty, not purpose. Kant's categorical imperative stated generally, 'Act only on the maxim which you can at the same time will to be a universal law,' brings to mind the 'golden rule'. Charles S. **Peirce**, although much influenced by Kant, considered the view that the unity of thought depends on the nature of the human mind rather than on 'things in themselves' to be a form of **nominalism**. (**NH**)

Further Reading

Körner, S. (1955) *Kant*, London: Penguin Books.

KINESICS Kinesics was introduced by **Birdwhistell** in 1952 to designate the study of body motion as communication in face-to-face interaction in which the actions of the face, head, hands and the whole body are viewed as culturally organized and learned by individuals as they become competent in the use of the unmediated communication systems of their culture. Kinesics was developed as part of an attempt to expand the scope of structural linguistic analytic techniques to cover all aspects of behaviour involved in face-to-face interaction. Birdwhistell proposed a terminology and conceptual framework paralleling that used in linguistics. The least discriminable unit of body motion effecting a contrast in **meaning** was called a *kineme* (analogous to **phoneme**). Kinemes combined into *kinemorphs* which in turn were proposed as components of *kinemorphic constructions*. Attempts to analyse body motion in these terms were rarely more than programmatic; however, the concept was highly influential in developing awareness of the importance of the role of visible bodily actions in communication. Today 'kinesics' may be found in English language dictionaries where it is defined as the study of how body movements convey meaning. It is also used to refer to those movements a person makes that are regarded as conveying meaning. (**AK**)

See also Stokoe (this volume), Sebeok (this volume) and GESTURE.

Further Reading

Birdwhistell, R. L. (1970) *Kinesics and Context*, Philadelphia: University of Pennsylvania Press.

KRESS Gunther Kress (b. 1942) has been central in forging social semiotics as a cutting edge mode of investigating the diversity of representational production in contemporary reality. Social semiotics is founded on a social theory of the **sign** and claims that the relationship between the **signifier** and the **signified** is not arbitrary, but motivated. Not only this, Kress insists that there is a relationship of motivation between the world of the sign-user and the signifier. This theory is based on the recognition that human beings produce signs as a result of their interested action as culturally and historically formed individuals within particular social contexts and relations of power. By placing human social and cultural environments at the centre of semiotic analysis, Kress emphasises **meaning** making as unstable, transformative action which produces change both in the object being transformed and in the individual who is the agent of the transformation. Meaning making is a constant process of re-designing available resources for representation, thus the making of signs is not an act of imitation but of creativity and innovation.

Kress's work on multimodality decentres written language as the dominant mode of representation in a contemporary world which is increasingly privileging multiple modes of communication, particularly the visual mode. Kress has applied many of these ideas to rethinking language and literacy education in a global, plural society in which the representational resources of all people need to be harnessed for productive, social and humane futures. (**PS**)

See also Kress (this volume) and HALLIDAY.

Further Reading

Kress, G. (1999) *Early Spelling*, London: Routledge.

KRISTEVA Julia Kristeva, born in Bulgaria in 1941, has been working in Paris since 1966 as a semiotician, psychoanalyst, writer, literary theorist and critic. She is editor of the famous journal *Tel Quel* and teaches at Paris University VII as well as at Columbia University in New York. She has authored three novels, *Samouraïs* which mirrors French society, *Le Vieil Homme et les loups*, and *Possession* and is now writing a trilogy, *La génie féminine*, devoted to Hannah Arendt, Melanie Klein and Colette (of which the first volume has already appeared).

In her book of 1969, *Le langage, cest inconnu*, Kristeva outlines the field of linguistics while pointing out its limits. These are traced to the history of linguistics and to its compromise with European culture, with phonocentrism, with the priority or exclusiveness accorded to the alphabetic script, etc. By taking into account the reflections on language offered by philosophy of language and **semiotics**, linguistics today has broadened its scope. At the same time, however, the epistemological paradigms adopted from the philosophical tradition at the birth of linguistics remain the same. Above all the notion of speaking *subject* is not called into question.

With her proposal of 'semanalysis' as formulated in *Semiotiké* (1969), Kristeva had already attempted a sort of short circuit by connecting the linguistic and the semiotic approach to the psychoanalytic. She confronts the Cartesian ego and the transcendental ego of Husserlian phenomenology, the subject of utterance linguistics, with the dual subject as theorized by Freud and his concept of the unconscious. In Kristeva's perspective the unconscious implies describing signification as a heterogeneous process. This is best manifested in literary writing.

In *La Révolution du langage poétique* (1974) Kristeva establishes a distinction between the *symbolic* and the *semiotic*. The symbolic designates language as it is defined by linguistics and its tradition, language in its normative usage. Semiotics refers to primary processes and to the pulsions that enter into contradiction with the symbolic. Literary writing is generated in the contradiction between the symbolic and the semiotic. Its value for semiotics, therefore, consists in its potential for exploring the experience of heterogeneity in signification processes.

Subsequently, Kristeva developed her distinction between the semiotic and the symbolic in a psychoanalytical framework. She analyses the heterogeneity of signification, which she also experiences directly in analytical practice, in her books, *Pouvoirs de l'horreur, Essais sur l'abjection* (1980), *Histoires d'amour* (1985) and *Soleil noir, dépression et mélancolie* (1987). But the questions of the speaking subject's identity and of heterogeneity of the **signification** process emerge just as well in situations of strangeness to language, analysed in *Étrangers à nous même*.

The question of strangeness is also dealt with in one of her most recent works, *Le temps sensible: Proust et l'expérience littéraire* (1994). Kristeva also analyses the role played by strangeness (racial: the Jew; the sexual: the homosexual) in Proust's *Recherche*. Literary writing can enrich our understanding of the outsider thanks to its dealings with heterogeneity in signification and with **alterity**. The more we recognize ourselves as strangers to ourselves, the more we are capable of greeting the strangeness of others. (**AP**)

Further Reading

Kristeva, J. (1981) *Desire in Language: A Semiotic Approach to Literature and Art*, trans. T. Gora, A. Jardine and L. S. Roudiez, Oxford: Blackwell.

Kristeva, J. (1982) *Powers of Horror: An Essay on Abjection*, trans. L. S. Roudiez, New York: Columbia University Press.

Kristeva, J. (1984) *The Revolution in Poetic Language*, trans. M. Waller, New York: Columbia University Press.

L

LABOV The sociolinguistic work of William Labov (b. 1927) takes the relation between social and linguistic structures as the primary object of inquiry. This can be read in two ways. On the one hand, it establishes through precise empirical work – in the analysis of phonetic variation, and in quantitative documentation and evaluation of variation – the close co-variation of linguistic form and social structure. On the other hand, it can provide the theoretical basis and detailed description of the mechanisms of linguistic change. It may be most productive to see Labov's work as integrating sociolinguistic and historical inquiry by a single powerful assumption, namely that the 'correlations' which he has described are produced by social forces and processes; and that they are the same for the differences visible at the micro-level of **phonetics** as for the macro-level that come to constitute separate languages.

Labov's method was to isolate an element subject to significant variation within a linguistic community, for instance the *r* sound which follows a vowel (post-vocalic *r*) in New York English (as in bea*r*, pa*r*ty). He manufactured texts which differed in terms of this variable alone. This enabled him to establish its function as a **marker** of socio-economic position, and to describe how it functioned as a prestige-marker, correlating significantly with judgements about the speaker's socio-economic status, or about the status of an occasion of speaking (ranging from formal to casual).

Labov found consensus by all members of groups (in a socially stratified structure) on certain **meaning**s. These meanings were assigned on the basis purely of chosen markers. All groups related users of the prestige forms as possessing higher earning power; in terms of physical power ('good in a fight'), those who were of high socio-economic status tended to rate users of low-prestige forms highly, and higher than did those who themselves used the forms.

This procedure opened up what had previously been impressionistically understood as (linguistic) prejudice to quantitative description: making available a precise, and new instrument, for studying the mechanisms and processes of group formation, and the complex social-ideological meanings which sustain them. In micro-analyses of this kind Labov could detect and describe evidence of ideological shifts and contradictions in group alliances, resistances by established groups to 'newcomers' – as for the residents of Martha's Vineyard who resented and rejected incoming 'outsiders' using hyper-corrected forms of the local **dialect**.

Labov's work has given rise to a large effort in linguistics: variation studies. His assumption that the processes which operate on the micro-level are effective in the same way at the macro-level has enabled him to work in both (as in his work on language in the inner city, on verbal duelling, for instance). In some of his work the use of the framework of transformational **generative grammar** with its incompatible theoretical assumptions has led him into positions at odds with his foundational work, as in his enormously influential article 'The logic of non-standard English' in which the attempt is made to erase, in the description, the difference between Black English and (White) middle-class forms. (**GRK**)

See also <u>Aitchison</u> (this volume), SOCIOLINGUISTICS, HISTORICAL LINGUISTICS and TRANSFORMATIONAL GRAMMAR.

Further Reading

Labov, W. (1972a) 'The logic of non-standard English', in P. P. Giglioli (ed.) *Language and Social Context*, Harmondsworth: Penguin.

Labov, W. (1972b) *Sociolinguistic Patterns*, Philadephia, PA: University of Pennsylvania Press.

Labov, W. (1994) *Principles of Linguistic Change*, vol. 1, Oxford: Blackwell.

LACAN Jacques Lacan was one of the three most creative and powerful contributors to psychoanalysis. Lacan, Sigmund Freud, and Melanie Klein together produced the most important of the conceptual and clinical foundations for the psychoanalytic movement. In Lacan's case, this entailed giving explicit formulations to philosophical, scientific, and linguistic themes that had often remained implicit in Freud's writings.

Lacan was born in 1901, and displayed an early interest in philosophy (particularly that of Spinoza), literature, and surrealism. He trained as a psychiatrist at the end of the 1920s before proceeding to train as a psychoanalyst with the *Société Psychanalytique de Paris* between 1932 and 1938. This society contained Edouard Pichon, who had a particular interest in the function and field of language in psychoanalysis, and Raymond de Saussure, the son of the linguist Ferdinand de **Saussure**. Lacan's interest in language developed alongside his friendships with Dalí, André Masson, and Picasso, and within a background of the work of Alexandre Koyré on the logic and methodology of the sciences. In the late 1940s his meetings and friendships with Claude **Lévi-Strauss** and Roman **Jakobson** led him to reformulations of the notion of unconscious structure, and to participate in work groups with mathematicians, initially with Georges-Théodule Guilbaud, and with Jacques Riguet. From 1953 he gave a public seminar over a period of twenty-six years; his collection of essays – *Écrits* – is only partially translated into English: a full translation is anticipated in the immediate future.

Lacan's work – from his first writings on hysteria in 1928 to his last public seminar in 1979 – spanned half a century. Its periodisation can be attempted in many ways, its themes being organised around a series of structures which took different forms from decade to decade. In all of these formulations Lacan repeatedly stressed that he drew on, and reconstructed, concepts and problems introduced into psychoanalysis by Freud. Lacan's work in the 1930s was focused on his attempt to make explicit a number of themes whose consequences are fundamental – but only broadly sketched – in Freud: narcissism, identification, misrecognition. This choice of themes led him to investigate the fictive aspects of the construction of reality, and to distinguish the ego, as the agency responsible for such fabrications, from the conditions and structures of subjectivity. The structure of language is what conditions subjectivity, and for Lacan, it is only this apparatus that can provide an approach to what is real. Language for Lacan is structured by the signifying chain.

The field of language, the field of narcissism, and the field of trauma, together span what by 1950 Lacan had begun to call the Symbolic, the Imaginary, and the Real. In his seminars of the early 1950s, Lacan tried to test the adequacy of these terms for the formulation of classical clinical and conceptual isssues in Freud. In these years his reformulation of the Oedipus complex stressed the primacy of desire; the aim of analysis, during this period of his work, was construed as the recognition of desire – and of its dependency on the matrix of the other.

From the late 1950s Lacan added to these signifying effects a further term: *jouissance*. This pair of terms – *jouissance* and the **signifier** – led him to study the relations between the excitation suffered by the human body, and its subjection to marks that provide or fail to provide 'the words to say it'. At the start of the 1960s Lacan's seminars focused for three years on Freud's concepts of transference, identification, and anxiety. This work consolidated Lacan's account of the structuring of subjectivity, and it was the formalisation of these concepts led Lacan to the development of his theory of **discourse**s by the end of that decade. In the 1970s Lacan proposed parallelisms between unconscious structure and mathematical structure, utilising knot theory, number theory and formal logic in studies of feminine and masculine sexuality, and of deficiencies in relations of love.

The years immediately following the Second World War had seen the French Psychoanalytic Society reconstituted as one of the most fruitful in the world. This Society split into two halves in 1953, one part being headed by Lacan. The split was presented as being about questions of technique, but actually was rather an index of the inability of the French Society to contain the originality and strengths of Lacan's theories. This same effect was to be repeated in 1963 when Lacan was effectively excommunicated from the International Psychoanalytic Association. In 1964 he founded his own school, the *École freudienne de Paris*, which achieved great successes in advancing the clinical and research frontiers of psychoanalysis before its dissolution by Lacan early in 1980. Over this period his Seminar and School made psychoanalysis available to a wide audience, and led to the construction of Franco-Hispanic schools of psychoanalysis which today represent one half of the psychoanalysis practised in the world. Lacan died in 1981, shortly after initiating

national and international associations to replace the activity of the *École freudienne de Paris*. (**BB**)

See also POSTSTRUCTURALISM.

Further Reading

Fink, B. (1997) *A Clinical Introduction to Lacanian Psychoanalysis: Theory and Technique*, Cambridge, MA: Harvard University Press.

Lacan, J. (1990) *Television*, New York: Norton.

Roudinesco, E. (1990) *Jacques Lacan & Co – A History of Psychoanalysis in France, 1925–1985*, London: Free Association Books (a translation of vol. 2 of E. Roudinesco, *La Bataille de Cent Ans – Histoire de la Psychanalyse en France; Vol 1: 1885–1939*, Paris, 1982, *Vol. 2: 1925–1985*, Paris, 1986).

LANGAGE Saussurean technical term, not to be confused with **langue**. According to the *Cours de linguistique générale*, *langage* is a human 'faculty', requiring for its exercise the establishment of a *langue* among the members of a community. (**RH**)

See also Harris (this volume), and *PAROLE*.

LANGUE Saussurean technical term, not to be confused with **langage**. According to the *Cours de linguistique générale*, *la langue* is 'a body of necessary conventions adopted by society to enable members of society to use their faculty of *langage*'. (**RH**)

See also Harris (this volume), and *PAROLE*.

LEGISIGN Charles S. **Peirce**'s term for the third division of his trichotomy of the **grounds** of signs. A legisign is a **sign** which, in itself, is a general law or type. Conventional signs, such as words, are legisigns. Legisigns signify through replicas or tokens (instances of their application). There are different kinds of legisigns distinguished principally by whether their underlying objects are represented **icon**ically (as in diagrams), **index**ically (as in demonstrative **pronoun**s), or **symbol**ically (as in common **noun**s, propositions, or arguments). (**NH**)

See also QUALISIGN, SINSIGN, RHEME, DICENT and ARGUMENT.

LEVINAS Emmanuel Levinas (Haunas 1906–Paris 1995), one of the most significant philosophers of the twentieth century, has profoundly contributed to semiotico-linguistic problematics by dealing with the question of **alterity** in terms of the critique of ontology. His work represents an original contribution, alongside Hartman, Block, Heidegger, Husserl, Sartre, Merleau-Ponty and **Bakhtin** to that multifaceted movement in philosophy concerned with the refoundation of ontology. Such refoundation contrasts with philosophies hegemonized by the logic of knowledge and reductively stated in epistemological terms. Levinas developed his thought in dialogue with Husserl and Heidegger whose works he was the first to introduce into France after having followed their courses in Freiburg between 1928 and 1929. (**AP**)

Further Reading

Levinas, E. (1990) *The Levinas Reader*, ed. S. Hand, Oxford: Blackwell.

LÉVI-STRAUSS Structuralist anthropologist Claude Lévi-Strauss – born in Brussels (of French parents) in November 1908 and still professionally active in his nineties – has been associated with the University of Paris and College of France throughout most of his life. His earliest training there, from 1927 to 1932, was in philosophy and law. In 1934 he accepted a position in sociology at the University of São Paulo in Brazil, from which post he ventured on several field trips into the

Amazon, intermittently between 1935 and 1938. From this background and in this crucible, fertile empirical fieldwork laid the foundation for a vast *œuvre* of ethnographic, ethnologic, and particularly theoretical, treatises. Anthropological **structuralism** took shape through Lévi-Strauss, but not without the integration of earlier and later influences in his life (**Marx**, **Kant**, Durkheim, Mauss, **Saussure**, **Jakobson**); he was also early to understand entropy in sociocultural systems.

At the outset of the Second World War, Lévi-Strauss lost an academic position due to the racial laws of the Vichy government. He relocated to the United States in 1941, holding a position at the New School for Social Research and serving, 1945–47, as French cultural attaché. While in New York, he met Roman Jakobson, Franz **Boas**, and innumerable other intellectuals from the USA and abroad (Sebeok 1991c). The contact with Jakobson and structural linguistics ignited Lévi-Strauss's intuitive handle on **synchronic** approaches to language and culture studies.

Lévi-Strauss's work until mid-century focused on kinship systems and marriage rules (e.g., 1949), while later he concentrated on belief systems embodied in myths and religion (e.g., his *Mythologiques* tetralogy 1964–71). In both realms, his aim was the same – to reveal the abstract systems with their internal logics of relations, rendering coherent the often chaotic and seemingly arbitrary practices and beliefs at the level of social life (Jenkins 1979; de Josseling de Jong 1952).

Inspired by linguistics and especially **phonology**, Lévi-Strauss developed a methodology to elicit principles pertaining to universal systems of marriage alliance and of narrated myth. One such principle is reciprocity (1944), fed by exchange/circulation/communication, whereby the process has value over and beyond what is exchanged. Restricted and generalized exchange not only elucidates the circulation of goods, women, and words, but goes further to explain the universal institution of incest prohibition. Proscription of sex and of marriage in the nuclear family and particular other entities leads to matrimonial alliances throughout the wider society; conversely, incest would extinguish reciprocity.

Lévi-Strauss abduced universal principles in abstract systems from empirical ethnographic observations and ethnological comparisons. His work is structural in its synchronic bias, and in its dissatisfaction with temporal (diffusionist and genealogical) explanations. History is relevant, but not because it is prior and certainly not because of authenticity claims. Between **diachronic** forms and between synchronic versions of cultural forms lie congruent transformational logics relying on the same intellectual techniques of analogy, homology, inversion, symmetry, and redundancy.

Lévi-Strauss asserts that human mentality and human culture are molar, linked, universal, symbolic processes. A controversial thinker having immeasurable impact on contemporary intellectual thought, Lévi-Strauss has raised the bar for all of the human sciences. (**MA**)

See also DOUGLAS and PIKE.

Further Reading

Hénaff, M. (1998) *Claude Lévi-Strass and the Making of Structural Anthropology*, trans M. Baker, Minneapolis: University of Minnesota Press.

Leach, E. R. (1970) *Lévi-Strauss*, London: Collins.

Rossi, I. (ed.) (1974) *The Unconscious in Culture: The Structuralism of Claude Lévi-Strauss in Perspective*, New York: E. P. Dutton.

LEXICON Sometimes used as an alternative to *dictionary*. In linguistics, the lexicon is the term used for the **component** of a **grammar** which contains informa-

tion about individual words: in particular, information which is idiosyncratic to that word and not predictable from some general rule. For instance, it is an accidental, idiosyncratic fact about English that the word *girl* means 'young female person'. The fact that the plural is *girls*, however, is the result of a general rule about plurals in English. The first fact would be part of the lexicon, the second would not. (**RS**)

LINGUISTIC SYSTEM In **structuralist** approaches, language is seen as a system of interrelated systems, arranged in a hierarchy of levels: the phonological system deals with regularities of sound; the grammatical system deals with regularities of form (both of elements such as words, and of structures); and the semantic system deals with elements and arrangements of **meaning**. (**GRK**)

LOCKE John Locke (1632–1704), English philosopher. By a tangled tale (L. J. Russell 1939; Sebeok 1971; Romeo 1977; Deely 1994a, Ch. 5; Deely 2000, Ch. 14), the word **'semiotics'** in English seems to derive as a transliteration from what would be the Latin ('semiotica') of the miscoined Greek term ΣΗΜΙΩΤΙΚΗ [sic] from the closing chapter of Locke's *Essay Concerning Human Understanding* of 1690. This original coinage Locke introduced to name what he also called 'the doctrine of signs', echoing the Latin expression 'doctrina signorum' widely circulated in the Latin university world of sixteenth-century Iberia, where, unknown to Locke, the idea had first been reduced to systematic foundations in the doctrine of triadic relation by John **Poinsot** (1632). Picked up by Charles S. **Peirce** as the nineteenth century reached its end, the term 'semiotics' gradually came into general usage over the course of the twentieth century, edging out its rival (**semiology**) as the term of popular culture for the new intellectual movement. In this way, to Locke has fallen the honor of naming the postmodern development that overthrew the modern epistemological paradigm (to which Locke himself in the main body of his *Essay* subscribed) in favor of, as Locke presciently put it, 'another sort of Logick and Critick, than what we have been hitherto acquainted with'. **(JD)**

Further Reading

Deely, J. (1978) 'What's in a name?', *Semiotica* 22 (1/2): 151–81.

LOCUTION, LOCUTIONARY In the terminological framework introduced by **Austin** (1962) to cope with the multifunctionality of all utterances (locution-**illocution-perlocution**), 'locution' is reserved for the act *of* saying something. This always involves the act of uttering certain noises, i.e. a *phonetic act*. Further, it is always connected with the act of pronouncing certain words belonging to and as belonging to a particular vocabulary, and certain constructions belonging to and as belonging to a particular **grammar**, i.e. a **phatic** act. Moreover, 'saying something' is generally the performance of a phonetic and phatic act with a more or less definite sense and reference (together adding up to 'meaning'), i.e. a *rhetic act*. In later versions of **speech act** theory (since Searle 1969) the term 'locution' is not in common use; it has generally been replaced by 'proposition' (covering reference and predication, and leaving out the aspects of sound, vocabulary, and grammar that were included by Austin). **(JV)**

Further Reading

Austin, J. L. (1962) *How to Do Things with Words*, ed. J. O. Urmson, Oxford: Oxford University Press.

LOGOS, LOGOCENTRIC Terms used by the Algerian-born French philosopher Jacques **Derrida** to describe the pre-eminence given to the spoken word in Saussurean linguistics. **Saussure**, says Derrida, equates *logos* with *phon* (sound), and by so doing, reinforces the belief (mistaken, according to Derrida) that spoken language is the expression of thought, and that thought can exist independent of language. **(RM)**

See PHONE, PHONIC, PHONOLOGISM.

LOTMAN Jurij (sometimes 'Yuri') Lotman (Petrograd 1922–Tartu 1993), scholar of literature and semiotician, co-founder of the Tartu–Moscow school. From 1939–40 and 1946–1950 he studied at the Leningrad State University (1940–45 in Soviet Army); from 1950 he was resident in Tartu and, from 1954, at the Tartu University (1960–77 Head of the Department of Russian Literature, from 1963 professor). During the period 1968–85 he was Vice President of the **IASS** (Terras 1985; Le Grand 1993).

Lotman's first explicitly 'semiotic' publication was 'Lectures on structural poetics' (1964) which formed the foundation to the series *Semeiotik: Sign Systems Studies*. Lotman's **semiotics** originated from distinguishing structure in language and texts (Lotman 1964, 1975), grounded by the notion of a '**modelling** system' as a structure of elements and their combinatory rules. The 'primary modelling system' is formed by **natural language** (cf. Sebeok 1989), while 'secondary modelling systems' are *analogous* to language, or use language as material (literature, fine arts, music, film, myth, religion, etc.). In culture these systems function together, aspiring to autonomy on the one hand, creolizing on the other. Thus, 'cultural semiotics' became, for him, 'the study of the functional correlation of different sign systems' (Lotman 1973).

Sign systems can be analysed individually, but their correlation is expressed best in the most important analytic unit – the text (Lotman 1976, 1977a). While culture 'is defined as a system of relationships established between man and the world' (Lotman and Uspenskij 1984; Lotman *et al.* 1985), the foundation of its description is a functional analogy between cerebral hemispheres, language, text and culture. From the primeval semiotic dualism – the splitting of the world in language and the doubling of the human in space – arises an asymmetric **binarism** of the minimal semiotic mechanism. Effectively, there is a division of systems into two main types: in 'discrete' systems (verbal, logical) the **sign** is basic and independent from behavior: in 'continual' systems (**icon**ic, mythological) there are texts in which signs are depictive and connected with behavior. In the first case language is created by signs, in the latter by the text. Thus text may simultaneously be a sign and one or more sign systems.

Understanding heterogeneity and coherence of text is inseparable from the notion of 'border'. The border segregates (guaranteeing structural cohesion) and unites (assuring dialogism with the extra-textual). Borders intertwining in time and space form a system of 'semiospheres' in a global semiosphere that is 'the result and the condition for the development of culture' (Lotman 1990; Deltcheva and Vlasov 1996; Mandelker 1994; Sturrock 1991).

Lotman's semiotics is characterized by a firm connection with empirical material: analyses of text, literary history and biography (Shukman 1987). (**PT**)

Further Reading

Lotman, Y. M. (1990) *Universe of The Mind*, trans. A. Shukman, London and New York: Tauris.

Lotman, J. M. and Uspenski, B. A. (1984) *The Semiotics of Russian Culture*, Ann Arbor, MI: Michigan Slavic Contributions 11.

Shukman, A. (1977) *Literature and Semiotics: A Study of the Writings of Ju. M. Lotman*, Amsterdam: North Holland Publishers.

M

MARKER General term capturing a range of linguistic phenomena whose task it is to 'mark' utterances as functionally related to context in a specific way. The full range goes from **illocutionary** force indicating devices (such as 'promise' in 'I promise to come tomorrow'), over contextualization cues (such as code switches symbolizing group adherence; see Gumperz 1982), to a multitude of '**discourse** markers' or 'pragmatic particles' (such as 'you know', 'I mean', 'anyway', etc.; see Schiffrin 1987). (**JV**)

MARX Karl Marx (1818–83). In the theoretical field as in politics 'Marxism' has interfered with an understanding of Marx's greatness as a thinker. Except for rare cases (such as **Vološinov/Bakhtin**, **Schaff** and **Rossi-Landi**), 'Marxist' theories of the sign and even 'Marxist linguistics (an example is the 'Marxist linguistics' practised by N. Ja. Marr – see Marcellese *et al.* 1978) have nothing to do with Marx's remarkable contribution to the study of language and social communication. It seems that Marx himself said: 'The only thing I can say is that I'm not a Marxist!' (see Enzensberger 1973, p. 456).

Marx suggests that, 'From the start the "spirit" is afflicted with the course of being "burdened" with matter, which here makes its appearance in the form of agitated layers of air, sounds, in short, of language' (Marx and Engels 1968, p. 42). Language occupies a very important part of Marx's philosophy. His materialism is not mechanistic and accepts the historical dimension; it maintains a balance between 'natural' and 'social' factors in order to preserve con-

tinuity between human and non-human animals as well as to assess the qualitative leap that distinguishes what is species-specifically human from the rest of life on the planet. Language is the requisite for the passage from 'mere life' to consciousness and consequently to the organisation of life. In other words, it is required for the move from **semiosis** to **semiotics**, from the mere passing of signs to the specific life of the human as a semiotic animal. Language is not one of several means of communication between the self and the other but the basis of the self and of one's relations, as self, with others. The possibility of 'having relations' and not merely of being in relation, which is a specifically human possibility, is founded on language.

> Language is as old as consciousness, language *is* practical consciousness that exists also for other men, and for that reason alone it exists for me personally as well . . . The animal does not 'have relations' . . . For the animal its relations do not exist as relations (Marx and Engels 1968, p. 42). . . . Language is the immediate actuality of thought . . . Neither the thought, nor the language exist in an independent realm from life.
> (Marx and Engels 1968, pp. 503–4)

Marxian critique concentrates on deciphering the 'language of commodities' (Marx 1962, vol. 1, chapter 1), and on explaining the entire process of the functioning of such commodities as messages. In tandem with this, the critique of the fetishistic vision of commodities aims at demonstrating that the relation among commodities, and among commodities and values, are relations of communication among human beings and are all founded on social relations. (AP)

Further Reading

Marx, K. (1973) *Grundrisse: Foundations of the Critique of Political Economy*, trans. M. Nicolaus, Harmondsworth: Penguin.

Marx, K. and Engels, F. (1974) *Über Sprache, Stil und Übersetzung*, ed. K. Ruschiski and B. Retzlaff-Kresse, Berlin: Dietz.

Ponzio, A. (1989) 'Semiotics and Marxism', in *The Semiotic Web 1988*, ed. T. A. Sebeok and J. Umiker-Sebeok, Berlin: Mouton de Gruyter.

MEANING 'Meaning' is at issue whenever something can be said to be a *culturally established* **sign** of something else, whether linguistic as in 'The French word "neige" means snow' or non-linguistic as in 'A white flag means surrender'. Meaning generated in the use of signs may be intentional or non-intentional (though some scholars would recognize only the intentional variety, thus emphasizing the production side). It may be literal (where the link between the sign and what the sign stands for is explicit and fully conventional) or figurative or indirect (where further inferencing is required, even though a degree of conventionality is often involved as well, as in the case of figures of speech and indirect speech acts). It may be seen as 'timeless' (sentence meaning and word meaning) or as occasion-specific (in which case **Grice** would use the term 'utterer's meaning').

Various theories of meaning can be distinguished. A referential or denotational theory views the meaning of an **expression** as that which it stands for. A mentalist theory would relate the meaning of an expression to the ideas or concepts it is associated with in the mind of anyone understanding it. A behaviorist theory views the stimulus evoking an expression or the response evoked by it as its meaning. The meaning-is-use theory holds that the meaning of an expression is a function of the way(s) in which it is used. According to the verificationist theory, the meaning of an expression is determined by the verifiability of the propositions that contain it. And a truth-conditional theory defines meaning as the contribution made by an expression to the truth conditions of a sentence. (**JV**)

See also BRÉAL, PROPOSITION, SEMANTICS, SPEECH ACT, DENOTATION, CONNOTATION, REFERENT, SIGNIFICATION and TRUTH.

Further Reading

Lyons, J. (1995) *Linguistic Semantics: An Introduction*, Cambridge: Cambridge University Press.

MEDIA DISCOURSE The main characteristic of media discourse is its diversity. Looking at different media in contemporary society it is evident that books, newspapers, magazines, radio, television and 'new media' like the Internet and the World Wide Web do not speak with one voice, neither in terms of content nor in terms of their modes of address. Media discourse, defined broadly as the way in which the media talk about social reality, is thus inherently a plural concept.

Diversity remains the main characteristic when one looks at the discourse of the individual media. Television, to take an example, spans a vast range of pure and hybrid **genres** such as news, current affairs, documentaries, comedy, soap opera, studio debate programmes, phone-in programmes, etc. whose language and other modes of **signification** defy uniform characterisation.

At the same time, however, it is evident that there are striking similarities between some of the media precisely at the level of the different genres. 'Interviews' are prominent in the printed press as well as in television and radio, although the interview genre has been adapted to the different technological and expressive modes of each medium. Other examples of genres shared between media are the various fiction formats like the western or the detective story, or advertising which is ubiquitous in all commercial media.

Because of this diversity people looking for a characterisation of media discourse should consult analytical works whose point of departure is the fundamental sign systems from which all media discourses build their **meanings** (Barthes [1957] 1973c; Eco 1979; Hodge and Kress 1988; Kress and Van Leeuwen 1996; Messaris 1997), or consult works that analyse the specific media or genres one is interested in (Crisell 1986; Bell 1991; Cook 1992; Scannell 1991; Livingstone and Lunt 1994; Turkle 1995; Olson 1999).

As a consequence of the inherent plurality of the phenomenon it designates the study of media discourse should be approached in a holistic manner (Schrøder 1994). One authoritative, synthesising approach, which draws on a range of academic traditions from linguistics to social theory, is that of Norman Fairclough (Fairclough 1995b). In this broadly social constructionist approach **discourse analysis** of the media is seen as consisting ideally of three interrelated steps: texts, discourse practices, and sociocultural practices. In practice, however, many analysts fall short of this ideal.

At the core of analytical activity stands the analysis of the texts carried by the media, i.e. the signifying structures of the verbal and visual signs that constitute the 'message', be this a newspaper report, an advertisement or a drama serial. The analysis proceeds according to the arsenal of tools developed in **semiotics** and linguistics, often with the aim of deducing through

textual analysis how the media text is likely to affect the audience's worldview or ideology and can thus be said to exercise power (Barthes 1964a; Fowler 1985).

It is widely recognised, however, that a fuller understanding of the social life of media texts is achieved by also looking at the **discourse** practices that surround the media text. These include both the institutional processes in which media texts are produced, or 'encoded', by journalists and other creative people, and the everyday, sometimes ritualised contexts in which people use, or 'decode', the texts according to their individual and social needs (Swales and Rogers 1995; Deacon *et al.* 1999).

Finally, one should consider the ways in which media discourses are related to the sociocultural practices that characterise the wider society, especially ways in which the media discourses contribute to social stability as well as social change. Among the salient communicative processes that characterise late modern societies Fairclough (1995b) suggests that particular attention should be paid to 'marketisation' and 'conversationalisation' of public discourse, and to an assessment of their ambivalent influence on mechanisms of social control and cultural democratisation. (**KCS**)

Further Reading

Briggs, A. and Cobley, P. (eds) (1998) *The Media: An Introduction*, Harlow: Longman (especially the essays in Section III, 'In the Media').

Fairclough, N. (1995b) *Media Discourse*, London: Arnold.

Myers, G. (1994) *Words in Ads*, London: Arnold.

METALANGUAGE Generally defined as the use of language to speak of language. In the Jakobsonian speech act model (1960), metalanguage is represented in the metalingual function, an ever-present aspect of any linguistic event, which is determined by reference to the **code** itself. The metalingual function is particularly important in child language acquisition and in any form of second or third language acquisition. Manifestations of metalingual breakdown are discussed at length in **Jakobson**'s 'Aspects of language and types of aphasic disturbances' (1956). Also relevant is Jakobson's discussion of the metalingual function in duplex linguistic structures in 'Shifters and verbal categories' (1957). (**EA**)

See also DEIXIS, METONYMY and HALLE.

METAPHYSICS Metaphysics is the backbone of the whole Western philosophical tradition, yet it has numerous potential definitions and has been the subject of considerable controversy. In general, metaphysics is concerned with 'how things are' in the universe and how relations between things are thought to inhere. Because humans' interaction with the things of the world is bound up with the mediating action of **signs**, **semiotics** has important findings to contribute to the debate about metaphysics. (**KB**)

See also REALISM and NOMINALISM.

METONYMY In Jakobsonian theory, metonymy is no longer a mere 'figure of speech', but rather becomes one of the two defining axes of human language. Each linguistic act requires a selection from a set of pre-existing units and a combination of these units into more complex **syntagm**s. The axis of selection is primarily based on similarity relations, which are metaphoric in their essence, while the axis of combination is based on contiguity relations, which are metonymic. All forms of aphasia for **Jakobson** rest between these two extremes. Jakobson's contiguity aphasic disorders are defined primarily by the loss of metonymic relations. No manifestation

of language of verbal art excludes metaphor and metonymy; however, one of the poles may be dominant (cf. Cubism and Eisenstein's cinematic art as examples of dominating metonymy). (**EA**)

MODE In the theory of **register**, mode refers to the channel of communication which is enacted in a speech **situation**. In a classroom, for example, the **field** or the social practices which inform the linguistic interaction will be the general ethos or process of education. The **tenor** will be the power relations between the teacher who might be active in imparting information and the student who might rely on the teacher for this purpose. These role relationships will take place through the mode: the specific channel of pedagogic communication, typical forms of which include lectures, seminars, brainstorming, and so on. (**PC**)

See also HALLIDAY.

MODELLING A process by which something is performed or reproduced on the basis of a model or schema, whether ideal or real. For example, Plato's world of ideas is used as a model by the demiurge to create the empirical world. In **semiotics** models are based on a relation of similarity or isomorphism and are therefore associated to the **icon**ic sign as understood by **Peirce**. The concept of 'modelling' is present in the term 'patterning' as used by **Sapir** (1916) to designate the original and specific organization of culture and language: *cultural patterning* and *linguistic patterning*. Among all social behaviors none is as dependent upon unconscious mechanisms as language. Unconscious patterning operates at all levels of natural language, phonological, syntactic, **semantic** and pragmatic. Natural language resists intervention by the individual and rationalization more than any other element in culture. However, it is also subject to transformation, but this is due to an internal 'drift' process. By comparison with all other cultural products, **natural language** is the most perfectly autarchic, unconscious and varied through internal 'drift' and for this reason it is the anthropologist's most important instrument for studies on the original patterning of culture.

'Modelling system' is used by the so-called Tartu–Moscow school. The expression 'primary modelling system' has been used since 1962 by A. A. Zaliznjak, V. V. Ivanov, and V. N. Toporov. In 1967 (English translation 1977) Ju M. **Lotman** specified that 'a modelling system can be regarded as a language'. 'Primary modelling system' is used to distinguish natural language from other semiotic systems. The expression 'secondary modelling system' is used by semioticians of the Tartu–Moscow school to denote human cultural systems other than natural language.

The concept of modelling as proposed by the Tartu–Moscow school comes very close to Sapir's. It confers upon language 'originariness' in modelling over other systems. As in Sapir, it involves the relativity of cultures with respect to such primary modelling and does not solve the problem of communicability among different languages and cultures, and of the multiplicity of languages, and still less the problem of language origin.

One way of developing and extending the Tartu conception is by connecting it to the biologist and semiotician Jakob von **Uexküll** and his concept of *Umwelt*, translatable as 'model'. This approach is adopted by **Sebeok** (1991a and Anderson and Merrell 1991) who attributes the capacity for primary modelling to *language* as distinct from speech. Language is specifically designed to produce and organize worldviews, whereas speech is an adaptive derivation in *Homo* arising for communicative purposes. *Homo* evolved into *Homo sapiens sapiens* thanks to this modelling device and its species-specific properties, language. All animal species construct their own worlds in which things assume a given sense; the distinctive feature of the human species rests in its capacity for conferring an infinite number of different senses upon a limited set of elements and, therefore, for constructing a great plurality of different possible worlds. Speech, with its specific communicative function, appears only subsequently in the evolutionary process. The plurality of languages and 'linguistic creativity' (**Chomsky**) testify to the capacity of language understood as a primary modelling device, for producing numerous possible worlds. On the contrary, verbal language and the natural languages in which it is differentiated, are the expression of *secondary modelling* processes. (**AP**)

Further Reading

Anderson, M. and Merrell, F. (eds) (1991) *On Semiotic Modeling*, Berlin and New York: Mouton de Gruyter.

Sebeok, T. A. and Danesi, M. (2000) *The Forms of Meaning: Modeling Systems Theory and Semiotic Analysis*, Berlin and New York: Mouton de Gruyter.

Zaliznjak, A. A. *et al.* (1977) 'Structural-typological study of semiotic modeling systems', in D. P. Lucid (ed.) *Soviet Semiotics: An Anthology*, Baltimore and London: Johns Hopkins University Press.

MORPHEME Words often consist of smaller meaningful parts. The word *climbers*, for instance, consists of three parts, each with its separate **meaning**: *climb* ('move upwards', -*er* ('person who does the action') and -*s* (plural). These minimal units with their own meaning are called *morphemes*. The word *daffodil* consists of a single morpheme, while *internationally* has four (*inter+nation+al+ly*). (**RS**)

MORPHOLOGY The study of the structure of words and **morphemes**.

Morphology covers inflection (different forms of the same word, such as *invent*, *invents*, *invented*, *inventing*) and word formation (the creation of new words by combining existing words and morphemes, such as *invention* from *invent + ion*). (**RS**)

MORRIS Charles Morris (Denver, Colorado, 1901–Gainesville, Florida, 1979) studied engineering, biology, psychology and philosophy. After having finished his science degree in 1922, he completed a PhD in philosophy at the University of Chicago in 1925, where he taught from 1931 to 1958.

Morris's **semiotics** offers a general description of **sign** as embracing all that belongs to the world of life. He aimed at developing an approach to semiotics that could deal with all kinds of signs, and to this end he constructed his terminology within a distinctly biological framework, as emerges particularly from his book of 1946, *Signs, Language and Behavior*. For this reason Ferruccio **Rossi-Landi** – who as early as 1953 had authored the monograph *Charles Morris* – described Morris's research in terms of 'behavioristic biopsychology'.

But Morris's interest in biology coincided with the beginning of his studies on signs, or, as he says in the 1920s, 'symbolism'. His PhD dissertation *Symbolism and Reality* (*SR*), of 1925 (but published only in 1993) includes a chapter entitled 'Some psychological and biological considerations'. Therefore, the terms 'symbolism' and 'biology' appear very early in his work. Also, in the preface to *Six Theories of Mind* (1932), he states his intention to develop a general theory of symbolism on the conviction that the mind and the symbolic process are identifiable.

On describing semiotics as a 'science of behavior', Morris was not referring to a philosophical–psychological trend known as behaviorism, but rather to a 'science', a discipline yet to be developed, a 'field', to use his own terminology. Morris underlines that his behaviorism derived mainly from George H. Mead as well as from Edward Tolman and Clark L. Hull. From Otto Neurath he took the term 'behavioristics' to name the science or field in question. And, indeed, differently to other behaviorists who apply psychology as developed in the study of rats to the study of men (as one of Morris's reviewers protested), these scholars attempted to develop a general theory of behavior, a 'behavioristics', says Morris, able to account for the behavior of both men and rats, while at the same time accounting for their differences.

Charles S. **Peirce**'s **pragmatism** played an important role in the development of Morris's semiotics. This is evident in the monograph entitled *Logical Positivism, Pragmatism and Scientific Empiricism* (1937). In 1938, in addition to *Foundations of a Theory of Signs*, his groundbreaking contribution to the science of signs, Morris also published 'Scientific Empiricism' (both in *International Encyclopedia of Unified Science*) as well as 'Peirce, Mead and Pragmatism' (*Philosophical Review*). In the latter Morris insists on the affinity between Peirce and Mead or between the original pragmatism of the former and the more recent version of the latter.

By comparison with *Foundations*, Morris in *Signs, Language and Behavior* (1946) consolidates the relation between biology, behaviorism and semiotics. His recourse to biology for semiotic terminology does not at all imply 'biologism', for there is no tendency to *reductionism* (the temptation of reducing a plurality of universes of **discourse** to only one, in this case the discourse of biology). From this point of view, his attitude was different from the reductionism of the logical empiricists or neo-positivists due to their explicitly physicalist orientation.

In *Signification and Significance* (1964), Morris develops his interest in values in addition to signs and indeed he establishes a close connection between semiotics and axiology. The word '**meaning**' has a dual meaning, not only the **semantic** (signification) but also the valuative (significance). At the same time, in this book Morris's semiotics confirms itself as an 'interdisciplinary enterprise' (ibid., p. 1) focusing on signs in all their forms and manifestations, relatively to human and nonhuman animals, normal and pathological signs, linguistic and nonlinguistic signs, personal and social signs. (**SP**)

Further Reading

Morris, C. (1938) *Foundations of the Theory of Signs*, Chicago: University of Chicago Press.

Morris, C. (1946) *Signs, Language and Behavior*, Englewood Cliffs, NJ: Prentice-Hall.

Morris, C. (1971) *Writings on the General Theory of Signs*, ed. T.A. Sebeok, The Hague and Paris: Mouton.

MUKAŘOVSKÝ Jan Mukařovský (1891–1975), one of the cofounders of the Prague Linguistics Circle (with R. **Jakobson**, N. **Trubetzkoy**, V. Mathesius, B. Havránek and S. Karcevskij) in 1926. His academic positions included a grammar school in Pilsen, a professorship at the University of Bratislava and, after 1937, a position as professor of aesthetics at Charles University. Scholarly works focus on the study of Czech poetics and the construction of a theory of structural aesthetics. Although Mukařovský was the only member of the Prague Linguistics Circle who was not a linguist, he is considered by many to be one of its more influential members. Mukařovský's more notable works include *Příspěvek k estetice českého verše* (1923), 'O jazyce básnickém' (1940), *Kapitoly z české poetiky* (1948). Mukařovský became quite active in politics in post-war Czechoslovakia as a pro-Communist supporter and apparently abandoned his intellectual (structuralist) roots. (**EA**)

See also PRAGUE SCHOOL.

Further Reading

Mukařovský, J. (1979) *Aesthetic Function, Norm and Value as Social Facts*, trans. M. Suino, Ann Arbor, MI: University of Michigan Slavic Contributions.

N

NATURAL LANGUAGE The phrase 'natural language' distinguishes languages used in actual communities from languages that individuals or committees invent to promote international harmony (e.g. Esperanto), or to serve a special population (e.g. the Paget-Gorman Sign Language, and numerous American sign systems for educating deaf children). Applied to language in general, however, the adjective 'natural' carries various **connotation**s.

In the tradition of Descartes and **Saussure**, some language scholars think that so arbitrary a system as language cannot have evolved naturally from other animals' communication (e.g. Chomsky 1957; Bickerton 1995). Others call language an instinct (e.g. Pinker, 1994), implying its use is as natural as any other instinctive behavior. But still others find evolutionary continuity by tracing language to **gesture**s, the meaningful movements that higher primates make and humans interpret syntactically as well as semantically (Armstrong *et al.* 1995; Stokoe [this volume]).

To the broad question, 'Does language happen naturally?' the answer appears to be, 'Yes; but only under certain conditions.' Natural or normal language acquisition requires both social interaction and functioning human physiology. Infants deaf from birth do not acquire a spoken language, at least not in the usual way. A review of many longitudinal studies of hearing and deaf children, in various language environments, finds that all children communicate gesturally for some months before they use the language others around them use (Volterra and Iverson 1996). Gestural communication appears to be a normal stage in an individual's acquisition of language – perhaps analogous to crawling before walking. (**WCS**)

See SIGN LANGUAGES and MODELLING.

Further Reading

Armstrong, D. *et al.* (1995) *Gesture and the Nature of Language*, Cambridge: Cambridge University Press.

NEUROLINGUISTICS The study of the neural basis of language. The main task for neurolinguists is to locate the regions of the brain which handle the various aspects of language. Two types of technique are used: the first one that developed was the study of people with brain damage, as a result of accident or illness. If a particular part of a person's brain is damaged and they mispronounce words, it is reasonable to suppose that this part of the brain is responsible for speech production. More recently, techniques for observing and measuring brain activity have provided a second type of technique for neurolinguistic investigation: these include computerised axial tomography and magnetic resonance imaging.

The main part of the brain associated with language appears to be the outer grey layer, known as the cerebral cortex. In most people it is the left hemisphere that is involved, though about 20 per cent of left-handed people have the language functions located in the right hemisphere (Caplan 1992, pp. 79–80). The location of particular functions of language in specific parts of the brain is a matter of some controversy, and the physiological and biochemical basis of language is still poorly understood. (RS)

Further Reading

Caplan, D. (1988) 'The biological basis for language', in F. Newmeyer (ed.) *Linguistics: The Cambridge Survey*, vol. 3, Cambridge: Cambridge University Press, pp. 237–55.

NOMINALISM The doctrine that whatever generality there is in the universe pertains to names and not to real things. Only particulars, or individuals, exist and universals, or generals, are merely creations of language for the purpose of referring to many things at once. In its most extreme form, nominalism takes the position that universals and abstract ideas do not exist in any sense except as empty names or words. This view does not necessarily imply that general terms are ineffectual or useless but only that they can always be reduced to expressions involving reference to nothing more than particulars or expressions that serve some logical purpose. On this view, universal terms of any kind are fictions. A more moderate form of nominalism, conceptualism, holds that while universals have no substantive existence they may have a subjective existence as mental concepts. Conceptualism is often regarded as a middle ground between nominalism and its principal opponent, Platonic **realism**.

The main arguments for nominalism emerged in the twelfth century with Roscellinus and Abelard and were further developed in the fourteenth century by **William of Ockham** in opposition to the realism of Duns Scotus. All of the main British empiricists were nominalists who, like Ockham, argued that general terms are in one way or another only linguistic

contrivances for referring to many particulars at once. Following the widespread acceptance of evolutionary theory in biology, nominalism tended to merge with materialism to support a mechanistic physicalist reductionism of the sort advanced by Herbert Spencer in the latter part of the nineteenth century and, more recently, so successfully advocated by philosophers like Willard van Orman Quine and Wilfrid Sellars. In continuing to guard against what they believe to be the unnecessary multiplication of entities, modern nominalists deny reality to all sorts of abstract entities from laws and possible states to properties, sets, and natural kinds. The denial that intentions and qualia are real and general is typical of contemporary nominalism.

With so many different abstract entities and generals now in the mix, there are many degrees and varieties of nominalism. Quine, for example, admits sets into his ontology, but otherwise only particulars. Although the traditional enemy of nominalism has been realism, some forms of realism are in fact quite compatible with nominalism. For example, what is now called external realism, the view that real things exist independently of all thought about them, is held by many contemporary nominalists. When nominalism is combined with external realism there is a tendency toward a Kantian isolation of fundamental reality from thought about it and to suppose that the principal content of thought is of linguistic or psychological origin. According to Charles S. **Peirce**, **Kant**'s view that all unity of thought depends upon the nature of the human mind, and does not belong to the 'thing in itself' is a form of nominalism.

Nominalism has significant ramifications for ethics, **semiotics**, and other disciplines. Nominalist ethics concerns itself exclusively with the interests of individuals and is built up without any reference to efficacious purposes or to universal goods or rights. Nominalist semiotics rejects any robust distinction between types and tokens, a core feature of Peirce's semeiotic. **(NH)**

See also METAPHYSICS.

Further Reading

Armstrong, D. M. (1978) *Universals and Scientific Realism*, 2 vols, Cambridge: Cambridge University Press.

Loux, M. J. (1998) 'Nominalism', *Routledge Encyclopedia of Philosophy*, London: Routledge.

Peirce, C. S. (1992) 'Some consequences of four incapacities', (1868) and 'Review of Fraser's *The Works of George Berkeley*', (1871) in *The Essential Peirce: Selected Philosophical Writings*, vol. 1, eds. N. Houser and C. Kloesel, Bloomington: Indiana University Press, pp. 83–105 and pp. 28–55.

NOUN Words like *table*, *cat* and *school* are called nouns. They can appear as part of the subject or object of a sentence (The *table* is empty; I hate *school*); they usually have plural forms (*cats*), and they can be preceded by an article (*the* school) or an adjective (a *full* table). Nouns typically refer to people, places, things or animals. **(RS)**

NOUN-PHRASE A group of words containing a **noun**, which behaves like a noun. An example is *the little room at the top of the stairs*: the main or 'head' noun is *room*, shown by the fact that if this noun phrase was the answer to the question *What did you see?*, the answer refers to a kind of room, with the other words in the phrase telling us something about the room. The subject or object of a sentence is usually a noun phrase rather than a noun on its own. **(RS)**

O

OBJECT Anything that can be sensed, reacted to, or thought about, either directly or indirectly. Often limited to that which stands in some relation as separate from or other than something else, but sometimes extended to include real things in themselves (independently of their relations). When taken in the first sense, objects can be distinguished from subjects. Objects may be of an intellectual (mental) nature, e.g. Plato's conception of justice, or they may be natural (external), e.g. the hemlock that Socrates drank. Also, a goal or purpose; that for which action is taken. As a **verb**: to oppose or raise an objection. In the semeiotic of Charles S. **Peirce**, an object is anything that is represented in a **sign**. If the object of a sign is of the nature of a character, the sign's **interpretant** will be a feeling. If the object is an existential thing or event, the interpretant will be a resistance or reaction. If the object is a law, the interpretant will be a thought. According to Peirce, signs involve two kinds of objects, immediate objects, which are just what signs represent them to be, and dynamical objects, which are instrumental in the determination of their signs but are not immediately represented in them. Signs cannot express dynamical objects but can only indicate them and leave it to interpreters to find them by 'collateral experience' (Peirce 1998, p. 498). (**NH**)

Further Reading

Réthoré, J. (ed.) (1993) *Variations sur l'objet*, special issue of *European Journal for Semiotic Studies*, 5 (1 and 2).

OCKHAM See **WILLIAM OF OCKHAM**.

OGDEN Charles Kay Ogden (1889–1957) was unquestionably a polymath, known above all for his book with Ivor A. **Richards**, *The Meaning of Meaning* (1923). As a student at Cambridge University, Ogden was one of the founders of the Heretic Society for the discussion of problems concerning not only religion but also topics related to philosophy, art, science, etc. He worked as editor of the *Cambridge Magazine* and subsequently of *Psyche* (1923–52), a journal of general and linguistic psychology. Among his various undertakings he founded the Orthological Institute and invented Basic English, an international language comprising 850 words for people with no knowledge of English.

The orientation and development of his research were significantly influenced by his relationship with Victoria Lady **Welby** and Richards. The unpublished correspondence between Ogden and Welby (1910–11) is of noteworthy interest from the viewpoint of the connection between Welby's **significs** and the conception of **meaning** proposed in the above mentioned book by Ogden and Richards (cf. Gordon 1990b; Petrilli 1995c, 1998a, 1998b). As a young university student Ogden was an enthusiastic promoter of significs and in 1911 he gave a paper for the Heretic Society on 'The Progress of Significs' (cf. Ogden 1994b). In the *Meaning of Meaning* Ogden and Richards (1923) propose a triadic schema of the **sign** where interpretation and meaning emerge as relational processes, ensuing from the dynamic interaction between sign (or **representamen**), **interpretant**, and **object**, or in the authors' terminology, between **symbol,** reference, and **referent**. In this book, while the importance of Charles S. **Peirce** for **semiotics** is recognized with the insertion of a section devoted to him in the Appendix with which his ideas were introduced and made to circulate for the first time in England alongside the name of other important figures, Welby is mentioned but the significance of her contribution is not sufficiently acknowledged.

Further Reading

Gordon, T. W. (1991) 'The semiotics of C. K. Ogden', in T. A. Sebeok and J. Umiker-Sebeok (eds) *Recent Developments in Theory and History: The Semiotic Web 1990*, The Hague and Berlin: Mouton de Gruyter, pp. 111–77.

ONOMATOPOEIA The process of forming a word based on the sound of what the word names. Examples in English are *cuckoo* and *hiss*. In other languages we find words like Hebrew *bak-buk* 'bottle' (from the sound that liquid makes as it comes out); Shona (a Zimbabwean language) *vhuvhuta* 'to blow like the wind', and German *knusprig* 'crisp, crunchy'. (**RS**)

OPEN TEXT In 1962, *L'opera aperta* (*The Open Work*, 1989) found many readers disagreeing on the innovative and somewhat controversial proposals of Umberto **Eco**. Today the expression 'open work' has become such a popular expression that it does not always refer to the original views of the Italian semiotician and novelist.

Eco's 'poetic of the open work' was a reaction to Benedetto Croce's idealistic aesthetics on inspiration, form and content; it was also the result of having studied under the supervision of Luigi Pareyson whose philosophical teachings on aesthetics focused on how art is a cognitive experience and how it knows the world through its formal structures.

The Open Work precedes a number of theoretical concepts on the dialectics between author, **text** and reader that in the 1960s and 1970s were revolutionizing literary criticism; and it announces a number of strategies foreseen by authors who regard readers as possible collaborators in the genesis of their work. In his essays we can easily detect elements of **Barthes'** notion of 'readers as collaborators', of 'reader reception theories' popularized by Wolfgang Iser and Roman Ingarden, and of the new approaches to art and literature proposed by the avant-garde and experimental 'Gruppo 63' in Italy.

The reflections on aspects and degrees of 'openness' begin with references to the musical compositions of Berio, Pousseur and Stockhausen which give complete (interpretative) freedom to artists who wish to perform them. What follows is a variety of observations on such diverse forms of expression as Caulder's mobiles, Baroque and Impressionist poetics, kitsch, Antonioni's movies, Mallarmé's poetry, and Joyce's novels, in order to examine what is meant by an 'open' structure. The remarks about composers, artists, movie directors, and audience are all implicitly linked to the views on open texts and readers.

The key words and expressions at the center of 'openness' are ambiguity, discontinuity, possibility, plurivocal, indeterminancy, movement, on-going process, performance, and free interplay. The underlining motif throughout the essays is that an open work does not suggest any conclusion or specific interpretation as it demands a free inventive response from the performer/reader.

An open work continuously transforms its **denotation**s in **connotation**s and its **signified**s in **signifier**s of other signifieds.

This process of decoding remains open and on-going, guaranteeing open readings of the text. With open works every reading/interpretation may explain a text but will not exhaust it because its inner laws are based on ambiguity (e.g. Joyce's *Finnegan's Wake*). Moreover, open texts are systems of relationships that emphasize the genesis of processes rather than messages. They also encourage an active collaboration with the author and invite a free play of associations that functions as divertissement and as an instrument of cognition. For Eco the openness of a work of art is the very condition of aesthetic pleasure and it is an epistemological metaphor of our society. Openness transcends historical parameters (an example might be the way that Dante's *Commedia*, though containing highly specific messages is still pleasurable today) and allows a work to remain valid for a long time. (**RC**)

See CLOSED TEXT.

Further Reading

Eco, U. (1989) *The Open Work*, trans. A. Cancogni, Cambridge, MA: Harvard University Press.

ORDINARY LANGUAGE PHILOSOPHY
Ordinary language philosophy is often referred to as 'Oxford Philosophy' because it was largely developed by a group of philosophers working in Oxford (from the 1930s till the 1960s), including J. L. **Austin**, P. F. Strawson, and H. P. **Grice** (who moved to the USA). This tradition emerged against the background of earlier forms of analytical philosophy (beginning in the late nineteenth century) which represented a 'linguistic turn' in philosophy, paying explicit attention to the problem of knowledge in its relation to language, as influenced by or represented in the work of G. Frege, G. E. Moore, B. Russell, the early **Wittgenstein**, and R. Carnap. In contrast to earlier analytical philosophy, ordinary language philosophy (to which the later Wittgenstein contributed strongly from Cambridge) shifted its concerns from reduction and reformulation to description and elucidation and switched from the language of science as its primary object to ordinary everyday language. In the context of this emphasis on actual language use, utterances also came to be viewed as forms of action, the basic observation that gave rise to **speech act** theory as first formulated by Austin and further developed by J. R. Searle. (**JV**)

Further Reading

Austin, J. L. (1961) *Philosophical Papers*, Oxford: Oxford University Press.

OTHERNESS See **ALTERITY**.

P

PARADIGM (PARADIGMATIC) Technical term in neo-Saussurean linguistics, but one which **Saussure** himself did not use. It often replaces Saussure's *série associative* ('associative series'), which is a set of signs linked by partial resemblances, either in form or in **meaning**. Saussure described such sets as being established 'in the memory' and the items thus associated as forming a 'mnemonic series'. Substituting paradigmatic for associative seems to place the emphasis rather on the notion (which Saussure discusses) of sets of items related by the possibilities of substititution in a particular position. The flexional paradigm familiar from Latin grammar (*dominus*, *dominum, domini*, etc.) is cited by Saussure as just one type of example of an associative series. (**RH**)

See also SYNTAGM.

PAROLE **Saussure**an technical term for the linguistic level at which individual **speech act**s occur. Two persons talking to each other constitute the minimum 'speech circuit' (*circuit de la parole*). The speech act (*acte de parole*) is entirely under the control of the individual, unlike *la langue*. (**RH**)

PEIRCE Charles Sanders Peirce (Cambridge, Massachussetts 1839–Milford 1914), an American scientist, historian of science, logician, mathematician and philosopher of international fame. He founded contemporary **semiotics**, a general theory of **sign**s which he equated with logic and the theory of inference, especially **abduction**, and later with **pragmatism**, or as he preferred, **pragmaticism**. Peirce

graduated from Harvard College in 1859 and then received an M.Sc. from Harvard University's newly founded Lawrence Scientific School in 1863. His thirty-one-year employment as a research scientist in the US Coast and Geodetic Survey ended in 1891. Apart from short-term lectureships in logic and philosophy of science at the Johns Hopkins University in Baltimore (1879–1884), at the Lowell Institute in Boston (1866), and at Harvard (1865, 1869–1870, 1903, 1907), as well as at private homes in Cambridge (1898 and in other years), Peirce worked in isolation, outside the academic community.

He had difficulty publishing during his lifetime. A selection of published and un-published writings were eventually pre-pared in the *Collected Papers*, the first of which appeared in 1931. But an anthology of his writings edited by M. R. Cohen and entitled *Chance, Love and Logic* had already been published in 1923. His works are now being organized chronologically into a thirty-volume critical edition under the general title, *Writings of Charles S. Peirce: A Chronological Edition* (Indianapolis, Indiana: Peirce Edition Project), the first volume having appeared in 1982.

In a letter to Victoria Lady **Welby** (1837–1912) of 23 December 1908, Peirce, who was nearly seventy, conveys a sense of the inclusive scope of his semiotic perspective when he says:

it has never been in my power to study anything – mathematics, ethics, metaphysics, gravitation, thermo-dynamics, optics, chemistry, compara-tive anatomy, astronomy, psychology,

phonetics, economics, the history of science, whist, men and women, wine, metrology, except as a study of semeiotic.

(in Hardwick 1977, pp. 85–6)

As anticipated in a paper of 1905, 'Issues of Pragmaticism', in Peirce's conception the entire universe, the universe of existents and the universe of our conceptual constructions about them, that wider universe we are accustomed to refer to as *truth* of which the universe of existents is only a part, 'all this universe is perfused with signs, if it is not composed exclusively of signs' (*CP* 5.448, n. 1).

While developing a general model of sign, Peirce was particularly interested in a theory of method. His research focused specifically on the sciences and therefore on the search for a scientific method. However, in the perspective of Peircean pragmatism, knowledge understood in terms of innovation and inventiveness is not conceived as a purely epistemic process. Knowledge presupposes ethical knowledge, responsiveness to the other, which the self listens to both as the other from self and as the other self: for there to be an interpreted sign, an **object** of interpretation, there must be an **interpretant**, even when we are dealing with cognitive signs in a strict sense. The sign as a sign is other; in other words it may be characterized as a sign because of its structural opening to the other and therefore as **dialogue** with the other. This implies that the sign's identity is grounded in the logic of **alterity**. Consequently, learning, knowledge, wisdom, understanding, and sagacity in their various forms are situated in a sign situation which, in the last analysis, is given over to the other, is listening to the other. Cognitive identity is subject to the other and as such is continually put into crisis by the restlessness of signs that the appeal of the other inexorably provokes. Therefore, insofar as it is part of the sign network by virtue of which alone it earns its status as sign, the cognitive sign is placed and modelled in a context that is irreducibly ethical. (**SP**)

See also <u>Merrell</u> (this volume), QUALISIGN, SINSIGN, LEGISIGN, ICON, INDEX, SYMBOL, RHEME, DICENT, ARGUMENT, REPRESENTAMEN, HABIT and GROUND.

Further Reading

Brent, J. (1998) *Charles Sanders Peirce: A Life*, rev. and enlarged edn, Bloomington: Indiana University Press.

Peirce, C. S. (1992) *The Essential Peirce: Selected Philosophical Writings*, vol. 1, eds. N. Houser and C. Kloesel, Bloomington: Indiana University Press.

Peirce, C. S. (1998) *The Essential Peirce: Selected Philosophical Writings*, vol. 2, ed. Peirce Edition Project, Bloomington: Indiana University Press.

PERFORMANCE The actual use of a language in concrete situations, as opposed to **competence**, the knowledge of a language. Although grammars and dictionaries describe competence, the study of performance is increasingly important, both for scientific reasons (sometimes performance has systematic features which do not directly reflect competence) and for practical reasons, since second language learners need help to perform authentically. (**RS**)

PERFORMATIVE In the contrast **constative**–performative, 'performative' refers to a category of utterances (such as 'I name this ship the Queen Elizabeth', 'I apologize', 'I welcome you', 'I advise you to do it') which do not just *say something* but which serve to *perform an action* (e.g. baptizing a ship, apologizing, welcoming, or offering advice). Performatives cannot be said to be true or false (even if a dimension of **truth** may be involved, as when someone is judged to be guilty of a crime), but they are liable to a dimension of criticism based on criteria of 'felicity'. Thus 'I name this ship the Queen Elizabeth' is felicitous only if the speaker has the proper authority to baptize the ship (otherwise the act is 'null' or 'void'), or 'I apologize' is felicitous only if the speaker intends to express regret (otherwise the utterance is 'abused').

J. L. **Austin** (1962) introduced a distinction between *primary* and *explicit* performatives. In contrast to primary performatives (such as 'I'll come tomorrow'), explicit performatives (such as 'I promise to come tomorrow') contain an explicit indication of the act that is being performed, e.g. a performative **verb** used in the first person singular indicative active ('promise' in this case). Often the term 'performative utterance' is reserved for the narrower category of 'explicit performatives' (e.g. in Searle 1989). (**JV**)

See also SPEECH ACT.

Further Reading

Verschueren, J. (1995) 'The conceptual basis of performativity', in M. Shibatani and S. Thompson (eds) *Essays in Semantics and Pragmatics*, Amsterdam and Philadelphia: John Benjamins, pp. 299–321.

PERLOCUTION, PERLOCUTIONARY In the terminological framework introduced by **Austin** (1962) to cope with the multi-functionality of all utterances (**locution-illocution**-perlocution), perlocution is reserved for the act performed *by* saying something. In Austin's words:

Saying something will often, or even normally, produce certain consequential effects upon the feelings, thoughts, or actions of the audience, or of the speaker, or of other persons: and it may

be done with the design, intention, or purpose of producing them.

(ibid., p. 101)

Arguing that such consequential effects are not part of the language system or that they are too random, unstable, and unpredictable to be handled as constitutive properties of types of speech acts, Searle (1969) decided to leave perlocutionary aspects largely undiscussed. Others have tried to preserve the role of the notion 'perlocution' in **speech act** theory by considering that all illocutionary act types must have certain effects that are typically associated with them even though their actual emergence is not predictable. Thus assertives are typically intended to inform an audience of a state of affairs, questions are typically intended to elicit answers, promises are typically intended to generate trust in the speaker's future course or action, just like directives are typically intended to make the hearer do something (which would even be regarded as their illocutionary point). (**JV**)

Further Reading

Austin, J. L. (1962) *How to Do Things with Words*, ed. J. O. Urmson, Oxford: Oxford University Press. (2nd rev edn, 1975, eds J. O. Urmson and M. Sbisà, Cambridge, MA: Harvard University Press.)

PETER OF SPAIN Peter of Spain (Petrus Hispanus) was born in Lisbon sometime before 1205. From 1220–29 he studied at the University of Paris, a famous centre for studies in logic, philosophy and theology. He studied medicine in Salerno or Montpellier and graduated circa 1235. He had already written his *Summule logicales* or *Tractatus* (critical ed. 1972), the work which gained him fame ('e Pietro Ispano/lo qual già luce in dodici libelli', Dante, *Paradise* XII, 134–35) some years before, in the early 1230s, presumably while living in the North of Spain. He taught medicine

235

at the University of Siena, Italy, from 1245–50. In 1276 he became Pope under the name of John XXI. He continued his pursuit of scientific studies in an apartment equipped for the purpose built alongside the Papal Palace at Viterbo, where he met his tragic death in 1277 under the roof of his study which collapsed in on him.

In the *Tractatus*, Peter of Spain systematized and explained logic as it had developed so far, in depth and with originality. He locates the **sign** within the complex process of **semiosis** identifying its fundamental aspects. His model of sign anticipated Charles S. **Peirce**'s (cf. Ponzio 1990c; Ponzio and Petrilli 1996). The correspondences that emerge are indicative of the orientation of the *Tractatus* and his anticipation of Peirce: *vox significativa* = **representamen**; *significatio* or *rapresentatio* = **interpretant**; *res significata* or *representata* = immediate **object**; *acceptio pro* = to stand for; *aliquid* (the referent of *acceptio*) = dynamic object. This explains Peirce's interest in Peter of Spain whom he cites on numerous occasions. (**AP**)

See also SEMIOTICS.

Further Reading

Ponzio, A. (1990) 'Meaning and referent in Peter of Spain', in *Man as a Sign*, trans., ed., intro. and appendices by S. Petrilli, Berlin and New York: Mouton de Gruyter.

PHATIC One of the six fundamental functions given in the **Jakobson**ian **speech act**, determined by the contact factor of the speech act. When the main goal of the utterance is to initiate, terminate or check the channel of communication, the phatic function may dominate. The only function to be shared by humans and birds. (**EA**)

PHILOLOGY As distinguished from *linguistics*, the term philology is usually applied to a more traditional form of language study, based on texts (particularly of bygone periods). Comparative philolology in the nineteenth century established the relationships between languages of the Indo-European family before the emergence of modern linguistics. (**RH**)

PHONE, PHONIC, PHONOLOGISM These terms all relate to the sounds of the spoken language, and are used by Jacques **Derrida** in his 'deconstruction' of the work of the linguist Ferdinand de **Saussure**. In his *Course in General Linguistics*, Saussure privileges speech over writing, and bemoans the fact that people attach more importance to writing than to speech, since 'the superficial bond of writing is much easier to grasp than the only true bond, the bond of sound' ([1916]1974, p. 25). As a result of this privileging of the phonic signifier, says Derrida, '*Phon* . . . is the signifying substance *given to consciousness* as that which is most intimately tied to the thought of the signified concept' (1981, p. 22). Thus, when we speak, the **signifier** and the **signified** seem to unite, so much so that the signifier seems to 'erase itself', to 'become transparent'. Hence we come to believe in the possibility of a concept 'simply present for thought, independent of a relationship to language', in what Derrida calls the 'transcendental signified' (ibid., pp. 19–22) – a possibility which Derrida rejects, as do a number of contemporary linguists (see Harris 1981, p. 9). (**RM**)

See also LOGOS, LOGOCENTRIC and *DIFFÉRANCE*.

Further Reading

Derrida, J. (1981) *Positions*, trans. A. Bass, Chicago: University of Chicago Press.

PHONEME The fundamental unit of sound in any language. For **Saussure** and others, differences between phonemes are crucial in generating **value**. A simple example of this is the difference between the sounds in the words *tin* and *kin* in English. The distinction of the phonemes designated by *k* and *t* enables different **meanings** to be engendered by each word. The study of such units is the subdomain of linguistics known as 'phonemics' (as opposed to **phonetics**). (**PC**)

PHONETICS The study of speech sounds: how they are produced by the organs of speech (articulatory phonetics), how they are perceived by the ear (auditory phonetics) and their physical properties (acoustic phonetics). Phoneticians have also developed systems for writing down the sounds of any language, the most widely used being the International Phonetic Alphabet (IPA). In IPA the word *phonetics* is written [fənetɪks]. (**RS**)
    See also PHONEME.

PHONOLOGY The study of the sounds and sound patterns of particular languages. Phonologists list the sounds that each language has (for instance, English has the sound *h* as in *hat*, but French does not), and how the sounds are structured (English *h* is only found at the beginning of a syllable). (**RS**)

PHRASAL VERB An **idiom** consisting of a **verb** and an adverb (e.g. *come round* in the sense of 'regain consciousness') or a verb and a preposition (e.g. *fall for someone* meaning 'start to like them'). Phrasal verbs are common in English, and are one of the major problems for people learning English as a second language. (**RS**)

PHRASE STRUCTURE **Clauses** consist of phrases: thus *The door opened very quietly* breaks down into [The door] and [opened very quietly]. These phrases sometimes consist of smaller phrases: *opened very quietly* can be analysed as [opened] + [very quietly]. The smaller phrases consist of individual words. This is the phrase structure of the original clause, and it is

sometimes conveniently represented using tree diagrams. (**RS**)

PIDGIN A language containing words from two or more languages, used for communication in trade or work between people who do not have a language in common. Pidgins often have a simple **grammar**, and their vocabulary is limited to the domains for which they are normally used. A pidgin which develops into a language that is used in all areas of life, and which is learned as a mother tongue by young people, is called a **creole**. (**RS**)

PIKE Kenneth Lee Pike (1912–2000), a long-time contributor to the Summer Institute of Linguistics, remains best recognized for his coinage (1954) and defence (1990) of the terms 'emic' (culture-bound) and 'etic' (culture-free), derived from 'phonemic' and 'phonetic', respectively, and for his adventurous deployment of metaphor in methodology and theory e.g. 'particle, wave, and field' (1959). An eclectic, Pike has published widely in all realms of linguistics. (**MA**)

POINSOT Eclipsed in modern philosophy by his contemporaries, Galileo and Descartes, John Poinsot nonetheless had the privilege historically of being the first to succeed in giving substance to **Augustine**'s proposal at the turn of the fifth century that **sign** be regarded as a mode of being indifferent to the distinction between nature and culture. Poinsot performed this intellectual feat by seizing upon two earlier achievements, then combining them with the contemporary realization (Araújo 1617) that signs are irreducibly triadic.
    First, he seized upon Boethius's translation of **Aristotle**'s problem in distinguishing between substances, which need to be understood relative to their environment (subjectivities, 'transcendental relatives'), and pure relations, which have no being other than that of linking substances

(suprasubjectivities, 'ontological relatives'). Next he seized upon Aquinas's realization (1266 Q. 28) that the pure relations identified by Aristotle are indifferent to their subjective basis, whence communication transcends the limits of finite being. In this way, Poinsot was the first to demonstrate systematically that the being proper to signs, as a relation irreducibly triadic, also transcends the distinction between being produced by the workings of nature and being produced by the workings of mind, making 'experience' an objective tapestry woven (or interwoven) from products of both workings. (JD)

See also SEMIOTICS.

Further Reading

Special Issue on John Poinsot, *American Catholic Philosophical Quarterly* 68 (3) (Summer 1994), pp. 363–93.

POINT DE CAPITON The 'points de capiton' are anchoring or mooring points by means of which the generation of endless shift of **meaning** is avoided. **Lacan** claims that while such 'quilting points' are operative in normal or neurotic states of thinking, they are deficient in a state of psychosis. Lacan speaks of the 'I' of a neurotic subject as being caught in this quilting. In 1953 Lacan took the quilting point effect to be produced by the 'no of the father'; later he used knot theory to formalise this function. (BB)

POLITENESS A means of showing courtesy, deference, consideration and social position in language. Politeness can consist of key words added to a freestanding utterance such as 'please'. It can also consist of words already coded as polite forms, for example the formal second person *Lei* in Italian as opposed to the informal *tu*. Because of the contextual factors which politeness embodies so commonly and so acutely, the phenomenon has been the object of considerable scrutiny in **pragmatics**. (PC)

POLYSEMY (POLYSEMIC) The capacity of **signs** or **texts** to have numerous meanings. The word 'crack', for example, is an instance of **onomatopeia** (an **icon** of a specific sound) both as a **verb** ('the fireworks began to crack') and as a **noun** ('a loud crack'). It is also a verb to do with breakage ('I decided to crack it open') and a noun ('the money fell into the crack'). It is a noun referring to sardonic remarks ('he made a crack about the prime minister's poor performance') or even as a verb designating the same ('he started to crack wise again'). In colloquial usage it refers to highly potent cocaine crystals ('crack'), to the join between the buttocks and, sometimes, to the vagina. In Ireland 'crack' often has a far more benign meaning to do with having a good time. These are just some of its possible decodings.

When extended to the level of larger texts and **discourse**, polysemy undoubtedly becomes more complex. In these cases, specific understandings of texts' potential meanings might be the result of a restriction of polysemy by **speech communities** or by the particular kinds of composition of texts (for example, a **closed text** or a text from a given **genre**). (PC)

See OPEN TEXT, UNLIMITED SEMIOSIS and ILLOCUTION.

Further Reading

Eco, U. (1979) *The Role of the Reader: Explorations in the Semiotics of Texts*, Bloomington: Indiana University Press.

PORT-ROYAL Name of a famous educational Jansenist foundation in seventeenth-century France, where Antoine Arnauld (1612–94) and Claude Lancelot (1615–95) produced an innovative French **grammar**, the *Grammaire générale et raisonée*

(1660), based on radical pedagogic principles. The 'rationality' of the method was based on the assumption that certain principles applied to all languages and that all languages could give expression to certain universal operations of the human mind. Arnauld and Pierre Nicole (1625–95) co-authored an accompanying *Art de penser*, commonly referred to as 'The Port-Royal Logic'. These works are often taken to epitomize the thesis that the structure of thought determines the structure of linguistic expression. (For the opposite thesis, see **Saussure**.) **(RH)**

Further Reading

Padley, G. A. (1985) *Grammatical Theory in Western Europe, 1500–1700: Trends in Vernacular Grammar I*, Cambridge: Cambridge University Press.

POSITIVISM The philosophical approach or movement, originating with Henri Comte de Saint-Simon (1760–1825) and Auguste Comte (1798–1857), which stressed the importance of basing knowledge on positive facts deriving from direct experience. Many features of the positivist program can be found in the work of earlier empiricists, including Hume and **Kant**, but positivism distinguished itself by its strict adherence to the methods of the exact sciences and by its sharp hostility to **metaphysics** and religion.

The proponents of positivism (positivists) were strongly opposed to basing knowledge claims on speculative beliefs and insisted that no hypothesis can be admitted for serious consideration unless it is capable of verification by direct observation. Positivists were much enamored with the successes of experimental science and were convinced that scientific method was the only route to truth for inquiry of any kind. The positivists wanted to remake philosophy and the social sciences in the image of the hard sciences.

Though hostile to traditional religion, positivism was promoted as a sort of secular religion, a religion of humanity. Human progress was described as the movement from a theological base, involving belief in the supernatural, through a metaphysical phase, involving much speculation and appeal to abstractions, to a final positive stage where metaphysical abstractions (e.g. final causes) are dismissed, and all knowledge is derived from experience and known scientific laws. As positivism developed after Comte, for example, in the work of John Stuart Mill, Herbert Spencer, and Ernst Mach, it ceased to be promoted as a secular religion, but it continued to be concerned with the advancement of society and the well-being of humankind. Positivists typically believed that the way to a better world is through mastery of nature, which can only be achieved through a sufficient increase in scientific knowledge.

Through related movements and programs, positivism was spread throughout philosophy. In Vienna a group of philosophers known as the Vienna Circle expanded on the ideas of Ernst Mach to develop logical positivism. This version of positivism continued to be staunchly opposed to metaphysics, but focused mainly on the process of verification by which knowledge claims can be justified. The *Tractatus Logico-philosophicus* of Ludwig **Wittgenstein** was a key text for logical positivists, among whom could be counted Moritz Schlick, Otto Neurath, Felix Kaufmann, Herbert Feigl, Philipp Frank, and Rudolf Carnap. Key members of the Vienna Circle emigrated to the United States in the early 1930s and, with Charles W. **Morris**, formed the Unity of Science Movement, dedicated to establishing a comprehensive empirical philosophy based on a rigorous scientific methodology guided by formal logic. Morris introduced semiotic principles to the members of this movement, in particular the important tripartite division of **semiotics** into syntactics, **semantics**, and **pragmatics**. In psychology and the philosophy of psychology, behaviorism incorporated the main principles of positivism. Through these and other outgrowths, positivism exerted an enormous influence on analytical and linguistic philosophy in the twentieth century.

Pragmatism, too, with its emphasis on scientific method and on practical consequences, and with its mission to improve society, bears some resemblance to positivism. But pragmatists never wanted to dismiss metaphysics wholesale, hoping, rather, to purify it, and in other ways deviated from positivism. **Peirce** believed that positivism was fatally nominalistic and he noticed that its insistence on verification by direct observation precluded historical knowledge (Peirce 1984, p. 45 n. 8). Other pragmatists, in particular John Dewey, and many contemporary philosophers, object to the many dichotomous distinctions positivists espoused, for instance, the distinction between metaphysics and science, facts and values, the analytic and the synthetic, and the verifiable and the non-verifiable. Recent philosophy has been, to a large extent, an undoing of the ill effects of positivism and a rethinking of its achievements. The international movement toward a Peircean brand of semiotics is largely a movement away from positivism. (NH)

Further Reading

Ayer, A. J. (1946) *Language, Truth and Logic*, rev. edn, New York: Oxford University Press.

Kremer-Marietti, A. (1998) 'Comte, Isidore-Auguste-Marie-François-Xavier', *Routledge Encyclopedia of Philosophy*, London, Routledge.

Peirce, C. S. (1984) 'Critique of positivism', (1867–68) in *Writings of Charles S. Peirce*, vol. 2, eds E. C. Moore, M. H. Fisch, *et al.*, Bloomington: Indiana University Press.

POSTSTRUCTURALISM, POSTSTRUCTURALIST Definitions of poststructuralism are infrequently found: this is partly because the phenomenon described by the term is so nebulous; partly because, as an intellectual current, it is especially difficult to periodize; and partly because many of its proponents purport to eschew definitions. Undoubtedly, it has a relation to '**structuralism**', but it is an uneasy one.

While structuralism might be said to embody the notion of a system of **sign**s in which humans can collectively participate – derived from the 'functionalist' aspect of **Saussure**'s concept of *langue* – poststructuralism envisages a fundamentally different relation between signs and humans. Structuralist approaches to cultural phenomena benefited from analyses which often took signs isolated from their contexts as the object of discussion. Poststructuralism, by contrast, stresses not only how signs are related to other signs but also how the human subject always apprehends signs in the plural, in chains, as **discourse**. As Silverman insists, 'signification occurs only through discourse . . . discourse requires a subject and . . . the subject itself is an effect of discourse' (1983, p. vii). Put another way, **signification** is not embodied in the '**meaning**' of one sign but in a sign as it is related to other signs; signification also has to be related to the human or humans who use the signs at a given moment; and, crucially, the sign user is not outside the discourse, using it in a perfectly controlled way, but is instead caught up in it, to the extent where s/he is actually a product of that discourse. These propositions are virtually axiomatic, albeit in nuanced ways, for all the major poststructuralists: **Lacan**, **Derrida**, **Kristeva**, Foucault, **Baudrillard**, Deleuze and Guattari.

However, the immediate Saussurean roots of the poststructuralist perspective actually *pre-date* those currents of thought in the humanities called structuralism which became popular in France in the 1950s and 1960s and in parts of the Anglo-Saxon intellectual world in the 1970s and 1980s. The father of poststructuralism was the French linguist, Emile **Benveniste**, whose writings of the 1940s made possible the critiques of Saussure and structuralism by Lacan in the late 1950s and Derrida in the 1960s.

Chiefly, Benveniste drew attention to some anomalies in Saussure's assertion of the *arbitrary* nature of the sign. That the sign was 'bipartite', made up of a *signifié*, concept and a *signifiant*, sound image (frequently translated in a misleading way which has become the norm as '**signified**' and '**signifier**' – for a corrective, see Harris 1987) was accepted. However, Benveniste located the arbitrary nature in *signification*; that is, in the relation between the sign and the reality (or, to use other terms, **referent** or **object**). The relations in the Saussurean *sign*, both parts being mental, were rather to be seen as *necessary*: the sound image and the concept were so close as to be almost one.

What Benveniste showed was that *sign* and *signification* were highly susceptible to conflation. The knowledge that the word *cat* only refers to the feline quadruped in an arbitrary way is omnipresent because it is clear that there are other ways of referring to the animal in different national languages: *chat*, *gatto*, etc. But the sign used for this purpose is composed of a relationship so strong and so close that its arbitrary nature in referring to reality can only be revealed 'under the impassive regard of Sirius' (Benveniste [1939] 1971, p. 44). In short, for the habitual user of the sign the way it refers *feels* unquestionably natural.

So, a linguistic sign might have **value** by virtue of its difference from other signs

in a system (*langue*), and this might be recognized through abstract thought. But the existence of this foundation for arbitrariness in signification is customarily overlooked because of the close, necessary relations in the sign. As a result, humans are subject to a system which they ultimately know to be constructed and arbitrary; in order to take their place and communicate with others they have to subscribe to a representation of the world which, however much they might feel it to be natural, is actually constructed. To use a typical poststructuralist trope, the subject is 'always already' constituted by the system.

The reverberations of this re-orientation of the sign were to be felt throughout the manifestations of poststructuralism. Notions such as 'deconstruction', 'the decentring of the subject', 'interpellation' and 'simulation' are all in some way derived from Benveniste's deflection of the aims of **semiology**.

Poststructuralism was never a movement recognized within its 'native' France (Easthope 1988, p. xxiii) and its success in parts of the Anglo-Saxon intellectual milieu was always unlikely to be mirrored within semiotics. On its home ground of **anthroposemiotics** the totalizing cultural pessimism which was characteristic of many brands of poststructuralism was already countered by the social semiotics which followed the work of **Halliday**. The very fundamentals of the latter, itself distantly related to the early critique of Saussure by **Vološinov** but largely based on empirical work, stressed conflict between sign systems and delineated a space for human resistance to pre-existing structures. On different grounds, poststructuralism was to fare even less well. The comprehensive version of the sign derived from **Peirce** which took hold outside of France and Britain in the closing decades of the twentieth century, coupled with the growing awareness of the importance of **biosemiotics**, only served to further reveal poststructuralism's semiological bias and anthropocentric limitations. (**PC**)

Further Reading

Benveniste, E. (1971) *Problems in General Linguistics*, trans. M. E. Meek, Coral Gables: University of Miami Press.

Derrida, J. (1976) *Of Grammatology*, trans. G. C. Spivak, Baltimore and London: Johns Hopkins University Press.

Lacan, J. (1977) *Écrits: A Selection*, trans. A. Sheridan, London: Tavistock.

PRAGMATICISM The term 'pragmaticism' was introduced in 1905 by Charles S. **Peirce** to distinguish his own conception of **pragmatism** from that of William James and Ferdinand C.S. Schiller (*CP* 5.414–415). Peirce rejected the idea of 'Doing' as 'the Be-all and the End-all of life' (*CP* 5. 429). Differently from vulgar pragmatism, meaning is a general law of conduct independent from the particular circumstances of action. As such, it is always general and communal. (**SP**)

PRAGMATICS In **Morris**'s theory of **semiosis**, the pragmatical dimension of the functioning of **sign**s pertains to 'the relation of signs to interpreters' (1938a, p. 6) and the study of this dimension is called pragmatics. In linguistics, pragmatics has often been treated as a waste basket to which problems were referred that could not be dealt with in **syntax** and **semantics**. As a result, in part of the pragmatic literature, its domain looks like a random selection of topics, in particular: **deixis**, presuppositions, implicatures, **speech act**s, and conversations (see Levinson 1983). It may be more useful, however, to go back to Morris's original definition and to view pragmatics as a general functional (i.e. cognitive, social, and cultural) perspective on language and language use, aimed at the investigation of processes of dynamic and negotiated meaning generation in interaction. Language use is then viewed as a form of action with real-world consequences and firmly embedded in a context. (**JV**)

See also AUSTIN, CONSTATIVE, ILLOCUTION, IPrA, LOCUTION, GRICE, MEANING, PERFORMATIVE, PERLOCUTION and RELEVANCE THEORY.

Further Reading

Verschueren, J. (1999) *Understanding Pragmatics*, London: Edward Arnold/ New York: Oxford University Press.

PRAGMATISM Pragmatism is a set of doctrines and methods elaborated by Charles S. **Peirce** and William James and continued above all by G. H. Mead, C. I. Lewis, Charles **Morris** and John Dewey. 'Pragmatism' makes its official entry into philosophical literature in 1898 when James held his conference 'Philosophical Conceptions and Practical Results', at G. H. Howinson's Berkeley Philosophical Union. But pragmatism was expounded for the first time in a series of six articles by Peirce, published in *Popular Science Monthly* between 1877–78 in the series 'Illustrations of the Logic of Science' (cf. *CP* 5.358–387, 5.388–410, 2.645–660, 2.669–693, 6.395–427, 2.619–644). However, as a thought system it may be traced back to an original nucleus of three writings by Peirce of 1868 (*CP* 5.213–263, 264–317, 318–357), subsequently developed in his writings of 1877–78. In his search for the origins, Peirce considers Nicholas St. John Green as the 'grandfather' of pragmatism (implicitly reserving the title of 'father' to himself). The latter, in turn, evoked the Scot, Alexander Bain, author of *Emotions and Will* (London 1859), urging the importance of applying his definition of belief as 'that upon which a man is prepared to act' (*CP* 5.12).

In general, pragmatism re-evaluates the importance of action in cognitive processes in the light of discoveries in biology, psychology and sociology traceable to Charles Darwin. Chauncey Wright who was a member of the 'Metaphysical Club' also recalled Darwin and it was in the meetings which took place between the end of 1871 and the beginning of 1872 in Cambridge, Massachusetts, that Peirce (cf. 'The Doctrine of Chances', *CP* 5.12) situated the birth of pragmatism. The 'Metaphysical Club' meetings were organized both in his and in James's study with the participation of scientists, theologians and lawyers. The influence of Darwinian biologism is obvious in Peirce's essay 'Fixation of Belief' (1877) where he states that logicality in regard to practical matters might result from the action of natural selection (cf. *CP* 5.366).

According to pragmatism, mind (or spirit or thought) is not a substance, as in Cartesian dualism, nor is it a process or act as understood by idealism, nor a set of relations as in classical empiricism, but rather it is a function exercised by verbal and nonverbal **sign**s. The study of signs and of verbal language in particular is therefore the condition for understanding mind (cf. Morris, *Six Theories of Mind*, 1932). Pragmatism is also a theory of meaning understood as the practical verifiability of the **truth** of an assertion. In 'How to Make our Ideas Clear' (1878), Peirce intended to demonstrate:

> how impossible it is that we should have an idea in our minds which relates to anything but conceived sensible effects of things . . . It appears, then, that the rule for attaining the third grade of clearness of apprehension is as follows: Consider what effects, that might conceivably have practical bearings, we conceive the object of our conception to have. Then, our conception of these effects is the whole of our conception of the object.
>
> (*CP* 5. 401–402)

This aspect was taken up but significantly modified by James who transformed pragmatism into a theory of truth. James interpreted pragmatism in terms of instrumentality and, therefore, of the dependency of knowledge on the needs of action and emotions (*The Will to Believe*, 1897). For James that which has satisfying practical consequences is true. Consequently he emphasizes the practical value of religious faith, of the will to believe, of the reasons of the heart (cf. also James's *Pragmatism*, 1907). Dewey also insisted on this aspect which he vigorously developed into his own version of pragmatism denominated 'experimentalism' or 'instrumentalism'. In Italy, pragmatism was developed along Peircean lines by Giovanni **Vailati** and Mario Calderoni and along Jamesian lines by G. Papini and G. Prezzolini. Ferdinand C.S. Schiller (cf. *Studies in Humanism*, 1907) oriented his approach in James's direction asserting the relativity of knowledge to personal or social utility.

Peirce returned to pragmatism in his set of seven conference-lessons held at Harvard at the iniative of James (cf. *CP* 5.14–40, 5.180–212), in which he identified pragmatism with the logic of **abduction** and with the theory of inquiry and implicitly, therefore, with logic and **semiotics**. In his *Monist* articles of 1905 (*CP* 5.411–437, 5.438–463, 4.530–572), Peirce established his distance from pragmatism as conceived by James and Schiller, identifying his own position with the substitute term **pragmaticism**. (SP)

Further Reading

Morris, C. (1937) *Logical Positivism, Pragmatism and Scientific Empiricism*, Paris: Hermann.

Murphy, J. P. (1990) *Pragmatism: From Peirce to Davidson*, Boulder, CO: Westview Press.

Peirce, C. S. (1907) 'Pragmatism', in Peirce (1998) *The Essential Peirce: Selected*

Philosophical Writings, vol. 2, ed. Peirce Edition Project, Bloomington: Indiana University Press, pp. 398–433.

PRAGUE SCHOOL Originally known as the Prague Linguistics Circle (PLC), founded in 1926 by V. Mathesius, B. Havránek, J. **Mukařovský**, R. **Jakobson**, N. **Trubetzkoy** and S. Karcevskij. Dedicated to the study of Slavic languages and literature, poetics, **phonology** and **morphology**. According to Waugh and Monville-Burston (1990, p. 6), it was Jakobson who coined the term '**structuralism**' for the group. The first detailed presentation of the PLC program occurred at the First International Congress of Slavists in 1929 in Prague. Also initiated in 1929 was the series, *Travaux du Cercle Linguistique de Prague*. For a clear statement of the fundamental propositions of the PLC, see 'Thèses' (with Bally, Jakobson, Mathesius, Sechehaye and Trubetzkoy, originally presented April 1928 and reprinted in Toman 1995).

According to the official by-laws of the PLC (dated 1 December 1930, translated and reprinted in Toman [1995, p. 265]), the primary purpose of the PLC 'is to work on the basis of functional-structural method toward progress in linguistic research'. Roman Jakobson was vice-president of the PLC until 1939 when he was obliged to leave as the Nazis invaded Czechoslovakia. In post-war years, the membership of the PLC changed considerably, in particular due to the absence of Jakobson and Bogatyrëv and the death of Trubetzkoy and Mathesius. In some accounts, the PLC is said to have ceased to exist in 1939. However, Mukařovský and others continued to lecture and conduct research. The post-Soviet era witnessed a revival of the Prague School in the 1990s. (**EA**)

Further Reading

Galan, F. W. (1985) *Historic Structures: The Prague School Project, 1828–1946*, Austin, TX: University of Texas Press.

Steiner, P. (ed.) (1982) *The Prague School: Selected Writings, 1929–1946*, Austin, TX: University of Texas Press.

Winner, T. G. (1995) 'Prague structuralism: neglect and resulting fallacies', *Semiotica* 105 (3/4), 243–76.

PRINCIPLES AND PARAMETERS THEORY A stage in the development of grammatical theory, pursued by **Chomsky** and his associates in the 1980s and early 1990s. The principles in question were claimed to be part of **Universal Grammar**, and were formulated as restrictions on the **grammar**s of individual languages. Parameters were principles which could vary in well-defined and limited ways across languages. A great deal of productive research into differences and similarities between languages was carried out in this framework, as well as research into first language acquisition and second language learning.

Because the grammars of particular languages were restricted by universal principles, it was possible to formulate very general rules like *Move-alpha*, which in effect said 'Move any word or phrase in a sentence'. Universal principles like the Structure-preserving Principle prevented Move-alpha from moving elements into all but the legitimate positions. The more recent elaboration of this work is minimalism, which proposes rules and principles of the utmost generality. (**RS**)

Further Reading

Culicover, P. W. (1997) *Principles and Parameters: An Introduction to Syntactic Theory*, Oxford, Oxford University Press.

PRONOUN A word like *she*, *it* or *they* which replaces a **noun** or (more exactly) a **noun phrase**. Often the noun phrase comes first, and the pronoun is used to avoid repetition: In *Paul washed the dishes and put them away*, the noun phrase *the dishes* is called the *antecedent* of the pronoun *them*. Occasionally the pronoun comes first, as in *When he left Blackburn, Shearer scored fewer goals*. (**RS**)

PROPOSITIONS Propositions differ from sentences and **speech act**s in that different sentences or speech acts (e.g. 'The cat is on the mat', 'Is the cat on the mat?', and 'Cat, on the mat!') may contain the same proposition, consisting of a *reference* (an **expression** identifying any thing, process, event, or action) and a *predication* (what is 'predicated' or said about a thing, process, event, or action identified by means of a referring expression). It is propositions, not sentences or speech acts, that are true or false. Assertive speech acts can nevertheless be said to be true or false because it is the nature of their **illocutionary** force to present a state of affairs as true or false. Thus one and the same sentence form (e.g. 'Napoleon was defeated at Waterloo') has different truth conditions associated with it, depending on the precise proposition it expresses (which will vary in relation to, e.g., the reference of 'Napoleon' which may be the name of a historical figure or the speaker's dog). (**JV**)
See also MEANING.

Further Reading

Lyons, J. (1995) *Linguistic Semantics: An Introduction*, Cambridge: Cambridge University Press.

PSYCHOLINGUISTICS The study of language and the mind, or the psychology of language. The mechanisms for producing and understanding language are a central concern of psycholinguists. Another is the way language might be stored in the brain. Many experimental methods have been devised to investigate these matters: they include measuring the time it takes for people to understand or respond to speech that has been distorted in various ways, and observing the speech errors that people make in different circumstances.

Another important concern of psycholinguists is the acquisition of language by young people. Acquisition of all languages seems to follow regular stages: infants produce single words first, followed by two-word sequences and then longer utterances with the beginnings of **syntax**. Speech and language pathology are related areas that have an important practical dimension. They also raise difficult issues about the relationship between language and other aspects of the mind, such as memory, general intelligence and emotion. A young person who has difficulty in learning to talk, or who later is slow at learning to read at school, may have a purely linguistic problem; often, though, there may be a link with other psychological problems that a young person is experiencing. (**RS**)

Further Reading

Garnham, A. (1989) *Psycholinguistics: Central Topics*, London: Routledge.

Q

QUALISIGN Charles S. **Peirce**'s term for the first division of his trichotomy of the **grounds** of **sign**s. A qualisign is a sign which, in itself, is a quality, and is thus fit only to represent **object**s with which it bears some similarity or has something in common. A paint chip represents its own color. All qualisigns are **icon**s and can only function when embodied. (**NH**)

See also LEGISIGN and SINSIGN.

R

REALISM The Platonic doctrine that universals or essences exist independently of individuals which instantiate them. Realism in this sense is opposed to **nominalism**. In its extreme form, it supposes that there is some kind of Platonic realm where universals exist timelessly and that particulars are imperfect copies of their universal counterparts. **Aristotle**'s realism was more moderate. He reversed the Platonic doctrine and held that the fullest reality is found in existing particulars in which universals inhere. But he also attributed reality to universals. Those who accept this doctrine today champion the reality of natural classes and abstract entities and such 'univerals' as laws and properties (including moral properties) rather than 'Platonic forms'.

Another form of realism, external realism, opposes idealism. The principal intuition of those who accept this kind of realism is that the external world exists independently of thought about it – reality exists separately from consciousness or mental representations. Since, on this view, the world is how it is independently of what we believe about it, then whether or not what we believe is true or false will depend on whether it corresponds with the facts of the matter. External realists accept that there may be unknowables, facts that we have no human capacity for cognizing. In its extreme from, external realism tends to merge with nominalism, the view that though the world is stocked with plenty of real things that are completely independent of what we think about them, our knowledge of the world cannot transcend its linguistic and psychological basis to meaningfully connect with 'things in themselves'. Michael Dummett has rounded out the modern form of external realism by further characterizing it as the view committed to the principle of excluded middle, and holding that, for any property, an object either must have that property or not. Any view that does not accept all of the assumptions of external realism is said to be anti-realism (Dummett 1978).

There are many other varieties of realism (or anti-realism). Internal realism, advocated by Hillary Putnam, denies that there are incognizables and rejects the correspondence theory of **truth** in favor of the view that truth must be understood, not as correspondence with the facts, but as the result of inquiry carried out long enough and in the right way (Putnam 1987). Scientific realism covers a wide variety of viewpoints including that scientific theories refer to real features of the world and, also, that a good and useful theory is not necessarily a true one.

Charles S. **Peirce** advocated a form of realism that resembles in some ways Putnam's internal realism, particularly in the view that truth must be understood in terms of the projected settlement of belief at the end of inquiry. But Peirce enriched the conception of realism by developing the position advocated by Duns Scotus that reality includes far more than the existent. Peirce identified three categories of reality: qualia or properties (**firstness**), facts or events (**secondness**), and types or laws (**thirdness**). The first and third categories are general, opposing Peirce to nominalism. It was Peirce's opinion that the 'battle' between nominalism and realism is one of the most crucial struggles in philosophy:

Though the question of realism and nominalism has its roots in the technicalities of logic, its branches reach about our life. The question whether the *genus Homo* has any existence except as individuals, is the question whether there is anything of any more dignity, worth, and importance than individual happiness, individual aspirations, and individual life. Whether men really have anything in common, so that the *community* is to be considered as an end in itself, and if so, what the relative value of the two factors is, is the most fundamental practical question in regard to every institution the constitution of which we have it in our power to influence.

(Peirce 1992, p. 105)

In the fine arts, realism usually refers to styles and techniques that emphasize common conceptions or ordinary experience. **(NH)**

See also METAPHYSICS and SEMIOTICS.

Further Reading

Armstrong, D. M. (1978) *Universals and Scientific Realism*, 2 vols, Cambridge: Cambridge University Press.
Haack, S. (1987) 'Realism', *Synthese* 73: 275–99.
Peirce, C. S. (1992) 'Review of Fraser's *The Works of George Berkeley*' (1871), in *The Essential Peirce: Selected Philosophical Writings*, vol. 1, eds N. Houser and C. Kloesel, Bloomington: Indiana University Press, pp. 83–105.

REFERENT Term commonly used to designate the thing in the world to which **sign**s refer. This consists of available things such as the real chair one is sitting on while one produces the sign, and unavailable things, for example Napoleon: 'in which case there may be a long list of sign-situations appearing in between the act and its referent: word – historian – contemporary record – eye-witness' (Ogden and Richards 1985, p. 11). In light of this definition certain similarities with the concepts of **Peirce** and certain dissimilarities with those of **Saussure** should be noted. Peirce's sign triad includes an **interpretant** and a **representamen** as well as an **object** which itself can be either immediate or, like a referent, dynamic – that is to say, existing in the world but not directly available at the same time and place as the sign. Saussure's dyadic sign, on the other hand, comprises a **signifier** and also a **signified**, the latter being a mental concept. In some accounts of **semiology**, the signified is confused with a referent or, more frequently, supplemented with the concept of referent as the entity that Saussure neglected. However, Saussure's *Cours* focuses on the relation in the sign between a mental sound pattern and a concept, not on the relation between linguistic signs and referents. **(PC)**

See also SEMIOTICS, STRUCTURALISM, POSTSTRUCTURALISM, OGDEN and RICHARDS.

Further Reading

Ogden, C. K. and Richards, I. A. (1923 [1985]) *The Meaning of Meaning: A Study of the Influence of Language on Thought and the Science of Symbolism*, London and Boston, MA: Ark.

REGISTER (TEXT VARIETY) A term deriving from (neo-) **Firth**ian linguistics which focuses on the relation of language and its social environments, and its variations in response to changes in context and use. It sees language as a resource through which its users (1) represent 'what is going on' in the world: the **field** of a text; (2) the characteristics of the social relations between the participants in linguistic interaction: the **tenor** of a text; and (3) the organization and shaping of language in communication: the **mode** of the text.

Register names the textual configuration which results from the combined interaction of each of the variables of field, tenor and mode. There may be relative stabilities of social **situation**, giving rise to relatively stable registers (the 'sermon', for instance). In general, register theory assumes a constantly dynamic and fluid arrangement for language in use. Register theory has been hugely influential for a range of developments concerned with language for special purposes, for **genre** theory, and in language planning. **(GRK)**

See also Coupland and Jaworski (this volume) and SOCIOLINGUISTICS.

Further Reading

Halliday, M. A. K. (1978) *Language as Social Semiotic*, London: Edward Arnold.

RELEVANCE THEORY One of **Grice**'s maxims of conversation was the maxim of relation, 'Be relevant' (Grice 1975). Some of the other maxims could be quite sensibly reduced to this notion of relevance. For instance, the statement 'There's a garage round the corner' in response to 'I am out of petrol', violates the maxim of quantity: the explicit **meaning** of the answer is not enough to guarantee the satisfaction of the expressed need; therefore, assuming the speaker's co-operativity, the utterance implicates that the garage has petrol for sale and is open. In other words, the response would not be *relevant* unless those aspects of implicit meaning can be assumed. Sperber and Wilson's (1986) relevance theory makes this generalized notion of relevance into the overriding principle to formulate a theory of communication and cognition intended to explain utterance understanding.

Relevance theory bears specifically on so-called 'ostensive communication', i.e. communication that is intentional and overt in such a way that the speaker does not only intend to convey a specific meaning but is also engaged in efforts to help the hearer recognize this intention. Such forms of communication are said to be governed by a 'principle of relevance', which holds that 'Every act of ostensive communication communicates the presumption of its own optimal relevance' (ibid. 1986, p. 158). In order for ostensive communication to be successful, an audience has to pay attention to the ostensive stimulus, and an audience will not pay attention unless the phenomenon to attend to seems relevant enough. In contrast to Grice's maxim, the principle of relevance is not formulated as a norm that can be adhered to or broken, but rather an exceptionless generalization about human cognition. Yet, the principle cannot guarantee that communication will always succeed. Success requires that the first accessible interpretation which a rational interlocutor selects as optimally relevant matches the intended one.

The theory of understanding based on these assumptions distinguishes between implicatures (of the Gricean type) and explicatures, which are the explicitly communicated **proposition**s that (could have) replace(d) those implicatures. It further hypothesizes that a principle is involved according to which needless cognitive effort is avoided. For that reason, expressions carrying implicatures may have additional meanings that can be said to be 'weakly implicated'. Thus there has to be a reason why a speaker puts a hearer to extra effort in the interpretation process by not expressing him/herself explicitly. For instance, if a speaker responds 'I have to study for an exam' in reaction to an invitation to go to the movies, this implicates that he/she does not accept. But the speaker could have said so directly. In addition to this implicature, therefore, the presumption of relevance in relation to the principle of least cognitive effort would dictate that a number of 'weak implicatures' – not intended specifically in the same way as the identified implicature – have to be added to the interpretation: the speaker wants to convey that there are good reasons for not accepting the invitation; or he/she wants to communicate a state of mind. (**JV**)

See also RULES.

Further Reading

Blakemore, D. (1992) *Understanding Utterances: An Introduction to Pragmatics*, Oxford: Blackwell.

Rouchota, V. and Jucker, A. H. (eds) (1998) *Current Issues in Relevance Theory*, Amsterdam/Philadelphia: John Benjamins.

Sperber, D. and Wilson, D. (1986) *Relevance: Communication and Cognition*, Oxford: Blackwell.

REPRESENTAMEN/SIGN A representamen conveys information about the **object** it represents. According to Charles S. **Peirce**, a representamen is a correlate in a triadic relation with an object and an **interpretant**. It determines the interpretant to stand in relation to the object as it does, so that the interpretant is mediately determined by the object. **Sign**s, which convey information to human minds, are the most familiar representamens, but perhaps not all representamens are signs. For example, a pathogen may be the representamen of some disease to an immune system without technically being a sign. Usually 'sign' is no longer restricted in this way and is used synonymously with 'representamen'. (**NH**)

RESTRICTED CODE Along with 'elaborated code', the term, introduced by sociologist Basil **Bernstein**, points to two phenomena: habitual use of language in a stable social environment leads to a particular orientation towards the use of the language which is a reflection of salient aspects of the characteristics of that environment; and habitual use leads to a **code**. Users of the restricted code are not excluded from full use of language, but this code requires effort to circumvent.

The code reflects the characteristics of the environment, like low geographical and social mobility, forms of knowledge which are those available in the immediate context. Such knowledge, which can be assumed to be known by all, need not be spoken. Where more is known in common, less needs to be spoken, leading to utterances in which more is left implicit, producing a lexically and syntactically simpler language.

The characteristics of the elaborated and restricted codes bear much similarity to characteristics that might be attributed to working-class and middle-class groups. This has led to challenges to this theory (see Labov 1972a). The terms may not have been particularly well chosen; they accurately express certain lexical and grammatical aspects of language use. However, they allow an interpretation of each term as characterizations of cognitive dispositions of users of codes. (**GRK**)

Further Reading

Bernstein, B. (1972) 'Social class, language and socialization', in P. P. Giglioli (ed.) *Language and Social Context*, Harmondsworth: Penguin.

RHEME Charles S. **Peirce**'s term for the first division of his trichotomy of **sign**s that concerns how they are interpreted. A rhematic sign (or rheme) is understood to represent its **object** in its characters and is thus interpreted as a sign of essence or possibility. Rhemes may be **icon**ic, **index**ical, or **symbol**ic, but they are always understood as representing a qualitative possibility of some sort rather than a fact of the matter or a reason. Rhemes are often associated with grammatical terms or with open predicates. (**NH**)

See <u>Merrell</u> (this volume), DICENT and ARGUMENT.

RHETORIC The art of using language, or elements of language such as tropes (figures of speech), effectively or persuasively; thus the study of how to influence the thoughts, emotions, or behaviour of others through the use of language. One of the three subjects of the Roman trivium: **grammar**, logic, and rhetoric. Classically, the art of rhetoric was divided into five parts: invention, disposition, elocution (diction and style), memory (mnemonics), and action (delivery). In Charles S. **Peirce**'s semeiotic, speculative (theoretical or pure) rhetoric is the third branch, after speculative grammar and speculative critic. According to Peirce, speculative rhetoric is 'the science of the essential conditions under which a **sign** may determine an interpretant sign of itself and of whatever it signifies, or may, as a sign, bring about a physical result' (1998, p. 326). Speculative rhetoric is the study of the necessary and sufficient conditions for the communication of information or of semeiotic content at any level of **semiosis** or information transfer, whether from person to person or even as a development of individual thought. Rhetoric is sometimes regarded as the imaginative or poetic use of language, that aspect of language that refuses to be limited to the rigorous demands of logic or rational discourse. In its most current sense rhetoric may be taken to be the general theory of linguistic expression or even the general theory of textuality. (**NH**)

See INTERPRETANT, GROUND and HABIT.

Further Reading

Liszka, J. J. (1996) *A General Introduction to the Semeiotic of Charles Sanders Peirce*, Bloomington: Indiana University Press (especially Chapter 4).

RICHARDS Ivor Armstrong Richards (1893–1979), literary theorist, linguist and cultural critic, taught at Cambridge and Harvard. Among his numerous books are *Principles of Literary Criticism* (1925), *Practical Criticism* (1929), *Coleridge on Imagination* (1935), *The Philosophy of Rhetoric* (1936), *How to Read a Page* (1942), *Poetries and Sciences* (1970) and *Beyond* (1975). In the field of **semiotics**, however, his most famous book remains his first, co-written with C. K. **Ogden**, *The Meaning of Meaning* (1923). In this volume the authors discussed an array of contemporary and near-contemporary theorists of signification including **Saussure**, **Peirce**, Russell and Frege, as well as precursors such as **William of Ockham** and **Humboldt**. They also outlined a three-fold version of signification which is not far removed from Peirce's triadic theory of the **sign**. Richards might also be best remembered in literary and sign theory for his investigation of metaphor and the distinction between 'vehicle' and 'tenor' in this trope.

I. A. Richards' approach to analysis was always eclectic, drawing on linguistics, literature and science, but invariably focusing on the vicissitudes of the sign. Interestingly, this has proved problematic for literary theory which has successively tried to claim his work as an early example of, on the one hand, New Criticism and, on the other, reader-response theory. (**PC**)

Further Reading

Richards, I. A. (1976) *Complementarities: Uncollected Essays*, ed. J. P. Russo, Manchester: Carcanet.

ROSSI-LANDI Ferruccio Rossi-Landi (Milan 1921–Trieste 1985) has contributed significantly to the development of **semiotics** and philosophy of language. In the early years of his intellectual formation, Rossi-Landi absorbed ideas and methodologies not only from Italian culture, but also from the cultural traditions of Austria and Germany as well as from British–American traditions of thought. Several of his essays and books were originally published in English. For many years he lived in countries other than Italy, especially in England and the United States. He taught at the University of Michigan, Ann Arbor (1962–63) and at the University of Texas, Austin (1963), which he revisited on several occasions, and acted as visiting professor at various universities in Europe as well as in America between 1964 and 1975. He also taught courses in philosophy and semiotics at the University of Havana and Santiago (Cuba). After a teaching appointment in Padova (1958–62), he only returned to the Italian academic world in 1975 as Professor of Philosophy of History at the University of Lecce (Southern Italy). In 1977 he became Full Professor of Theoretial Philosophy at the University of Trieste.

As an editor and translator as well as author, Rossi-Landi made significant contributions to intellectual life. He served as editor or member of the editorial board of various journals, some of which he had in fact founded: *Methodos* (1949–52), *Occidente* (1955–56), *Nuova corrente* (1966–68), *Dialectical Anthropology* (from 1975), *Ideologie* (1967–74), and finally *Scienze umane* (1979–81), which contain numerous contributions to the theory of **sign**s.

Rossi-Landi's studies may be divided into three phases (cf. Ponzio 1986, 1989). The first concerns the 1950s and includes the monographs: *Charles Morris* (1953, revised and enlarged in an edition of 1975; see also Rossi-Landi's correspondence with Morris published in 1992); *Significato, comunicazione e parlare comune* (1961, but which in fact was the conclusion of his work of the 1950s, republished in 1980 and again in 1998 in a volume edited by A. Ponzio).

The second phase belongs to the 1960s

and includes: *Il linguaggio come lavoro e come mercato* (1968, Eng. trans. 1983), which proposes a theory of linguistic production and of sign production in general which is also a theory of linguistic work and of general sign work, thereby laying the foundations to study the semiotic homology between linguistics and economics. *Semiotica e Ideologia* (1972, reprinted in 1974, 1994) completes the preceding volume with the addition of important essays like 'Ideologia della relatività linguistica'. The latter was also published as an independent volume in English under the title *Ideologies of Linguistic Relativity* (1973). Finally, *Linguistics and Economics* (1975), written in English in 1970–71 for the book series *Current Trends in Linguistics*, vol. 12, and reprinted as an independent volume in 1975 and 1977.

The third period covers the 1970s and includes the book *Ideologia* (1978, 1982), where Rossi-Landi discusses the problem of the connection between ideology and language with particular reference to linguistic alienation. During this third phase he also authored various essays which were subsequently collected in the volume, *Metodica filosofica e scienza dei segni* (1985).

Several essays from all three periods, including those which had originally appeared in English, were collected posthumously in the volume *Between Signs and Non-signs* (1992a, ed. S. Petrilli). This volume had been planned by Rossi-Landi himself but was among the many that remained unpublished during his lifetime. (**AP**)

Further Reading

Rossi-Landi, F. (1977) *Linguistics and Economics*, The Hague: Mouton.

Rossi-Landi, F. (1990) *Marxism and Ideology*, trans. R. Griffin, Oxford: Clarendon.

Rossi-Landi, F. (1992) *Between Signs and*

Non-signs, ed. S. Petrilli, Amsterdam: John Benjamin.

RULES In *logic* two types of rules have been traditionally distinguished: formation rules, determining the way in which logical formulae are built from basic expressions, and rules of inference or deduction which detemine the steps by means of which one formula can be deduced from another in such a way that truth conditions are preserved. In *linguistics* the term 'rule' has been in popular use since **Chomsky** (1957), mainly in order to cope with recursiveness: rules determine how one pattern can be expanded into another one. Thus it is possible to speak of rules of **grammar**; in the area of language use, however, the term 'rule' is usually disfavored and replaced, rather, by principle or strategies (e.g. Leech 1983). In *philosophy* a distinction is made between regulative rules (regulating pre-existent forms of behavior, such as rules or etiquette) and constitutive rules (defining forms of behavior, such as the rules of football); Searle (1969) uses this distinction and describes the rules formulated for **speech act**s as constitutive rules (thus the act of 'promising' is constituted, created, or defined by the fact that under certain conditions the uttering of 'I promise to come tomorrow' counts as the undertaking of an obligation on the part of the speaker). (**JV**)

See also GRICE.

Further Reading

Bartsch, R. (1987) *Norms of Language*, London: Longman.

RUSSIAN FORMALISM A trend in literary theory developed in Russia between 1915–25. The most important continuator of this movement in terms of originality and critique is Mikhail **Bakhtin**. With the latter's collaboration, Pavel N. Medvedev weighs up Russian Formalism in his book of 1928, *The Formal Method in Literary Scholarship*. Formalism was condemned under Stalin as a bourgeois conception which contrasted with Marxist orthodoxy. The formalists were above all 'specifiers' who dealt with the problem of the 'specificity of the poetic text' for the first time ever. Two prominent figures in Russian Formalism are R. **Jakobson** and L. Jakubinsky. One of the inaugurating texts of this movement is V. B. Shklovsky's booklet *The Resurrection of the Word* (1914), while the first attempt at a historical sketch of formalism is B. M. Eikhenbaum's 'Teoriia "formal" nogo metoda' (1926, Eng. trans. in Todorov 1965).

Russian Formalism developed in three phases. Its guiding theoretical principles were established in the first phase (1914–19). 'Poetic language' was the specific object of research and to this problematic was dedicated the Society for the Study of Poetic Language (*Opoiaz*). Poetic language is a special linguistic system. A relation of opposition was established between the laws of *poetic* and *practical language* on the basis of specific linguistic characteristics, especially phonetic. *Poetic construction* was differentiated from practical language and considered extraneous to it through a process of 'foreignization'. In poetic construction the *plot* is central whereas the *story (fabula)* is only an expedient. An important contribution consists in explaining the art work in terms of literary **genre** instead of referring to the author and his/her life. The second stage (1920–23) is characterized by a lack of unity and a failure to reconcile itself with Marxist orthodoxy. The third (1924–25) was the time of disintegration into different theories to the point of engendering as many formalisms as there were formalists. (**AP**)

Further Reading

Steiner, P. (1984) *Russian Formalism: A Metapoetics*, Ithaca, NY and London: Cornell University Press.

S

SAPIR Edward Sapir (1884–1939) was an American linguist and anthropologist. Born in Germany, his family moved to the United States when he was five. While studying at Columbia University he met the anthropologist Franz **Boas**, who encouraged Sapir to study native American languages and cultures. Sapir worked in Ottawa for fifteen years, researching the indigenous peoples of Canada. He later taught at the Universities of Chicago and Yale.

Sapir did important pioneering work in **phonology** and **historical linguistics**, and on the classification of the indigenous languages of America. His introductory textbook *Language* (1921) is an elegant and attractive book that is still often recommended as an introduction to linguistics. Sapir often made use of the notion of a grammatical process, not in the sense of a historical change over time but as a way of describing relationships between different variants of the same word or **morpheme**. For instance, the **noun** *nation* has a related adjective *national*. Thinking of this relationship as a process, one could say that the adjective is formed by adding *-al* onto the end of the noun and changing the pronunciation of the first vowel from the one in *hate* to the one in *hat*. Many American structuralists were suspicious of this way of describing linguistic relationships, preferring a strictly distributional method (see **American structuralism**). **Chomsky**'s work in **generative grammar** reintroduced processes into grammatical theory.

Sapir's name is sometimes linked with that of **Whorf**, though statements rejecting the 'Whorf hypothesis' can be found in his writings. He made important contributions to anthropology, notably on the relation between culture and society, and to Jewish studies. He read widely in psychiatry and psychoanalysis, and wrote papers on the relation between culture and personality. His poems appeared in many places, and he wrote several musical works.

Although Sapir and **Bloomfield** are usually regarded as the main architects of structuralist linguistics in America, Sapir's broader range of scholarly interests meant that much of his influence was in anthropology and cultural studies, leaving Bloomfield as the more dominant figure in linguistics. As Chomsky's prestige grew in the second half of the century, however, Sapir was named more often as a major intellectual precursor, while the weaknesses of Bloomfield's work were emphasised. One reason for this was that Bloomfield avoided linking language and the mind, whereas Sapir was keen to connect linguistics and psychology. The various brands of linguistics which use 'cognitive' as label (see **cognitive linguistics**) see themselves as continuing Sapir's work in different ways.

Sapir was a rare combination: a rigorous scholar with a broad humanist range of interests and achievements. For appreciations of his work, see Koerner (1984). **(RS)**

Further Reading

Koerner, K. (1984) *Edward Sapir: Appraisals of his Life and Work*, Amsterdam: John Benjamins.

Sapir, E. (1921) *Language*, London: Hart-Davis MacGibbon (reprinted 1978).

Sapir, E. (1949) *Selected Writings in Language, Culture and Personality*, ed. D. G. Mandelbaum, Berkeley, CA: University of California Press (reprinted 1985).

SAPIR–WHORF HYPOTHESIS See **SAPIR and WHORF**.

SAUSSURE Ferdinand-Mongin de Saussure (1857–1913), Swiss linguist, one of the twentieth-century's most influential thinkers on language. His posthumously published *Cours de linguistique générale* (1916), edited by colleagues on the basis of students' notes, became the Magna Carta of modern linguistics. It is a key text not only in the development of language studies but also in the establishment of '**semiology**', a more general science of signs, of which linguistics was to be one special branch and in the formation of that broader intellectual movement which came to be known as '**structuralism**'.

Saussure's revolutionary proposal was that instead of language being seen as peripheral to an understanding of reality, our understanding of reality revolves around language. This idea later became commonplace in various areas of intellectual inquiry, from anthropology to philosophy and psychology; but in Saussure's *Cours* it is clearly articulated, and also expounded in some detail, for the first time.

The basis of Saussure's thinking is a new conception of how the speaker, by uttering certain sounds, is able to articulate ideas. How are these two activities related? In a famous comparison, Saussure likens a language to a sheet of paper. Thought is one side of the sheet and sound the reverse side. Just as it is impossible to cut the paper without cutting corresponding shapes on both sides, so it proves to be impossible in the linguistic case, he held, to isolate thought from sound or sound from thought.

The two matching configurations are back and front of a single form of experience. They are not separate things artificially brought together for purposes of linguistic expression. On the contrary, their indissoluble unity is a *precondition* for the possibility of linguistic expression.

The minimal unit of correlations between sound and thought is the linguistic **sign**, which exists in the speaker's mind as a pairing of *signifiant* (sound pattern) with *signifié* (concept). The linguistic sign is both arbitrary and linear. Arbitrariness implies that the relation between *signifiant* and *signifié* is determined by no external factors. Linearity implies the sequential concatenation of signs in linguistic messages, where they enter into '**syntagmatic**' relations with signs preceding and following.

Saussure held that each language correlates sound and thought in its own unique way. In this sense, speakers of language A do not inhabit the same mental world as speakers of a different language B, even if they live in the same physical space. He insisted on distinguishing the individual linguistic act (*parole*) from the linguistic system underlying it (*langue*), and both of these from the human language faculty in general (*langage*). Langue he saw as a system belonging to society, i.e. to the collectivity of its speakers, and even said that it is never complete in any individual. He also insisted that it be studied as a '**synchronic**' phenomenon (i.e. without reference to the passage of time) and relegated the study of linguistic change to '**diachronic**' linguistics. In his view the failure to distinguish synchronic from diachronic facts had vitiated large areas of nineteenth-century language studies. **(RH)**

See also SIGNIFIED and SIGNIFIER.

Further Reading

Harris, R. (1987) *Reading Saussure*, London: Duckworth.

Saussure, F. de ([1916] 1972) *Cours de linguistique générale*, ed. T. de Mauro, Paris: Payot.

Saussure, F. de (1983) *Course in General Linguistics*, trans. R. Harris, London: Duckworth.

SCHAFF Adam Schaff (b. 1913, Lwów) Polish philosopher. Of his numerous books, several treat problems of **semantics**, philosophy of language, logic, theory of knowledge and ideology. According to Schaff, language is a social product as well as a genetic phenomenon and is functional to human praxis. This is the basis of the 'active role' of the human subject both at the level of cognitive processes as well as of practical action. Language is not only an instrument for the **expression** of **meaning**, but also the material which goes to form meaning and without which meaning could not exist. Consequently Schaff criticizes the reductive innatist and biologistic interpretation of language as proposed by linguist Noam **Chomsky** and biologist Eric H. Lenneberg (see Schaff 1978).

According to Schaff, we must free ourselves from what he calls (1962) the 'fetishism of **sign**s' (a direct echo of **Marx**'s 'fetishism of commodities'). The 'fetishism of signs' is reflected in the reified conception of the relations among signs as well as between **signifier** and **signified**; analysis must begin from the social processes of communication, and sign relations must be considered as relations among humans who use and produce signs in specific social conditions. In Schaff's opinion, by contrast with naïve materialism, we must recognize the superiority of language theories which stress the active function of language in the cognitive process; the connection between language and *Weltanschauung*; and the connection between language and the 'image of reality'. However, the human being should be considered as the result of social relations, and language as inseparable from social praxis (Ponzio 1974).

In studies of human **semiosis**, this leads us to a new vision of issues related to sign and language: the problem of the connection between language and knowledge (see Schaff 1973, 1975); language and consciousness; language, ideology and stereotypes; and language and responsibility. Conversely, it is apparent that theories of knowledge are theories in need of support from studies on language; in order to maintain an adequate consideration of the concepts of 'choice', 'responsibility', 'individual freedom', and such problems as the 'tyranny of words', 'linguistic alienation' and its causes must also be taken into account. (**AP**)

Further Reading

Ponzio, A. (1990) 'Humanism, language and knowledge in Adam Schaff', in A. Ponzio (ed.) *Man as a Sign*, Berlin: Mouton de Gruyter.

Schaff, A. (1973) *Language and Cognition*, New York: McGraw-Hill.

Schaff, A. (1978) *Structuralism and Marxism*, Oxford: Pergamon Press.

SEBEOK Thomas A. Sebeok was born in Budapest in 1920. He emigrated to the United States in 1937, and became a citizen in 1944. He has been a faculty member of Indiana University since 1944 and is General Editor of *Semiotica*, the journal of the International Association for Semiotic Studies (**IASS**), founded in Paris in 1969. Sebeok must be counted among the figures who have most contributed to the institutionalization of **semiotics** internationally, and to its configuration as 'global semiotics'. His work is largely inspired by Charles S. **Peirce**, but also by Charles **Morris** and Roman **Jakobson**. His numerous and diversified research interests cover a broad expanse of territories, ranging from the natural sciences to the human sciences.

A fundamental conviction deriving from Peirce and subtending Sebeok's general research method is that the entire universe is perfused with **sign**s. By virtue of this 'global' or 'holistic' approach, Sebeok's research into the 'life of signs' may be immediately associated with his concern for the 'signs of life'. In his view, **semiosis** and life coincide. Semiosis originates with the first stirrings of life, which leads to the formulation of an axiom he believes cardinal to semiotics: 'semiosis is the criterial attribute of life'. Semiotics provides a point of confluence and observation post for studies on the life of signs and the signs of life.

Moreover, Sebeok's global approach to sign life presupposes his critique of anthropocentric and glottocentric semiotic theory and practice. In his explorations of the boundaries and margins of the science or (as he also calls it) 'doctrine' of signs he opens the field to include **zoosemiotics** (a term he introduced in 1963) or even more broadly **biosemiotics**, on the one hand, and endosemiotics, on the other. In Sebeok's conception, the sign science is not only the 'science qui étude la vie des signes au sein de la vie sociale' (**Saussure**), that is the study of communication in culture, but also the study of communicative behavior in a biosemiotic perspective.

Sebeok's opening remarks to *The Sign and Its Masters* (1979), which he defines as 'transitional', may be extended to all his research considered in the light of current debate in philosophico-linguistic and semiotic theory. A transition is now generally occurring from '**code** semiotics' to 'interpretation semiotics', that is, from semiotics centred on linguistics to one which is autonomous from it.

Even in an earlier theoretical work, *Contributions to the Doctrine of Signs* (1976), Sebeok clearly privileges interpretation semiotics, while in *The Play of Musement* (1981), he explores the efficacy of semiotics as a methodological tool and therefore its extensibility to varying fields in more discursive and applicative terms.

Other important volumes have followed in rapid succession and include: *I Think I Am a Verb: More Contributions to the Doctrine of Signs* (1986), *Essays in Zoosemiotics* (1990), *A Sign is Just a Sign* (1991), *Semiotics in the United States* (1991), and *Signs: An Introduction to Semiotics* (1994). (**SP**)

See also Sebeok (this volume).

Further Reading

Sebeok, T. A. (1976) *Contributions to the Doctrine of Signs*, Bloomington: Indiana University Press.

Sebeok, T. A. (1989) *The Sign and its Masters*, 2nd edn, Lanham, MD: University Press of America.

Sebeok, T. A. (1994) *Signs: An Introduction to Semiotics*, Toronto: University of Toronto Press.

SECONDNESS Secondness is one of Charles S. **Peirce**'s three categories of phenomena, the other two being **firstness** and **thirdness**. The category of secondness (obsistence, over-againstness), together with firstness and thirdness are the omnipresent categories of mind, **sign** and reality (*CP* 2.84–2.94).

Secondness is the category according to which something is considered relative to, or over against something else. It involves binarity, a relation of opposition or reaction. From the viewpoint of signs, secondness is connected with the **index**. The index is a sign that signifies its object by a relation of contiguity, causality or by some other physical connection. However, this relation also depends on a **habit** or convention. For example, the relation between hearing a knock at the door and someone on the other side of the door who wants to enter. Whereas the **icon**, which is governed by firstness, presents itself as an *original* sign, and the **symbol**, which is governed by *thirdness*, as a *transuasional* sign, the index, which is governed by secondness, is an *obsistent* sign (*CP* 2.89–92).

From the viewpoint of logic, inference regulated by secondness corresponds to deduction. In fact, in the case of an Obsistent Argument or Deduction the conclusion is *compelled* to acknowledge that the facts stated in the premises, whether in one or both, are such as could not be if the fact stated in the conclusion were not there (cf. *CP* 2.96).

From the viewpoint of ontology, that is, of being, secondness is present in the law of *anancasm* or necessity which, on Peirce's account, regulates the evolutionary development of the universe together with *agapasm* (creative love, which corresponds to firstness) and *tychasm* (casuality, which corresponds to thirdness) (cf. *CP* 6.287–317; Petrilli 1999d).

Therefore, on the level of logic, firstness, secondness and thirdness correspond to **abduction**, deduction and induction; on the level of the typology of signs they correspond to the icon, index and symbol; and on the level of ontology to agapism, anancism and tychism.

To secondness or obsistence, a binary category, there corresponds a relation of relative **alterity** in which the terms of the relation depend on each other. Effective alterity, the possibility of something being-on-its-own-account, *absolute per se*, autonomously, presents itself under the category of firstness, or orience, or originality, according to which something '*is what it is without reference to anything else* within it or without it, regardless of all force and of all reason' (*CP* 2.85). An effective relation of alterity would not be possible if there were only binarity, secondness, and therefore obsistence (cf. Ponzio 1990a, pp. 197–214). Relations of alterity would not be possible in a system regulated exclusively by secondness and, therefore, by binarity, where an element exists only on the condition that it refers to another element and would not exist should this other element be negated.

Take, for example, a husband and wife. Here there is nothing but a real twoness; but it constitutes a reaction, in the sense that the husband makes the wife a wife in fact (not merely in some comparing thought); while the wife makes the husband a husband.

(*CP* 2.84) (**SP**)

Further Reading

Peirce, C. S. (1955) 'The principles of phenomenology', in *Philosophical Writings of Peirce*, ed. J. Buchler, New York: Dover.

Peirce, C. S. (1958) 'Letter to Lady Welby, 12 October 1904', in *Charles S. Peirce: Selected Writings*, ed. P. Wiener, New York: Dover.

Petrilli, S. (1999) 'About and beyond Peirce', *Semiotica* 124 (3/4), 299–376.

SEMANTICS In **Morris**'s theory of **semiosis**, the semantical dimension of the functioning of **signs** pertains to 'the relation of signs to the objects to which the signs are applicable' (1938a, p. 6) and the study of this dimension is called semantics. In linguistics, this translates into a view of semantics as the component of a linguistic theory dealing with **meaning**, whether at the word level (lexical semantics) or at the sentence or propositional level. Often, semantics is said to study meaning out of context, whereas **pragmatics** studies meaning in context (Levinson 1983). However, most sentences can only be understood against a set of background assumptions which effectively define a context (Searle 1978). A more useful distinction may be, therefore, to regard the province of semantics as the properties of the language system that directly enable the generation of meaning in language use, a process which is itself within the realm of pragmatics. (**JV**)

See also BRÉAL and GRICE.

258

Further Reading

Lyons, J. (1995) *Linguistic Semantics: An Introduction*, Cambridge: Cambridge University Press.

SEMIOLOGY Not to be confused either with **semantics** or with **semiotics**, despite the fact that the latter term is often loosely treated as synonymous with semiology. The English word is a translation of French *sémiologie*, coined by Ferdinand de **Saussure** in 1894 and intended as the designation for a (then non-existent) discipline devoted to studying 'the life of signs as part of social life'. In Saussure's *Cours de linguistique générale* this discipline is presented as a branch of social psychology. Saussure did not conceive of semiology as a general science of signs of every kind. From his Geneva lectures, it seems clear that he excluded from semiology all signs dependent on or controlled by the decisions of individuals. Nor did he include so-called 'natural' signs (storm clouds, blushing, etc.). Semiology was apparently to be confined to the study of public institutional signs, particularly those in which the relation between form and **meaning** was 'arbitrary': of these Saussure regarded linguistic signs as constituting the most important class.

Followers of Saussure later extended the definition of the term. Buyssens equated semiology with the study of communication processes in general (at least when conceived of as actions intended to influence others, and recognized as such by the 'others' in question). **Barthes** reversed Saussure's view of the relations between semiology and linguistics, treating the former as part of the latter. **Lévi-Strauss** considered anthropology to be a branch of semiology. None of these later developments corresponds to Saussure's original conception. (**RH**)

See Harris (this volume), HJELMSLEV, STRUCTURALISM and POSTSTRUCTURALISM.

Further Reading

Saussure, F. de (1983) *Course in General Linguistics*, trans. R. Harris, London: Duckworth.

SEMIOSIS Semiosis is the name given to the action of **signs**. **Semiotics** might therefore be understood as the study of semiosis or even as a 'metasemiosis', producing 'signs about signs'. Behind this simple definition lies a universe of complexity. In general parlance, and sometimes in semiotics, signs are conceived only as inanimate objects which are utilised for the purpose of sending messages. However, semiosis occurs in many different ways and in places where signs are not necessarily apparent to humans. Whereas human semiosis has been the object of the many investigations which make up **anthroposemiotics**, there is an enormous variety of semiosis which is non-human in character. Moreover, anthroposemiosis should not be considered as separate from the wider-ranging actions of signs between all kinds of cells. Instead, it should be understood as being *contained* within the latter, its vicissitudes merely being differently ordered than that of its neighbours: 'Thus, physics, biology, psychology and sociology each embodies its own peculiar level of semiosis' (Scbcok 1994, p. 6).

Morris famously defines semiosis as a 'process in which something is a sign to some organism' (1946, p. 366). Like **Peirce**, he identifies a threefold operation of semiosis consisting of the *sign vehicle*, the ***designatum*** and the *interpretant* (equivalent to **representamen**, **object** and **interpretant**), in which the first acts as a sign, the second is what is referred to and the third is the effect of, and the effector of, the relationship between the other two (Morris 1938). Morris's work is a good example of how simple sign relations entail semiosic complexity. He envisages three realms of semiosis: these are the relations between sign vehicles, to which he gives the name *syntactics* (or **syntax**); the relations between each different sign vehicle and its designatum, named **semantics**; and the relations between signs and their users – **pragmatics**. With adjustments, this triad of approaches to semiosis in general has provided the agenda for much of modern linguistics.

The relations between the terms 'semiosis' and 'communication' should also be noted. It is well known that Peirce used the term 'semiosis' and seldom invoked concepts of 'communication' and 'intentionality' (although, see Johansen 1993, p. 189 ff.). The latter, however, are often taken as axiomatic in anthroposemiotics. **Saussure**, for example, in his *Cours*, outlines the 'speech circuit'. A diagram of two human heads is shown, passing coded speech to each other and thus connecting the contents of two minds in an act of 'telementation' (1983, p. 11; cf. Harris 1987, p. 205 ff.).

Such emphasis on the 'success' of human semiosis characterizes much communication theory. Much later in the twentieth century, for example, **relevance theory** questioned **code** models suggesting that:

> most human communication is intentional, and it is intentional for two good reasons. The first reason is the one suggested by **Grice**: by producing direct evidence of one's informative intention, one can convey a much wider range of information than can be conveyed by producing direct evidence for the basic information itself. The second reason humans have for communicating is to modify and extend the mutual cognitive environment they share with one another.
>
> (Sperber and Wilson 1995, p. 64)

The code in Saussure's speech circuit and the ostension and inference in relevance theory are powerful components in the act of human communication. Both imply the manifest transaction in the verbal transmission of signs. However, this should not be allowed to obscure the fact that communicative acts and intentionality are only a small part of the universal semiosic repertoire. Semiosis is simply ineffable and many semioses, like the action of subatomic particles (Sebeok 1994, p. 8), can only be discerned through a **model** of their activity. (**PC**)

See also Sebeok, Coupland and Jaworksi and Verschueren (this volume), SIGNIFICATION and BIOSEMIOTICS.

Further Reading

Merrell, F. (1998) *Sensing Semiosis: Toward the Possibility of Contemporary Cultural Logics*, London: Macmillan.

Morris, C. (1938) *Foundations of the Theory of Signs*, Chicago: University of Chicago Press.

Sebeok, T. A. (1994) *Signs: An Introduction to Semiotics*, Toronto: University of Toronto Press.

SEMIOTICS   Semiotics may be understood as indicating

1   the specificity of human **semiosis**;
2   the general science of **signs**.

Concerning (1) in the world of life which coincides with semiosis, human semiosis is characterized as *metasemiosis*, that is, as the possibility of reflecting on signs, of making signs not only the object of interpretation not distinguishable from the response to these signs, but also of interpretation as reflection on signs, as suspension of response and possibility of deliberation. We may call this specific human capacity for metasemiosis 'semiotics'. Developing **Aristotle**'s correct observation made at the beginning of his *Metaphysics*, that man tends by nature to knowledge, we could say that man tends by nature to semiotics. Human semiosis, anthroposemiosis, is characterized by its presenting itself as semiotics. Semiotics as human semiosis or anthroposemiosis, can (a) venture as far as the entire universe in search of **meanings** and senses, considering it therefore from the viewpoint of signness. Or, (b) absolutize anthroposemiosis by identifying it with semiosis itself.

Concerning (2), semiotics as a discipline or science (**Saussure**) or theory (**Morris**) or doctrine (**Sebeok**) presents itself in the first case (a) as 'global semiotics' (Sebeok) extensible to the whole universe insofar as it is perfused by signs (**Peirce**); whereas in the second case (b) it is limited and anthropocentric.

The origins of semiotics as a field of knowledge are identified above all in the origins of medical semiotics, or symptomatology, the study of symptoms. In truth, since man is a 'semiotic animal' all human life has always been characterized by knowledge of a semiotic order. If, therefore, medical semeiotics may be considered as the first branch of development in semiotics, this is only because in contrast to Hippocrates and Galen, hunters, farmers, navigators, fisherman, and women with their wisdom and sign practices relative to the production and reproduction of life, have always been involved in semiotics, but without writing treatises.

Given that verbal signs, oral and written, are unique in the sense that they carry out nothing other than a sign function, reflection on verbal signs since ancient times represents another pillar in the semiotic science. Indeed, the study of verbal signs has greatly oriented the criteria for determining what may be considered as a sign.

This explains how in very recent times (the beginning of the twentieth century), semiotics presents itself, on the basis of its linguistico-verbal interests, in the form of *sémiologie* with the task, in Saussure's view, of studying the life of signs 'dans le sein de la vie sociale'. And though linguistics was included as merely a branch of

semiology, *sémiologie* in its totality was profoundly influenced by it. Saussure only recognized signs in entities which carry out an intentionally communicative function in a social context. From the limits of this conception, *communication semiotics*, a transition takes place to *signification semiotics* (**Barthes**) which also recognizes signs in what is not produced with the intention of functioning as such, and finally to the phase which with Barthes (1975) may be called 'third sense semiotics', or 'text semiotics', or *significance semiotics*. But parallel to all this, other semiotic perspectives have developed in different fields of interest as well. Without claiming to exhaust the list, consider the following perspectives together with the names of their main representatives: the psychological (Freud, **Bühler**, Vygotsky), philosophical (**Peirce**, **Welby**, **Ogden** and **Richards**, **Wittgenstein**, Morris, Cassirer), literary critical (**Bakhtin**), biological (Romanes, Jakob and Thure von **Uexküll**, Jacob, Monod), mathematical–topological (René Thom). By making the 'semiosphere' (**Lotman**) consist in the 'semiobiosphere', Sebeok's 'global scmiotics' has offered the most exhaustive account of signs: this perspective is the most capable of questioning the presumed totalities of semiotics and showing them up for what they really are, its parts. (**SP**)

See also ANTHROPOSEMIOTICS and BIOSEMIOTICS.

Further Reading

Deely, J. (1994) *The Human Use of Signs, or Elements of Anthroposemiosis*. Lanham, MD: Rowman and Littlefield.

Hoffmeyer, J. and Emmeche, C. (eds) (1999) *Biosemiotica*. Special issue of *Semiotica* 126.

Nöth, W. (1990) *Handbook of Semiotics*, Bloomington: Indiana University Press.

SHIFTER See DEIXIS.

SIGN A sign is a factor in a process conceived either dyadically (**signifier/signified**) in accord with **Saussure** and his followers or triadically (sign (**representamen**)/**object**/**interpretant**) in accord with **Peirce** and his.

The fundamental terms of a sign include what we may call the *interpreted* sign, on the side of the object, and the *interpretant* in a relation where the interpretant is what makes the interpreted sign possible. The interpreted becomes a sign component because it receives an interpretation, but the interpretant in turn is also a sign component with the potential to engender a new sign: therefore, where there is a sign, there are immediately two, and given that the interpretant can engender a new sign, there are immediately three, and so forth as described by Charles S. Peirce with his concept of **unlimited semiosis**, the chain of deferrals from one interpretant to another.

To analyse the sign beginning from the object of intepretation, that is, the interpreted, means to begin from a secondary level. In other words, to begin from the object-interpreted means to begin from a point in the chain of deferrals, or semiosic chain, which cannot be considered as the starting point. Nor can it be privileged by way of abstraction at a theoretical level to explain the workings of sign processes.

An example: a spot on the skin is a sign insofar as it may be interpreted as a symptom of sickness of the liver: this is already a secondary level in the interpretation process. At a primary level, retrospectively, the skin disorder is an interpretation enacted by the organism itself in relation to an anomaly which is disturbing it and to which it responds. The skin disorder is already in itself an interpretant response.

To say that the sign is first an interpretant means that the sign is first a response. We could also say that the sign is a reaction: but only on the condition that by 'reaction' we intend 'interpretation' (similarly to Charles **Morris**'s behaviorism, but differently from the mechanistic approach).

The expression 'solicitation-response' is preferable to 'stimulus-reaction' to the end of avoiding superficial associations between the approaches that they recall respectively. Even a 'direct' response to a stimulus, or better solicitation, is never direct but 'mediated' by an interpretation: unless it is a 'reflex action', formulation of a response involves identifying the solicitation, situating it in a context, and relating it to given behavioral parameters (whether a question of simple types of behaviour, e.g., the prey-predator model, or more complex behaviours connected to cultural values, as in the human world). Therefore, the sign is first of all an interpretant, a response beginning from which something is considered as a sign and becomes its interpreted and is further able to generate an unlimited chain of other signs.

A sign presents varying degrees of plurivocality and univocality. A signal may be defined as a univocal sign, or better as a sign with the lowest degrees of plurivocality.

(Note, also, that 'sign' is the usual shorthand term given to the formal **sign language** used by the deaf.) (**SP**)

See also <u>Merrell</u> and <u>Sebeok</u> (this volume), SEMIOSIS, SEMIOTICS, SEMIOLOGY and SIGNIFICATION.

Further Reading

Morris, C. (1938) *Foundations of the Theory of Signs*, Chicago: University of Chicago Press.

Peirce, C. S. (1955) 'Logic as semiotic: the theory of signs', in *Philosophical Writings of Peirce* ed. J. Buchler, New York: Dover.

Sebeok, T. A. (1994) *Signs: An Introduction to Semiotics*, Toronto: University of Toronto Press.

SIGNANS The signans is, with the signatum, a sign component. These recently revived Augustinian terms are preferable to the Saussurean *signifiant* and *signifié*, 'acoustic image' and 'concept', since they do not imply a psychologistic and phonocentric (see **phone**) version of **sign**.

The signans is an object which, once interpreted, becomes material of the signatum. The sign is the totality and should not be confused with the signans as in the current expression 'to be a sign of' which would be better said with 'to be a signans of': something is interpreted as that which *stands for*, or *refers to*, or is a *vehicle of a signatum* – or *designatum* (Morris 1938a), or **significatum** (Morris 1946), or **signification** (Morris 1964) – to be distinguished from **denotatum**. Instead, when a whole sign acts as a new signans of a signatum at a secondary level, we then have the case of **connotation** (Hjelmslev 1961).

The materiality of the signans (cf. Rossi-Landi 1992b, pp. 271–99; Petrilli 1990b, pp. 365–401) is not only extrasign materiality, physical materiality (the body of the signans) and instrumental materiality (nonverbal signs, their nonsign uses and functions), but also semiotic materiality: that is, historico-social materiality at more or less high levels of complexity, elaboration and/or articulation (elaboration materiality); ideological materiality; extra-intentional materiality, that is, objectivity independent from consciousness and volition; and also signifying otherness materiality, that is, the possibility of other signata with respect to the signatum of any one specific interpretive path. (**SP**)

Further Reading

Rossi-Landi, F. (1992) 'Signs and material reality', in *Between Signs and Non-signs*, ed. and introduced by S. Petrilli, Amsterdam: John Benjamins.

SIGNIFICATION/SIGNIFICANCE Charles **Morris** distinguishes between signification and significance, thereby indicating two different aspects of '**meaning**': the **semantic** and the axiological. Victoria **Welby**, instead, uses significance (see **significs**) for the third term of her meaning triad, the other two being 'sense' and 'meaning'. Both authors (in the same way as others who work on the same concepts, e.g. Barthes 1975) relate sense to value and, therefore, semiotics to axiology. In the words of Morris (1964, p. vii): 'if we ask what is the meaning of life, we may be asking a question about the signification of the term "life", or asking a question about the value or significance of living – or both'. And the fact that usage of such terms as 'meaning' (with the polarity suggested) is so widespread suggests, continues Morris, that there is a fundamental relation between what he distinguishes as signification and significance. (**SP**)

SIGNIFICATUM Use of the term significatum in **semiotics** is explained by Charles **Morris** in *Signs, Language, and Behavior* (1949). The **sign**, or better, the **signans**, *signifies* its significatum. To signify, to have **signification** and to have a significatum are synonyms. In the words of Morris: 'Those conditions which are such that whatever fulfills them is a denotatum will be called a *significatum* of the sign' (1971, p. 94). In his description of the conditions which allow for something to be a sign, the significatum is distinct from the **denotatum**. If something satisfies the conditions such that something else functions as a sign, while this second something is a denotatum, the first something is the significatum.

All signs signify, that is, have a significatum, but not all signs denote. The significatum of the bell (sign) which attracts the attention of Pavlov's famous dog (interpreter) is that something edible is available; the food found by the dog which enables it to respond in a certain way (**interpretant**) as provoked by the sign, is the denotatum. The latter, however, may actually not exist, to the dog's great disappointment. In *Foundations of the Theory of Signs* (1938a, Ch. 2), Morris uses the term designatum instead of significatum. Every sign insofar as it is a sign has a designatum, but not every sign has a denotatum, because not every sign refers to something which actually exists: where what is referred to (significatum or designatum) actually exists as referred to, the object of reference is a denotatum. In other words, the significatum is what the sign or signans refers to, a set of qualities forming a class or type of objects or events to which the interpreter reacts independently of the fact that what is referred to actually exists (denotatum) according to the existence value attributed to it by the sign (cf. Ponzio 1981a). In *Signification and Significance* (1964) he replaces the term 'significatum' with 'signification' while the term 'denotatum' is dropped altogether. (**SP**)

Further Reading

Morris, C. (1971) *Writings on the General Theory of Signs*, ed. T.A. Sebeok, The Hague and Paris: Mouton.

SIGNIFICS Significs was a neologism introduced by Victoria **Welby**, after first trying *sensifics*, for her approach to the study of **sign**s, **meaning** and interpretation. A provisional definition of significs was formulated by Welby in *Significs and Language* (1911): 'the study of the nature of significance in all its forms and relations' (Welby [1911] 1985a, p. vii), with a practical bearing 'not only on language but on every possible form of human expression in action, invention, and creation' (ibid., p. ix). But see her own dictionary definition of 1902 and encyclopaedia entry of 1911 (now Welby 1977). In contrast to '**semantics**', 'semasiology' and '**semiotics**', 'significs' was free from technical associations, thus making it suitable to signal the connection between meaning and value in all its aspects (pragmatic, social, ethic, esthetic, etc.) (cf. Welby 1983, 1985a; Schmitz 1985). It takes account of the everyday expression 'What does it signify?', with its focus on the sign's ultimate value and significance (see **signification/significance**) beyond semantic meaning. In addition to a theory of meaning, significs proposes a 'significal method' that transcends pure descriptivism and strictly logico-epistemological boundaries in the direction of axiology and of the study of the conditions that make meaningful behaviour possible (cf. Petrilli 1988, 1998a). Central to significs is Welby's analysis of meaning into three main levels: 'Sense' – 'the organic response to environment'; 'Meaning' – the specific sense which a word 'is intended to convey'; 'Significance' – 'the far-reaching consequence, implication, ultimate result or outcome of some event or experience' (cf. Hardwick 1977, p. 169). According to Charles S. **Peirce**, the triad of sense, meaning and significance relates closely to his own triad of Immediate **Interpretant**, Dynamical Interpretant and Final Interpretant, respectively (Hardwick 1977, pp. 109–11). (**SP**)

Further Reading

Welby, V. (1985) *Significs and Language: (The Articulate Form of Our Expressive and Interpretative Resources)* (1911), with additional essays, ed. and introduced H. W. Schmitz, Amsterdam and Philadelphia: John Benjamins.

SIGNIFIED A common but bad English translation for the **Saussure**an technical term *signifié* (= the conceptual component of the linguistic sign). It is *not*, as the English mistranslation suggests, the 'thing signified' (i.e. the **referent**). (**RH**)

SIGNIFIER A common but bad English translation for the **Saussure**an technical term *signifiant* (= the mental sound pattern associated with the *signifié* to form the linguistic sign). It is neither the sign-user nor the material manifestation of the sign (i.e. the sounds uttered). **(RH)**

See SIGNANS

SIGN LANGUAGE Phenomena to which the term sign language has been, or might be, applied are numerous indeed. A great many species in the animal kingdom survive by interpreting and using what they see. For many of them, the most important information comes from interpreting the visible actions of conspecifics (e.g. von Frisch on the language of honey bees). The broadest views of the phenomena are taken by **semiotics** (see also Sebeok, this volume) and biology. But when the behavior is human, researchers in anthropology, linguistics, psychology, and sociology also take note of portions of this behavior. They may label their selection as **gesture**, gesticulation, **kinesics**, surrogate speech, nonverbal behavior, or something else; but sign language is the designation that frequently seems to have the most appeal to the public and the broadest scope.

The amount and variety of such phenomena cause great variation in what is covered by the terms used for them. Philosophers from ancient times regarded gesture either as a forerunner of speech or dismissed it and saw language as spoken only. It was only in the middle of the twentieth century that social scientists came to recognize that the signing of deaf people serves in all respects as does the speaking of hearing people, to make the primary signs of a language, in short, that a sign language is a language. When members of a social group sign instead of speaking their first or only language, their signing expresses a language. Their manual, facial, and body actions constitute language signs just as vocal actions do. This is true also of sign languages people use as alternatives to the languages they normally speak (Kendon 1988; Farnell 1995). But circumstances keep apart the groups using these 'primary' and 'alternate' sign languages (SLs) even more than they keep apart groups using spoken languages (see **sign languages [alternate]**). Different groups of people use different languages, whether they speak or sign them.

Although humans who share no common language can communicate with gestures, no common nor universal sign language exists. **(WCS)**

See also Sebeok (this volume), BIO-SEMIOTICS and SIGN LANGUAGES (PRIMARY).

Further Reading

Wilson, F. R. (1998) *The Hand: How its Use Shapes the Brain, Language, and Human Culture*, New York: Pantheon.

SIGN LANGUAGES (ALTERNATE) A century ago studies of alternate **sign language**s (SLs) tended to concentrate on what has come to be known as Plains Indian Sign Language. The work of Mallery (1881) provides much otherwise unobtainable data about the signs used in various Native American tribes. However, virtually all linguistic studies of Native American languages have been focused on their spoken languages, their possible relationship, and their linguistic typology. These tribes may have used (and still use: see Farnell 1995) their SLs as alternatives to the languages they normally speak, but linguists have so far failed to treat their SLs as languages too.

Apart from works by Kendon (1988) and Farnell (1995), there is a dearth of research on alternative SLs. This may result from the tendency in the social sciences to rely on Aristotelian or rigorous logic – something is either language or is not language. With such a mind set, it becomes impossible to determine whether what one is looking at in an exotic population is the gesturing everyone is likely to do while speaking or the signing that expresses a sign language. Logical categorization puts out of reach the possibility that gesturing and signing are related by evolution (see Stokoe, this volume). (**WCS**)

See also SIGN LANGUAGES (PRIMARY).

Further Reading

Farnell, B. (1995) *Do You See What I Mean? Plains Indian Sign Talk and the Embodiment of Action*, Austin, TX: Texas University Press.

SIGN LANGUAGES (PRIMARY) Languages where signing is the primary mode of communication. There are many primary **sign languages** (SLs), and when a widely distributed population uses one of them, it may be marked by **dialects**. That is, deaf signers may have **signs** that differ from those used in other parts of the country, but they share a **grammar**.

Signers of the dialects still use the same key grammatical **markers**: like signs for 'and', 'but', 'to', 'for', 'not', 'because', etc. but usually do so differently. This variety in national SLs comes about from the same causes that make spoken languages different – separation and contact of populations. But another factor operates with deaf SLs. In the eighteenth and nineteenth centuries, changes in attitudes towards deaf people led great innovators to provide effective formal education for those who could not hear. Most notable was the institute founded in Paris (1755) by the Abbé Charles Michel de l'Epée (1712–89).

Its success, based on the use of the pupils' own sign, led rapidly to establishment of schools for the deaf in most European capitals and as early as 1817 in Hartford, Connecticut, USA. Consequently, deaf persons educated in Paris became leaders in the arts, printing and publishing, and other fields. They carried their successes – and their sign language – to other places, where their language and that used in the national schools inevitably led local signers to adopt new signs. This process continues today: deaf signers in Asian countries are rapidly adopting signs from American Sign Language. Modern Thai SL differs greatly from that used by deaf signers of an older generation, and the difference is the use of signs from ASL.

Apart from Woodward's lexicostatistic studies of the relatedness of primary SLs, little has been done to compare primary SLs. Instead, recent attempts by linguists to find a **Universal Grammar** of language have led some sign language researchers to ignore differences and look for similarities among SLs, and between SLs and spoken languages. Much current post-Chomskyan theory has it that language comes from an organ in the human brain not from social interaction. This has turned SL research towards treating deaf signs and infants' gestures as automatic products of innate mechanisms. In this view, differences in SLs and comparative study have little to offer, as the goal is not sought for in bodies of visible data but in the intricacies of the brain. (**WCS**)

Further Reading

Journal of Deaf Studies and Deaf Education.

Sign Language Studies (1972–1996).

Stokoe, W. C. (1972) *Semiotics and Human Sign Languages*, The Hague: Mouton.

SINSIGN Charles S. **Peirce**'s term for the second division of his trichotomy of the **grounds** of signs. A sinsign is a sign which, in itself, is an existent thing or event. There are different kinds of sinsigns distinguished principally by whether they represent their **referents iconically**, e.g. an individual diagram (an iconic sinsign), or **index**ically, e.g. a cry of pain or a weathervane (*dicent* sinsigns). Iconic sinsigns inform of essences while indexical sinsigns only inform of causes or actual facts. A sinsign may be a token of a type. (**NH**)

See also QUALISIGN and LEGISIGN.

SITUATION Utterances, spoken or written, always occur in (social) situations. In socially oriented theories of language the assumption is that features of the situation (who is involved, in what social relations, for what purposes, in what institutional settings) will be reflected in aspects of the utterance. (**GRK**)

See also FIELD, TENOR and MODE.

SOCIAL STRUCTURE Social theories of language (or of representation more generally) explicitly or implicitly refer to the structurings of the social environment. These may be structures of class; of 'stratification'; of derived or dependent categories, such as power, gender or family. The type of structure assumed will affect assumptions about language (use). (**GRK**)

See also SITUATION.

SOCIOLINGUISTICS Sociolinguistics deals with the variability of language given changes in social circumstances. Three distinct approaches are discernible: one sees language and its uses as a reflection of social factors; a second treats the social as an effect of the linguistic; and a third accounts for relations between social and linguistic structures, where both are seen as autonomous. Instances of the first describe the language (use) of professions; of social **dialect**s or 'codes'; of **genre**s and **register**s of all kinds; or the language uses associated with gender, age, class. Instances of the second are forms of **discourse analysis** which see social organizations – the law, medicine, science – as the result of linguistic action. Here too belong studies which deal with 'language about' genders, races, classes, or ethnicities, producing the social facts of gender as sexism, or of race as racism. Attempts to change the social by changing linguistic behaviours, the struggles of feminism to change naming practices, for instance, rest on this approach. The third approach treats language and society as autonomous, but sees regularities in interrelations between them: code-switching shows how changes in social circumstances lead to a switch from one language (or dialect) to another; studies in phonological variation show how speakers pronounce the same word differently in an informal and a formal environment. (**GRK**)

See Aitchison, Kress and Coupland and Jaworski (this volume), DISCOURSE, LABOV and BERNSTEIN.

Further Reading

Hudson, R. A. (1996) *Sociolinguistics*, 2nd edn, Cambridge: Cambridge University Press.

SPEECH ACT The term 'speech act' was first introduced by **Austin** (1962) to draw attention to the fact that people perform actions when saying something. It was Searle's (1969) further elaboration of this idea that made 'speech act theory' into a popular domain of research not only in the philosophy of language but also in linguistics. The general form of a speech act is F(p), where 'p' stands for a **proposition** (a reference and a predication) and 'F' for the **illocutionary** *force* of the utterance. Speech acts can be described in terms of *constitutive* **rule**s which bear on the *necessary and sufficient conditions* for the felicitous performance of an act of a certain type. Thus a 'propositional content condition' for a promise is that the speaker predicates a future act on his/her own part; 'preparatory conditions' for promising include that the hearer would prefer the speaker to perform this act to his/her not performing it, and that it is not obvious to both speaker and hearer that the speaker would perform this act in the normal course of events; the 'sincerity condition' for promising is that the speaker intends to do what he/she promises; and the 'essential condition' is that the speaker intends his/her utterance to place him/her under an obligation to do as promised.

An important distinction is made between direct and indirect speech acts (Searle 1975). Indirect speech acts such as 'Can you reach the salt?' have a double illocutionary force: there is a primary illocutionary act (a request to pass the salt in this case) and a secondary act (i.e. the one by means of which the primary force is indirectly obtained, in this case a question pertaining to one of the preparatory conditions for the speakers being able to make the request). (**JV**)

Further Reading

Searle, J. R. (1969) *Speech Acts: An Essay in the Philosophy of Language*, Cambridge: Cambridge University Press.

SPEECH COMMUNITY A language is not uniformly the same throughout: there are differences of geographical and social **dialect**; of specialist languages, the language of the law, of medicine, of motor mechanics; of differences in levels of formality; and others. One can assume either that these just exist: 'In this part of the country this dialect is spoken, in this part that dialect is spoken', or one can attempt to understand the causes of that difference.

The term 'speech community' locates the origins of difference in the fact that members of groups are characterized, among other things, by a greater density/ frequency of interaction than others; that the occasions of their interaction within the community, the 'speech events', are marked by greater similarity than those

of interaction 'outside' the community or across communities; that certain 'speech events' in the group occur frequently; that the substance/content of interaction has relative persistence and stability. A number of factors of this kind will lead to the emergence of very similar pronunciations, of words used, of **grammar**, **syntax**, and of **genres**. All these mark the group as a 'community', are *reinforced* by the community, and make its language uses recognizably distinct. (**GRK**)

See also Aitchison (this volume).

Further Reading

Gumperz, J. J. (ed.) (1982) *Language and Social Identity*, Cambridge: Cambridge University Press.

STOICS AND EPICUREANS Zeno of Citium (*c*.336–260 BCE) founded a movement of thought that came to be known as Stoicism, because of the location at which he originally taught, the famous *stoa poecille* or 'painted porch'. The Stoic philosophy encouraged involvement in public affairs and the performance of great deeds as fulfilling the mission of human existence. A nearly opposite view was proposed in Epicurean philosophy, the movement of thought founded at nearly the same historical moment by Epicurus of Samos (341–270 BCE).

Epicurus taught withdrawal from public notice and the 'cultivation of one's own garden' where, with like-minded friends and associates, one could explore the realm of reason (so far as wisdom is given to humankind) in the peace that only avoidance of the currents of public life can provide. Stoics and Epicureans tended to agree on the basically material nature of the world. But whereas Stoics saw the universe suffused with divine reason which they called, after the usage attributed to the poem of Heraclitus (*c*.540/535–*c*.480/475 BCE), the λογος, the 'fertilizing wisdom of

God', and which they saw as the purpose of human reason to grasp, Epicureans saw the universe rather, after the teachings of Democritus (*c*.460–370/362 BCE), as a dance of atoms in a void.

Reconstruction of Stoic views in particular represents a problem, because the report of their theoretical views survives for us only in the reports of their enemies, notably, the skeptic Sextus Empiricus (*c*.150–*c*.225) and the follower of Epicurus Philodemus of Gadara (*c*.110–40 BCE). As far as concerns **semiotics**, by far the most important testimony concerning both the Stoics and the Epicureans is that which shows a crossing of their theoretical paths in the understanding of natural **sign**s. The main source of this testimony is the mid-first century BCE tract *On the Sign and Inferences Therefrom*, Περὶ σημείων καί σημειώσεων, by Philodemus. Philodemus intended that his tract prove the Epicurean position correct on all matters at issue. Even so, in present hindsight, what is fundamentally interesting about the tract (variously referred to by a Latin plural title, *De Signis*, or by the English title under which it was in fact published, *On Methods of Inference*, which omits the σημείον even in the singular) is the evidence it provides of a controversy rooted in the notion of **sign**, σημείον, toward the dawn of the Christian era, a controversy whose terms reveal that at this late period there did not exist in Greek philosophy a general notion of sign in which the two orders of nature and culture (linguistic communication in particular) are unified. The sign still belonged to the order of nature, language to the order of convention.

As we might expect in a controversy between Epicureans and Stoics over the subject matter of logical inference, the Epicureans view everything in *a posteriori*, experiential terms, the Stoics in *a priori* terms of rational necessity. In the Stoic and the Epicurean analysis alike the σημείον is a material object or natural event accessible to sense, a *tynchánon* (in the transliteration of Manetti, for a Stoic actual sensible **referent**). To such an **object** a linguistic expression, *sēmainon* in the Stoic logic, *onoma* in Epicurean, is mediately related; in the former case by what the Stoics call the *sēmaínomenon* or *lekton*, in the latter case by prolepsis (προλήψις, 'preconception' or 'anticipation').

Hence, within the agreement 'about the validity of particular signs', this great theoretical difference emerges: 'while the Stoics considered an object to be a sign beginning from the consequent (or rather from what was referred to), the Epicureans considered it from the point of view of the antecedent' (Manetti 1993, pp. 128–9). Much more than this as a firm general conclusion we have no evidence of to state particulars. All that appears definitive is that in both the Stoic and the Epicurean cases the link between any theory of linguistic expressions and signs as such remains indirect and implicit in their time.

What Manetti (1993, p. 98) remarks of the Stoics applies equally to the Epicureans, to wit, they 'do not reach the point of saying that words are signs (**Augustine** is the first to make such a statement)', and, in the particular case of the Stoics, 'there remains a lexical difference between the sēmaínon/ sēmaínomenon pair and sēmeíon'. Concerning this triad of terms, **Eco** (1984, p. 32) had already remarked that 'the common and obvious etymological root is an indication of their relatedness'; so that perhaps (Jackson 1972, p. 136) we see in the sēmaínon/sēmaínomenon pairing some semantic drift in the direction Augustine will mark out as a unique path for philosophy to pursue in its Latin language development. But this suggestion seems unlikely and, in any event, exceeds actual evidence from existing texts. Much more obvious than any such imputed or implicit drift is the approximation to isomorphism between the Stoic sēmaínon/sēmaínomenon pair and the *signifiant/signifié* pair proposed by late modern **semiology** as the technical essence of 'sign'. This similarity would also, and perhaps better, explain why Mates' version of Stoic logic (e.g. Mates 1961, p. 20) proves so congenial to the logical theories of Frege and Carnap.

Speculations to one side, the present evidence from Greek antiquity requires us to hold that the eventual suggestion for sign as a general notion by Augustine (354–430) will mark an original Latin initiative in philosophy, the one which will most distinctively mark the speculative character of the Latin Age from its origin in Augustine's day to its culmination in the 1632 work of John **Poinsot** (1589–1644), where Augustine's general notion, for the first time, is reduced systematically to its foundations in the theory of relative being. After Poinsot, the Latin Age gives way to the development of modern times. Attention turns to the work of Galileo and Descartes, and Latin gives way to the national languages. The crossing of ways of the Stoics and Epicureans will not be of interest again till the contemporary development of semiotics makes the historical ancestry of notions of sign a matter of general interest and scholarly urgency. (**JD**)

See also SIGNANS, SIGNIFIER, SIGNIFIED and SIGNIFICATION.

Further Reading

Fisch, M. H. (1986). 'Philodemus and Semeiosis (1879–1883)', section 5 (pp. 329–30) of the essay 'Peirce's General Theory of Signs', reprinted in M. H. Fisch *Peirce: Semeiotics and Pragmatism*, Bloomington: Indiana University Press, pp. 321–56.

Mates, B. (1949) 'Stoic logic and the text of Sextus Empiricus', *American Journal of Philology* LXX (3): 290–8.

Philodemus (*c.*110–*c.*40BC). i.54–40 BCE. Περὶ σημειώσεων (*De Signis*), trans. as *On the Methods of Inference* in the edition of P. H. De Lacy and E. Allen De Lacy, rev. with the collaboration of M. Gigante, F. Longo Auricchio, and A. Tepedino Guerra, Naples: Bibliopolis, 1978, Greek text pp. 27–87, English 91–131.

STRUCTURALISM,   STRUCTURALIST The term 'structuralism' designates a number of things. **American structuralism** refers to tendencies in linguistics associated with the names of **Bloomfield**, **Sapir**, **Harris** and, more problematically, **Chomsky**. Structuralism also refers to a tendency in anthropology instanced by contemporary anthropologists such as **Douglas**. Then there is the 'structural linguistics' or structuralism of the **Prague School** which focused upon different functional levels in language and was carried from **Russian Formalism** through the Prague Linguistic Circle and into his later work by Roman **Jakobson** (for example, Jakobson 1960). Most often, however, structuralism is associated with a widespread movement in the human sciences whose heyday was the 1950s and 1960s in France and the late 1960s and 1970s in the Anglo-American world (see, for example, Macksey and Donato 1972; de George and de George 1972). The term 'structure' is undoubtedly latent in 'structuralism' but is not always explicit; what is quite frequently implicit is a set of semiological principles derived from **Saussure**'s notion of *langue*.

Crudely put, structuralism entertained a common method across disciplines whereby surface manifestation of phenomena were interrogated in order that they might reveal a limited set of underlying principles. The anthropology of **Lévi-Strauss** is a good example of this, particularly his approach to myth. Essentially, his approach is akin to searching through numerous examples of *parole* (the various myths under study) in order to discover a universal *langue* (a master **code** which makes possible all myths). In the process, a given myth might therefore be stripped bare to reveal its own structure in relation to the master code. Famously, Lévi-Strauss took the Oedipus myth and treated it 'as an orchestra score would be if it were unwittingly considered as a unilinear series' (1977, p. 213). The result was a table of columns showing the distribution of various narrative functions in a fashion almost resembling the cross-section of a cell and certainly fulfilling the **synchronic** remit set by Saussure. This was not just an abstract exercise, however; as a result of such work Lévi-Strauss was able to posit theories about the recurrent – or even universal – features of the human mind in such activities as mythmaking and storytelling.

A broadly similar approach can be seen in the work of **Greimas**, Bremond and even 'proto-structuralists' such as the Russian folklorist Vladimir Propp (about whose work Lévi-Strauss wrote an incisive critique in 1961 – see Lévi-Strauss 1978). The early writings of Roland **Barthes** might also be said to be structuralist in their orientation. Such works as his 1957 collection *Mythologies* ([1957] 1973) have become famous for the skilful way in which they show some of the most 'obvious' and 'natural' artefacts of popular culture to have been generated by a more or less coherent system that is ideological through and through.

Even though Barthes undoubtedly harboured a critical purpose in his structuralism what underlies his approach and that of the others mentioned above is the belief in a semiological master code governing the appearance and immediate nature of phenomena. For this reason structuralism is often associated with functionalism, a tendency in sociological thinking which is already present in Saussure's *langue*, a concept which itself is frequently thought to have been influenced by the functionalist sociology of Durkheim. In functionalism, the machinery of society works to facilitate human interaction and its different branches are largely

believed to operate with a minimum of conflict. (Work deriving from **Vološinov** and the tradition of **sociolinguistics** posits virtually the opposite theory: see Vološinov [1929] 1973.) As such, humans are frequently seen in structuralism to be the 'bearers' or 'arbitrators' of systems rather than their controllers. Where **poststructuralism** breaks with structuralism is precisely on this point, seeing humans, instead, as largely the *effect* of systems and structures. However, the distinction here is subtle and it is usually difficult to immediately identify such a break between the two movements. (**PC**)

Further Reading

Lévi-Strauss, C. (1987) *The View from Afar*, Harmondsworth: Penguin.
Sturrock, J. (ed.) (1979) *Structuralism and Since*, Oxford: Oxford University Press.
Sturrock, J. (1993) *Structuralism*, 2nd edn, London: Paladin.

SURFACE STRUCTURE   In early **generative grammar**, the level of analysis after transformations have applied. The basic idea was that the grammatical structure of complex sentences is best described by decomposing them into more transparent representations called **deep structure**s to which a series of operations called transformations apply. Surface structures are thus the grammatical structures that are immediately discernible in sentences: it is not quite true to say that they are 'the sentences we see or hear', since phonological rules apply to surface structures to produce actual sequences of sounds, sometimes called phonetic form (PF).

In more recent work the role of deep structure was reduced and more work was done by surface structure. The most recent theory proposed by **Chomsky** and his associates, known as minimalism, suggests that surface structure can be dispensed with. (**RS**)

271

Further Reading

Chomsky, N. (1965) *Aspects of the Theory of Syntax*, Cambridge, MA: MIT Press.

SYLLOGISM A syllogism is a deductive argument consisting of two categorical premises with a conclusion resulting from the elimination of a common term, as in: All men are born of women; Anything born of a woman is mortal; therefore, All men are mortal. Traditional Logic focused on the study of the forms of syllogism and rules for valid inferences. The principle of transivity (if *a* then *b*, and if *b* then *c*, then if *a* then *c*) is the key to syllogistic reasoning. (**NH**)

SYMBOL This term is **polysemic** both in everyday discourse and in philosophical–scientific discourse including the semiotic one. We may distinguish between the following two main acceptations: symbol is

1   A synonym for **sign**; or
2   a special type of sign.

As regards (1):

- The notion of symbol is used by Ernst Cassirer in *Philosophy of Symbolic Forms* (1921–29) to refer to signs. The human being constructs culture through signs and is an *animal symbolicum*. Symbol is connected to symbolic form which leads to Cassirer's *critique of symbolic reason* or of the diverse aspects of culture including language, myth, religion, etc.

- In **Ogden** and **Richards** (1923) as well, 'symbol' stands for *sign* which presents **meaning** in terms of the interactive relation between so-called *symbol*, *thought* or *reference*, and **referent**.

As regards (2):

- For Freud and subsequent psychoanalytically oriented thinkers the symbol is a particular type of sign which indicates all psychic or oniric activity *insofar as it reveals the unconscious*. The unconscious, by presenting consciousness with the symbol of the symbolized object, exerts a screening and protective function.
- The symbol is also a particular type of sign in the typology described by Charles S. **Peirce**: the symbol is the sign 'in consequence of a **habit** (which term I use as including a natural disposition)' (*CP* 4.531).
- According to Charles **Morris**, it is a sign which replaces another as a guide for behavior (cf. Morris 1946, I, 8).
- In John Dewey's account (1938, 'Introduction'), it is an arbitrary or conventional sign.
- The symbol is a particular type of sign for **Saussure** (1916, ch. I) as well. However, on the latter's account it is not completely arbitrary and therefore it is distinct from the verbal sign. In contrast to verbal signs, the relation between **signifier** and **signified** in the symbol is always to a degree conventional (as in the case of scales acting as a sign of justice), though not wholly arbitrarily.
- With reference to the encyclopaedic entry 'Symbol' by S. S. Averincev (1971), M. **Bakhtin** (1974) describes the symbol as the sign which most requires answering comprehension, given the dialectic correlation between identity and **alterity**. The symbol includes the warmth of mystery that unites, juxtaposition of one's own to the other, the warmth of love and the coldness of extraneousness, juxtaposition and comparison: it is not circumscribable to an immediate context but relates to a remote and distant context, which accounts for its opening to alterity. (**AP**)

Further Reading

Ponzio, A. (1985) 'The symbol, alterity, and abduction', *Semiotica* 56 (3/4): 261–77.

SYNCHRONY (SYNCHRONIC) Synchrony is the Saussurean technical term for a theoretical perspective in which a (linguistic) sign system is seen as a self-contained structure not subject to change. The study of linguistic change **Saussure** relegated to '**diachronic**' linguistics. The opposition between synchronic and diachronic is often loosely but wrongly interpreted as merely contrasting relations between linguistic phenomena which happen to be contemporaneous with relations between linguistic phenomena which happen to be separated in time but phylogenetically connected. Thus 'diachronic' becomes (misleadingly) equated with 'historical'. For Saussure *langue* is an exclusively synchronic concept, and diachronic linguistics does not study *langue* in any sense. Saussure's alternative term for synchronic linguistics was 'static linguistics', i.e. the study of linguistic states (*états de langue*). (**RH**)

SYNTAGM, SYNTAGMATIC In **Saussu**rean terminology, syntagmatic relations are those into which a linguistic unit enters in virtue of its linear concatenation in a speech chain. Thus the word *unbeatable* is a syntagm comprising three syntagmatically related signs: (i) *un*, (ii) *beat*, and (iii) *able*. The **meaning** of a syntagm is always more than the sum of its parts. Syntagmatic relations are contrasted in Saussurean theory with 'associative' relations (see **paradigm**). Syntagmatics should not be confused with **syntax**, in the sense in which that term is usually understood in traditional **grammar** or non-Saussurean linguistics. (Saussure's editors warned explicitly against this confusion, but it is commonly made.) Saussure described syntagmatic relations as holding *in praesentia*, as opposed to associative relations, which hold *in absentia*. (**RH**)

SYNTAX, SYNTACTIC Syntax is the part of a **grammar** which deals with the arrangement of words in sentences. An important part of syntax is the order of words. Compare these English and German sentences:

(1) Max has read the book
(2) Max hat das Buch gelesen
    Max has the book read

The two sentences have the same **meaning**, but the two languages have different syntactic rules of word order: in English, the object normally comes after the **verb** (*read + the book*), whereas in this kind of German sentence the object comes before the verb (*das Buch + gelesen*).

Syntax also deals with operations on sentences. English and German have a way of turning statements like (1) and (2) into questions by moving the first **auxiliary** verb to the front of the sentence, giving us:

(3) Has Max read the book?
(4) Hat Max das Buch gelesen?
    Has Max the book read?

In French, however, the syntax of questions is different, since French does not allow (5) to be turned into a question like (6):

(5) Max a lu le livre
(6) *A Max lu le livre?

(The asterisk in (6) indicates that this sentence is not possible in French.) Since the meaning of the sentences is the same in each language, these rules of syntax are independent of meaning. (**RS**)

Further Reading

Fabb, N. (1994) *Sentence Structure*, London: Routledge.

SYSTEMIC GRAMMAR Systemic grammar is an approach to language which puts function first: the emphasis is on what people do with language, rather than analysing the structure of language in isolation (for this reason it is also known as Functional Grammar (cf. Halliday 1994)). The driving force is Michael **Halliday**, a British linguist who has worked in Australia for many years. Any single utterance or longer **text** is seen as the result of choices by speakers or writers, and systemic grammarians try to classify these choices in terms of three basic functions of language: the **ideational** function is the use of language to convey information; the **textual** function is the creation of links between different parts of a text; and the **interpersonal** function is the use of language to create and maintain social relations between people.

Systemic grammar is one of the few frameworks which analyses whole texts, identifying the words and structures which makes texts coherent (cf. Halliday and Hasan 1976). It is also distinctive in giving a central place to links between language and social processes. Because of this it has been influential in stylistics, in **sociolinguistics** and in education. (**RS**)

Further Reading

Halliday, M.A.K. (1994) *An Introduction to Functional Grammar*, 2nd edn, London: Arnold.

T

TEL QUEL *Tel Quel* is the name of a Parisian quarterly journal which ran from 1960 to 1980. It is also the name attached to an intellectual quasi-movement associated with the periodical. Neither were really concerned with direct questions of **semiotics** and linguistics but they have become renowned for being the crucible of **poststructuralism**.

Despite the currency from 1968 onwards of **Barthes'** notion of the 'death of the author' (Barthes 1977a), *Tel Quel* thrived on the celebrity status of the names connected with it. The one constant was its editor, the novelist, Philippe Sollers; the others most associated with the journal were Julia **Kristeva** (who joined the editorial committee in 1970) and Jacques **Derrida**.

The journal was committed to translating into French the works of foreign authors (including T. S. Eliot, Virginia Woolf, Gunther Grass, Charles Olson and Philip Roth), publishing fiction by French authors (Alain Robbe-Grillet, Michel Butor, George Bataille, Antonin Artaud *et al.*), and presenting theoretical essays by the great and the good of the Gallic intelligentsia (Roland Barthes, Michel Foucault, Luce Irigaray and René Girard, among others). One of the main themes of the journal echoed what Barthes called, within its pages in 1971, a 'euphoric dream of scientificity' (Coward and Ellis 1977, p. 25), although this was tinged by typical poststructuralist anti-scientism. *Tel Quel*'s invocation of 'science' revolved around the nexus of **Marx**–Freud–**Saussure** (refracted, arguably, through the prism of Althusser–**Lacan**–**Derrida**). The other

major figure in Western thought of the previous hundred and fifty years – and a *bona fide* scientist – Darwin, was conspicuous by his absence.

The slavish devotion to Maoism, including the publication of translations of some of Mao's works, can sometimes obscure *Tel Quel*'s residual pioneering spirit. The journal occasionally published some key works on the **sign** and signification: a long extract from **Eco**'s *The Open Work*, for example, was included in an issue on Joyce. (PC)

Further Reading

ffrench, P. and Lack, R.-F. (eds) (1998) *The Tel Quel Reader*, London: Routledge.

TENOR In the theory of **register**, tenor refers to the set of role relationships among participants in a speech **situation**. In a classroom, for example, the **field** or the social practices which inform the linguistic interaction will be the general ethos or process of education. The tenor will be the power relations between the teacher who might be active in imparting information and the student who might rely on the teacher for this purpose. These role relationships will take place through the **mode**: typical forms of pedagogic communication including lectures, seminars, brainstorming, and so on. (PC)

See HALLIDAY.

TEXT As a result of the increased recognition of the importance of semiotics and linguistics to so many disciplines in the later part of the twentieth century, the term 'text'

275

has become widely used. It is a neutral way of acknowledging that different kinds of semiotic phenomena are connected by virtue of their **sign**-based character. This includes texts such as films, speeches, novels, short stories, advertisements, drama, paintings, virtual reality environments, instruction manuals, opera, historical writing, statuary, conversation, and so on.

In the sphere of **biosemiotics**, the presence of entities classifiable as texts has not always been clear until quite recently. However, such facts as the proliferating knowledge of the properties of the DNA strand have encouraged some to consider biological processes and their results as akin to texts (Pollack 1994).

In the theory of **discourse** (see Coupland and Jaworski, this volume) and **discourse analysis** text continues to have specific **meaning**s. Sometimes text is considered as synonymous with that notion of discourse which simply means many signs joined together; in **Saussure**'s terms, for example, a lengthy instance of *parole*. In these linguistic cases, text is usually conceived as more extensive than a sentence. Sometimes, in a way similar to treatments of discourse, text is conceptualized only as a collection of signs which displays definite **rule**s or structures.

In **Halliday**'s social semiotics text refers to 'actualized meaning potential'. It 'represents choice. A text is "what is meant", selected from the total set of options that constitute what can be meant' (1978, p. 109). In this version, text is a potential for meaning which suffuses collections of signs as a result of the enabling and constraining forces of **situation** and the general culture in which those signs appear. **(PC)**

Further Reading

Beaugrande, R. de and Dressler, W. (1981) *Introduction to Text Linguistics*, Harlow: Longman.

TEXTUAL The textual function deals with the organization of language as message. It refers to text-internal relations, between and across sentences and paragraphs; to the relations of text to its context; and to the overall shape of the text as an effect of its social function. **(GRK)**

See IDEATIONAL, INTERPERSONAL, SYSTEMIC GRAMMAR and HALLIDAY.

THEME For **Vološinov** the theme of an utterance is contrasted to its **meaning**. An utterance such as 'What is the time?' has a general meaning which is applicable to all social situations. It is like the strict dictionary definition which might be thrown up by an investigation of the construction of the question. In this example, the definition or meaning of 'What is the time?' might be 'an inquiry into temporal passage'. The theme, on the other hand, changes from moment to moment and from situation to situation. 'What is the time?' has a different theme for (a) the person with a tyrannical boss who is late for work and asks the question of a passer-by; (b) his/her fellow employees who ask each other the question because they are appalled by the way that time drags in the work-place; and, (c) the profit-obsessed bosses who survey what they consider to be the poor production-rate of their workforce and ask the question in disgust.

Theme is hence the significance of a whole utterance in relation to a specific historical situation. As such, it is traversed by a social **accent**. **(PC)**

See also Verschueren (this volume), DIALOGUE, LOCUTION and ILLOCUTION.

Further Reading

Vološinov, V. N. (1973) *Marxism and the Philosophy of Language*, New York: Seminar Press.

THIRDNESS Thirdness is a category introduced by Charles S. **Peirce**, the other two being **firstness** and **secondness**. Firstness (in-itselfness, originality), secondness (over-againstness, obsistence) and thirdness (in-betweenness, transuasion) are universal categories. Together with the other two categories, thirdness guides and stimulates inquiry and therefore has a heuristic value. The inferential relation between premises and conclusion is based on mediation, that is, on thirdness. And since for Peirce all mental operations are **sign** operations, not only are his categories universal categories of the mind but also of the sign. And, furthermore, given that all of reality, in other words, being itself, is perfused with signs, they are also ontological categories. A sign, says Peirce, exemplifies the category of thirdness; it embodies a triadic relation among itself, its **object** and the **interpretant**. A sign always plays the role of third party, for it mediates between the interpretant and its object.

Any sign may be taken as something *in itself*, or in relation *to something else* (its object), or as a go-between (mediating between its object and interpretant). On the basis of this threefold consideration, Peirce establishes the following correspondences between his trichotomy of the categories which includes thirdness (but all his trichotomies contain thirdness insofar as they are trichotomies) and three other important trichotomies in his semiotic system: *firstness*: **qualisign, icon, rheme**; *secondness*: **sinsign, index**, dicisign (or **dicent** sign); *thirdness*: **legisign, symbol, argument** (cf. *CP* 2.243).

Thirdness regulates continuity which, according to Peirce, subsists in the dialectic relation among symbolicity, indexicality and iconicity. The symbol is never pure but contains varying degrees of indexicality and iconicity; similarly, as much as a sign may be characterized as an index or icon, it will always maintain the characteristics of symbolicity, that is, a sign to subsist as such requires the mediation of an interpretant and recourse to a convention. Symbolicity is the dimension of sign most sharing in thirdness, it is characterized by mediation (or in-betweenness), while iconicity by firstness or immediacy (or in-itselfness), and indexicality by secondness (or over-againstness).

Peirce foresees the possibility of tracing signs in nature, intrinsically, that is, independently from the action of an external agent. From this viewpoint, the universe is perfused with signs antecedently to the action of an interpretive will. Genuine *mediation* – irreducible thirdness – is an inherent part of the reality we encounter in experience, which imposes itself on our attention as sign reality and reveals itself in interpretive processes. Thirdness characterizes the relation (of mediation) among signs throughout the whole universe. From this viewpoint, Peirce identifies a close relation between thirdness and 'synechism', his term for the doctrine of *continuity* (cf. *CP* 7.565, 7.570, 7.571), which while excluding all forms of separateness does not deny the discrete unit, secondness. Therefore, while recognizing the discrete unit, the principle of continuity does not allow for irreducible distinctions between the mental and the physical, between self and other (cf. *CP* 6.268). Such distinctions may be considered as specific units articulated in existential and phenomenological semiosic streams.

Gérard Deledalle (1987) establishes a series of correspondences between the categories of firstness, secondness and thirdness, on the one hand, and transcendentalism, methodological **pragmatism** and metaphysical pragmatism, on the other. (**SP**)

Further Reading

Peirce, C. S. (1955) 'The principles of phenomenology', in *Philosophical Writings of Peirce*, ed. J. Buchler, New York: Dover.

Peirce, C. S. (1958) 'Letter to Lady Welby, 12 October 1904', in *Charles S. Peirce: Selected Writings*, ed. P. Wiener, New York: Dover.

Petrilli, S. (1999) 'About and beyond Peirce', *Semiotica* 124 (3/4), 299–376.

TRACE A term used by the Algerian-born French philosopher, Jacques **Derrida** in his deconstruction of the work of the linguist Ferdinand de **Saussure**. In his *Course in General Linguistics*, Saussure proposed that a basic principle in the study of language was the rule of difference which states that 'concepts are purely differential and defined . . . by their relations with other terms of the system' (Saussure [1916] 1974, p. 117). Thus language can be studied in terms of combination (the **syntagmatic** axis) or choice (the **paradigmatic** axis). On the basis of this, Derrida asserts that the origin of all **meaning**-making lies in the trace, that is, the echoes carried by a **signifier** of all the preceding or subsequent signifiers, and of all the choices that could have been made but were rejected. But Derrida goes further: in discussing Saussure's remark that 'a sound-image . . . is not the material sound . . . , but the pychological imprint of the sound' ([1916] 1974, p. 66), Derrida suggests that the trace is part of the process that transforms the chaos of the material world into the world organised through language, the *'différance* which opens appearance and signification' (1976, p. 65). (**RM**)

Further Reading

Derrida, J. (1976) *Of Grammatology*, trans. G. C. Spivak, Baltimore and London: Johns Hopkins University Press.

TRANSFORMATIONAL GRAMMAR A term sometimes misleadingly used to refer to **Chomsky**'s theory of **grammar**. The term was used in the 1950s and 1960s because transformational **rule**s were one of the major innovations introduced by Chomsky into grammatical theory. The term is unfortunate for several reasons. First, Chomsky and his colleagues have introduced many types of rule into grammatical theory, and it is not helpful to pick out one in particular. Second, even Chomsky's opponents often had no objection to transformations, which are a convenient descriptive device. Third, since the mid-1960s Chomsky and his associates have been concerned to reduce the formal power of transformations (see Salkie, this volume, for discussion). Finally, in recent work specific transformations proposed earlier have all been subsumed under one rule called *Move*.

This leaves the question of what a better label might be for Chomsky's linguistics. Chomsky often describes his enterprise as 'using language to investigate cognitive aspects of human nature', but this is a long mouthful and we may be left with no alternative to the expression 'Chomsky's linguistics'. (**RS**)

TRANSLATION '*Strictu sensu*', translation is the transposition of a **text** from one historical language to another. However, in a semiotic perspective such authors as Victoria **Welby**, Charles S. **Peirce** and Roman **Jakobson** recognize the importance of translation in **semiosis** and in semiotic processes at large. Translation, understood as a process where one sign entity is considered as equivalent to another which it replaces, presupposes:

(1) *translating*; a series of operations whereby one semiotic entity is replaced by another; and
(2) *translatability*, inter-replaceability, interchangeability among semiotic entities.

We must underline that (1) and (2) are prerogatives of *semiosis* and of the **sign**. Translation, therefore, is a phenomenon of sign reality and as such it is the object of study of **semiotics** (cf. Petrilli 1992a, 1998e, 1998f, 1999b, 1999c; Ponzio 1981b, 1997b, pp. 158–63). With Jakobson we may distinguish between three types of translation: *interlingual* translation (between two semiotic entities from two different verbal languages; *intralingual* translation (between two semiotic entities within the same verbal language); and *intersemiosic* translation (between two semiotic entities from two different sign systems, whether one of them is verbal or not). The absence of a fourth type: *intrasemiosic* translation (that is, internal to one and the same nonverbal sign system) is justified by the lack of a metalinguistic capacity in nonverbal sign systems. (**SP**)

See also WHORF.

Further Reading

Merrell, F. (1999–2000) 'Neither matrix nor redux, but reflux: translation from within semiosis', *Athanor* X (2).

TRUBETZKOY Prince Nikolaj Sergeevič Trubetzkoy (1890–1938). Most prominent scholarly works devoted to the defining principles of **phonology** and morphophonology and a theory of **distinctive features** using markedness. His 1939 *Grundzüge der Phonologie* is still considered to be a landmark work in phonological theory. Close colleague of and friend to Roman **Jakobson**. Trubetzkoy and Jakobson were two of the co-founders of the Prague Linguistics Circle (see **Prague School**) and co-authors of the defining propositions of the Prague Circle. (**EA**)

TRUTH A statement or body of knowledge that accords with or conforms to the facts. Although truth is often loosely ascribed to the facts themselves, or what is the case, it really pertains to representations of

a certain kind: **propositions**. Propositions are usually expressed in sentences, which in Charles S. **Peirce**'s semeiotic are **dicent symbol**s, but Peirce allows that a painted portrait with the subject's name written at the bottom is a proposition, in effect representing that so-and-so looks like this. We can also think of an article or even an entire book as 'a proposition' in an extended sense, and thus as 'a truth' if the world is satisfactorily represented. In a way, all propositions represent the world, or some part of it – their object, to be 'like this,' namely, as described in the predicate. So a truth is a proposition that represents its object, however complex and whether real or fictional, in the right way, namely, as it really is. Thus we can say that truths accord with reality. In Peirce's view, a proposition is true if it represents its object in the way inquiry would settle on if carried on long enough. We can say that truths correspond to the facts, but for a Peircean pragmatist such correspondence means only that the set of experiential expectations associated with a truth, if they have grown out of an indefinitely long inquiry into the facts of the matter, will be met. It must be remembered that propositions are **sign**s and that significance always depends on the interrelations of signs with their **object**s and interpreters. There can be no truth that is not of something for someone.

According to Peirce, truth as that which conforms to the facts is not the highest kind of truth; a higher kind is conformed to by the facts. Such truths would be laws of nature. (**NH**)

Further Reading

Saatkamp, H. J. Jr. (ed.) (1995) *Rorty and Pragmatism*, Nashville: Vanderbilt University Press. (See especially the exchange between Susan Haack and Richard Rorty, pp. 126–53.)

U

UEXKÜLL Jakob von Uexküll (1864, Keblaste [now Mihkli], Estonia – 1944, Capri, Italy) was a biologist, and the founder of **biosemiotics**. He studied zoology at the University of Tartu (then Dorpat), Estonia from 1884 to 1889; after that he worked at the Institute of Physiology of the University of Heidelberg in the group led by Wilhelm Kühne (1837–1900), and at the Zoological Station in Naples. In 1907 he was given an honorary doctorate from the University of Heidelberg for his studies in the field of muscular physiology and tonus. One of his results from these years became known as Uexküll's law, which is probably one of the first formulations of the principle of negative feedback occurring inside an organism. His later work was devoted to the problem of how living beings subjectively perceive their environment, how they build the inner model of the world, and how this model is linked to their behaviour. He introduced the term *Umwelt* (1909) to denote the subjective world of an organism. This is the notion according to which Uexküll is most frequently cited in the contemporary literature. Uexküll developed a specific method of the experimental study of behaviour which he termed '*Umwelt*-research'. Between 1927 and 1939, Uexküll was the director of the *Institut für Umweltforschung* (also founded by him) at the University of Hamburg, spending his summers with his family on Puhtu peninsula (western coast of Estonia) in his summer cottage, where he wrote many of his works (Brock 1934a, 1934b: G. v. Uexküll 1964).

Uexküll's field of research was the behaviour of living organisms and their interaction as cells and organs in the body or as subjects within families, groups, and communities (T. v. Uexküll 1987). He is recognised as one of the founders of behavioural physiology and ethology, and a forerunner of biocybernetics.

Of particular interest to Uexküll was the fact that **signs** and **meanings** are of prime importance in all aspects of life processes. His concept of functional cycle (*Funktionskreis*) can be interpreted as a general model of sign processes (**semiosis**).

Uexküll considered himself a follower of the biologists Johannes Müller (1801–1858) and Karl Ernst von Baer (1792–1876). His philosophical views were based on the works of **Kant**.

Uexküll wrote one of the first monographs on theoretical biology (1920, 1928). The fields in which he also made a remarkable contribution include comparative physiology of invertebrates, comparative psychology, philosophy of biology. He is recognised as the founder of the semiotic approach in biology (1940, translation 1982). In **semiotics**, his work became widely known after the publications of **Sebeok** (1979) and J. v. Uexküll's son T. v. Uexküll (1987), followed by republications of earlier works (Uexküll 1980, 1982, 1992). Since 1993, the Uexküll Centre in Tartu, Estonia, has organised work on Uexküll's legacy. (**KK**)

Further Reading

Sebeok, T. A. (1989) *The Sign and its Masters*, Lanham, MD: University Press of America.

Uexküll, G. von (1964) *Jakob von Uexküll,*

seine Welt und seine Umwelt: Eine Biographie, Hamburg: Christian Wegner Verlag.

Uexküll, T. von (1987) 'The sign theory of Jakob von Uexküll', in M. Krampen, *et al.* (eds) *Classics of Semiotics*, New York: Plenum Press, pp. 147–79.

UMWELT *Umwelt* is the subjective world of an organism. The concept has been introduced by Jakob von **Uexküll** (1909) and Uexküll and Kriszat (1934), who also distinguished between simple *Umwelten* which may consist of only a few inter-related **sign**s (e.g., in ticks, and protozoans), and complex *Umwelten* which include space and time. The *Umwelten* with imaginary objects, which exist to the subject alone and are bound to no experiences, or at most are related to one single experience, are called magic *Umwelten* (these include also genetically inherited *Umwelten*).

Umwelt is the conjunction of perceptual world (*Merkwelt*) and operational world (*Wirkwelt*) through the functional cycle (*Funktionskreis*). *Umwelt* as the individual (internal) world is opposed to the environment as the external world which is the same for different organisms. *Umwelt* is a subjective **model** of the world. *Umwelt* is the world as represented in the sign system of an organism.

The description of *Umwelten* is possible through the study and comparison of sense and effector organs of living organisms. In addition to this, comparative behavioural studies and behavioural experiments can shed light on the categorisation of forms in the structure of *Umwelt*, which it may not be possible to describe on the basis of anatomical data.

The notion of *Umwelt* is nowadays also widely used in anthropology and comparative psychology. (**KK**)

See also BIOSEMIOTICS.

Further Reading

Kull, K. (1998) 'On semiosis, *Umwelt*, and semiosphere', *Semiotica* 120 (3/4): 299–310.

UNIVERSAL GRAMMAR Chomsky's term for those parts of our **competence** in a particular language which are innate, transmitted via our genes, apply to all languages, and therefore do not need to be learned by young people acquiring a language. Chomsky argues that it is a reasonable initial assumption that some aspects of language are genetically encoded, and that they are specific to language, i.e., not general aspects of human cognition. He proposes that linguists can formulate specific hypotheses about universal grammar by investigating parts of **grammar**s of individual languages which can be shown to be impossible to learn on the basis of the data available to young people. These hypotheses must be general enough to apply to all languages but specific enough to account for the relative ease with which young people acquire their particular first language.

Universal Grammar is seen by Chomsky as a system of principles (see **principles and parameters**) which limit the range of hypotheses which young people have to try out in the process of acquiring a language.

For Chomsky, it is the possibility of finding out about Universal Grammar that makes linguistics interesting. If his approach is correct, then studying linguistics enables us to discover fundamental things about the human mind. (**RS**)

Further Reading

Salkie, R. (1990) *The Chomsky Update*, London: Unwin Hyman.

UNLIMITED SEMIOSIS Charles S. **Peirce**'s definition of '**sign**' (with its dynamic triadic relationship between sign or **representamen**, **interpretant** and **object**) contains implicitly an ongoing semiosic process that can be defined as infinite or unlimited semiosis. For Peirce:

a sign or representamen is something which stands to somebody for something in some respect or capacity. It addresses somebody, that is, creates in the mind of that person an equivalent sign, or perhaps a more developed sign. That sign which it creates I call the interpretant.

(*CP* 2.228)

It is important to note that the interpretant of the sign becomes in itself a sign or representamen and thus, we initiate a series characterized by an 'interpretant becoming in turn a sign, and so on ad infinitum' (*CP* 2.303).

Peirce has also defined a sign as 'something by knowing which we know something more' (*CP* 8.332) implicating an endless cognitive process that develops as we follow the chain of signs/interpretants. For Peirce every act of cognition is determined by previous ones and cognition, being of the nature of a sign, must be interpreted in a subsequent cognition and so on.

In the 1980s these notions of 'infinite semiosis', combined with those of 'unlimited intertextuality', became quite popular especially with semioticians and narratologists. We recall that **Eco** in *The Name of the Rose* underlines frequently the idea that 'often texts speak of other texts'. Radical deconstructionists go as far as to maintain that there is nothing outside of a text except other words pointing to other texts, and so on. And thus, infinite semiosis, like intertextuality, often accompanies images and metaphors of libraries, labyrinths, encyclopedias, rhizomes, and of the theoretically infinite 'web' of possible links on the Internet, in order to illustrate the potentially unlimited chains of definitions, explanations, quotations, or allusions employed in the process of acquiring and conveying knowledge. (**RC**)

See also <u>Merrell</u> (this volume) DERRIDA, *DIFFÉRANCE* and POSTSTRUCTURALISM.

Further Reading

Eco, U. (1990) 'Unlimited semiosis and drift', in *The Limits of Interpretation*, Bloomington: Indiana University Press.

Merrell, F. (1995) *Peirce's Semiotics Now: A Primer*, Toronto. Canadian Scholars Press.

Peirce, C. S. (1931–1958) *Collected Papers of Charles Sanders Peirce*, vol. 1–8., eds. C. Hawthorne, P. Weiss and A. Burks, Cambridge, MA: Harvard University Press.

VAILATI Giovanni Vailati (1863–1909), mathematician, logician and pragmatist philosopher. A pupil of Giuseppe Peano, Vailati lectured in mathematics and physics at the University of Turin (in 1892 and 1899) and subsequently taught in various state schools. He corresponded with such thinkers as Franz Brentano and Victoria **Welby** whose **significs** he appreciated and developed. He acknowledged the importance of **Peirce**'s **pragmatism** which he introduced in Italy. In his short lifetime he distinguished himself as an innovative thinker in philosophy of language, history of science, and epistemology.

The aim of Vailati's work is to reveal expressive ambiguity and verbal fallacies. In his articles (collected in *Scritti* 1911 and 1987) Vailati calls our attention to linguistic anarchy ensuing from the incorrect use of language, and proposes to search for 'effectual pedagogic contrivances for creating the habit of perceiving the ambiguities of language' (letter to Welby of 12 July 1898 in Vailati 1971, p. 141).

In 'Sull'arte dell'interrogare' (1905) Vailati proposes to replace questions of the 'what is it?' kind – which produce stereotyped sentences and mechanical definitions – with those of the series 'What would you do, if . . .' or 'in order that', which emphasize the connection between concepts or definitions and behaviours, contexts and expectations. For Vailati, as for Welby, the question 'what does it signify for you/us?' is fundamental (see Ponzio 1990d, 1990e).

In 'I tropi della logica' (1905) Vailati shows that metaphors are not only present in ordinary language, in **rhetoric**, and in poetry, but also in logic and in mathematics (in such expressions as 'to be based', 'to descend', etc.). In 'La grammatica dell'algebra' (1908) Vailati compares verbal language to the language of algebra from a semiotic viewpoint. Independently of Peirce, Vailati was conscious of the importance of **abduction** in discovery and in innovation.

In Italy the explicit and programmatic continuation of language studies in the direction indicated by Vailati is the work of **Rossi-Landi**. **(SP)**

Further Reading

Petrilli, S. (1990e) 'The critique of language in Vailati and Welby', in A. Ponzio, *Man as a Sign*, ed. S. Petrilli, Berlin: Mouton de Gruyter, pp. 339–47.

VALUE English translation of the Saussurean technical term *valeur*, to which an entire chapter is devoted in the *Cours de linguistique générale*. **Saussure** distinguishes between the value of a sign and all its other properties. The value of a **sign** is determined by the network of contrasts it enters into with all other signs in the system. In the case of linguistic signs, *la langue* is itself 'a system of pure values', i.e. confers a value on every constituent sign within it. This notion plays a key role in the whole theory of Saussurean **structuralism**, and sets it apart from the cruder versions of structuralism which became current in American linguistics during the inter-war and post-war periods. The value of a term is *not* its '**meaning**', although this equation, which Saussure explicitly rejects, is nowadays commonplace. (**RH**)

VERB Words like *consider, construct* and *prevent* are called verbs. Only verbs take *-s* in the third person singular (*she considers . . .*), *-d* to form the past tense (*We constructed . . .*) and *-ing* to make the present participle (*preventing*). Verbs can be modified by adverbs: we say *They considered carefully . . .* Verbs typically express actions or states. (**RS**)

VERB PHRASE A group of words containing a **verb** and which behaves like a verb. An example is the words after *Maxine* in the sentence *Maxine has often organised charity events*. The verb that is the 'head' of the verb phrase is *organised*: the other words indicate the time of the verb (*has*), tell us how many times the action took place (*often*), and tell us what the action of organising was applied to (*charity events*). (**RS**)

VOLOŠINOV Valentin Nikolaevich Vološinov (1895–1936) graduated in law from St Petersburg. He was a poet and musical critic, with interests in philosophy of language, literary criticism and psychology. He was a friend and collaborator of Mikhail M. **Bakhtin** and a member of his 'Circle' during the 1920s. His two books, *Freudianism: A Critical Sketch* (1927) and *Marxism and the Philosophy of Language* (1929), and his essays published between 1925 and 1930, the most important of which is 'Discourse in life and discourse in art' (1926), were probably written with Bakhtin's collaboration.

Vološinov's texts share Bakhtin's recognition of the **alterity** relation as the fundamental character of the word. The problem of the relation between one's own word and the word of the other is a constant and unitary focus in all the former's writings. Part III of *Marxism and the Philosophy of Language* analyses this relation in its various forms as it is manifested in different **discourse genre**s and in different **natural language**s. But this problematic is also dealt with in his critique of 'Freudian philosophy' just as it is present in his conception of expression as the manifestation of autonomous interiority, independently from the interlocutor as well as from receiver-oriented intentionality. (**AP**)

Further Reading

Vološinov, V. N. (1987) *Freudianism: A Critical Sketch*, trans. I. R. Titunik, Bloomington: Indiana University Press. (This edition also contains 'Discourse in life and discourse in art' as an appendix.)

VOWEL A speech sound in which the breath is not significantly obstructed. The term is also used for letters which represent vowel sounds, but unfortunately alphabets are not always consistent: the word *happy* has a vowel sound at the end, but the letter *y* is also used in other words like *yellow* to represent an initial **consonant** sound. (**RS**)

WELBY Victoria Lady Welby (1837–1912), independent scholar, philosopher, originator of **significs**, and founding mother of 'semiotics', was born into the highest circles of English nobility. She was not educated in any conventional sense and in her early years travelled widely with her mother (cf. Hardwick 1977, pp. 13–14), publishing her travel diary in 1852. After her marriage to Sir William Earle Welby in 1863, she began her research fully aware of her exceptional status as an open-minded female intellectual of the Victorian era.

She introduced the neologism 'significs' for her theory of **meaning** which examines the relation among **sign**s, sense in all its signifying implications, and values as well as their practical consequences for human behaviour. Initially her interest was directed towards theological questions which lead to her awareness of the problems of language, meaning and interpretation. In 1881 she published *Links and Clues*, considered unorthodox by official opinion in religious circles. In it she reflects on the inadequacies of religious discourse which, she believed, was cast in outmoded linguistic forms. In her examination of language and meaning she found a pervasive linguistic confusion which largely stemmed from a misconception of language as a system of fixed meanings, and which could be resolved only by the recognition that language must grow and change as does human experience generally. She proposed a critique of figurative language and insisted on the need to adequately develop a critical linguistic consciousness (cf. Welby 1891, 1892, 1893, 1897, 1898). She made a serious study of the sciences with special reference to biology and evolutionary theory which she read critically, with the conviction that important scientific discoveries supplied the new experiences in the light of which all **discourse**, including the religious, could be updated and transformed into something more significant. Her main publications on these topics include *What is Meaning?* ([1903] 1983), her most sophisticated theoretical work, *Significs and Language* ([1911] 1985a), which is more of an appeal for significs, and her articles 'Meaning and Metaphor' (1893) and 'Sense, Meaning and Interpretation' (1896), both included in the volume of 1985, *Significs and Language*, with a selection from her other previously unpublished writings.

Besides numerous articles in newspapers, magazines and scientific journals, Welby published a long list of privately printed essays, parables, aphorisms, and pamphlets on a large range of subjects addressed to diverse audiences: science, mathematics, anthropology, philosophy, education, and social issues. She promoted the study of significs, announcing the Welby Prize for the best essay on significs in the journal *Mind* (1896), awarded to Ferdinand Tönnies (1899–1900) in 1898 (cf. Welby and Tönnies 1901). Important moments of official recognition for Welby's research are represented by publication of the entry 'Significs', co-authored with J. Baldwin and F. Stout (1902) for Baldwin's *Dictionary of Philosophy and Psychology* (1901–5), followed by the entry 'Significs' in the *Encyclopaedia Britannica*, in 1911 (cf. Welby 1977).

She wrote regularly to over 450 correspondents, developing a vast epistolary network through which she developed her ideas and exerted her influence, though mostly unrecognized – as in the case of C. K. **Ogden** – over numerous intellectuals of her times. Charles S. **Peirce** reviewed *What is Meaning?* for *The Nation* in 1903 alongside Russell's *Principles of Mathematics* (cf. Peirce 1977). The correspondence thus begun lasted until 1911, influencing the focus of his research during the last decade of his life; indeed, some of his best semiotic expositions are in letters to Welby (cf. Fisch 1986a; Hardwick 1977). Part of her correspondence was edited and published by her daughter Mrs Henry (Nina) Cust (cf. Welby 1929 and 1931), including letters exchanged with B. Russell, C. K. Ogden, J. M. Baldwin, H. Spencer, T. A. Huxley, M. Müller, B. Jowett, F. Pollock, G. F. Stout, H. G. Wells, M. E. Boole, H. and W. James, H. L. Bergson, M. **Bréal**, A. Lalande, J.-H. Poincaré, F. Tönnies, R. Carnap, O. Neurath, H. Höffding, F. van Eeden, G. **Vailati** and many others.

The Signific Movement in the Netherlands originated from Welby's research through the mediation of Frederik van Eeden (1860–1932) (cf. Schmitz 1990b; Heijerman and Schmitz 1991). The results of her research, including her many unpublished writings, are to be found in the Welby Collection in the Archives of Toronto's York University and the Lady Welby Library in the University of London Library (cf. Schmitz 1985; Petrilli 1998a). (**SP**)

Further Reading

Hardwick, C. (1977) *Semiotic and Significs: The Correspondence Between Charles S. Peirce and Victoria Lady Welby*, Bloomington and London: Indiana University Press.
Welby, V. (1983) *What is Meaning?*, ed. A.

Eschbach, introduced by G. Mannoury, Amsterdam and Philadelphia: John Benjamins (originally 1903).
Welby, V. (1985) *Significs and Language. (The Articulate Form of Our Expressive and Interpretative Resources)*, with additional essays, ed. and introduced H. W. Schmitz, Amsterdam and Philadelphia: John Benjamins.

WHORF Benjamin Lee Whorf (1897–1941) was an American linguist and anthropologist. After training as a chemical engineer, Whorf worked for many years in the insurance business. His interest in language led him to study linguistics under Edward **Sapir**, and his publications were widely read. His main writings were republished posthumously as *Language, Thought and Reality* (1956).

Whorf is best known for his view that the language you speak influences the way you think, a view known as the linguistic relativity hypothesis or the 'Whorf hypothesis'. Since Sapir sometimes expressed similar views, it is sometimes called the '**Sapir–Whorf hypothesis**'. Whorf was struck by the enormous differences between native American languages like Hopi and European languages. He published several papers claiming that the world view encoded in each language determines the way its speakers perceive and understand the world.

This 'strong' form of the Whorf hypothesis does not seem justifiable. If it were correct, **translation** between languages would be impossible much of the time. Translation is certainly difficult on occasion, but it is clearly possible most of the time. This leaves a weaker form of the hypothesis, which asserts that the influence of language on thought is less pervasive.

It is probably true to say that Whorf's reputation is higher today outside linguistics than within it. For a more positive assessment, see Gumperz and Levinson (1996). (**RS**)

Further Reading

Gumperz, J. and S. Levinson (eds) (1996) *Rethinking Linguistic Relativity*, Cambridge, Cambridge University Press.

WILLIAM OF OCKHAM Along with Scotus before and **Poinsot** after, though not with equal merit, Ockham (*c*.1285–1349) is a defining figure of the later Latin Age (Deely 1994b). He was notable for applying the designation 'natural **sign**' to concepts (Ockham 1323; McCord Adams 1978). Followers, beginning with Pierre d'Ailly (a.1396), inspired by this actually baffling designation (Gilson 1955, p. 491), further distinguished concepts as 'formal signs' from objects as 'instrumental signs' (Meier-Oeser 1997, pp. 114, 119). This new terminology marked a turning point (Deely 2000, Ch. 8) in the identification of signs as consisting essentially in or 'being' relations in precisely the sense Ockham notoriously denied, namely, suprasubjective in nature independently of human thought ('ontological relation', as it came to be known after Boethius, Aquinas, and Poinsot). Ockham himself affirmed 'but one mode of being, the being of an individual thing or fact, the being which consists in the object's crowding out a place for itself in the universe, so to speak' (Peirce 1903: *CP* 1.17) – in a word, subjectivity. This doctrine, called '**Nominalism**', was viewed by **Peirce** (e.g. *c*.1902; *CP* 2.167 ff.) as incompatible alike with science and the doctrine of signs. Modern in what he anticipated, Ockham stands antiquated among the Latins by the postmodern anticipations of Scotus and Poinsot. (**JD**)

Further Reading

Maurer, A. (1999) *The Philosophy of William of Ockham in the Light of Its Principles*. Toronto: Pontifical Institute of Mediaeval Studies.

WITTGENSTEIN Ludwig Josef Johann Wittgenstein (1889–1951) was born into a wealthy, talented Austrian family. He spent most of his working life in Engand, teaching philosophy at Cambridge. The *Tractatus Logico-Philosophicus* (1922) is the only extended work published during his lifetime. His *Philosophical Investigations* appeared posthumously in 1953. Wittgenstein exerted an enormous influence on Anglo-American philosophy and is a living force in international studies on verbal language and **sign**s.

Wittgenstein began his work on language–thought production processes and on semiotic–cognitive procedures in his *Tractatus*. However, this aspect of his research is subsequently left aside in his *Philosophical Investigations* where attention is focused on **meaning** *as use* and on linguistic conventions (linguistic games). The importance attributed to the 'turn' operated by the *Philosophical Investigations*, especially by the analytical philosophers must not lead one to lose sight of the importance of the *Tractatus*, particularly as regards the **icon**ic aspect of language (cf. Ponzio, 'Segno e raffigurazione in Wittgenstein', in Ponzio 1997b, pp. 309–13). In fact, in the *Tractatus*, Wittgenstein distinguishes between names and **proposition**s: the relation between names or 'simple signs' used in the proposition and their objects or meanings, is of the conventional type. The relation between whole propositions or 'propositional signs' and what they signify, is a relation of similarity. The proposition is a logical picture (cf. *CP* 4.022 and 4.026). As much as propositions are also conventional-symbolic, they are fundamentally based on the relation of representation, that is, the iconic relation; and, similarly to **Peirce**'s 'existential graphs', this relation is of the proportional or structural type. (**AP**)

Further Reading

Wittgenstein, L. (1953) *Philosophical Investigations*, Oxford: Blackwell.

ZOOSEMIOTICS See **BIOSEMIOTICS**.

REFERENCES

d'Ailly, P. (a.1396 [1980]) *Destructiones Modorum Significandi (secundum viam nomi-nalium), nach Inkunabelausgaben in einer vorlaufigen Fassung neu zusammengestellt und mit Anmerkungen versehen von Ludger Kaczmarek*, Munster: Munsteraner Arbeitskreis für Semiotik.

Aitchison, J. (2001) *Language Change: Progress or Decay?*, 3rd edn, Cambridge: Cambridge University Press.

Aitchison, J. (1995) 'Language contact and models of change', in J. Fisiak (ed.) *Linguistic Change Under Contact Conditions*, Berlin and New York: Mouton de Gruyter.

Aitchison, J. (1996) *The Seeds of Speech: Language Origin and Evolution*, Cambridge: Cambridge University Press.

Alford, H. (1864) *A Plea for the Queen's English,* 2nd edn, London: Strahan.

Almeder, R. (1980) *The Philosophy of Charles S. Peirce: A Critical Introduction,* Totowa, NJ: Rowman and Littlefield.

Anderson, M. and Merrell, F. (eds) (1991) *On Semiotic Modeling*, Berlin and New York: Mouton de Gruyter.

Aquinas, T. ([*c*.1266–1273] 1982) 'Summa theologiae', in R. Busa (ed.) *S. Thomae Aquinatis Opera Omnia ut sunt in indice thomistico*, Stuttgart-Bad Cannstatt: Frommann-Holzboog, vol. 2, pp. 184–926.

Araújo, F. de (1617) *Commentariorum in universam Aristotelis Metaphysicam tomus primus*, Burgos and Salamanca: J. B. Varesius.

Armstrong, D. (1999) *Original Signs: Gesture, Signs, and the Sources of Language,* Washington, DC: Gallaudet University Press.

Armstrong D., Stokoe, W. and Wilcox, S. (1995) *Gesture and the Nature of Language*, Cambridge: Cambridge University Press.

Armstrong, D. M. (1978) *Universals and Scientific Realism*, 2 vols, Cambridge: Cambridge University Press.

Ashby, W. (1981) 'The loss of the negative particle *ne* in French: a syntactic change in progress', *Language* 57: 674–87.

Asher, R. E. (ed.) (1994) *The Encyclopedia of Language and Linguistics*, Oxford: Pergamon.

Atkinson, M. and Heritage, J. (eds) (1984) *Structures of Social Action: Studies in Conversation Analysis*, Cambridge: Cambridge University Press.

Atkinson, P. (1985) *Language, Structuralism and Reproduction: An Introduction to the Sociology of Basil Bernstein*, London: Methuen.

Auer, P. and Di Luzio, A. (eds) (1992) *The Contextualization of Language*, Amsterdam and Philadelphia: John Benjamins.

Austin, J. L. (1957) 'A plea for excuses', *Proceedings of the Aristotelian Society* LVII (new series), pp. 1–30.

Austin, J. L. (1962) *How to Do Things with Words*, ed. J. O. Urmson. Oxford: Oxford

University Press. (2nd rev. edn, 1975, eds. J. O Urmson and M. Sbisà, Cambridge, MA: Harvard University Press.)

Averincev, S.S. (1971) 'Simbolo' ('Sinvol', in *Kratkaja literaturnaja enciclopedija*, vol. VII, Moscow 1971), It. trans in A. Ponzio and P. Jachia (eds) *Bachtin e . . .* , Bari and Rome: Laterza, 1993.

Ayer, A. J. (1946) *Language, Truth and Logic,* rev. edn, New York: Oxford University Press.

Bach, E. and Harms, R. T. (eds) (1968) *Universals in Linguistic Theory*, New York: Holt, Rinehart and Winston.

Bakhtin, M. M. (1929) *Problemi dell'opera di Dostoevskij*, It. trans. M. De Michiel, intro. A. Ponzio, Bari: Edizioni dal Sud, 1997.

Bakhtin, M. M. (1963) *Problems of Dostoevsky's Poetics*, trans. C. Emerson Minneapolis: University of Minnesota Press, 1984.

Bakhtin, M. M. (1965) *Rabelais and His World*, trans. H. Iswolsky, Bloomington: Indiana University Press, 1984.

Bakhtin, M. M. (1974) 'Toward a methodology for the human sciences', in M. Bakhtin, *Speech Genres and Other Late Essays*, Austin, TX: University of Texas Press, 1986, pp. 159–72.

Bakhtin, M. M. (1975) *Estetica e romanzo. Un contributo fondamentale alla scienza della letteratura*, ed. C. Strada Janovic, Turin: Einaudi, 1979.

Bakhtin, M. M. (1979) *L'autore e l'eroe. Teoria letteraria e scienze umane*, ed. C. Strada Janovic, Turin: Einaudi, 1988.

Bakhtin, M. M. (1981) *The Dialogic Imagination: Four Essays*, ed. M. Holquist, trans. C. Emerson and M. Holquist, Austin, TX: University of Texas Press.

Bakhtin, M. M. (1986) *Speech Genres and Other Late Essays*, trans. V. McGee, ed. C. Emerson and M. Holquist, Austin, TX: University of Texas Press.

Bakhtin, M. M. (1990) *Art and Answerability. Early Philosophical Essays*, ed. M. Holquist and V. Liapunov, trans. and notes V. Liapunov, suppl. trans. K. Brostrom, Austin, TX: University of Texas Press.

Bakhtin, M. M. (1998) *La scrittura e l'umano. Saggi, dialoghi, conversazioni*, M. De Michiel and A. Ponzio eds, Bari: Edizioni dal Sud.

Bakhtin, M. M. and Medvedev, P. N. (1928) *The Formal Method in Literary Scholarhip*, trans. A. J. Werle, Cambridge, MA: Harvard University Press, 1985.

Barlow, J. P. (1996) 'A Cyberspace Independence Declaration'. URL is http://www.eff. org/Publications/John_Perry_Barlow/barlow_0296.declaration

Barnet, V. (1972) 'Learning the spoken language', in V. Fried (ed.) *The Prague School of Linguistics and Language Teaching*, Oxford: Oxford University Press, pp. 29–42.

Barnett, D. (1987) *The Art of Gesture: The Practices and Principles of 18th Century Acting,* Heidelberg: Carl Winter.

Barthes, R. ([1947] 1953) *Le Degré zero de l'écriture*, Paris: Seuil.

Barthes, R. (1963) *Sur Racine*, Paris: Seuil.

Barthes, R. (1964a) 'La rhétorique de l'image', *Communications*, Paris. Published in English as 'The rhetoric of the Image', in *Image-Music-Text*, ed. and trans. S. Heath, London: Fontana, 1977.

Barthes, R. (1964b) *Éléments de sémiologie*, Paris: Seuil.

Barthes, R. (1964c) *Essais critiques*, Paris: Seuil.

Barthes, R. (1966a) *Critique et Vérité*, Paris: Seuil.

Barthes, R. (1966b) 'L'introduction à l'analyse structurale des récits', *Communications* 8, pp. 1–27.

Barthes, R. (1967a) *Elements of Semiology,* trans. R. Howard, London: Cape.

Barthes, R. (1967b) *Système de la mode*, Paris: Seuil.

Barthes, R. (1970a) *S/Z*, Paris: Seuil.

Barthes, R. (1970b) *L'Empire de Signes*, Geneva: Skira.

Barthes, R. (1971) *Sade, Fourier, Loyola*, Paris: Seuil.

Barthes, R. (1973a) 'Myth today', in *Mythologies*, trans. A. Lavers, London: Paladin.

Barthes, R. (1973b) *Le Plaisir du texte*, Paris: Seuil.

Barthes, R. ([1957] 1973c) *Mythologies*, trans. A. Lavers, London: Paladin.

Barthes, R. (1975) *Roland Barthes*, Paris: Seuil.

Barthes, R. (1977a) 'The death of the author', in *Image-Music-Text*, trans. and ed. S. Heath, London: Collins.

Barthes, R. (1977b) *Image-Music-Text*, trans. S. Heath, London: Collins.

Barthes, R. (1977c) *Fragments d'un discours amoureaux*, Paris: Seuil.

Barthes, R. (1977d) *Leçon*, Paris: Seuil.

Barthes, R. (1980) *La Chambre claire*, Paris: Seuil.

Barthes, R. (1982) *L'Obvie et l'obtus. Essais critiques III*, Paris: Editions du Seuil.

Barthes, R. (1993–1995) *Œuvres complètes*, ed. E. Marty, Paris: Seuil.

Barthes, R. (1998) *Scritti. Società, testo, comunicazione,* ed. G. Marrone, Turin: Einaudi.

Battison, R. (1978) *Lexical Borrowing in American Sign Language*, Burtonsville, MD: Linstok Press.

Baudrillard, J. (1975) *The Mirror of Production*, trans. M. Poster, St. Louis: Telos.

Baudrillard, J. (1981) *For a Critique of the Political Economy of the Sign*, trans. C. Levin, St. Louis: Telos.

Baudrillard, J. (1983a) *Simulations,* New York: Semiotext(e).

Baudrillard, J. (1983b) *In the Shadow of the Silent Majorities*, trans. P. Foss, J. Johnston, and P. Patton, New York: Semiotext(e).

Baudrillard, J. (1988) *The Ecstasy of Communication*, trans. B. Schutze and C. Schutze, New York: Semiotext(e).

Baudrillard, J. (1995) *Simulacra and Simulation*, trans. S. F. Glaser, Ann Arbor, MI: University of Michigan Press.

Beaken, M. (1996) *The Making of Language*, Edinburgh: Edinburgh University Press.

Beaugrande, R. de (1994) 'Text linguistics', in R. E. Asher, *The Encyclopedia of Language and Linguistics*, Oxford: Pergamon, pp. 4573–8.

Bell, A. (1991) *The Language of News Media*, Oxford: Blackwell.

Benveniste, E. (1971) *Problems in General Linguistics,* trans. M. E. Meek, Coral Gables: University of Miami Press.

Bernstein, B. (1962) 'Linguistic codes, hesitation phenomena and intelligence', *Language and Speech* 5: 221–40. Reprinted in B. Bernstein, (1971) *Class, Codes and Control Vol 1: Theoretical Studies Towards a Sociology of Language*, London: Routledge and Kegan Paul.

Bernstein, B. (1971) 'Introduction', in *Class, Codes and Control Vol 1: Theoretical Studies Towards a Sociology of Language*, London: Routledge and Kegan Paul.

Bickerton, D. (1981) *Roots of Language,* Ann Arbor, MI: Karoma.

Bickerton, D. (1995) *Language and Human Behavior*, Seattle: University of Washington Press.

Billig, M. (1990) 'Stacking the cards of ideology: the history of the Sun Royal Album', *Discourse and Society* 1 (1): 17–37.

Billig, M. (1991) *Ideologies and Beliefs*, London: Sage.

Billig, M. *et al.* (1988) *Ideological Dilemmas*, London: Sage.

Bloch, B. (1948) 'A set of postulates for phonemic analysis', *Language* 24 (1): 3–46.

Blommaert, J. and Verschueren, J. (1998) *Debating Diversity: Analysing the Discourse of Tolerance*, London: Routledge.

Bloomfield, L. (1935) *Language*, London: Allen and Unwin.

Boas, F. ([1911] 1963) *The Mind of Primitive Man,* rev. edn, New York: Collier.

Boden, D. and Zimmerman, D. H. (eds) (1991) *Talk and Social Structure: Studies in Ethnomethodology and Conversation Analysis*, Oxford: Polity Press.

Bonfantini, M. A. (1987) *La semiosi e l'abduzione*, Milan: Bompiani.

Bonfantini, M. A. and Ponzio, A. (1986) *Dialogo sui dialoghi,* Ravenna: Longo.

Bonfantini, M. A. *et al.* (1996) *I tre dialoghi della menzogna e della verità*, Naples: Edizioni Scientifiche Italiane.

Bouissac, P. *et al.* (eds) (1986) *Iconicity: Essays on the Nature of Culture.* Festchrift for Thomas A. Sebeok on his 65th birthday, Tübingen: Stauffenburg.

Bourdieu, P. (1991) *Language and Symbolic Power*, Cambridge: Polity Press.

Bourdieu, P. (1999) 'Language and symbolic power', in A. Jaworski and N. Coupland (eds) *The Discourse Reader*, London: Routledge, pp. 502–13. [Originally published as part of Bourdieu 1991.]

Braine, M. D. W. (1963) 'Grammatical structure in the speech of two-year-olds', *Proceedings of the Washington Linguistics Club* 1.1 (Fall): 7–16.

Brantlinger, P. (1990) *Crusoe's Footprints: Cultural Studies in Britain and America*, London: Routledge.

Bréal, M. (1897) *Essais de sémantique: science des significations*, Paris: Hachette.

Bremmer, J. and Roodenberg, H. (eds) (1992) *A Cultural History of Gesture*, Ithaca: Cornell University Press.

Brent, J. (1998) *Charles Sanders Peirce: A Life*, 2nd edn, Bloomington: Indiana University Press.

Briggs, C. L. and Bauman, R. (1992) 'Genre, intertextuality, and social power', *Journal of Linguistic Anthropology* 2: 131–72.

British Council (1995) *English in the World: The English 2000 Global Consultation.* Manchester: British Council.

Brock, F. (1934a) 'Jakob Johann Baron von Uexküll: Zu seinem 70. Geburtstage am 8. September 1934', *Sudhoffs Archiv für Geschichte der Medizin und der Naturwissenschaften* 27: 193–203.

Brock, F. (1934b) 'Verzeichnis der Schriften Jakob Johann von Uexexternal und der aus dem Institut für Umweltforschung zu Hamburg hervorgegangenen Arbeiten', *Sudhoffs Archiv für Geschichte der Medizin und der Naturwissenschaften* 27: 204–12.

Brøndal, V. (1932) *Morfologi og Syntax*, Copenhagen: Bianco Luno.

Brøndal, V. (1943) *Essais de linguistique générale*, Copenhagen: Munksgaard.

Brøndal, V. ([1928] 1948) *Les parties du discours,* Copenhagen: Munksgaard.

Brøndal, V. ([1940] 1950) *Théorie des prépositions*, Copenhagen: Munksgaard.

Brown, P. and Levinson, S.C. (1987) *Politeness: Some Universals in Language Usage*, Cambridge: Cambridge University Press.

Bühler, K. (1990) *Theory of Language: The Representational Function of Language,* trans. D. Fraser Goodwin, Amsterdam and Philadelphia: John Benjamins.

Bull, T. (1996) 'Spørsmål og svar i språk-og-kjønn-forskinga', in T. Bull *et al.*, *Sprog og Køn – Oplæg fra et seminar på RUC 30.5.1994* (Skrifter fra Dansk og Public Relations), Roskilde: University of Roskilde.

Bullowa, M. (1977) 'From performative act to performative utterance: an ethogical perspective', *Sign Language Studies* 16: 193–218.

Cairns-Smith, A. G. (1996) *Evolving the Mind*, Cambridge: Cambridge University Press.

Cameron, D. (1995) *Verbal Hygiene*, London: Routledge.

Cameron, D. (1999) 'Performing gender identity: young men's talk and the construction of heterosexual identity', in A. Jaworski and N. Coupland (eds) *The Discourse Reader*, London: Routledge, pp. 442–58.

Cameron, D. *et al.* (1999) 'Power/knowledge: the politics of social science', in A. Jaworski and N. Coupland (eds) *The Discourse Reader*, London: Routledge, pp. 141–57.

Candlin, C. N. (1997) 'General editor's preface', in B-L. Gunnarsson, P. Linell and B. Nordberg (eds) *The Construction of Professional Discourse*, London: Longman, pp. xii–xiv.

Caplan, D. (1992) 'Neural structures', in W. Bright (ed.) *International Encyclopedia of Linguistics*, vol. 3, Oxford: Oxford University Press, pp. 79–84.

Caramazza, A. and Miozzo, M. (1997) 'The relation between syntactic and phonological knowledge in lexical access: evidence from the "tip-of-the-tongue" phenomenon', *Cognition* 64: 309–43.

Carroll, J. B. (ed.) (1956) *Language, Thought, and Reality: Selected Writings of Benjamin Lee Whorf*, Cambridge, MA: MIT Press.

Chambers, I. (1986) *Popular Culture: The Metropolitan Experience*, London: Methuen.

Cheney, D. and Seyfarth, R. (1990) *How Monkeys See the World*, Chicago: University of Chicago Press.

Cheshire, J. (1982) *Variation in an English Dialect*. Cambridge: Cambridge University Press.

Chierchia, G. and McConnell-Ginet, S. (1990) *Meaning and Grammar: An Introduction to Semantics*, Cambridge, MA: MIT Press.

Chomsky, N. (1957) *Syntactic Structures*, The Hague: Mouton.

Chomsky, N. (1959) 'Review of Skinner 1957', *Language* 35: 26–58.

Chomsky, N. (1964a) *Current Issues in Linguistic Theory*, The Hague: Mouton. Also in J. Fodor and J. J. Katz (eds) *The Structure of Language: Readings in the Philosophy of Language*, Englewood Cliffs, NJ: Prentice-Hall, pp. 50–118.

Chomsky, N. (1964b) 'Review of B. F. Skinner, "Verbal Behaviour"', in J. Fodor and J. J. Katz (eds) *The Structure of Language: Readings in the Philosophy of Language*, Englewood Cliffs, NJ: Prentice-Hall, pp. 547–78.

Chomsky, N. (1965) *Aspects of the Theory of Syntax*, Cambridge, MA: MIT Press.

Chomsky, N. (1972) *Language and Mind*, New York: Harcourt, Brace and World.

Chomsky, N. (1980) *Rules and Representations*, Oxford: Basil Blackwell.

Chomsky, N. (1981) *Lectures on Government and Binding*, Amsterdam: Foris.

Chomsky, N. (1988) *Language and Problems of Knowledge*, Cambridge, MA: MIT Press.

Chomsky, N. (1995) *The Minimalist Program*, Cambridge, MA: MIT Press.

Chomsky, N. (1996) *Powers and Prospects*, London: Pluto Press.

Chomsky, N. and Miller, G. A. (1963) 'Introduction to the formal analysis of natural languages', in *Handbook of Mathematical Psychology*, vol. II, ed. R. D. Luce *et al.*, New York: Wiley, pp. 269–322.

Chouliaraki, L. and Fairclough, N. (1999) *Discourse in Late Modernity: Rethinking Critical Discourse Analysis*, Edinburgh: Edinburgh University Press.

Clahsen, H. and Almazan, M. (1998) 'Syntax and morphology in Williams syndrome', *Cognition* 68: 167–98.

Clark, H. H. (1996) *Using Language*, Oxford: Oxford University Press.

Clark, K. and Holquist, M. (1984) *Mikhail Bakhtin*, Cambridge, MA: Belknap Press.

Coates, J. (1989) 'Gossip revisited: language in all-female groups', in J. Coates and D. Cameron (eds) *Women in their Speech Communities*, London: Longman, pp. 94–121.

Coates, J. (1996) *Women Talk: Conversations between Women Friends*, Oxford: Blackwell.

Colapietro, V. (1989) *Peirce's Approach to the Self*, Albany, NY: State University of New York Press.

Collins English Dictionary (1994) Third updated edition, Glasgow: HarperCollins.

Cook, G. (1992) The discourse of advertising, London: Routledge.

Corballis, M. C. (1999) 'The gestural origins of language', *American Scientist* 87 (2): 8–16.

Cottingham, J. (1988) *The Rationalists* (A History of Western Philosophy, vol. 4), Oxford: Oxford University Press.

Coulmas, F. (ed.) (1997) *The Handbook of Sociolinguistics*, Oxford: Blackwell.

Coupland, J. (ed.) (2000) *Small Talk*, London: Longman.

Coupland, J. and Coupland, N. (2000) 'Selling control: ideological dilemmas of sun, tanning, risk and leisure', in S. Allan *et al.* (eds) *Communication, Risk and the Environment*, London: UCL Press.

Coupland, J. *et al.* (1991) 'Intergenerational discourse: contextual versions of ageing and elderliness', *Ageing and Society* 11: 189–208.

Coupland, N. (2000) 'Other representation', in J. Verschueren (ed.) *Handbook of Pragmatics*, Amsterdam and Philadephia: John Benjamins.

Coupland, N. and Nussbaum, J. F. (eds) (1993) *Discourse and Lifespan Identity*, Newbury Park, CA: Sage.

Coward, R. and Ellis, J. (1977) *Language and Materialism: Developments in Semiology and the Theory of the Subject,* London: Routledge and Kegan Paul.

Crick, F. (1994) *The Astonishing Hypothesis: The Scientific Search for the Soul*, New York: Charles Scribners and Sons.

Crisell, A. (1986) *Understanding Radio*, London: Methuen.

Croft, W. (1994) 'Universals, Linguistic', in R. E. Asher, *The Encyclopedia of Language and Linguistics* Oxford, Pergamon, pp. 4850–2.

Crystal, D. (1985) *Linguistics*, 2nd edn, Harmondsworth: Penguin.

Culicover, P. (1997) *Principles and Parameters*, Oxford: Oxford University Press.

Curtiss, S. (1977) *Genie: A Linguistic Study of a Modern-day 'Wild Child',* New York: Academic Press.

Darwin, C. (1872) *The Expression of the Emotions in Man and Animals*, London: John Murray.

Darwin, C. ([1872] 1998) *The Expression of the Emotions in Man and Animals*, Intro., Afterword and Commentaries P. Ekman, New York: Oxford University Press.

Deacon, D., Fenton N. and Bryman, A. (1999) 'From inception to reception: the natural history of a news item', *Media, Culture and Society* 21.

Deacon, T. (1996) *The Symbolic Species*, New York: Norton.

Deely, J. (1985) 'Editorial afterword', to J. Poinsot (1632) *Tractatus de Signis: The Semiotic of John Poinsot*. Berkeley, CA: University of California Press, pp. 395–514.

Deely, J. (1994a) *New Beginnings: Early Modern Philosophy and Postmodern Thought*, Toronto: University of Toronto Press.

Deely, J. (1994b) 'What happened to philosophy between Aquinas and Descartes?', *The Thomist* 58 (4): 543–68.

Deely, J. (1994c) *The Human Use of Signs, or Elements of Anthroposemiosis*, Lanham, MD: Rowman and Littlefield.

Deely, J. (2001) *Four Ages of Understanding: The First Postmodern Survey of Philosophy from Ancient Times to the Turn of the Twenty-first Century*, Toronto: University of Toronto Press.

Deely J. and Petrilli, S. (eds) (1993) *Semiotics in the United States and Beyond: Problems, People, and Perspectives*, Semiotica 97 (3/4).

de George, R. and de George, F. (eds) (1972) *The Structuralists: From Marx to Lévi-Strauss*, New York: Doubleday and Co.

de Josseling de Jong, J.P.B. (ed.) (1952) *Lévi-Strauss's Theory on Kinship and Marriage*, *Mededelingen van het Rijksmusem voor Volkenkunde* 10, Leiden: Brill.

Deledalle, G. (1987) *Charles S. Peirce: Phénomenologue et sémioticien*, Amsterdam: John Benjamins; trans. *Charles S. Peirce: An Intellectual Biography*, trans. and intro. S. Petrilli, Amsterdam: John Benjamins, 1990.

Deltcheva, R. and Vlasov, E. (1996) 'Lotman's *Culture and Explosion*: a shift in the paradigm of the semiotics of culture', *Slavic and East European Journal* 1 (40): 148–52.

de Mauro, T. (1972) *Édition critique du 'Cours de linguistique générale' de F. de Saussure*, Paris: Payot.

Denison, D. (1993) *English Historical Syntax*, London: Longman.

Dennett, D. C. (1991) *Consciousness Explained*, New York: Little, Brown.

Derrida, J. ([1967] 1976) *Of Grammatology*, trans. G. C. Spivak, Baltimore and London: Johns Hopkins University Press.

Derrida, J. (1977) 'Limited Inc abc . . .', trans. S. Weber, *Glyph* 2: 164–254.

Derrida, J. (1981) *Positions*, trans. A. Bass, Chicago: University of Chicago Press.

Derrida, J. (1982) 'Signature, event, context', in *Margins of Philosophy*, trans. A. Bass, Chicago: University of Chicago Press.

Dewey, J. (1938) *Logic, the Theory of Inquiry*, New York: Henry Holt.

Dik, S.C. (1994) 'Functional grammar', in Asher, R.E. *The Encyclopedia of Language and Linguistics*, Oxford: Pergamon, pp. 1318–23.

Discourse and Society (1999) 'Debate: critical discourse analysis and conversation analysis: an exchange between Michael Billig and Emanuel A. Schegloff', *Discourse and Society* 10 (4): 543–82.

Donald, M. (1991) *Origins of the Modern Mind: Three Stages in the Evolution of Culture and Cognition*, Cambridge, MA: Harvard University Press.

Dorian, N. (1981) *Language Death: The Life Cycle of a Scottish Gaelic Dialect*, Philadelphia, PA: University of Pennsylvania Press.

Douglas, M. T. (1966) *Purity and Danger: An Analysis of Concepts of Pollution and Taboo*, London: Routledge.

Douglas, M. T. (1970) *Natural Symbols: Explorations in Cosmology*, New York: Pantheon Books.

Douglas, M. T. and Isherwood, B. (1979) *The World of Goods: An Anthropological Theory of Consumption*, New York: Basic Books.

Douglas, M. T. and Wildavsky, A. (1982) *Risk and Culture*, Berkeley, CA: University of California Press.

Drew, P. and Heritage, J. (eds) (1992) *Talk at Work: Interaction in Institutional Settings*, Cambridge: Cambridge University Press.

Dummett, M. (1978) *Truth and Other Enigmas*, Cambridge, MA: Harvard University Press.

Duranti, A. and Goodwin, C. (eds) (1992) *Rethinking Context*, Cambridge: Cambridge University Press.

Easthope, A. (1988) *British Post-structuralism Since 1968*, London: Routledge.

Eckert, P. (1989) *Jocks and Burnouts: Social Categories and Identity in the High School*, New York: Teachers College Press.

Eco, U. (1973) 'Social life as a sign system', in C. Norris (ed.) *Structuralism: An Introduction,* Oxford: Oxford University Press.

Eco, U. (1975) *Trattato di semiotica generale*, Milan: Bompiani.

Eco, U. (1976) *A Theory of Semiotics*, Bloomington: Indiana University Press.

Eco, U. (1979a) *The Role of the Reader: Explorations in the Semiotics of Texts*, Bloomington: Indiana University Press.

Eco, U. (1979b) *A Semiotic Landscape*, The Hague: Mouton.

Eco, U. (1984) *Semiotics and the Philosophy of Language*, Bloomingtonp: Indiana University Press.

Eco, U. (1989) *The Open Work*, trans. A. Cancogni, Cambridge, MA: Harvard University Press (abridged translation of *Opera Aperta*, Milano: Bompiani, 1962).

Eco, U. (1990) *The Limits of Interpretation*, Bloomington: Indiana University Press.

Eco, U. (1997) *The Search for the Perfect Language*, London: Fontana.

Eco, U. (1997) *Kant e l'ornitorinco*, Milano: Bompiani. English trans. *Kant and the Platypus*, (1999).

Eco, U. (2000) *Kant and the Platypus*, trans. A. McEwan, Harcourt: New York.

Edelman, G. (1989) *The Remembered Present: A Biological Theory of Consciousness*, New York: Basic Books.

Edelman, G. (1998) 'Building a picture of the brain', *Dædalus* 127(2): 37–70.

Eikhenbaum, B. M. (1926) 'Teoriia "formal" nogo metoda', trans. in T. Todorov (ed.) *Théorie de la Littérature*, Paris: Seuil.

Elman, J. (1990) 'Finding structure in time', *Cognitive Science* 14: 179–211.

Elman, J. *et al.* (1996) *Rethinking Innateness*, Cambridge, MA: MIT Press.

Emerson, C. (1997) *The First Hundred Years of Mikhail Bakhtin*, Princeton, NJ: Princeton University Press.

Enzensberger, H. M. (1973) *Gespräche mit Marx und Engels*. Frankfurt am Main: Insel Verlag.

Erlich, V. (1964) *Russian Formalism*, The Hague: Mouton.

Eschbach, A. (1988) *Karl Bühler's Theory of Language: Proceedings of the Conferences Held at Kirchberg, August 26, 1984 and Essen, November 21–24, 1984,* Amsterdam and Philadelphia: John Benjamins.

Fairclough, N. (1989) *Language and Power*, London: Longman.

Fairclough, N. (1992) 'Introduction', in N. Fairclough (ed.) *Critical Language Awareness*, London: Longman, pp. 1–29.

Fairclough, N. (1995a) *Critical Discourse Analysis: The Critical Study of Language*, London: Longman.

Fairclough, N. (1995b) *Media Discourse*, London: Arnold.

Fairclough, N. (1999) 'Linguistic and intertextual analysis within discourse analysis', in A. Jaworski and N. Coupland (eds) *The Discourse Reader*, London: Routledge, pp. 183–211.

Farnell, B. (1995) *Do You See What I Mean? Plains Indian Sign Talk and the Embodiment of Action*, Austin, TX: University of Texas Press.

Fillmore, C. J. (1975) *Santa Cruz Lectures on Deixis*, Bloomington: Indiana University Linguistics Club.

Firth, J.R. (1957) *Papers in Linguistics 1934–1951*, Oxford: Oxford University Press.

Fisch, M. H. (1986a) *Peirce: Semeiotics and Pragmatism*, Bloomington: Indiana University Press.

Fisch, M. H. (1986b) 'Philodemus and Semeiosis (1879–1883)', section 5 of the essay 'Peirce's General Theory of Signs' in M. H. Fisch, *Peirce: Semeiotics and Pragmatism*, Bloomington: Indiana University Press.

Fischer, S. D. and Siple, P. (1990) *Theoretical Issues in Sign Language Research*, vol. 1, Chicago: University of Chicago Press.

Fiske, J. (1989a) *Understanding Popular, Culture*, London: Unwin Hyman.

Fiske, J. (1989b) *Reading the Popular*, London: Unwin Hyman.

Fiske, J. (1991) *Introduction to Communication Studies*, London: Routledge.

Foley, R. (1997) *Humans Before Humanity: An Evolutionary Perspective*, Oxford: Blackwell.

Foucault, M. (1972) *The Archaeology of Knowledge*, trans. S. Smith, London: Tavistock.

Foucault, M. (1977) *Power/Knowledge*, Hemel Hempstead: Harvester.

Foucault, M. (1979) *Discipline and Punish: The Birth of the Prison*, New York: Vintage/Random House.

Foucault, M. (1999) 'The incitement to discourse', in A. Jaworski and N. Coupland (eds) *The Discourse Reader*, London: Routledge, pp. 514–22.

Fought, J. G. (1994) 'American structuralism', in R. Asher and J. Simpson (eds) *The Encyclopedia of Language and Linguistics*, vol. 1, Oxford: Pergamon Press, pp. 97–106.

Fouts, R. with Mills, S. T. (1997) *Next of Kin: What Chimpanzees Have Taught Me About Who We Are*, New York: William Morrow.

Fowler, R. (1981) *Literature as Social Discourse: The Practice of Linguistic Criticism*, London: Batsford Academic.

Fowler, R. (1985) 'Power', in T. van Dijk (ed.) *Handbook of Discourse Analysis*, vol. 4, London: Academic Press, pp. 61–82.

Fowler, R. *et al.* (eds) (1979) *Language and Control*, London: Routledge and Kegan Paul.

Frege, G. (1892) 'Über Sinn und Bedeutung' [On sense and reference], English translation in D. Davidson and G. Harman (eds) *The Logic of Grammar*, Encino, CA: Dickenson, pp. 116–28.

Freud, S. (1899) *Die Traumdeutung*, Leipzig and Vienna.

Freud, S. (1905 [1960]) *Jokes and Their Relation to the Unconscious*, in *The Standard Edition of the Complete Psychological Works of Sigmund Freud*, vol. VIII, Hogarth: London.

Fried, V. (ed.) (1972) *The Prague School of Linguistics and Language Teaching*, Oxford: Oxford University Press.

Fromkin, V. and Rodman, R. (1978) *An Introduction to Language*, 2nd edn, New York: Holt, Rinehart and Winston.

Gabelentz, G. von der (1891) *Die Sprachwissenschaft: Ihre Aufgaben, Methoden und bisherigen Erbegnisse*, Leipzig: Weigel.

Gadamer, H.-G. (1975) *Truth and method*, Bloomington: Indiana University Press.

Galasiński, D. and Jaworski, A. (forthcoming) 'Meeting the local Other: representations of local people in British press travel sections'.

Gardner, B. T. and Gardner, A. (1971) 'Two way communication with an infant chimpanzee', in Schrier and Stollnitz (eds) *Behavior of Non-human Primates*, vol. 4, New York: Academic Press.

Gardner, H. (1993) *Frames of Mind: The Theory of Applied Multiple Intelligence*, London: HarperCollins.

Garfinkel, H. (1967) *Studies in Ethnomethodology*, Englewood Cliffs, NJ: Prentice-Hall.

Garfinkel, H. (1974) 'On the origins of the term "ethnomethodology"', in R. Turner (ed.) *Ethnomethodology*, Harmondsworth: Penguin.

Giddens, A. (1991) *Modernity and Self-identity: Self and Society in the Late Modern Age*, Cambridge: Polity Press.

Gilbert, G. N. and Mulkay, M. (1984) *Opening Pandora's Box: A Sociological Analysis of Scientists' Discourse*, Cambridge: Cambridge University Press.

Giles, H. (1994) 'Accommodation in communication', in R. E. Asher, *The Encyclopedia of Language and Linguistics*, Oxford: Pergamon, pp. 12–15.

Gilson, E. (1995) *History of Christian Philosophy in the Middle Ages*, New York: Random House.

Givón, T. (1995) *Functionalism and Grammar*, Amsterdam: John Benjamins.

Godel, R. (1957) *Les sources manuscrites du Cours de Linguistique Générale de F. de Saussure*, Geneva: Droz and Paris: Minard.

Goffman, E. (1959) *The Presentation of Self in Everyday Life*, New York: Anchor Books.

Goffman, E. (1967) *Interaction Ritual: Essays on Face-to-Face Behavior*, New York: Doubleday.

Goffman, E. (1974) *Frame Analysis: An Essay on the Organization of Experience*, New York: Harper and Row.

Goffman, E. (1983) 'The interaction order', *American Sociological Review* 48: 1–17.

Goldschmidt, W. R. (ed.) (1959) *The Anthropology of Franz Boas: Essays on the Centennial of his Birth*, American Anthropological Association, Memoirs, No. 89. Menasha, WI: American Anthropological Association.

Goodwin, C. (1994) 'Professional vision', *American Anthropologist* 96: 606–33.

Gopnik, M. (1999) 'Some evidence for impaired grammars', in R. Jackendoff *et al.* (eds) *Language, Logic, and Concepts: Essays in Memory of John Macnamara*, Cambridge, MA: MIT Press, pp. 263–84.

Gordon, T. W. (1990a) 'Significs and C.K. Ogden: the influence of Lady Welby', in W. H. Schmitz (ed.), *Essays on Significs*, Amsterdam: John Benjamins, pp. 179–96.

Gordon, T. W. (1990b) *C.K. Ogden. A Bio-bibliographic Study*, London: Scarecrow and New Jersey: Metuchen.

Gordon, T. W. (1991) *The Semiotics of C.K. Ogden*, in T. A. Sebeok and J. Umiker-Sebeok (eds), *Recent Developments in Theory and History: The Semiotic Web 1990*, The Hague and Berlin: Mouton de Gruyter, pp. 111–77.

Graddol, D. (1996) 'The semiotics of a wine label', in S. Goodman and D. Graddol (eds) *Redesigning English: New Texts, New Identities*, London: Routledge in association with The Open University, pp. 73–81.

Greenberg, J. H. (ed.) (1966) *Universals of Language*, 2nd edn, Cambridge, MA., MIT Press.

Greimas, A. J. (1966) *Sémantique structurale*, Paris: Larousse.

Greimas, A. J. (1970) *Du sens*, Paris: Seuil.

Greimas, A. J. (1987) *On Meaning: Selected Writings in Semiotic Theory*, trans. and ed. P. Perron and F. Collins, Minneapolis: University of Minnesota Press.

Grice, H. P. (1957) 'Meaning', *Philosophical Review* 66: 377–88.

Grice, H. P. (1968) 'Utterer's meaning, sentence-meaning and word-meaning', *Foundations of Language* 4: 1–18.

Grice, H. P. (1969) 'Utterer's meaning and intentions', *Philosophical Review* 78: 147–77.

Grice, H. P. (1975) 'Logic and conversation', in P. Cole and J. L. Morgan (eds) *Syntax and Semantics 3: Speech Acts*, New York: Academic Press, pp. 41–58.

Grice, H. P. (1978) 'Further notes on logic and conversation', in P. Cole (ed.) *Syntax and Semantics 9: Pragmatics*, New York: Academic Press, pp. 113–27.

Grice, H. P. (1981) 'Presupposition and conversational implicature', in P. Cole (ed.) *Radical Pragmatics*, New York: Academic Press, pp. 183–98.

Gumperz, J. J. (1982) *Discourse Strategies*, Cambridge: Cambridge Univerity Press.

Gumperz, J. and Levinson, S. (eds) (1996) *Rethinking Linguistic Relativity*, Cambridge: Cambridge University Press.

Haack, Susan (1987) 'Realism', *Synthese* 73: 275–99.

Hadamard, J. (1945) *The Psychology of Invention in the Mathematical Field*, Princeton, NJ: Princeton University Press, Appendix II, titled 'A testimonial from Professor Einstein'.

Hale, K. *et al.* (1992) 'Endangered languages', *Language* 68: 1–42.

Hall, E. T. (1994) in J. Erting *et al.* (eds) *The Deaf Way: Perspectives from the International Conference on Deaf Culture*, Washington, DC: Gallaudet University Press.

Hall, S. (1996) 'The problem of ideology: Marxism without guarantees', in D. Morley and K. H. Chen (eds) *Stuart Hall: Critical Dialogues in Cultural Studies*, London: Routledge, pp. 25–46.

Halliday, M. A. K. (1973) 'Foreword', in B. Bernstein (ed.) *Class, Codes and Control Vol 2: Applied Studies Towards a Sociology of Language*, London: Routledge and Kegan Paul.

Halliday, M. A. K. (1978) *Language as Social Semiotic: The Social Interpretation of Language and Meaning*, London: Edward Arnold.

Halliday, M. A. K. (1985) *An Introduction to Functional Grammar,* London: Edward Arnold.

Halliday, M. A. K. (1994) *An Introduction to Functional Grammar*, 2nd edn, London: Arnold.

Halliday, M. A. K. and Hasan, (1976) *Cohesion in English*, London: Longman.

Hardwick, C. S. (ed.) (1977) *Semiotic and Significs: The Correspondence Between Charles S. Peirce and Victoria Lady Welby*, Bloomington and London: Indiana University Press.

Harris, R. (1981) *The Language Myth*, London: Duckworth.

Harris, R. (1987) *Reading Saussure*, London: Duckworth.

Harris, R. (1992) 'On scientific method in linguistics', in G. Wolf (ed.), *New Departures in Linguistics*, New York: Garland, pp. 1–26.

Harris, R. (1995) *Signs of Writing*, London: Routledge.

Harris, R. (1998) *Introduction to Integrational Linguistics*, Oxford: Pergamon.

Harris, Z. ([1951] 1984) 'Review of *Selected Writings* by Edward Sapir (Berkeley, University of California Press, 1949)', *Language* 27(3): 228–333.

Harris, Z. (1991) *A Theory of Language and Information*, Oxford: Clarendon Press.

Hart, B. and Risley, T. R. (1995) *Meaningful Differences*, Baltimore: P. H. Brookes.

Headland, T. N., Pike, K. L. and Harris, M. (eds) (1990) *Emics and Etics: The Insider/Outsider Debate*, Newbury Park, CA: Sage.

Hebdige, D. (1979) *Subculture: The Meaning of Style*, London: Methuen.

Hediger, H. (1980) *Tiere verstehen: Erkenntnisse eines Tierpsychologen* [*Understanding Animals: Experiences of an Animal Psychologist*], Munich: Kindler.

Hediger, H. (1998) 'Biosemiotics' in P. Bouissac (ed.) *Encyclopedia of Semiotics,* New York: Oxford University Press, pp. 82–5.

Hediger, H. and Emmeche, C. (eds) (1999) *Biosemiotica, Semiotica* 126 [Special issue].

Heijerman, E. and Schmitz, W. H. (eds) (1991) *Significs, Mathematics and Semiotics. The Significs Movement in the Netherlands,* Proceedings of the International Conference, Bonn, 19–21 Nov., 1986 Munster, Nodus Publikationen.

Heisenberg, W. (1958) *Physics and Philosophy,* Ann Arbor: University of Michigan Press.

Heritage, J. (1984a) 'A change-of-state token and aspects of its sequential placement', in J. Atkinson and J. Heritage (eds) *Structures of Social Action: Studies in Conversation Analysis*, Cambridge: Cambridge University Press, pp. 299–345.

Heritage, J. (1984b) *Garfinkel and Ethnomethodology*, Oxford: Blackwell.

Hjelmslev, L. (1928) *Principes de grammaire générale*, Copenhagen: Det Kongelige Danske Videnskabernes Selskab.

Hjelmslev, L. (1932) *Études baltiques*, Copenhagen: Munksgaard.

Hjelmslev, L. (1935–1937) *La catégorie des cas*, vols 1–2, Aarhus: Universitetsforlaget.

Hjelmslev, L. (1959) *Essais linguistiques,* Copenhagen: Nordisk Sprog- og Kulturforlag.

Hjelmslev, L. (1961) *Prolegomena to a Theory of Language*, rev. edn, trans. F. J. Whitfield, Madison, WI: University of Wisconsin Press.

Hjelmslev, L. (1973) *Essais linguistiques*, vol. II, Copenhagen: Nordisk Sprog-og Kulturforlag.

Hjelmslev, L. (1975) *Résumé of a Theory of Language,* Copenhagen: Nordisk Sprog- og Kulturforlag.

Hobsbawm, E. J. (1992) *Nations and Nationalism Since 1780: Programme, Myth, Reality*, 2nd edn, Cambridge: Cambridge University Press.

Hodge, R. and Kress, G. (1988) *Social Semiotics*, Oxford: Polity Press.

Hodge, R. and Kress, G. (1993) *Language as Ideology*, 2nd edn, London: Routledge.

Holmes, J. (1999) 'Women, men and politeness: agreeable and disagreeable responses', in A. Jaworski and N. Coupland (eds) *The Discourse Reader*, London: Routledge, pp. 336–45.

Holmes, J. and Meyerhoff, M. (1999) *Communities of Practice in Language and Gender Research*, Special Issue of *Language in Society*, 28 (2).

Holquist, M. (1990) *Dialogism: Bakhtin and His World,* London and New York: Routledge.

Hookway, C. (1992) *Peirce,* London: Routledge and Kegan Paul.

Hoopes, J. (ed.) (1991) *Peirce on Signs,* Chapel Hill, NC: University of North Carolina Press.

Hopper, P. (1994) 'Phonogenesis', in W. Pagliuca (ed.), *Perspectives on Grammaticalisation*, Amsterdam and Philadelphia: John Benjamins.

Hubel, D. and Wiesel, T. (1968) 'Receptive fields and functional architecture of monkey striate cortex', *Journal of Physiology (Lond.)* 195: 215–43.

Husserl, E. (1938) *Erfarhrung und Urteil*, Praha: Akademia.

Husserl, E. ([1900–01] 1968) *Logische Untersuchungen*, vols 1–2, Tübingen: Niemeyer.

Hutchby, I. (1999) 'Power in discourse: the case of arguments on a British talk radio show', in A. Jaworski and N. Coupland (eds) *The Discourse Reader*, London: Routledge, pp. 576–88.

Hutchby, I. and Wooffitt, R. (1998) *Conversation Analysis*, Cambridge: Polity Press.

Hymes, D. (1974) *Foundations in Sociolinguistics: An Ethnographic Approach*, London: Tavistock.

Jackendoff, R. (1983) *Semantics and Cognition*, Cambridge, MA: MIT Press.

Jackendoff, R. (1994) *Patterns in the Mind*, New York: Basic Books.

Jackendoff, R. (1996) 'How language helps us think', *Pragmatics and Cognition* 4: 1–24.

Jackendoff, R. (1997) *The Architecture of the Language Faculty*, Cambridge, MA: MIT Press.

Jackson, B. D. (1972) 'The theory of signs in Augustine's *De Doctrina Christiana*', in *Augustine: A Collection of Critical Essays*, ed. R. A. Markus, Garden City, NY: Doubleday and Co, pp. 92–147.

Jakobson, R. (1960) 'Closing statement: linguistics and poetics', in T. A. Sebeok (ed.) *Style in Language*, Cambridge, MA: Harvard University Press.

Jakobson, R. ([1956] 1990a) 'Two aspects of language and two types of aphasic disturbances', in *On Language*, ed. L. R. Waugh and M. M. Burston, Cambridge, MA and London: Harvard University Press.

Jakobson, R. ([1957] 1990b) 'Shifters and verbal categories', in *On Language*, ed. L. R. Waugh and M. M. Burston, Cambridge, MA and London: Harvard University Press.

James, W. (1897) *The Will to Believe*, 1979; It. trans. *La volontà di credere*, Intro. C. Sini, Milan: Principato, 1984.

James, W. ([1907] 1981) *Pragmatism*, Indianapolis: Hackett, 1981.

Jaworski, A. and Coupland, N. (eds) (1999) *The Discourse Reader*, London: Routledge.

Jaworski, A. and Galasiński, D. (1998) 'The last Romantic hero: Lech Walesa's image-building in TV presidential debates', *Text* 18 (2): 525–44.

Jaworski, A. and Galasiński, D. (1999) 'Vocative address forms and ideological legitimisation in political debates', *Discourse Studies* 2 (1): 65–83.

Jaworski, A., Coupland, N. and Galasiński, D. (eds) (forthcoming) *Metalanguage: Social and Political Perspectives*.

Jenkins, A. (1979) *The Social Theory of Claude Lévi-Strauss*, New York: St. Martin's Press.

Jespersen, O. (1905) *Growth and Structure of the English Language*, Leipzig: Teubner.

Jespersen, O. (1909–1949) *A Modern English Grammar on Historical Principles*, Copenhagen: Munksgaard and London: Allen and Unwin.

Jespersen, O. (1916) *Nutidssprog hos börn og voxne* [*Contemporary Child and Adult Language*], Copenhagen and Christiania: Gyldendal.

Jespersen, O. (1922) *Language: Its Nature, Development and Origin*, London: Allen and Unwin.

Jespersen, O. (1924) *The Philosophy of Grammar*, London: Allen and Unwin.

Jespersen, O. (1941) *Efficiency in Linguistic Change*, Copenhagen: Munksgaard.

Johansen, J. D. (1993) *Dialogic Semiosis: An Essay in Signs and Meaning*, Bloomington: Indiana University Press.

Juul, A. *et al.* (eds) (1995) *A Linguist's Life: An English Translation of Otto Jespersen's Autobiography with Notes, Photos and a Bibliography*, trans. D. Stoner, Odense: Odense University Press.

Kanaev, I. I. (1926) 'Contemporary vitalism', It. trans. 'Il vitalismo contemporaneo', in M. Bakhtin *et al.*, *Bachtin e le sue maschere*, ed. A. Ponzio *et al.*, Bari: Dedalo, 1995, pp. 175–98.

Kapor, M. (1993) 'Where is the digital highway really heading?', *Wired* (July–Aug): 53–9, 94.

Karttunen, L. (1974) 'Presupposition and linguistic context', *Theoretical Linguistics* 1: 3–44.

Kegl, J. *et al.* (1999) 'Creation through contact: sign language emergence and sign language change in Nicaragua', in M. DeGraff (ed.), *Language Creation and Language Change*, Cambridge, MA: MIT Press.

Kendon, A. (1988) *Sign Languages of Aboriginal Australia*, Cambridge: Cambridge University Press.

Kinsbourne, M. (1998) 'Unity and diversity in the human brain: evidence from injury', *Dædalus* 127(2): 233–56.

Klima, E. and Bellugi, U. (1979) *The Signs of Language*, Cambridge, MA: Harvard University Press.

Knowlsen, J. R. (1965) 'The idea of gesture as a universal language in the XVIIth and XVIIIth centuries', *Journal for the History of Ideas*, 26: 495–508.

Koerner, K. (1984) *Edward Sapir: Appraisals of his Life and Work*, Amsterdam: John Benjamins.

Köhler, W. (1927) *The Mentality of Apes*, London: Routledge and Kegan Paul.

Körner, S. (1955) *Kant*, London: Penguin Books.

Kremer-Marietti, A. (1998) 'Comte, Isidore-Auguste-Marie-François-Xavier', *Routledge Encyclopedia of Philosophy*, London, Routledge.

Kress, G. and van Leeuwen, T. (1996) *Reading Images: The Grammar of Visual Design*, London: Routledge.

Kristeva, J. (1969a) *Le langage, cet inconnu*, Paris: Seuil.

Kristeva, J. (1969b) *Semeiotiké: recherches pour une sémanalyse*, Paris: Seuil.

Kristeva, J. (1974) *La révolution du langage poétique*, Paris: Seuil.

Kristeva, J. (1979) *Les Samouraïs*, Paris: Fayard.

Kristeva, J. (1980) *Pouvoirs de l'horreur: essais sur l'abjection,* Paris: Seuil.

Kristeva, J. (1983) *Histoires d'amour*, Paris: Denoël.

Kristeva, J. (1987) *Soleil noir. Dépression et mélancolie*, Paris: Gallimard.

Kristeva, J. (1988) *Étrangers à nous-mêmes*, Paris: Fayard.

Kristeva, J. (1991) *Le Viel Homme et les loups*, Paris: Fayard.

Kristeva, J. (1994) *Le temps sensible. Proust et l'expérience littéraire*, Paris: Gallimard.

Kristeva, J. (1999) *Le génie féminine, Tome premier: Hannah Arendt,* Paris: Fayard.

Kuiper, K. (1991) 'Sporting formulae in New Zealand English: two models of male solidarity', in J. Cheshire (ed.) *English Around the World*, Cambridge: Cambridge University Press, pp. 200–9.

Labov, W. (1972a) 'The study of language in its social contexts', in P. P. Giglioli, *Language and Social Context: Selected Readings*, Harmondsworth: Penguin Books, pp. 283–307.

Labov, W. (1972b) *Language in the Inner City: Studies in the Black English Vernacular*, Philadelphia, PA: University of Pennsylvania Press.

Labov, W. ([1972c] 1978) *Sociolinguistic Patterns*, Philadephia, PA: University of Pennsylvania Press.

Labov, W. (1994) *Principles of Linguistic Change: Vol. 1. Internal Factors*, Oxford: Blackwell.

Lakoff, G. (1973a) 'Fuzzy grammar and the performance-competence terminology game', *Papers from the Ninth Regional Meeting, Chicago Linguistic Society*, pp. 271–91.

Lakoff, G. (1973b) 'The logic of politeness: or minding your p's and q's', *Proceedings of the Ninth Regional Meeting of the Chicago Linguistic Society*, pp. 292–305.

Lakoff, G. (1987) *Women, Fire, and Dangerous Things*, Chicago: University of Chicago Press.

Lakoff, R. (1975) *Language and Woman's Place*, New York: Harper and Row.

Langacker, R. (1987) *Foundations of Cognitive Grammar*, Vol. 1, Stanford, CA: Stanford University Press.

Larsen, S. E. (1988) 'Gods, ghosts, and objects: Brøndal and Peirce', *Semiotica* 70 (1/2): 49–58.

Larsen, S. E. (1993) 'Patriarchal hierarchies', *Semiotica* 94 (1/2): 35–54.

Lecourt, D. (1973) *The Case of Lysenko*, London: New Left Books.

Ledgerwood, M. D. (1995) 'The visual and the Auditory: poetry on CD ROMs', *Semiotics 1994*, University Press of America, pp. 381–91.

Ledgerwood, M. D. (1997) 'Hypertextuality and Multimedia Literature', *Semiotics of the Media: State of the Art, Projects and Perspectives*, Berlin: Mouton de Gruyter.

Ledgerwood, M. D. (1998a) 'The semiotics of cyberspace: Part One, persona', *Signs and Space, Raum und Zeichnen: An International Conference on the Semiotics of Space and Culture in Amsterdam*, Tübingen: Günter Narr Verlag, pp. 273–9.

Ledgerwood, M. D. (1998b) 'The end of narrative? Multimedia literature and hypertext', *Signs and Space, Raum und Zeichnen: An International Conference on the Semiotics of Space and Culture in Amsterdam*, Tübingen: Günter Narr Verlag, pp. 279–90.

Ledgerwood, M. D. (1999) 'Multimedia Literature, "Exploratory Games" and their Hypertextuality', in S. Inkinen (ed.) *Mediapolis: Aspects of Texts, Hypertexts and Multimedial Communication*, Berlin: Walter de Gruyter, pp. 547–58.

Leech, G. N. (1983) *Principles of Pragmatics*, London: Longman.

Le Grand, E. (1993) 'Lotman', in I. M. Makaryk (ed.) *Encyclopedia of Contemporary Literary Theory: Approaches, Scholars, Terms,* Toronto, Buffalo, London: University of Toronto Press.

Lemke, J. L. (1995) *Textual Politics: Discourse and Social Dynamics*, London and Bristol, PA: Taylor and Francis.

Lenneberg, E. (1967) *Biological Foundations of Language*, New York: Wiley.

Levinas, E. (1961) *Totalité et Infini*, La Haye: Nijhoff.

Levinas, E. (1974) *Autrement qu'être ou au-delà de l'essence,* La Haye: Nijhoff.

Levinson, S. C. (1983) *Pragmatics*, Cambridge: Cambridge University Press.

Levinson, S. C. (1996) 'Frames of reference and Molyneux's question: crosslinguistic evidence', in P. Bloom *et al.* (eds), *Language and Space*, Cambridge, MA: MIT Press, pp. 109–70.

Lévi-Strauss, C. (1944) 'Reciprocity and hierarchy', *American Anthropologist* 46(2): 266–8.

Lévi-Strauss, C. (1949) *Les Structures Élémentaires de la Parenté*, Paris: Presses Universitaires de France.

Lévi-Strauss, C. (1964) *Le Cru et le Cuit. Mythologiques*, Vol. 1, Paris: Plon. Trans. *The Raw and the Cooked*, New York: Harper and Row, 1969.

Lévi-Strauss, C. (1966) *Du Miel au Cendres. Mythologiques*, Vol. 2, Paris: Plon. Trans. *From Honey to Ashes*, New York: Harper and Row, 1973.

Lévi-Strauss, C. (1968) *L'Origine des Manières de Table: Mythologiques*, Vol. 3, Paris: Plon. Trans. *The Origin of Table Manners*, New York: Harper and Row, 1978.

Lévi-Strauss, C. (1971) *L'Homme nu. Mythologiques*, Vol. 4, Paris: Plon. Trans. *The Naked Man*, New York: Harper and Row, 1981.

Lévi-Strauss, C. (1977) *Structural Anthropology 1*, Harmondsworth: Penguin.

Lévi-Strauss, C. (1978) 'Structure and form: reflections on a work by Vladimir Propp', in *Structural Anthropology 1*, Harmondsworth: Penguin.

Lévi-Strauss, C. (1987) *The View from Afar*, Harmondsworth: Penguin.

Li, P. and Gleitman, L. R. (2000) *Turning the Tables: Explorations in Spatial Cognition*, Technical Report no. 2000–3, Institute for Research in Cognitive Science, University of Pennsylvania.

Liszka, J. J. (1996) *A General Introduction to the Semeiotic of Charles Sanders Peirce*, Bloomington: Indiana University Press, esp. Ch. 4.

Livingstone, S. and Lunt, P. (1994) *Talk on Television: Audience Participation and Public Debate*, London: Routledge.

Lotman, J. (1964) 'Sur la délimitation linguistique et littéraire de la notion de structure', *Linguistics* 6: 59–72.

Lotman, J. (1975) 'Notes on the structure of a literary text', *Semiotica* 15 (3): 199–205.

Lotman, J. (1976) *Analyses of the Poetic Text: Verse Structure*, Ann Arbor: Ardis.

Lotman, J. (1977a) *Structure of the Artistic Text*, Ann Arbor: Michigan Slavic Contributions 7.

Lotman, J. (1977b) 'Primary and secondary communication-modeling systems', in D. Lucid, (ed.) *Soviet Semiotics: An Anthology*, Baltimore: Johns Hopkins University Press.

Lotman, J. (1990) *Universe of the Mind*, trans. A. Shukman, London and New York: Tauris.

Lotman, J. M. and Uspenskij, B. A. (1984) *The Semiotics of Russian Culture*, Ann Arbor: Michigan Slavic Contributions, 11.

Lotman, J. *et al.* (1973) 'Theses on the semiotic study of cultures (as applied to Slavic texts)', in J. van Eng (ed.) *Structure of Texts and Semiotics of Culture*, The Hague and Paris: Mouton.

Lotman, J. *et al.* (1985) *The Semiotics of Russian Cultural History*, eds. A. D. Nakhimovsky and A.S. Nakhimovsky, Ithaca, NY and London: Cornell University Press.

Loux, M. J. (1998) 'Nominalism', *Routledge Encyclopedia of Philosophy*, London, Routledge.

Lucid, D. P. (ed.) (1977) *Soviet Semiotics: An Anthology*, Baltimore: Johns Hopkins University Press.

McClelland, J., and Rumelhart, D. (1986) *Parallel Distributed Processing*, vol. 1, Cambridge, MA: MIT Press.

McCord Adams, M. (1978) 'Ockham's theory of natural signification', *The Monist* 61: 444–59.

Macksey, R. and Donato, E. (eds) (1972) *The Structuralist Controversy: The Languages of Criticism and the Sciences of Man*, Baltimore and London: Johns Hopkins University Press.

McNeill, D. (1992) *Hand and Mind: What Gestures Reveal About Thought*, Chicago: Chicago University Press.

Maher, J. (1996) *Seeing Language in Sign: The Work of William C. Stokoe*, Washington, DC: Gallaudet University Press.

Mallery, G. ([1881] 1972) *Sign Language among the North American Indians Compared with That of Other Peoples and Deaf Mutes,* The Hague: Mouton.

Malotki, E. (1983) *Hopi Time: A Linguistic Analysis of the Temporal Concepts in the Hopi Language*, Berlin: Mouton.

Mandelker, A. (1994) 'Semiotizing the sphere: organicist theory in Lotman, Bakhtin, and Vernadsky', *PMLA* 3 (109): 385–96.

Manetti, G. (1993) *Theories of the Sign in Classical Antiquity* trans. C. Richardson, Bloomington: Indiana University Press.

Marcellesi, J.-B. *et al.* (1978) *Linguaggio e classi sociali. Marrismo e stalinismo*, ed. A. Ponzio, Bari: Dedalo.

Marcus, G. (2001) *The Algebraic Mind*, Cambridge, MA: MIT Press.

Martinet, A. (1984) 'Double articulation as a criterion of linguisticity', *Language Sciences* 6 (1): 31–8.

Martinet, A. (1994) 'Functional grammar: Martinet's model', in R. E. Asher, *The Encyclopedia of Language and Linguistics*, Oxford: Pergamon, pp. 1323–7.

Marx, K. (1962) *Capital*, Book I, 2 vols, trans. E. and C. Paul, introd. G. D. H. Cole, London: Dent.

Marx, K. and Engels, F. (1968) *The German Ideology*, ed. S. Rayzankaya, Moscow: Progress Publishers.

Mates, B. (1961) *Stoic Logic*, Berkeley, CA: University of California Press.

Matthews, P. H. (1979) *Generative Grammar and Linguistic Competence*, London: Allen and Unwin.

Mehan, H. (1999) 'Oracular reasoning in a psychiatric exam: the resolution of conflict in language', in A. Jaworski and N. Coupland (eds) *The Discourse Reader*, London: Routledge, pp. 559–75.

Meier-Oeser, S. (1997) *Die Spur des Zeichens. Das Zeichen und seine Funktion in der Philosophie des Mittelalters und der frühen Neuzeit,* Berlin: Walter de Gruyter.

Merleau-Ponty, M. (1966) *Sens et non sens* (1948), Paris: Nagel.

Merquior, J. G. (1986) *From Prague to Paris: A Critique of Structuralist and Post-Structuralist Thought*, London: Verso.

Merrell, F. (1995a) *Semiosis in the Postmodern Age,* West Lafayette: Purdue University Press.

Merrell, F. (1995b) *Peirce's Semiotics Now: A Primer,* Toronto: Canadian Scholars' Press.

Messaris, P. (1997) *Visual Persuasion: The Role of Images in Advertising*, London: Sage.

Mey, J.L. (1994) 'Pragmatics', in R. E. Asher, *The Encyclopedia of Language and Linguistics*. Oxford: Pergamon, pp. 3260–78.

Mills, S. (1997) *Discourse*, London: Routledge.

Milroy, J. (1992) *Linguistic Variation and Change*, Oxford: Blackwell.

Milroy, J. and Milroy, L. (1985) 'Linguistic change, social network and speaker innovation', *Journal of Linguistics* 21: 339–84.

Milroy, J. and Milroy, L. (1998) *Authority in Language: Investigating Language Prescription and Standardisation*, 3rd edn, London: Routledge.

Milroy, L. (1987) *Language and Social Networks*, Oxford: Blackwell.

Morris, C. (1932) *Six Theories of Mind,* Chicago: University of Chicago Press.

Morris, C. (1937) *Logical Positivism, Pragmatism and Scientific Empiricism*, Paris: Hermann.

Morris, C. (1938a) *Foundations of the Theory of Signs* [= *International Encyclopedia of Unified Science* 1, 2], Chicago: University of Chicago Press.

Morris, C. (1938b) 'Scientific Empiricism', in *Encyclopedia and Unified Science* [= *International Encyclopedia of Unified Science* 1, 2], Chicago: University of Chicago Press, pp. 63–75.

Morris, C. (1938c) 'Peirce, Mead, and Pragmatism', *Philosophical Review* XLVII: 109–27.

Morris, C. (1946) *Signs, Language and Behavior*, Englewood Cliffs, NJ: Prentice-Hall.

Morris, C. (1964) *Signification and Significance: A Study of the Relations of Signs and Values,* Cambridge MA: MIT Press.

Morris, C. (1971) *Writings on the General Theory of Signs*, T. A. Sebeok ed., The Hague and Paris: Mouton.

Morris, C. (1993 [1925]) *Symbolism and Reality: A Study in the Nature of Mind*, A. Eschbach ed. and pref., Amsterdam: John Benjamins.

Morris, D. (1977) *Manwatching: A Field Guide to Human Behaviour*, London: Jonathan Cape.

Morson, G. S. and Emerson, C. (eds) (1989) *Rethinking Bakhtin: Extensions and Challenges*, Evanston, ILL: Northwestern University Press.

Morson, G. S. and Emerson, C. (1990) *Mikhail Bakhtin: Creation of a Prosaics,* Stanford, CA: University of California Press.

Murphy, J. P. (1990) *Pragmatism: From Peirce to Davidson*, Boulder, CO: Westview Press.

Myers-Scotton, C. (1998) 'A way to dusty death: the Matrix Language turnover hypothesis', in L. A. Grenoble and L. J. Whaley (eds), *Endangered Languages: Current Issues and Future Prospects*, Cambridge: Cambridge University Press.

Newmeyer, F. J. (1994) 'Autonomous linguistics', in R. E. Asher, *The Encyclopedia of Language and Linguistics*, Oxford: Pergamon, pp. 283–4.

Newmeyer, F. J. (1998) 'On the supposed "counterfunctionality" of Universal Grammar: some evolutionary implications', in J. Hurford *et al.* (eds) *Approaches to the Evolution of Language*, Cambridge: Cambridge University Press.

Newport, E. (1990) 'Maturational constraints on language learning', *Cognitive Science* 14: 11–28.

Nunes, M. (1995) 'Baudrillard in cyberspace: Internet, virtuality, and postmodernity', *Style* 29: 314–27.

Ockham, William of (1323) *Summa Logicae*, vol. I of the *Opera Philosophica* in the 17-volume critical edition *Guillelmi de Ockham Opera Philosophica et Theologica*, St Bonaventure, NY: Editions of the Franciscan Institute of the University of St. Bonaventure, 1974–1988.

Ogden, C. K. (1994a) *C. K. Ogden and Linguistics*, 5 vols, ed. T. W. Gordon, London: Routledge-Thoemmes Press.

Ogden, C. K. (1994b) 'The progress of Significs', in *C.K. Ogden and Linguistics*, vol. 1, *From Significs to Orthology*, London: Routledge-Thoemmes Press, pp. 1–47.

Ogden, C. K. and Richards, I. A. ([1923] 1985) *The Meaning of Meaning: A Study of the Influence of Language upon Thought and of the Science of Symbolism*, with supplementary essays by B. Malinowski and F. G. Crookshank, London: Routledge and Kegan Paul; New York: Harcourt Brace Jovanovich, 1989.

Olson, S. R. (1999) *Hollywood Planet: Global Media and the Competitive Advantage of Narrative Transparency*, Mahwah, NJ: Lawrence Erlbaum Associates.

Ong, W. (1982) *Orality and Literacy*, London: Methuen.

Östman, J.-O. (1986) *Pragmatics as Implicitness*, Ann Arbor: University Microfilms International.

Parret, H. (1983) *Semiotics and Pragmatics: An Evaluative Comparison of Conceptual Frameworks*, Amsterdam: John Benjamins.

Pateman, T. (1983) 'What is a language?', *Language and Communication* 3, (2): 101–27.

Payne, J.R. (1994) 'Universals of language', in R. E. Asher, *The Encyclopedia of Language and Linguistics*, Oxford: Pergamon, pp. 4847–50.

Pêcheux, M. (1982) *Language, Semantics and Ideology*, Basingstoke: Macmillan.

Peirce, C. S. (1868) 'Some consequences of four incapacities', in C. S. Peirce, *The Essential Peirce*, vol. 1, Bloomington: Indiana University Press, 1992, pp. 28–55.

Peirce, C. S. (1871) 'Review of Fraser's *The Works of George Berkeley*', in C. S. Peirce, *The Essential Peirce*, vol. 1, Bloomington: Indiana University Press, 1992, pp. 83–105.

Peirce, C. S. (*c*.1902) *Minute Logic*, draft for a book complete consecutively only to Chapter 4. Published in *CP* in extracts scattered over six of the eight volumes, including 1.203–283, 1.575–584; 2.1–202; 4.227–323, 6.349–352; 7.279, 7.374n10, 7.362–387 except 381n19.

Peirce, C. S. (1905a) 'What pragmatism is', in C. S. Peirce *The Essential Peirce*, vol. 2, Bloomington: Indiana University Press, 1998, pp. 331–45.

Peirce, C. S. (1905b) 'Issues of pragmaticism', in C. S. Peirce *The Essential Peirce*, vol. 2, Bloomington: Indiana University Press, 1998, pp. 346–59.

Peirce, C. S. (1907) 'Pragmatism', in C. S. Peirce *The Essential Peirce*, vol. 2, Bloomington: Indiana University Press, 1998, pp. 398–433.

Peirce, C. S. (1923) *Chance, Love and Logic,* ed. M. R. Cohen, New York: Harcourt.

Peirce, C. S. (1931–1958) *Collected Papers of Charles Sanders Peirce,* ed. A. Burks, C. Hartshorne and P. Weiss, Cambridge, MA: The Belknap Press of Harvard University Press.

Peirce, C. S. (1966) 'Letter to Lady Welby, 23 December 1908', in *Charles S. Peirce: Selected Writings*, ed. P. Wiener, New York: Dover.

Peirce, C. S. (1977) *What is Meaning?* By V. Welby. *The Principles of Mathematics.* By Bertrand Russell (1903, Review article), *The Nation* 77. 15/Ott./1903, 308–9; in C. S. Peirce (1931–58), vol. VIII; now in C. S. Hardwick (ed.) *Semiotics and Significs*, Bloomington: Indiana University Press, 1977, pp. 157–9.

Peirce, C. S. (1982–) *Writings Of Charles Sanders Peirce: A Chronological Edition*, vols. 1–6. Bloomington: Indiana University Press.

Peirce, C. S. (1984) 'Critique of positivism', (1867–68) in *Writings of Charles S. Peirce,* vol. 2, ed. E. C. Moore, M. H. Fisch, *et al.*, Bloomington: Indiana University Press.

Peirce, C. S. (1992) *The Essential Peirce: Selected Philosophical Writings,* vol. 1, ed. N. Houser and C. Kloesel, Bloomington: Indiana University Press.

Peirce, C. S. (1998) *The Essential Peirce: Selected Philosophical Writings,* vol. 2, ed. Peirce Edition Project, Bloomington: Indiana University Press.

Petrilli, S. (1986) 'Introduzione', in V. Welby, *Significato, metafora, interpretazione,* trans. and ed. S. Petrilli, Bari: Adriatica, 1986, pp. 7–77.

Petrilli, S. (1988) *Significs, Semiotica, Significazione*, Bari: Adriatica.

Petrilli, S. (1989) 'La critica del linquaggio in Giovanni Vailati e Victoria Welby', in M. Quaranta (ed.), *Giovanni Vailati nelia cultura del '900*, Bologna: Forni, pp. 87–101.

Petrilli, S. (1990a) 'The problem of signifying in Welby, Peirce, Vailati, Bakhtin', in A. Ponzio, *Man as a Sign*, trans. ed., intro. and Appendices S. Petrilli, Berlin and New York: Mouton de Gruyter, pp. 313–63.

Petrilli, S. (1990b) 'On the materiality of signs', A. Ponzio, *Man as a Sign*, trans. ed., intro. and appendices S. Petrilli, Berlin and New York: Mouton de Gruyter, pp. 365–401.

Petrilli, S. (1990c) 'Sign and meaning in Victoria Welby and Mikhail Bakhtin: a confrontation', in W. H. Schmitz ed., *Essays on Significs*, Amsterdam and Philadelphia: John Benjamins, 1990, pp. 197–215.

Petrilli, S. (1990d) 'Dialogue and Chronotopic Otherness: Bakhtin and Welby', *Discours social/Social Discourse* 1/2, pp. 339–350.

Petrilli, S. (1990e) 'The critique of language in Vailati and Welby', in A. Ponzio, *Man as a Sign*, ed. S. Petrilli, Berlin: Mouton de Gruyter.

Petrilli, S. (1992a) 'Translation, semiotics and ideology', *TTR. Etudes sur le texte et ses transformations* V, 1, pp. 233–64.

Petrilli, S. (1992b) (ed. and introd.) *Semiotica. Social Practice, Semiotics and The Sciences of Man: The Correspondence between Charles Morris and Ferruccio Rossi-Landi, Semiotica* 8 (1/2).

Petrilli, S. (1995a) *Materia segnica e interpretazione*, Lecce: Milella.

Petrilli, S. (1995b) 'La metafora in Charles S. Peirce e Victoria Lady Welby', in S. Petrilli, *Materia segnica e interpretazione*, Lecce: Milella, 1995, pp. 323–59.

Petrilli, S. (1995c) 'Between Semiotics and Significs. C.K. Ogden and V. Welby', *Semiotica*, 105–3/4: 277–309.

Petrilli, S. (1996a) *Che cosa significa significare?*, Bari: Edizioni dal Sud.

Petrilli, S. (1998a) *Su Victoria Welby: Significs e filosofia del linguaggio*, Naples: Edizioni Scientifiche Italiane.

Petrilli, S. (1998b) 'La significs e il significato di "significato": la corrispondenza di Welby con Charles K. Ogden', in S. Petrilli *Su Victoria Welby*, Naples: Edizioni Scientifiche Italiane, pp. 281–98.

Petrilli, S. (1998c) 'Linguaggio figurato, processo linguistico e processi del significare', in S. Petrilli, *Su Victoria Welby: Significs e filosofia del linguaggio*, Naples: Edizioni Scientifiche Italiane, pp. 173–219.

Petrilli, S. (1998d) *Teoria dei segni e del linguaggio*, Bari: Graphis.

Petrilli, S. (1998e) 'Intersemiosi e traduzione', in S. Petrilli, *Teoria dei segni e del linguaggio*, Bari: Graphis, pp. 49–82.

Petrilli, S. (1998f) 'Translation and ideology', *Signs of Research on Signs, Semiotische Berichte*, ed. S. Petrilli, Jg. 22, 3, 4/1998, pp. 127–39.

Petrilli, S. (1999a) 'Semiotic phenomenology of predicative judgement', *S – European Journal for Semiotic Studies, Trajectories in Semiotic Studies from Bari*, Special Issue ed. S. Petrilli, forthcoming.

Petrilli, S. (1999b) 'Traduzione e traducibilità', in S. Gensini (ed.), *Manuale di comunicazione*, Rome: Carocci, pp. 419–49.

Petrilli, S. (1999c) ed. and introd. 'Traduzione e semiosi: considerazioni introduttive', *Athanor: Semiotica, Filosofia, Arte, Letteratura* X, ns. 2, 1999–2000.

Petrilli, S. (1999d) 'About and Beyond Peirce', *Semiotica* 124–3/4: 299–376.

Petrilli, S. (forthcoming) 'Welby', in H. C. G. Matthew (ed.), *New Dictionary of National Biography*, Oxford: Oxford University Press.

Petrus Hispanus (1972) *Tractatus: Called afterwards Summule logicales* (1230[?]), L. M. De Rijk ed., Assen: Van Gorcum; *Tractatus. Summule logicales*, It. trans. and ed. A. Ponzio, Bari: Adriatica, 1985.

Philodemus (*c*.110–*c*.40BC) i.54–40 BCE. Περὶ οημειώσεων (*De Signis*), trans. as *On the Methods of Inference* in the edition by P. H. De Lacy and E. Allen De Lacy, rev. with the collaboration of M. Gigante, F. Longo Auricchio and A. Tepedino Guerra, Naples: Bibliopolis, 1978, Greek text pp. 27–87, English 91–131.

Pike, K. L. (1954) *Language in Relation to a Unified Theory of the Structure of Human Behaviour*, Part 1, Glendale: Summer Institute of Linguistics.

Pike, K. L. (1959) 'Language as particle, wave, and field', *Texas Quarterly* 2 (2): 37–54.

Pinker, S. (1994) *The Language Instinct*, New York: William Morrow.

Pinker, S. and Bloom, P. (1990) 'Natural language and natural selection', *Behavioral and Brain Sciences* 13: 707–26.

Poinsot, J. (1632) *Tractatus de Signis*, subtitled *The Semiotic of John Poinsot*, arranged in bilingual format by J. Deely in consultation with R. A. Powell. First edition Berkeley, CA, University of California Press, 1985; available in electronic form as a text database, Charlottesville, VA: Intelex Corp., 1992.

Pollack, R. (1994) *Signs of Life: The Language and Meanings of DNA*, Harmondsworth: Penguin.

Ponzio, A. (1974) *Persona umana, linguaggio e conoscenza in Adam Schaff*, Bari: Dedalo.

Ponzio, A. (1980a) *Michail Bachtin: Alle origini della semiotica sovietica*, Bari: Dedalo.

Ponzio, A. (1980b) Introduzione, in V. N. Vološinov and M. Bakhtin, *Il linguaggio come pratica sociale*, essays 1926–30, collected and cd. A. Ponzio, Bari: Dedalo, pp. 5–17.

Ponzio, A. (1981a) 'Das Problem der Bezeichnung bei Morris und in der zeitgenössischen Semiotik', A. Eschbach ed., *Zeichen über Zeichen über Zeichen*, Tübingen: Günter Narr, 1981, pp. 162–72.

Ponzio, A. (1981b) 'Polisemia e traduzione', in A. Ponzio, *Segni e contraddizioni. Fra Marx e Bachtin*, Bertani, Verona, pp. 15–42.

Ponzio, A. (1985) 'The symbol, alterity, and abduction', *Semiotica* 56, 3/4: 261–77.

Ponzio, A. (1986) 'On the signs of Rossi-Landi's work', *Semiotica* 62–3/4: 207–21.

Ponzio, A. (1989) *Rossi-Landi e la filosofia del linguaggio*, Bari: Adriatica.

Ponzio, A. (1990a) *Man as a Sign*, trans., ed., intro. and Appendices S. Petrilli, Berlin and New York: Mouton de Gruyter.

Ponzio, A. (1990b) 'Signs to talk about signs', in A. Ponzio *Man as a Sign*, Berlin and New York: Mouton de Gruyter, pp. 16–74.

Ponzio, A. (1990c) 'Meaning and referent in Peter of Spain', in A. Ponzio, *Man as a Sign*, Berlin and New York: Mouton de Gruyter, pp. 77–93.

Ponzio, A. (1990d) 'Significs and semiotics. Victoria Welby and Giovanni Vailati', in A. Ponzio, *Man as a Sign*, ed. S. Petrilli, Berlin: Mouton de Gruyter.

Ponzio, A. (1990e) 'Theory of meaning and theory of knowledge: Vailati and Welby', in W. H. Schmitz ed., *Essays on Significs*, Amsterdam: John Benjamins, pp. 165–78.

Ponzio, A. (1992a) *Tra semiotica e letteratura. Introduzione a Michail Bachtin*, Milano: Bompiani.

Ponzio, A. (1992b) 'Intervista a Julia Kristeva', in J. Kristeva, *Il linguaggio, questo sconosciuto*, Bari, Adriatica, pp. 9–27.

Ponzio, A. (1993) *Signs, Dialogue and Ideology*, Amsterdam: John Benjamins.

Ponzio, A. (1994) *Scrittura, dialogo, alterità tra Bachtin e Lévinas*, Florence: La Nuova Italia.

Ponzio, A. (1995a) *I segni dell'altro. Eccedenza letteraria e prossimità*, Naples: Edizioni Scientifiche Italiane.

Ponzio, A. (1995b) 'Nel segno di Barthes', in A. Ponzio *I segni dell'altro*, Naples: Edizioni Scientifiche Italiene, pp. 76–86.

Ponzio, A. (1996) *Sujet et altérité. Sur Lévinas*, Paris: L'Harmattan.

Ponzio, A. (1997a) 'Treating and mistreating semiotics: Eco's treatise on semiotics', *S-European Journal for Semiotic Studies* 9 (3, 4): 641–60.

Ponzio, A. (1997b) *Metodologia della formazione linguistica*, Bari: Latera.

Ponzio, A. (1998a) *La revolución Bajtiniana. El pensamiento de Bajtín y la ideología contemporánea*, Madrid: Ediciones Cátedra.

Ponzio, A. (1998b) 'Bakhtin's semiotics as philosophy of language', *Semiotische Berichte* Jg. 22, 3, 4: 19–33.

Ponzio, A. (ed.) (1998c) *Lévinas vivant. Riflessioni sul pensiero di Emmanuel Lévinas*, Bari: Edizioni dal Sud.

Ponzio, A. and Petrilli, S. (1996) 'Peirce and medieval semiotics', in V. M. Colapietro and T. M. Olshewsky (eds) *Peirce's Doctrine of Signs: Theory, Applications, and Connections*, Berlin and New York: Mouton de Gruyter, pp. 351–64.

Ponzio, A. and Petrilli, S. (1998) *Signs of Research on Signs, Semiotische Berichte*, mit Linguistik Interdisziplinär, Jg. 22, 3, 4/1998.

Ponzio, A. and Petrilli, S. (1999) *Fuori campo. Il segni del corpo tra rappresentazione ed eccedenza*, Milan: Mimesis.

Ponzio, A. and Petrilli, S. (2000) *Il sentire della comunicazione globalizzata*, Rome: Meltelmi.

Ponzio, A. *et al.* (1985) *Per parlare dei segni/Talking about Signs*, trans. S. Petrilli, Bari: Adriatica.

Ponzio, A. *et al.* (1999) *Fondamenti di filosofia del linguaggio*, Bari: Laterza.

Postal, P. (1968) *Aspects of Phonological Theory*, New York: Harper and Row.

Potter, J. (1996) *Representing Reality: Discourse, Rhetoric and Social Construction*, London: Sage.

Potter, J. and Wetherell, M. (1987) *Discourse and Social Psychology: Beyond Attitudes and Behaviour*, London: Sage.

Prince, A. and Smolensky, P. (1993) *Optimality Theory: Constraint Interaction in Generative Grammar*, Piscataway, NJ: Rutgers University Center for Cognitive Science.

Prodi, G. (1988) 'La biologia come semiotica naturale [biology as nature semiotics]', in M. Herzfeld and L. Melazzo, (eds) *Semiotic Theory and Practice*, Vol. II, Berlin: Mouton de Gruyter, pp. 929–51.

Pullum, G. (1991) *The Great Eskimo Vocabulary Hoax,* Chicago: University of Chicago Press.

Pulvermüller, F. (1999) 'Words in the brain's language', *Behavioral and Brain Sciences* 22: 253–79.

Pustejovsky, J. (1995) *The Generative Lexicon*, Cambridge, MA: MIT Press.

Putnam, H. (1987) *The Many Faces of Realism*, LaSalle, IL: Open Court.

Quaranta, M. (ed.) (1989) *Giovanni Vailati e la cultura del 1900*, Bologna: Arnaldo Forni.

Quintilian, M. F. (1924) *The Institutio Oratoria of Quintilian with an English Translation*, trans. H. E. Butler. London: W. Heinemann.

Recherches structurales 1949. Interventions dans le débat glossématique. Publiées à l'occasion di cinquantenaire de M. Louis Hjelmslev, Copenhagen: Nordisk Sprog- og Kulturforlag.

Réthoré, J. (ed.) (1993) *Variations sur l'objet*, special issue of *European Journal for Semiotic Studies* 5 (1/2).

Robertson, G. *et al.* (eds) (1996) *FutureNatural: Science, Nature, Culture*, London: Routledge.

Robins, R. H. and Uhlenbeck, E. M. (eds) (1991) *Endangered Languages*, Providence: Berg.

Romeo, L. (1977) 'The derivation of "semiotics" through the history of the discipline', *Semiosis* 6 (2): 37–49.

Rossi-Landi, F. (1953) *Morris e la semiotica novecentesca*, Milan: Feltrinelli, 1975.

Rossi-Landi, F. (1961) *Significato, comunicazione e parlare comune*, Venice: Marsilio, 1998.

Rossi-Landi, F. (1968) *Il linguaggio come lavoro e come mercato*, Milan: Bompiani, 1992. trans. M. Adams *et al. Language as Work and Trade*, South Hadley, MA: Bergin and Garvey, 1983.

Rossi-Landi, F. (1972) *Semiotica e ideologia*, Milan: Bompiani, 1994.

Rossi-Landi, F. (1973) *Ideologies of Linguistic Relativity*, The Hague: Mouton.

Rossi-Landi, F. (1975) *Linguistics and Economics,* The Hague: Mouton, 1977.

Rossi-Landi, F. (1978) *Ideologia*, Milan: Mondadori, 1982; trans. R. Griffin, *Marxism and Ideology*, Oxford: Clarendon, 1990.

Rossi-Landi, F. (1985) *Metodica filosofica e scienza dei segni*, Milan: Bompiani.

Rossi-Landi, F. (1992a) *Between Signs and Non-signs*, intro. and ed. S. Petrilli, Amsterdam: John Benjamins.

Rossi-Landi, F. (1992b) 'Signs and material reality', in F. Rossi-Landi *Between Signs and Non-signs*. Amsterdam: John Benjamins, pp. 271–99.

Rossi-Landi, F. (1992c) *Semiotica. Social Practice. Semiotics and the Sciences of Man: The Correspondence between Charles Morris and Ferruccio Rossi-Landi*, ed. and intro. S. Petrilli, *Semiotica*, 1/2.

Ruesch, J. and Kees, W. (1956) *Nonverbal Communication: Notes on the Visual Perception of Human Relations*, Berkeley, CA: University of California Press.

Russell, B. (1948) *Human Knowledge: Its Scope and Limits*, London: Allen and Unwin.

Russell, L. J. (1939) 'Note on the Term ΣΗΜΙΩΤΙΚΗ [sic] in Locke', *Mind* 48, 405–6.

Saatkamp, H. J., Jr. (ed.) (1995) *Rorty and Pragmatism*, Nashville: Vanderbilt University Press.

Sacks, H., Schegloff, E. and Jefferson, G. (1974) 'A simplest systematics for the organization of turn-taking for conversation', *Language* 50: 696–735.

Sacks, O. (1984) *Seeing Voices,* London: Picador.

Said, E. (1995) *Orientalism: Western Conceptions of the Orient*, Harmondsworth: Penguin.

Salkie, R. (1990) *The Chomsky Update: Linguistics and Politics*, London: Unwin Hyman.

Sapir, E. (1916) 'Time perspective in Aboriginal American culture: a study in method', in D.G. Mandelbaum (ed.) *Selected Writings of Edwards Sapir in Language Culture and Personality*, Berkeley and Los Angeles: University of California Press, 1962.

Sarangi, S. and Slembrouck, S. (1996) *Language, Bureaucracy, and Social Control*, London: Longman.

Saussure, F. de (1916) *Cours de linguistique générale*, (ed.) C. Bally and A. Sechehaye, Paris: Payot

Saussure, F. de ([1916] 1974) *Course in General Linguistics*, trans. W. Baskin, London: Peter Owen.

Saussure, F. de (1983) *Course in General Linguistics*, trans. R. Harris, London: Duckworth.

Savage-Rumbaugh, S. *et al.* (1998) *Apes, Language, and the Human Mind,* Oxford: Oxford University Press.

Savan, D. (1987–88) *An Introduction to C. S. Peirce's Full System of Semeiotic,* Toronto: Victoria College.

Scannell, P. (1991) *Broadcast Talk*, London: Sage.

Schaff, A. (1962) *Introduction to Semantics*, Oxford: Pergamon Press.

Schaff, A. (1973) *Language and Cognition*, New York: McGraw-Hill.

Schaff, A. (1975) *Humanismus: Sprachphilosophie-Erkenntnistheorie des Marxismus*, Vienna: Europa Verlag.

Schaff, A. (1978) *Structuralism and Marxism*, Oxford: Pergamon Press.

Schegloff, E. A. and Sacks, H. (1999) 'Opening up closings', in A. Jaworski and N. Coupland (eds) *The Discourse Reader*, London: Routledge, pp. 263–74.

Schieffelin, B. B. *et al.* (eds) (1998) *Language Ideologies: Practice and Theory*, Oxford: Oxford University Press.

Schiffrin, D. (1987) *Discourse Markers*, Cambridge: Cambridge University Press.

Schiller, F. C. S. (1907) *Studies in Humanism*, London and New York: Macmillan.

Schmitz, W. H. (1985) 'Victoria Lady Welby's Significs: The origin of the Signific movement', in V. Welby *Significs and Language*, Amsterdam, John Benjamins, pp. ix–cclxvii.

Schmitz, W. H. (ed.) (1990a) *Essays on Significs. Papers Presented on the Occasion of the 150th Anniversary of the Birth of Victoria Lady Welby*, Amsterdam and Philadelphia: John Benjamins.

Schmitz, W. H. (1990b) 'The Signific movement in the Netherlands', in W. H. Schmitz (ed.) *Essays on Significs*, Amsterdam and Philadelphia: John Benjamins, pp. 219–72.

Schrøder, K. C. (1994) 'Media language and communication', in *The Encyclopedia of Language and Linguistics*, vol. 5, Oxford: Pergamon Press.

Searle, J. (1980) 'Minds, brains, and programs', *Behavioral and Brain Sciences* 3: 417–58.

Searle, J. R. (1969) *Speech Acts: An Essay in the Philosophy of Language*, Cambridge: Cambridge University Press.

Searle, J. R. (1975) 'Indirect speech acts', in P. Cole and J.L. Morgan (eds) *Syntax and Semantics 3: Speech Acts*, New York: Academic Press, pp. 59–82.

Searle, J. R. (1976) 'A classification of illocutionary acts', *Language in Society* 5: 1–23.

Searle, J. R. (1978) 'Literal meaning', *Erkenntnis* 13: 207–24.

Searle, J. R. (1989) 'How performatives work', *Linguistics and Philosophy* 12: 535–58.

Sebeok, T. A. (1971) '"Semiotic" and its congeners', as reprinted in J. Deely *et al.* (eds) *Frontiers in Semiotics*, Bloomington: Indiana University Press, 1986, pp. 255–63.

Sebeok, T. A. (1976a) *Contributions to the Doctrine of Signs*, Bloomington: Indiana University Press.

Sebeok, T. A. (1976b) 'Iconicity', *Modern Language Notes*, 91, pp. 1427–56.

Sebeok, T. A. (ed.) (1977) *A Perfusion of Signs*, Bloomington: Indiana University Press.

Sebeok, T. A. (1979) *The Sign and Its Masters*, London: University of Texas Press.

Sebeok, T. A. (1981) *The Play of Musement*, Bloomington: Indiana University Press.

Sebeok, T. A. (1986a) 'The problem of the origin of language in an evolutionary frame', *Language Sciences* 8 (2): 168–74.

Sebeok, T. A. (1986b) *I Think I am a Verb*, New York and London: Plenum Press.

Sebeok, T. A. (1989) *The Sign and its Masters*, 2nd edn, Lanham, MD: University Press of America.

Sebeok, T. A. (1990) *Essays in Zoosemiotics*, ed. M. Danesi, Toronto: Toronto Semiotic Circle.

Sebeok, T. A. (1991a) 'In what sense is language a "primary modeling system"?', in *A Sign is Just a Sign*, Bloomington and Indianapolis: Indiana University Press.

Sebeok, T. A. (1991b) *A Sign is Just a Sign*, Bloomington: Indiana University Press.

Sebeok, T. A. (1991c) *Semiotics in the United States*, Bloomington: Indiana University Press.

Sebeok, T. A. (1991d) *American Signatures: Semiotic Inquiry and Method*, ed. I. Smith, Norman and London: University of Oklahoma Press.

Sebeok, T. A. (1994) *Signs: An Introduction to Semiotics*, Toronto: University of Toronto Press.

Sebeok, T. A. (1996a) 'Galen in medical semiotics', *Interdisciplinary Journal for Germanic Linguistics and Semiotic Analysis* 1: 89–111.

Sebeok, T. A. (1996b) 'Signs, bridges, origins', in J. Trabant (ed.) *The Origins of Language*, Budapest: Collegium Budapest Institute for Advanced Study.

Sebeok, T. A. (1997) 'The evolution of semiosis', in R. Posner and T. A. Sebeok (eds) *Semiotics: A Handbook on Sign-Theoretic Foundations of Nature and Culture*, vol. 1, Berlin: Walter de Gruyter, pp. 436–46.

Sebeok, T. A. (1998a) *A Sign is Just a Sign and La semiotica globale* [*Global Semiotics*], Milan: Spirali.

Sebeok, T. A. (1998b) *Come comunicano gli animali che non parlano* [*How Speechless Creatures Communicate*], Modugno: Edizioni dal Sud.

Sebeok, T. A. and Umiker-Sebeok, J. (eds) (1991) *Biosemiotics*, Berlin: Mouton de Gruyter.

Seigel, J. P. (1969) 'The Enlightenment and the evolution of a language of signs in France and England', *Journal for the History of Ideas* 30: 96–115.

Semiotics in the Biosphere: Reviews and a Rejoinder (1998), *Semiotica* 120 (3/4). [Special issue].

Shear, J. (ed.) (1998) *Explaining Consciousness: The Hard Problem*, Cambridge, MA: MIT Press.

Sheriff, J. K. (1989) *The Fate of Meaning: Charles Peirce, Structuralism, and Literature*, Princeton, NJ: Princeton University Press.

Sheriff, J. K. (1994) *Charles Peirce's Guess at the Riddle*, Bloomington: Indiana University Press.

Short, T. L. (1998) 'What's the use?', *Semiotica* 122, 1/2: 1–68.

Shotter, J. (1993) *Conversational Realities*, London: Sage.

Shotter, J. and Gergen, K. J. (eds) (1989) *Texts of Identity*, London: Sage.

Shukman, A. (1987) 'Semiotic Aspects of the Work of Jurij Michailoviè Lotman', in *The Semiotic Web 1987*, Berlin: Mouton de Gruyter.

Silver, I. (1993) 'Marketing authenticity in Third World countries', *Annals of Tourism Research* 20: 302–18.

Silverman, K. (1983) *The Subject of Semiotics*, Oxford: Oxford University Press.

Silverstein, M. (1993) 'Metapragmatic discourse and metapragmatic function', in J. A. Lucy (ed.) *Reflexive Language*, Cambridge: Cambridge University Press, pp. 33–58.

Sinclair, J. (1991) *Corpus, Concordance, Collocation*, Oxford: Oxford University Press.

Sinclair, J. M. and Coulthard, M. (1976) *Towards an Analysis of Discourse: The English Used by Teachers and Pupils*, London: Oxford University Press.

Skinner, B. F. (1957) *Verbal Behavior*, New York: Appleton-Century-Crofts.

Snow, C. P. (1993) *The Two Cultures*, Cambridge: Cambridge University Press.

Sonea, S. (1990) 'Bacterial communication', in T. A. Sebeok and J. Umiker-Sebeok (eds) *The Semiotic Web*, Berlin: Mouton de Gruyter, pp. 639–62.

Sonea, S. and Panisset, M. (1983) *A New Bacteriology*, Boston: Jones and Bartlett.

Spang-Hanssen, H. (1954) *Recent Theories on the Nature of the Language Sign*, Copenhagen: Nordisk Sprog-og Kulturforlag.

Spence, N. C. W. (1957) 'A hardy perennial: the problem of *langue* and *parole*', *Archivum Linguisticum*, 9.

Sperber, D. and Wilson, D. (1986) *Relevance: Communication and Cognition*, Oxford: Blackwell.

Sperber, D. and Wilson, D. (1995) *Relevance: Communication and Cognition*, 2nd edn, Oxford: Basil Blackwell.

Stocking, G. W., Jr. (1966) 'Franz Boas and the culture concept in historical perspective', *American Anthropologist* 68: 867–82.

Stocking, G. W., Jr. (ed.) (1996) Volksgeist *as Method and Ethic: Essays on Boasian Ethnography and the German Anthropological Tradition*, History of Anthropology, vol. 8, Madison, WI: University of Wisconsin Press.

Stockwell, R. P. (1977) Motivations for exbraciation in Old English', in C.N. Li (ed.) Mechanisms of Syntactic Change, Austin, TX: University of Texas Press.

Stokoe, W. C. *et al.* (1965, rev. 1976) *A Dictionary of American Sign Language on Linguistic Principles*, 2nd edn, Silver Spring: Linstok Press.

Stubbs, M. (1983) *Discourse Analysis*, Oxford: Blackwell.

Sturrock, J. (1991) 'Inside the Semiosphere', *TLS*, 3 May.

Swales, J. M. and Rogers, P. S. (1995) 'Discourse and the projection of corporate culture: the Mission Statement', *Discourse and Society*, 6 (2).

Swift, J. (1966) 'A proposal for correcting, improving and ascertaining the English Tongue' (1712), in W.F. Bolton (ed.) *The English Language: Essays by English and American Men of Letters 1490–1839*, Cambridge: Cambridge University Press.

Tannen, D. (1999) 'New York Jewish conversational style', in A. Jaworski and N. Coupland (eds) *The Discourse Reader*, London: Routledge, pp. 459–73.

Tarski, A. (1956) 'The concept of truth in formalized languages', in A. Tarski, *Logic, Semantics and Metamathematics*, London: Oxford University Press, pp. 152–97.

Tasca, N. (ed.) (1995) *Essays in Honour of Thomas A. Sebeok*, Cruzerio Sémiotico 22–5.

Terras, V. (1985) 'Lotman', in V. Terras (ed.) *Handbook of Russian Literature*, New Haven, CT and London: Yale University Press.

Thompson, J. B. (1991) 'Editor's introduction', in P. Bourdieu, *Language and Symbolic Power*, Cambridge: Polity Press, pp. 1–31.

Todorov, T. (ed.) (1965) *Théorie de la littérature*, Paris: Seuil.

Todorov, T. (1981) *Le principe dialogique, Mikhail Bakhtine*, Paris: Editions du Seuil.

Toman, J. (1995) *The Magic of a Common Language: Jakobson, Mathesius, Trubetzkoy, and the Prague Linguistic Circle*, Cambridge, MA: The MIT Press.

Tomasello, M. (1999) *The Cultural Origins of Human Cognition*, Cambridge, MA: Harvard University Press.

Tomlin, R. S. (1986) *Basic Word Order: Functional Principles*, London: Croom Helm.

Tracy, K. and Coupland, N. (1990) 'Multiple goals in discourse: an overview of issues', in K. Tracy and N. Coupland (eds) *Multiple Goals in Discourse*, Clevedon: Multilingual Matters, pp. 1–13.

Trudgill, P. and Hannah, J. (1982) *International English*, London: Arnold.

Turkle, S. (1995) *Life on the Screen: Identity in the Age of the Internet*, New York: Simon and Schuster.

Turner, G. (1990) *British Cultural Studies*, London: Unwin Hyman.

Turner, R. (1974) *Ethnomethodology*, Harmondsworth: Penguin.

Tylor, E. (1865) *Researches into the Early History of Mankind*, London: John Murray.

Uexküll, G. von (1964) *Jakob von Uexküll, seine Welt und seine Umwelt: Eine Biographie*, Hamburg: Christian Wegner Verlag.

Uexküll, J. von (1909) *Umwelt und Innenwelt der Tiere*, Berlin: Verlag von Julius Springer.

Uexküll, J. von (1940) *Bedeutungslehre*, Leipzig: Verlag von J.A. Barth.

Uexküll, J. von. ([1920, 1928] 1973) *Theoretische Biologie [Theoretical Biology]*, Frankfurt: Suhrkamp.

Uexküll, J. von (1980) *Kompositionslehre der Natur: Biologie als undogmatische Naturwissenschaft. Ausgewählte Schriften*, T. von Uexküll, ed., Frankfurt am Main: Verlag Ullstein GmbH.

Uexküll, J. von (1982) 'The theory of meaning', *Semiotica* 42 (1): 25–82.

Uexküll, J. von (1992) 'A stroll through the worlds of animals and men: a picture book of invisible worlds', *Semiotica* 89 (4): 319–91.

Uexküll, J. von, and Kriszat, G. (1934) *Streifzüge durch die Umwelten von Tieren und Menschen: Ein Bilderbuch unsichtbarer Welten*, Berlin: J. Springer.

Uexküll, T. von. (1986) 'Medicine and semiotics', *Semiotica* 61: 201–17.

Uexküll, T. von. (1987) 'The sign-theory of Jakob von Uexküll', M. Krampen *et al.* (eds) *Classics of Semiotics*, London: Plenum Press, pp. 147–79.

Uexküll, T. von. (1997) 'Biosemiose' ['Biosemiosis'], in R. Posner and T. A. Sebeok (eds) *Semiotics: A Handbook on Sign-Theoretic Foundations of Nature and Culture*, vol. 1, Berlin: Walter de Gruyter, pp. 447–57.

Uexküll, T. von. *et al.* (1993) 'Endosemiosis', *Semiotica* 96: 5–51.

Uldall, H. J. (1944) 'Speech and writing', *Acta Linguistica* 4: 11–17.

Uldall, H. J. (1957) *Outline of Glossematics,* Copenhagen: Nordisk Sprog-og Kulturforlag.

Vachek, J. (ed.) (1964) *A Prague School Reader in Linguistics*, Bloomington: Indiana University Press.

Vailati, G. (1971) *Epistolario*, Turin: Einaudi.

Vailati, G. (1972) *Scritti filosofici*, ed. G. Lanaro, Florence: La Nuova Italia.

Vailati, G. (1987) *Scritti*, ed. M. Quaranta, Bologne: Arnaldo Forni.

Vailati, G. (2000) *Il metodo della filosofia: Saggi di critica del linguaggio*, ed. A. Ponzio, Bari: Graphis.

van Dijk, T.A. (ed.) (1985) *Handbook of Discourse Analysis*, London: Academic.

van Dijk, T. A. (1992) 'Discourse and the denial of racism', *Discourse and Society* 3 (1): 87–118.

van Dijk, T.A. (1993a) *Elite Discourse and Racism*, London: Sage.

van Dijk, T.A. (ed.) (1993b) *Discourse and Society* 4 (2) (special issue on Critical Discourse Analysis).

van Dijk, T. A. (1998) *Ideology*, London: Sage.

Van Leeuwen, T. (1993) 'Genre and field in critical discourse analysis', *Discourse and Society* 4 (2): 193–225.

Vargha-Khadem, F. *et al.* (1995) 'Praxic and nonverbal cognitive deficits in a large family with a genetically transmitted speech and language disorder', *Proceedings of the National Academy of Sciences* 92: 930–3.

Verschueren, J. (1999) *Understanding Pragmatics*, London: Edward Arnold; New York: Oxford University Press.

Vološinov, V. N. (1926) 'Discourse in life and discourse in art (Concerning Sociological Poetics)', trans. in V. N. Vološinov, *Freudianism: A Critical Sketch*, trans. I. R. Titunik, ed. I. R. Titunik with N. H. Bruss, Indianapolis: Indiana University Press, 1987, pp. 93–116; and as 'Discourse in life and discourse in poetry: questions of sociological poetics', trans. J. Richmond, in *Bakhtin School Papers*, ed. A. Shukman, RPT Publications in association with Dept. of Lit., University of Essex: Colchester 1988, pp. 5–30.

Vološinov, V. N. ([1927] 1987) *Freudianism: A Critical Sketch*, trans. I. R. Titunik, ed. I. R. Titunik with N. H. Bruss, Indianapolis: Indiana University Press.

Vološinov, V. N. ([1929] 1973) *Marxism and the Philosophy of Language*, trans. L. Matejka and I. R. Titunik, Cambridge, MA: Harvard University Press, 1976.

Volterra, V. and Iverson, J. (1996) 'When do modality factors affect the course of language acquisition?', in K. Emmorey and J. S. Reilly (eds) *Language, Gesture and Space*, 371–390.

Vygotsky, L. (1978) *Mind in Society: The Development of Higher Psychological Processes*, Cambridge, MA: Harvard University Press.

Warnock, G. J. (1953) *Berkeley*, London: Penguin Books.

Watson, J. B. (1913) 'Psychology as the behaviorist views it', *Psychological Review* 20: 158–77.

Waugh, L. and Monville-Burston, M. (1990) 'Introduction', in R. Jakobson *On Language*, Cambridge, MA: Harvard University Press.

Welby, V. (1852) *A Young Traveller's Journal of a Tour in North and South America during the Year 1850*, London: T. Bosworth.

Welby, V. (1881) *Links and Clues*, London: Macmillan and Co, 1883.

Welby, V. (1891) *Witnesses to Ambiguity: A Collection,* Grantham: W. Clarke (Late L. Ridge).

Welby, V. (1892) *The Use of 'Inner' and 'Outer' in Psychology: Does the Metaphor Help or Hinder? A Small Collection of Extracts Bearing upon this Question Respectfully Submitted to the International Congress of Experimental Psychology, August 1892,* Grantham: W. Clarke (Late L. Ridge).

Welby, V. (1893) *A Selection of Passages from 'Mind' (Jan. 1876, to July 1892), 'Nature' (1870 and 1888 to 1892), 'Natural Science' (1892), Bearing on Changes and Defects in the Significance of Terms and in the Theory and Practice of Logic,* Grantham: W. Clarke (Late L. Ridge).

Welby, V. (1897) *Grains of Sense*, London: J.M. Dent.

Welby, V. (1898) *The Witness of Science to Linguistic Anarchy*, a Collection of Extracts, chiefly from *Nature, Science* and *Natural Science*, Grantham: W. Clarke.

Welby, V. (1902) 'Translation', in J. M. Baldwin (ed.) *Dictionary of Philosophy and Psychology in Three Volumes, 1901–1905*, New York and London: Macmillan, vol. 2, p. 712.

Welby, V. (1929) *Echoes of Larger Life: A Selection from the Early Correspondence of Victoria Lady Welby,* Mrs Henry Cust ed., London: Jonathan Cape.

Welby, V. (1931) *Other Dimensions: A Selection from the Later Correspondence of Victoria Lady Welby*, Mrs Henry Cust ed., introd. L. P. Jacks. London: Jonathan Cape.

Welby, V. (1977) 'Significs' (1911), in *The Encyclopedia Britannica*, 11th edn, vol. XXV, pp. 78–81, Cambridge: Cambridge University Press; now in C. Hardwick, *Semiotic and Significs: The Correspondence Between Charles S. Peirce and Victoria Lady Welby*, Bloomington and London: Indiana University Press, 1977, pp. 167–75.

Welby, V. (1983) *What is Meaning?* (1903), A. Eschbach (ed. and pref., ix–xxxii), G. Mannoury (intro., pp. xxxiv–xlii, Amsterdam and Philadelphia: John Benjamins.

Welby, V. (1985a) *Significs and Language: (The articulate form of our expressive and interpretative resources)* (1911), with additional essays, W. H. Schmitz (ed. and intro.), Amsterdam and Philadelphia: John Benjamins.

Welby, V. (1985b) 'Meaning and metaphor' (1893), *The Monist* 3(4): 510–25. Now in V. Welby, *Significs and Language*, Amsterdam and Philadelphia: John Benjamins.

Welby, V. (1985c) 'Sense, Meaning and Interpretation' (1896), *Mind* 5(17): 24–37. 5(18): 186–202. Now in V. Welby, *Significs and Language*, Amsterdam and Philadelphia: John Benjamins.

Welby, V. (1986) *Significato, metafora, interpretazione,* intro. trans. and ed. S. Petrilli, Bari: Adriatica.

Welby, V. and Tönnies, F. (1901) 'Notes on the "Welby Prize Essay"', *Mind* 10 (38): 188–209.

Welby, V. *et al.* (1902) 'Signific', in J. M. Baldwin (ed.) *Dictionary of Philosophy and Psychology in Three Volumes, 1901–1905*, New York and London: Macmillan, vol. 2, p. 529.

Wells, G. A. (1987) *The Origin of Language: Aspects of the Discussion from Condillac to Wundt*, La Salle, ILL: Open Court Publishing Co.

Whorf, B. L. (1997) 'The relation of habitual thought and behavior to language', in N. Coupland and A. Jaworski (eds) *Sociolinguistics: A Reader and Coursebook*, London: Macmillan, pp. 443–63.

Williams, V. J. Jr. (1996) *Rethinking Race: Franz Boas and his Contemporaries*, Lexington, MA: University Press of Kentucky.

Wilson, F. R. (1998) *The Hand: How its Use Shapes the Brain, Language, and Human Culture*, New York: Pantheon.

Wittgenstein, L. (1922) *Tractatus Logico-Philosophicus*, trans. D. F. Pears and B. F. Guinness, introd. B. Russell, London: Routledge and Kegan Paul.

Wittgenstein, L. (1953) *Philosophical Investigations,* Oxford: Blackwell.

Woodward, K. (ed.) (1997) *Identity and Difference*, London and Thousand Oaks, CA: Sage/Open University.

Woolhouse, R. S. (1988) *The Empiricists* (A History of Western Philosophy, vol. 5), Oxford: Oxford University Press.

Young, K. (1999) 'Narrative embodiments: enclaves of the self in the realm of medicine', in A. Jaworski and N. Coupland (eds) *The Discourse Reader*, London: Routledge, pp. 428–41.

Zimmerman, D. H. and West, C. (1975) 'Sex roles, interruptions and silences in conversation', in B. Thorne and N. Henley (eds) *Language and Sex: Difference and Dominance*, Rowley, MA: Newbury House, pp. 105–29.

INDEX

Items in **bold** also have their own entry in Part II; page references in bold indicate where the entry is located.